Practicing Catholic

BOOKS BY JAMES CARROLL

Fiction

MADONNA RED

MORTAL FRIENDS

FAULT LINES

FAMILY TRADE

PRINCE OF PEACE

SUPPLY OF HEROES

FIREBIRD

MEMORIAL BRIDGE

THE CITY BELOW

SECRET FATHER

Nonfiction

AN AMERICAN REQUIEM

CONSTANTINE'S SWORD

TOWARD A NEW CATHOLIC CHURCH

CRUSADE

HOUSE OF WAR

PRACTICING CATHOLIC

Practicing CATHOLIC

James Carroll

MARINER BOOKS
HOUGHTON MIFFLIN HARCOURT
BOSTON • NEW YORK

First Mariner Books edition 2010

www.hmhbooks.com

Library of Congress Cataloging-in-Publication Data
Carroll, James, date.
Practicing Catholic / James Carroll.
p. cm.
Includes bibliographical references and index.
ISBN 978-0-618-67018-5
1. Carroll, James, date. 2. Catholics — Biography. 3. Catholic Church — History — 20th century. 4. Catholic church — History — 21st century. 5. Catholic Church—Doctrines. I. Title.
BX4705.C327A3 2009
282.092 — dc22 [B] 2008037386

ISBN 978-0-547-33626-8 (pbk.)

Printed in the United States of America

Book design by Robert Overholtzer

DOC 10 9 8 7 6 5 4 3 2 1

The author is grateful for permission to quote from "Howl," from *Collected Poems, 1947–1980* by Allen Ginsberg. Copyright © 1955 by Allen Ginsberg. Reprinted by permission of HarperCollins Publishers.

FOR LEXA

CONTENTS

INTRODUCTION

PRACTICING CATHOLIC

WHY AM I A CATHOLIC? There are a thousand ways to answer that question, and this book will take up many of them. By its end, there will be one answer. I will move through the three phases of my life as a Catholic—from my youthful formation, in an immigrant family that magnificently achieved its assimilation; to my time as a seminarian and priest, which coincided with the unexpected hope of the Second Vatican Council; to life after the priesthood, a time when the limits of assimilation into the American consensus showed themselves, and the reforms of the council were repudiated, but when I discovered a far deeper meaning of the faith.

This book has the form of a personal and historical essay about the Catholic Church in my lifetime—from the full flower of the faux-medieval Catholicism into which I was christened, through the heady arrival of an Irish-American subculture in the Kennedy era, the glorious witness of a humanist pope, the frightening dislocations of assassination and war, the crisis of authority over sexual morality, the political power-brokerage symbolized by a pope who helped end the Cold War, the ironic collapse of post–Vatican II Catholic identity after that "arrival," the stunning betrayal of the priestly sexual-abuse scandal, to the end of narrow denominationalism that sets Catholic Christians against Orthodox and evangelical Christians. After 9/11, fundamental assumptions of Islam came quickly into question, but so did the assumptions of every religion. Like millions of Catholics, my faith has been shaken by the events of our time. We have had to announce,

"The Church is dead," while searching for a way to declare, "Long live the Church."

I trace the large drama of major shifts that affect the whole American people, but do so by telling a personal story that is firmly located in part of the nation's life. Though centered in one person's experience, *Practicing Catholic* is less a family memoir than a religious and cultural history, addressed to everyone concerned with questions of belief and disbelief. Apart from the museums that anchor the great cities of Europe and America, the Roman Catholic Church is what remains of "Christendom," the generating aesthetic and intellectual tradition of Western civilization. Offshoots of the Protestant Reformation claim that same Christian heritage, but the Catholic Church, in its institutional DNA if not its ideology, has served as the vehicle for carrying key elements of the Roman Empire forward into history, much as Rome carried the achievements of ancient Greece forward. Even today, in its organization, judicial system, official language, attachment to material culture, and elevation of the classic virtues, the Church embodies that first *Romanitas.*[1]

Leaving theology aside for the moment, this worldly rootedness has been a source of the Church's exceptional longevity as well as of its global reach. The diocesan structure of its organization, for example—with bishops and cardinals exercising over local churches an authority derived from the transcendent power center—is a repetition of Rome's proconsul method of governance. The way the Church's finances are organized, with independent dioceses feeding support to that center; the way the Church's diplomacy is structured, with papal legates dispatched to world capitals; the way the cult of the leader is maintained, with the bishop of Rome regarded as the deity's vicar—all of this echoes the methods of the imperium, a system that is otherwise long gone.

St. Peter's Basilica, after all, is an architectural duplication of the palace of the emperor; indeed, the word "basilica" derives from the basil wreath with which, in primordial Rome, the ruler was crowned. Meanwhile, Catholic doctrine is grounded in philosophical propositions that came into their own in the ancient world, which is why any revision of that doctrine—is it even possible?—would amount to an extraordinary intellectual and spiritual transformation. Down through the ages, the tension between the papacy and the councils of the Church, which across two thousand years were convened, on average, once each century, can be seen to have been analogous to the tension between Caesar and the Roman Senate, which ended tragically. Indeed, the Church has, if only accidentally, carried forward the internal conflict between republic and empire, a tension that, in the Church's case, while yet to be resolved, has become dramatic in the contemporary push-pull between the laity and lower clergy on one side, and the hierarchy on the other. For all of these reasons, Catholicism continues to be an object of fascination. And, admittedly, of repugnance.

Grave moral failings of the Church became evident in the era since my birth, and those historic failings were compounded by further mistakes in recent years. I reflect on this dark legacy, showing what it meant to me as I was repeatedly forced to confront it. But I aim less at judgmental criticism than at a loving act of remembrance, recalling Catholics—and myself—to what they have been at their best. A tradition centered on social justice, accommodation of immigrants, the work of peace, sacramental respect for creation, liturgical beauty, a global vision, and the consolations of faith—all of this weighs as much in the scale of history as spiritual imperialism, scandal, and hypocrisy. One theme of *Practicing Catholic* is loss, but another—through the embrace of change—is renewal. Catholic history is nothing but a saga of glory and tragedy, corruption and reform, false starts and new beginnings. In our time, this age-old pattern has been compressed and sped up, with an edge that cuts deeper than ever before.

I bring a Catholic sensibility to bear on this experience, but equally I bring an American sensibility, which is something else entirely. American Catholicism, which has been profoundly influenced by the nation's predominantly Protestant ethos, is a subject of its own here, with tension running in both directions—against the broader national culture, which is overtly secular but implicitly pietistic,[2] and against European Catholicism, which in the past was established, hierarchical, and antimodern, but is at present in a state of near collapse. European Catholicism came to the United States and became something new, as it is today becoming something new in Africa and Asia. Third World religiosity may define the Catholic future, much as Europe defines its past. But American Catholicism stands decisively on its own ground, even if Rome has never fully accommodated that.

At its peak, just as I entered the seminary in the early 1960s, the Catholic Church in the United States was an astounding success story. Perhaps as much as a third of the nation's population—more than fifty million people—were Catholics, and nearly three-quarters of them reported attending Mass every week.[3] Since then, "success story" is not the way the Church would be described, yet a vast number of people continue to understand themselves either in its terms or against them. Today there are about seventy million self-identified Catholics in the United States, about a quarter of the nation's population, registered in about twenty thousand parishes. They put a billion dollars a year in collection baskets.[4] This may not seem like a decline, but these numbers are bolstered by a huge percentage of newly arrived immigrants, mainly from Latin America. In the past thirty years, the number of native-born U.S. Catholics has plummeted; about one-third of those born into the faith have left it behind, meaning that fully ten percent of Americans are former Catholics.[5] But whether they have abandoned the Church or remain with it, the religious identities of all of these people have undergone transformation—the kind of tectonic shifts in meaning and practice that this book will report. Many American Catholics and former Catholics will recognize their stories in this work, but so might all Americans whose religious identities have undergone transformation or obliteration in these tumultuous years.

I was born in 1943. Numerous global eruptions have upended religious and political assumptions in the decades since then. Europe, after two acts of continental self-destruction, yielded to the United States as the power center of the West. The United States, in turn, defined itself, theologically as well as politically, against communism abroad and at home. Basic flaws were laid bare in Western civilization (the Holocaust) and in America (continuing racism), with the recognition that hatred of the Other (whether Jews, blacks, or, say, Muslims) is still virulent. Women came to a new self-understanding, from the workforce jolt of World War II to the claustrophobia of the suburbs in the 1950s to the liberation of the 1960s (the birth control pill) and 1970s (*Roe v. Wade*). Sexual sensibility itself was upended, with gay rights, the loosening of marriage, male insecurity, and the eroticizing of mass culture. Europe and Japan embraced pacifism while America was so much at the mercy of an arms race that, even when the Soviet Union disappeared, the economic, psychological, and political grip of war did not give up its hold on the United States. All of this weighed heavily on religion in general, and on American Catholicism in particular.

During my lifetime, America fully embraced the ethos of global empire, fulfilling what had begun in the merely continental notion of Manifest Destiny. A shift in the nation's religious self-understanding occurred, too, with its Christian character being more openly proclaimed by politicians while preachers blatantly advanced political agendas.[6] Up until the time of my birth, American Protestants, particularly fundamentalists, had been, as we will see, unbridled in their contempt for Catholics, but that changed. As "faith-based" initiatives marked both domestic and foreign policy, a new coalition was formed between politically motivated evangelical Christians, who supplied the fervor, and so-called neoconservative Catholics, who supplied a newfound intellectual gravitas.[7] Together they represented a major new strain of public influence in America, defined by nothing so much as political moralism. This book tells the astounding story of that shift, with reactionary Catholics and Protestants alike regarding the secular United States as an infidel nation, and their program one of massive cultural resistance.

The most striking instance of this new alliance centered on the U.S. Supreme Court, which had long been a hostile forum to Roman Catholics. Only one of the first fifty-four justices was a Catholic. Then, for many years, there was a single "Catholic seat" on the nation's highest bench, occupied most recently by Justice William Brennan, Jr., a moderate liberal whose appointment by the moderate Republican Dwight Eisenhower in 1956, when I was thirteen, gave me my first feeling of personal connection to the court. But then, under a succession of conservative Republican presidents, a string of Catholic conservatives was appointed, until, with the naming of Samuel Alito in 2006, the Supreme Court had a Catholic majority for the first time, a majority composed of right-wing Catholics who were poised to reverse precedents on antidiscrimination statutes, conservation, women's rights, free speech, and government intrusions in the private lives of citizens.[8]

But the brand of Catholicism represented by the court majority was out of step with the generally progressive social teachings of the Church (the Catholic justices were not, for example, opposed to the death penalty). Indeed, the court's five Catholics could be seen as holding out not only against the dominant current of contemporary American life but also against a new Catholic mainstream that had been set running in the mid-twentieth century, a fountain of renewal that will form the wellspring of this book.[9]

But Supreme Court or not, right-wing Catholicism does not define the heart of this tradition even now. I know this from my own experience and the experience of countless fellow Catholics. In steadfastly asserting my Catholic identity, I am not describing mere membership in a group. There is more to being Catholic than that, as I and many others learned over the decades that are the subject of this book, a time when our Church's own leaders first called us to profound reforms in our ways of being religious, and then warned us off those reforms. By now we find ourselves caught, in effect, between an increasingly vocal group of "neo-atheists"[10] and religious reactionaries, some of whom want to teach creationism in schools and some of whom vie for control of our own Catholic Church.

When the likes of Richard Dawkins, Sam Harris, and Christopher Hitchens,[11] citing insights of science or the rise of sectarian violence, denounce the very idea of God, Protestant and Catholic fundamentalists strike back by attacking the pillars on which such modern criticism stands. Yet religious people make a big mistake to dismiss those who warn, even mockingly, of the dangers of irrational belief or of religiously sponsored intolerance. Instead, such criticism should be taken as a challenge to purify faith of its dehumanizing elements, and this book aims to be an instance of that. Dawkins and company share one common conviction with religious reactionaries—that religion is a primitive impulse, unable to withstand the challenge of contemporary thought.[12]

Rather than feel intimidated by secular or scientific criticisms of religion, a believer can insist that faith in God is a fulfillment of all that fully modern people affirm when they assent to science—or object to violence. From Marx, Nietzsche, and Freud forward, religion's critics have insisted that faith is mere superstition, a province of the illiterate masses. When educated people cling to the faith, it is supposed that they are merely protecting unexamined, if closely held, notes of identity. Smart folks, too, have their irrational needs—although not the smart folks who have jettisoned belief. Grossly fervent popular religion and cooler, more sophisticated belief systems are, to the critics, alike in their dependence on ignorance, their encouragement of resignation in the face of injustice, and their deep complicity in intolerance and even violence.

Against all this, it is embarrassing to the critics of religion that so many passionate advocates of justice in this world are motivated by expressly spiritual concerns; that peace defines the work of so many believers around the globe; that so many otherwise intellectually astute people cling to their doctrinaire mumbo-jumbo despite all the quite evident reasons not to. The critics steadily manage to avoid the clear fact of human experience—that "evident reasons" forever fall short of fully accounting for human experience. "Naïve atheism is as difficult to sustain," the Catholic scholar Peter Steinfels has written, "as naïve theism."[13] Critical religion, while always aiming to submit to tests of reason, never defines itself exclusively in terms of evidence or reason. And in that, critical religion is pointing toward the essential depth of living that science by itself cannot address. The test of reason, that is, includes the acknowledgment of reason's limit—and that test is one to which religion submits.

At the same time, a believer can advance the Dawkins-Harris-Hitchens critique (and the Marx-Nietzsche-Freud critique) to say that most articulations of traditional religion of all stripes fall far short of doing God justice. The world has changed, and with it the way humans think of the world. Inevitably, that means the way humans think of God has changed. As will become clear in this book, the God who has repeatedly been pronounced dead is not one for whom all religious people mourn. The God whom atheists aggressively deny (the all-powerful, all-knowing, unmoved Mover; the God of damnation, supernatural intervention, salvation-through-appeasement, patriarchy, puritanism, war, etc.) is indeed the God enshrined in many propositions of the orthodox tradition. But this God is also one whom more and more believers, including Catholics, simply do not recognize as the God we worship. Such people regard the fact that God is unknowable as the most important thing to know about God. Traditional propositions of the creed, therefore, must be affirmed neither rigidly nor as if they are meaningless, but with thoughtful modesty about all religious language, allowing for doubt as well as respect for different creeds—and for no creed.[14]

This is not an entirely new way of being religious. One sees hints of it in the wisdom of many thinkers, from Augustine in ancient times to Nicholas of Cusa in the Renaissance to Kierkegaard in the modern period. But, in fact, the contemporary religious imagination has been transformed by understanding born of science. Once a believer has learned to think historically and critically, it is impossible any longer to think mythically. That is the ground on which this book stands; its subject is the positive transformation of religious thought that has defined much of Christianity, including Catholicism, during my lifetime. I intend to offer a defense of that transformation.

In truth, however, that transformation has had profoundly negative aspects. For Catholics of my generation, there was a particular epiphany attached to the clergy sexual-abuse scandal that came to light in the first five years of the new millennium. In the chronology traced here, that tragic story must inform the climactic period, for it was then that the Catholic laity had no choice but to face the harsh reality of our Church's situation. Although a small minority of sexually exploitative priests had actually betrayed the young people in their care, almost the entire rank of bishops, from the pope down, had moved with alacrity to protect the abusive priests instead of the children.[15] In the name of "avoiding scandal," the crimes of the exploiters were covered up. These priests were typically given new assignments, which meant they could repeat their assaults. Psychologically disturbed men were enabled *by their bishops* to become serial rapists of boys and girls. Their offenses were perverse and far more extensive than anyone imagined. But what the bishops did in response revealed a systemic corruption, an indictment of the whole clerical culture.

Rather than deal with that dysfunction, and with inevitable questions about the place and power of the laity, mandatory celibacy, and the priesthood's male exclusivity, the bishops engaged in denial, putting their own power ahead of the welfare of the Church's most vulnerable members. By "scandal," it became clear, the bishops meant anything that might undermine their authoritarian control. With that, the Catholic people saw what had happened to the Church we loved. The magisterium of the Church, from its unmagisterial margin, was seen to exercise a sham authority, with little real influence over the inner or outer lives of the faithful, who had been forced in all of this to claim a new kind of Catholic identity. That new identity is my subject.[16]

I say new identity, but actually the Catholic people have long affirmed their faith in ways that maintain a certain independence from the authority structure of the Church. Often, indeed, the Church is discussed as if its clerical aspect were all there is. But that is not, and never was, the half of it. There are more than a billion Catholics around the world, and we are far from slavish—or even uniform—in the way we express our beliefs. Yet in the basic creed to which—rich and poor, north and south, high-tech savvy and illiterate—we devote ourselves, can we all be wrong? The very size of the Catholic Church is perhaps its anchor in history, the reason both to take it seriously and to understand it as involving far more than a relatively small clerical establishment. As councils and popes vied with one another for supremacy, and as theologians and philosophers debated fine points of the triune "persons" of the Godhead or the two "natures" of Jesus Christ, ordinary Christians kept the substance of Jesus Christ's meaning at the center of practice, the Gospel narratives paramount, the rite of initiation into his death and resurrection as the basic symbol, with regular gatherings to remember him at Mass as the main note of communal identity. And always Catholics understood what every ethic had to be measured against: the Lord's central command to love each other and the stranger, his radical option in favor of the powerless over princes.

Thus hospitals, schools, universities, peace movements, social welfare organizations, labor unions, healthy family cultures, and humanistic art forms all emerged with creative regularity from the Catholic experience. (Today the Roman Catholic Church is the largest and most productive nongovernmental organization in the world, accomplishing good works, without strings, around the globe.[17]) The laity, producing most of this, knew full well, even in eras of widespread illiteracy, what membership in Christ implied, no matter the pronouncements coming from on high.

If there is a surprise in this story, it is in how, after a century of decline and disillusionment, religion reemerged as a major factor in the new millennium's future, and how questions of Catholic identity surfaced with profound relevance not only for me but for the world.

Yet the dominant tone of what I recount, as it turns out, is wonder at the privilege of living through a period of such momentous significance. And in the telling, I discover that the most important personal note is gratitude for the way in which this profound and profoundly conflicted tradition presents itself anew, inviting a fresh embrace and affirming a place of welcome.

So here is the faith of a "practicing Catholic," which is the way we like to define ourselves. The label holds several meanings. "Practical" describes someone who is both concerned with matters of fact and good at solving problems—two characteristics necessary for survival in today's Catholic Church. And, of course, we laugh that we are "practically Catholic," too, depending on who is doing the defining. But fundamentally our religious life is a practice, like the practice of medicine. This religious practice involves practical disciplines, like acquaintance with a tradition, regular observance of rituals, and attendance, as we say, at Mass. Attending physician, attending Catholic. The sacramental life is not to be confused with subservience, although even dissenting Catholics are steadily in search of authority figures who show themselves worthy of respect. But for us, the primary meaning of "practicing" is that, through these disciplines, rituals, and searches, we have some prospect of getting better. This, therefore, is practice like the practice of an art or sport. That we are practicing means, above all, that we are not perfect—not in faith, hope, or charity. Not in poverty, chastity, or obedience. Not in the cardinal virtues, the works of mercy, or the acts of contrition. Not in peace or justice. Not in the life of prayer, which is nothing but attention to the presence of God. In all of this we are practicing, which is the only way we know to be Catholic. The main form that my practice takes, since I am a Catholic writer, is this book.

CHAPTER ONE

BORN CATHOLIC

1. PAST, PRESENT, FUTURE

"WHO MADE YOU?" I was asked in catechism class by the nuns at St. Thomas More School. I knew the answer.

"And why did God make you?" The answer to that question remains the very marrow of my being: "To know, love, and serve Him in this life, and to be happy with Him in the next." Knowledge plus love plus service equals happiness—such was my first arithmetic, and its simplicity formed my *lives.* There are two lives, I was taught, and they are divided by the moment of death. And, though by now the content of my faith in that next life is thoroughly undefined, it remains the punctuation mark of time as I experience it, making the idea of the future as permanent as the past and the present. And I say "the" future, not "a" future, preferring the article that implies no particularity, exactly because I do not know *what* to expect. I know only *to* expect.

As a way to measure the weight of the past, and to carry it forward into the future, belief in Jesus Christ, mediated through the Latin Church, has defined my existence, and still does. In *Slaughterhouse-Five* Kurt Vonnegut's Billy Pilgrim writes that on the planet of Tralfamadore, "all moments, past, present, and future, always have existed, always will exist." But what about the problem of transience here on earth? Is there any way a human can locate himself in eternity? The way I have found to do that is by asking three questions about Jesus: Who was he? Who is he? Who will he be?

So I begin with history, the memory of an actual man about whose actuality I know little but that, in an age of empire, he preferred service over sovereignty, a choice that led the empire to murder him. I know that, because of that preference, and despite his murder, he was recognized by his friends as having unique significance as God's son, an awareness that struck them during the simple act of eating the meals he had regularly prepared. At table, the serving Jesus insisted that we are all God's sons and daughters. After his death, that insistence took hold of his friends' imagination—a taking-hold that, leaving doctrinal questions aside for now, is called the Resurrection. They, too, embraced service over sovereignty.

Jesus was a peasant of no social standing, but his actions and words were compelling. His friends, responding to him as a teacher of Jewish faith and as a resister of Roman occupation, were devoted to him and continued to revere him after death. Because the first followers of Jesus let him down when he needed them most, the community that grew out of their inability to let go of their affection for him was defined above all by its awareness of failure. Yes, what we call sin is a fact, but so is forgiveness. Those followers had forgiveness from Jesus himself, as so many of the stories about him declare. Therefore the Church is the community in which forgiveness is always necessary and always possible.

It matters that only gradually did his friends come to think of Jesus as the Jewish Messiah, and, even more gradually, as the Son of God. It matters that their sacred texts evolved slowly out of oral traditions, and then that the sacred texts themselves were only gradually selected from among many others, equally honored but never officially deemed "inspired." This book will take up the story of these developments. The point here is that once we understand that doctrines evolved over time, we stop regarding them as timeless. The evolution of doctrine can continue.

In Jesus, after the fact, believers saw the presence of God, and in that faith, what we call Incarnation, they established the key idea of this religion—that human experience, far from being untrustworthy or contemptible, is itself God's way of being in the world. The Church gives concrete expression to this idea by organizing itself around sacraments, which turn the key moments of life—birth, maturity, marriage, illness, death—into openings to transcendence. God the Great Unknown is nevertheless as routinely present as bread, wine, and a common word of love.

The illuminating meal with Jesus continues as the Eucharist, the

Mass, the ritual to which we Catholics make our way each week in order to renew that first awareness. Sovereignty remains the great temptation, as nothing shows more eloquently than the Church's own history, especially once it embraced the ethos of empire against which Jesus had set himself. But the Church is judged by its foundation, and is continually recalled to service by the memory of its founder. That is why we Catholics go to the table as much to be forgiven as to be fed.

Because all religious language is indirect, a matter of metaphor more than metaphysics, we know precious little about the present life of Jesus—his "presence"—except that at Mass it is "real." How that is explained—from the first enthusiastic reports of resurrection to the philosophical conceit of transubstantiation—is less important than the visceral conviction that, in the sacrament, Jesus lives. The conviction is sustained by the presence of all those others at the table, which is why we Catholics prefer not to eat alone.

The past of history and the present of ritual point to a future fulfillment, which remains as undefined as it is, in faith, certain. With creation, God has begun something that includes its own forward momentum. When creation became aware of itself in the human person, that awareness carried an invitation to trust the momentum, without knowing where it goes. As we do not understand life's origins, we cannot predict life's ultimate fate. Enough to know, with Jesus, that God is God of this creation, and in the very act of creating life out of nothing, God forbids the return of nothing. The one who creates *ex nihilo* is no nihilist. Life is worthy of trust. The future belongs to God, but so does God's creation. Therefore God's creation has the future, too.

Without the Church—its memory of the past, its present ritual, its insistence on a future—I would be an orphan in time, and a prisoner of it. The past is a foreign country, yes, but Catholicism makes me one of its citizens, with my Irish forebears but with all the others, too. The Church is my time machine, taking me back through Rome's tragic glory, the source of our vitality and vanity; through Christianity's roots in Jewishness, the tradition that gave Jesus his measure of meaning (and which continues to this day as another mode of God's presence to creation); through history into myth and all the way back to Adam and Eve, in whom human life itself, including fallibility, could be reckoned as the image of God. So with the future—forward not to spaceships but, according to the faith, to an undefined but sure life with the One who is life's source and sustenance, a life in which nothing valuable of the past is lost.

"Absolute future" is another name for God, whom we more typically assign to the past.[1] But human experience is essentially a matter of an ever-expanding awareness, which is awareness of both the world and the self. That expansion is what drives the imagination forward, out of memory and into expectation. All of this unfolds in a relationship, for no person comes to awareness alone. The one in relation to whom this expansion of awareness ultimately unfolds, the one we continually expect, is the one we call God. In God the temporal categories of past, present, and future, which seem always to fall apart, fall together. Indeed, they do so in our experience, too, with the present being nothing but the instant intersection of the past and future, with the transitory character of all three being what makes them permanent. The myth of paradise is usually regarded as a story of the old days, but the Golden Age is the one that has not yet come.

Paradise, as Genesis portrays it, is the present moment in which the past and future both are lost. The story of the mistake of Adam and Eve provides us with the doctrine of Original Sin, a peculiarly Catholic reference, given compelling expression by St. Augustine in the fourth century. In fact, Genesis nowhere uses the word "Fall," and it is important to acknowledge that the dogma of human fallenness, attached to the disobedience of Adam and Eve, comes not from the revealed Word of God but from its early interpreters.[2] For Catholics, the chief interpreter, in this regard, was Augustine. But sin was not all of it for him.

The first great theologian of the Western Church, Augustine elevated self-consciousness into an occasion of grace, and he did that through his self-consciousness as a writer. In his works[3] Augustine defined, in effect, the markers of the momentum of creation, from simple being to being alive to being aware to being self-aware. From *Homo sapiens,* that is, comes *Homo sapiens sapiens*—the creature that knows it knows.[4] Each individual human, however modest his or her circumstances, is *all of creation aware of itself,* across all of time and space. Human consciousness, even in its finitude, is unbounded in its reach. In that unboundedness Genesis saw an "image" of God, and Augustine saw God's way of being in the world.

Augustine's *Confessions* is a monument to one man's exploration of his own experience, and his bold assertion is that in such exploration, the man can find his way to God. If the book I am writing has a license, it comes from Augustine—however short of Augustine's achievement this work falls. Its premise is opposed to all those—from Augustine's time to our own—who insist that the only way to God is through the authorized dogmas of orthodoxy, which are overseen by an ordered hierarchy. Augustine, ever alert to the dangers of narcissism, was a defender of orthodoxy, but at a deeper level, "winding down through the spirals of memory," he was an exemplar of the search through human experience as the surest path to sacred illumination. The tensions we have already noted between past, present, and future gave shape in Augustine, for example, to a threefold mode of temporal consciousness in which he recognized nothing less than traces of the Trinity.

In Augustine's supremely self-aware writing, the outrageous proclamation of Genesis, that human life is the very image of God, is applied to one life; one man applying it to himself. Augustine is a treasure not only of the Catholic tradition but of Western civilization, for in taking individual experience so seriously, as divinity's own analogue, he planted seeds that sprouted into the literary genre of autobiography—and ultimately into the idea of democracy, which assumes the primacy of *self*-evidence. ("We hold these truths to be self-evident, that all men are created equal, that they are endowed by their Creator with certain unalienable Rights . . .")

Yet Augustine's reading of the Adam and Eve story is remembered as having put a cold stamp on the Christian mind, and that—more than his glorious celebration of self-exploration—must give this book its starting point.[5] For him and others under the influence of philosophies that disdained physical existence in favor of the spiritual, the fateful sin, which Genesis defined only symbolically—eating fruit of the tree of knowledge—had a decidedly sexual component.[6] That its first consequence was the shame Adam and Eve felt at their nakedness—"I was afraid because I was naked, so I hid"[7]—seemed to prove the point, and Catholicism was suspicious of sex ever after. "Concupiscence" is Augustine's word for that suspicion, and I am sure it was the first four-syllable word I was ever taught to say.

There is an irony in the Catholic doctrine of Original Sin. A primordial fallenness was a shadow descending on the millennia to darken every life, even at its conception. But the expectation of moral disappointment is so thoroughly drummed into us that the Church's own fallenness, evident most in its laughable claim to be unfallen, is not finally disqualifying. Speaking generally, Protestants believe that a church (small *c*, the visible institution) should seek to replicate the Church (large *C*, God's invisible creation). When a church fails to do this, Protestants feel commissioned to leave the church (small *c*) to start a new and better church (again, small *c*). Catholics take for granted the universal condition of self-centeredness from which every person and institution needs to be redeemed. Yet the Church is always rendered as capital *C*. It's imperfections do not disqualify it from being God's. The Church, that is, is only its people. What's the point of leaving? "To whom shall we go, Lord?" Peter asks Jesus.[8] This can lead to a quietist tendency to acquiesce in the face of scandalous behavior, and Roman Catholics often do. Tyrannical popes? Abusive priests? The hypocrisies of the annulment game? Mafia money in the collection basket? Catholics hold to the principle of *ex opere operato*, which literally means "by the work worked." Just by the proper performance of the ritual, an officiant in the state of mortal sin nevertheless validly enacts the sacraments. The priest at Mass can be drunk, but the bread is holy. Braced for the worst, we are not as surprised as we should be when it comes. That, too, is central to the story this book tells.

2. *DE PROFUNDIS*

I was born in a hospital named Little Company of Mary, on the South Side of Chicago, but really I was born in Original Sin. I associate the idea, in my first sense-memory, with the stench of the nearby stockyards, which gave me my dominating metaphor for hell. The yards were laid out, fifty years before I was born, in a perfect square, a mile on each side, straddling the terminal points of three great railroads. Their multitudinous activities, all designed to turn flesh into coin, were organized in a huge maze of animal pens. Tens of thousands of cattle, sheep, and hogs were daily run through long rutted chutes into one of two mammoth slaughterhouses from each of which tall graceful chimneys rose like the upraised fingers of a man going down for the third time. Into the air from those chimneys streamed tons of ash and smoke, the only unused vestige of animals that had been turned into hams and dressed beef as well as glue, brushes, and fertilizer. A cloud of sulfur dioxide poured into the prevailing winds that carried it across Chicago, but the most ferocious stench suffocated my neighborhood, Back of the Yards. It was the concentration of all the foulness. The odor was in the very wood of the floors I learned to crawl on. My nostrils first opened to the stink of death.[9]

The doctrine of Original Sin was the idea in the presence of which my religious awareness first opened. The cries of animals being sacrificed are part of this story, as are the cries of children being born. "Out of the depths I cry unto Thee, O Lord," Psalm 130 begins, and I am sure that was the first psalm that ever registered with me. I knew what crying was, and I could guess what "depths" were. *De profundis:* even the Latin phrase by which the psalm is known is like a rod in my memory. The past has us by the throat even as we come into the world awash in blood. The stockyards give me my religion.

Animal sacrifice, after all, was the moral improvement, whatever the stench, that replaced human sacrifice, the breakthrough in consciousness, embodied in the story of Abraham, Isaac, and the miraculous ram that took the boy's place upon the altar. The story was taken as God's signal that the blood of a human person would never be required again. *De profundis* must have been the music I was hearing when I began to think this way. The line from that psalm takes me back so far in memory, and the Abraham-Isaac story pushes back even further.

But memory itself is the revelation. The past has the very future by the throat. How did I first learn this? Once again, memory tells me—a specific memory. It is a memory, intriguingly, of something that occurred at Mass, which is the symbolic sacrifice in which the animal—the Lamb of God—has itself been replaced by a man.[10] God wills human sacrifice after all, but the beloved son this time is God's own. Judging by the fact that, when I was on my knees at Church that morning, my chin did not come up as high as the edge of the pew in front of me, I could have been no more than five or six years old when the thing happened. I was next to my father. My mother was on the other side of him, and beside her was my brother Joe. The car-sized radiators on the nearby wall were hissing, a sound I attached to the other peculiar aroma, besides the yards, that stamped my youth—the perfume of candles and incense. It was the early morning Mass.

What I knew to wait for from other Masses I had attended was the happy jangling that broke the gloom when an altar boy shook his fist full of brass bells, filling the air. At last the ringing came, but this time, instead of craning toward the altar to see where the sound was coming from, I glanced up at the people around me. Just as I did, they all brought their closed fists sharply against their breasts while muttering something I did not understand. The bells faded, and I realized that the people having hit themselves was somehow tied to that glad sound. Then, before I could begin to take in what was happening, the bells rang out again, and once more the congregants slammed their fists against their breasts, saying something. This time I saw the blows for what they were, acts of real violence, cued to the bells. The bells rang and the people hit themselves. It happened once more. Three times the bent worshipers struck themselves hard enough to make me feel the pain. *Domine, non sum dignus,* they were saying, in unison with the priest. *Domine, non sum dignus. Domine, non sum dignus.* Much later, I would understand: "Lord, I am not worthy . . . Lord, I am not worthy . . . Lord, I am not worthy . . ."

An adaptation of what a Roman soldier said to Jesus, the full pre-Communion affirmation continues, " . . . but only say the word, and my soul shall be healed."[11] But the people around me never made it as far as that act of hope, much as the prayer of *de profundis* never, in my hearing, went on to the promise of redemption. Unworthiness was all there was for these people, the depths their only home. Such explicit meaning eluded my consciousness, of course, but its emotional truth landed on me with full force. Associating the abject gesture of fist on breast with voices crying *de profundis,* I knew that something of enormous importance, as much for me as for the people I was part of, was happening right then. An oceanic question opened in my breast: *What are you doing? And why?*

The people from whom I spring were defined by the Chicago stockyards. They were its shitkickers, pipefitters, knife wielders, men whose job was to keep the blood flowing through the bowels of the slaughterhouses. Those were "the depths" out of which they came. When the drain holes clotted, the crimson soup would back up in the pipes, bubbling out onto the killing lines, covering the ankles of the butchers, forcing a stop, which in turn caused commotion in the pens, risking the animal panic of stampede. When that happened, the beasts would climb over each other before finding no escape, and then their common wail would replace the stench as the manifestation of stockyards horror. The stampede cry of twenty thousand caged animals, as from the throat of one creature, would carry out across the South

Side, and drivers would stop their cars to listen, and worry. Out of the depths, the cry. But the uproar was the sound of meat being manufactured, the dead opposite of the muted anguish of the Auld Sod, where peasants and their children had sunk silently into the stupor of starvation. The Irish in Chicago, well fed because of the blood, never complained of the stink.

During the Great Famine, the population of Ireland had shrunk by something like six million—a holocaust of starvation and exile.[12] It followed the blight of the potato, a crop on which the Irish had become overly dependent because, unlike other crops, the British could not burn it. The famine drove the emigration that brought my people to America. They were in flight from a vast fetid killing field, though it could only be spoken of as the green land of leprechauns. The Emerald Isle. Yet no one emerging from the fog of such a past presumed to have left it behind. The most the children and grandchildren of the famine could do was hollow out all memory with the spade of denial, digging an emotional abyss out of which nothing would come but an unslaked thirst and the barbed wit that passed for Irish humor. That abyss would always be there as the black hole into which they and their children and their children's children—myself—would be forever terrified of falling back. Out of those depths no cry had come, which is why the grief-struck psalm could itself seem an act of hope.

The stockyards defined the famine's antidote, but at a terrible cost. At the end of each workday, the South Siders stood under a scalding shower, trying to scrub the stench of slaughter from their skin. If they left the neighborhood, they always sensed their fellow passengers on the El squinting their noses at them. Indeed, the sensation of foul odors never fully left the nostrils of my people, and the permanent fear was that they themselves were the source of it.[13] My Irish-American forebears spent their lives trying to escape the claws reaching up for them out of the starvation grounds of their ancestors, and out of the blood pits and shit holes of their own youths, to pull them back down where they belonged. Into the depths, not out of them. *Who do you think you are!*[14]

Those fists against those breasts were the most eloquent religious expression I ever saw, and alas, it shaped my faith. I was born into an unworthy people. A mere symbol, yet I knew an act of self-hating violence when I saw one, and that it was carried out to the glad music of bells taught me all I needed to know about the contradiction that adheres to my religion. When, later, I asked my mother what the people were doing when they hit themselves in church, she waved me off: "It's just a prayer, Jimmy."

What my mother knew was the other side of the story, how that bent people was just then coming into its own. The great democratic mixing of World War II had just occurred, and immigrant Catholicism was already being triumphantly transformed. The GI Bill of Rights was sending a generation of Micks, Wops, Polacks, and Krauts to college. The postwar economic boom was giving them a foretaste of real prosperity. The institutions of American Catholicism were thriving, with nearly fifty thousand priests, three times that number of nuns, four hundred seminaries across the country, and almost ten thousand parochial schools—including hundreds of high schools staffed by teaching brothers. In 1950 there were almost a million infant baptisms, which was a signal of the famously fertile birthrate. But that year, more significantly, there were well over a hundred thousand adult baptisms, showing that conversion to the Catholic Church was now a mark of American life.[15] By every measure, the Catholic people were strong and succeeding, the furthest thing from the legion of breast beaters among whom I found myself.

And yet success, I was learning, was not to be trusted. My first lesson in religion was that we humans are born with a feeling of existential inadequacy. I am not certain if I believe in other expressly Catholic orthodoxies—God's intervention in nature through miracles, say, or the survival of the individual personality after death—and I actively disbelieve in some—the infallibility of the pope, sexuality as the condition of concupiscence. But I firmly believe in the Catholic doctrine of Original Sin, which is the way I understand my own limits, my inbred sadness, and my unshakable suspicion that, even before setting out on life's journey, I had lost my way. I say "my own," but this accumulated insecurity is inherited, and in these grim feelings I recognize my patrimony. Inbred, indeed. A feeling of unworthiness is the core of my selfhood, and I know exactly where I get it.

The clue is the slaughterhouse and animal sacrifice. So the mind leaps, again, to Abraham and Isaac. If *de profundis* was the psalm that first registered with me, the tale of that father and son was my first Bible story. The boy follows his father up the hill. He loves his father, and his father loves him. Their love for each other is the ground on which each one walks. From his father, the son has learned trust. Or rather, from his own absolute confidence in his father, the son knows what trust is. Trust is the feeling he has whenever he and his father are together.

Like now. The boy is carrying a load of wood for the father. He has done this before, whenever he has followed his father up the mountain of sacrifice. He carries the wood because his father must carry the offering. The wood is for the fire in which the offering will be consumed, as the Holy One requires. The son does not know why the Holy One requires sacrifice. It is enough to know that his father does as the Holy One requires. It is not the Holy One in whom the boy has placed his trust. It is his father in whom he trusts.

But wait. Something is different. The boy looks up from beneath the burden of the bundled wood he carries on his back. His father, as usual, goes ahead. But today his father is not carrying an offering. No first fruits. No lamb for the slaughter. His father's arms are empty. *Where is the offering, Father?* the boy would like to ask. *Where is the young animal or the bushel of crops to be consumed by the fire you will build with this wood that I carry? When we reach the top of the mountain, the place of sacrifice, what will you burn?* These are the questions the boy has, but he cannot ask them. That is also strange. He has never hesitated to ask questions of his father before. This question feels different. *What, Father, will you set afire?*

The Abraham-Isaac story in Genesis is an elaboration of the meaning of Original Sin.[16] Original, in Genesis, however, refers not to the primal offense but to a blessing that precedes it. There was Original Sin, but before that there was a Creator beholding creation and saying, *This is good. This is very good.*[17] That, too, is of the story. *In the beginning God* is how the Bible starts, the most implication-laden phrase not in the text but in the language. The word "God" and the word "good" go together, which is why God says it. But in pronouncing the creation good, perhaps the Creator was, in fact, making an argument more than an affirmation, declaring it good when there were already reasons to think otherwise.

What does it take for a parent to slay his child? For a long time I could plumb this mystery only from the point of view of the son. But then I became a father. When my daughter and son were small, the absolute truth of my life—and this is every parent's absolute truth—was that I would protect them from everything, forever. As they grew up, I grew, too. We all grew into the knowledge that I could not do it. There is a tragedy at the heart of human existence from which there is no protection. *Is that tragedy good?* Not only would I be unable to shield my precious ones from what awaited them; from a certain point on, it would hurt them if I tried. That certain point is their adulthood, and when a parent comes to it, the parent comes into a second maturity.

Surely this was what Abraham knew. Leave aside the particular mystery of the *Akedah* (for "binding," as in "the binding of Isaac") story: How could the Holy One even seem to require the slaughter of the son by the father? How could Abraham even contemplate obeying such a commandment? At an even more primal level, what Abraham and Isaac were both confronting was the ultimate human dilemma that each of them was fated to be slain by the structure of life itself. *How can that be good, very good?* Isaac was spared his fate by a ram, but in truth his fate was only postponed. Now, of course, it matters if a parent is the actual agent of the slaughter of the child; it matters if one generation sends its juniors off to war. But these crimes and tragedies unfold within the larger crime and tragedy that is human life itself.

Or is it? I spoke earlier of trust. The One who creates *ex nihilo* is no nihilist. To me, that is what this story concerns. A child's trust in a parent, so complete, so unquestioning, must be outgrown. Questions are the essence of wisdom: *What is this wood for, Father? What will we be burning?* This story is not about Isaac's trust in Abraham, but about Abraham's trust in the Holy One. The Holy One, creator of life that ends in death, the Holy One who was already doing to Abraham what the Holy One was asking Abraham to do to Isaac. Knowing what we know about this existence, can we trust it anyway? Can we trust the author of the story that is unfolding here, in our experience day by day?

The biblical tradition, as I read it now, and the living religious traditions that are nourished by that tradition—my own Christianity and, as I understand them, rabbinic Judaism and Islam—suggest an answer to this question. And the answer is yes. *Out of the depths I cry unto Thee, O Lord. For with Thee there is mercy and plenteous redemption.*[18] Life is trustworthy, though it ends in death, the ultimate in depths. Death is at the service of life. There is no glib or easy way to say that. And, with Isaac, who has every right to feel betrayed, as with every child who has ever been sent by a parent into the maw of war, we know that there are good reasons never to trust anyone or anything again. Were it otherwise, trust would not be trust, for the trust of maturity, as opposed to childhood, is the act of affirmation that is made despite, not because.

So, yes: *In the beginning God . . . And God said this is good, very good.*

3. JIMMY MARCHING

My mother and father—their names were Mary and Joseph. Given the character of this son they had—no Messiah—their names should perhaps have been Adam and Eve, and I wish they were. If I am Abel, I am also Cain—the favored son who hates himself for being favored. But at least I would not be what, for the first years of my pious association, I was by definition, the son of Mary and Joseph who was not worthy of the family names.

But that was not my mother's thought. To her I was the anointed one, that's all. "*Did you see my little Jimmy marching . . .*" She would sing the Irving Berlin ditty as she bounced me on her knee. The memory is sensuous. The light of a morning sun is washing the parquet floor and sound fills the air, her voice in synchrony with my own pleasured laughing. Pleasure was to be the sole object of her attention. "*. . . With the soldiers up the avenue?*" The bouncing and the singing were a regular feature of my earliest years, and I knew the lyrics of that oft-repeated song long before I understood them. The words described an entire regiment of heroes heading off to war:

> There was Jimmy just as stiff as starch,
> Like his Daddy on the seventeenth of March . . .
> Away he went,
> To live in a tent;
> Over in France with his regiment.

This music remains in my mind as the very structure of rhythm, the ground of order. "*Were you there, and tell me, did you notice? They were all out of step but Jim.*" I took in what those words meant, but it was years before I got the joke.

That song was the most condensed affirmation I ever received. My mother was simply telling me that if the whole world stood against me, I was right and the world was wrong. She had found a song to say so, and it addressed me by name. Her voice, her fingers around mine, the trustworthy thrill of her dancing knee, the defense against all my accusers, the morning sun on the polished floor—this one memory remains the standard against which I measure every experience of happiness.

Now, in reading the lyrics, I notice that Jimmy is heading off to war: *"It made me glad, to gaze at the lad; Lord help the Kaiser if he's like his Dad."* But I heard the song as concerning only me, and what was it but the answer to *Domine, non sum dignus?* If I believed that my being out of step was all right, instead of yet another signal of unworthiness, it was only because of her saying it was so. "*They were all out of step but Jim.*" The purity of insinuation in her voice made the affirmation absolute. Those who were out of step were the ones slamming their fists into their breasts. I did not need to do that. If I believe that affirmation still—and in some part, given the choices I have made (some of which involved a refusal of war), I must—it is still, in that same part, because of her.

To a child being brought into the mystery of the storied Holy Family, there were no coincidences. If I have laid claim to a deep capacity for trust, which, despite all contradiction, most profoundly defines the Catholic faith (trust in God defined, first, as trust in the self), I know where it comes from. Mary, the mother of Jesus, is called in the tradition a second Eve, because, by the fruit of her womb, she turned the Original Sin back against itself. Opposing these two women, Eve and Mary, as occupying polarities of sin and salvation, one defined as sex, the other as virginity, is the foundational mistake of the Catholic narrative, and I would internalize it. But even so, Mary as the answer to Eve was the great story of a second chance, and as much as I was born in Original Sin, I was born, son of my own Mary, into the warm aura of that redemption. That is what it meant when I learned that my mother had another name than Mom, and of course I thought of her, then, when she told me the name of our hospital, the place where she gave birth to me, the Little Company of Mary.

The name referred to the order of nursing nuns who ran the place, but I thought the company was of "Marys." Hadn't Mom been admitted to that particular hospital because she was one of them? Every Catholic has a confusion of Marys—there is the Blessed Virgin and there is Mary Magdalen, remembered as the repentant whore, yet another Eve—but in my case the name Mary, even double-barreled like that, was an *Open Sesame!* I now realize that the transcendent associations of her name defined my mother as the counterbalance to the inbred sense of unworthiness I sensed at church, just as the slaughter yards were balanced by a hospital, as I myself was balanced on her dandling knee.

This is the common territory of human development, how infants learn trust from the mother's smile, and how children move through the gates of a growing independence, supported by, and in conflict with, their parents—and ultimately finding a place among the larger group outside the family. In my case, this normalcy came cloaked in the language of religion, with the names of saints and martyrs invoked as the audience for our progression and the sponsors of it. I moved, as everyone does, from believing my parents were God to believing them, by virtue of the accident of their names, to be the parents of God, to understanding them, finally, as poor banished children of Eve like all of us. The point is, my parents, through our version of the ancient cycle, brought me into the way of choosing that is trusting by bringing me into a way of knowing that is believing. Where they brought me is where I remain.

4. GROWING UP WITH JESUS

In the beginning God . . . And in the middle God, and at the end as well. We are still in the shade of Billy Pilgrim's question about time, but time opens into space. *Where is God?* the nuns asked me, and I knew the answer: *Everywhere.* It was the core truth of my first awareness: *God is everywhere. Even here.* Catholicism is the language I was given to know that, and to know everything else that mattered. Election was the core of it, but not the whole of it. If I invoke memories of my first people here, it is because they taught me the religious lesson par excellence—how every people of God regards itself as the Chosen People. Jews do this, Catholics do it, born-again Christians do it, Muslims do it. And the catechism word for this affirming prodigality is "everywhere." God belongs to every place and every person, yet without getting lost in an abstract universality. *God is everywhere. Even here.*

It takes a balancing mind to say such a thing. Soon enough, I began to think that balance was the business of Catholicism, and just in time. I had to discover a way to live with what I had inherited, finding balance between being unworthy and being chosen. Between the stench of the slaughter yards and the sweet aroma of candles and incense. Between the self-doubt that my pew-mates showed me and the willed affirmation that I still associate with my mother. But because she was "Mary," I received an invitation to identify myself with Mary's son, who was the Son of God. This can be the warm bath of mere narcissism, a Christian version of the Jewish-mother joke, but there was more to it than my being ushered into a false sense of myself as Messiah.

About the time my infantile gaze was shifting away from the company of Marys, the figure of Jesus presented itself as an object of contemplation. This man came into my awareness when I was very young, and he did so as a point of automatic identification. Despite being the son of Mary and Joseph, and despite sharing a pair of initials with him, I never confused myself with Jesus, but neither did I imagine a life apart from him. I grew up with Jesus. He was a pole around which my consciousness turned, a mysterious figure in relation to whom, bit by bit, I constructed a sense of self.

Jesus was a friend and a stranger. He was a god and a human. He was a stern judge and a forgiver. Above all, even in being raised from the dead, he was mortal. Wherever I looked, I saw him. And when I saw him, I saw something of the man I wanted to be. And never would be. A man of virtue, and a keeper of bad company. An itinerant, and a man at home in alien rooms. A lover of women, and of loneliness. The balancing of such contradictions—wasn't balance the skill that defined the lad who had to carry the bundle of wood up the mountain of sacrifice? In that Isaac story, too, I saw Jesus, how he trailed his Father through desolation, noticing too late that his Father's arms were empty. *Where is the object of sacrifice, Father?* What struck me early and strong—and surely this was the main point of my first full identification with him—was the complexity of the relationship between Jesus and his Father. My young mind exploded to learn that, from the top of that mountain of sacrifice, also known as Golgotha, the son hurled an accusation against his beloved Father: *My God, my God, why have you abandoned me?*[19]

I did not know until years after they had branded my soul that these words of Jesus were from a psalm (Psalm 22) and were therefore, perhaps, less a cry of despair than an anguished prayer—his own *de pro-*

fundis. That the Gospel of Mark, composed in Greek, put this one line in the Aramaic—*Eloi Eloi, lama sabachthani*—suggests that the desperate prayer may well have been wrenched from the disillusioned Jesus himself and not necessarily supplied after the fact by Gospel writers drawing on Jewish Scripture, as is true of so many other details of the Passion story. We will see more in this book of how the Gospels were composed, and why it matters, but here we should note that this accusing plea very likely points to an experience of forsakenness belonging to the historical Jesus. He expected some kind of protection from God and did not get it. I took the line that way in my first naïve readings, and still do.

My God, my God, why have you abandoned me? The literal meaning of these words still defines the moment of my identification with Jesus. God is everywhere, we are told, but God was not with Jesus when he needed God. Christianity was born in the broken hopes not first of the followers of Jesus ("We were hoping he was the one to save Israel," the devastated disciple tells the stranger on the road to Emmaus[20]), but of Jesus himself. *Why, Father, have you chosen to make a sacrifice of me?* That heart-crushing note, evoking an experience of absolute existential betrayal, is what made the story of the Galilean so closely mine.

I was born a white American male near the middle of the twentieth century, which puts me in history's charmed circle. I have no illusions about my privilege. Yet that election makes my sensitivity to the furious injustices of the human condition all the more acute. From an early age, I sensed broken hopes all around me, even among the well fed with whom I lived. It was my legacy, reaching back past slaughter yards and famine. An unsettled wind was blowing in the world into which I was born,[21] and I felt it on my neck. *Lord, I am not worthy.* Then the poor banished child of Eve nudges his neighbor to whisper, *And if I'm not worthy, neither are you, bub.* But if the generations do this awful thing to one another, then how can the One who generated the generations remain unaccused? *Where is God? Nowhere.* Here is the beginning of our story.

That the first half of the double-barreled but contradictory climax of the greatest story ever told renders the shock of God's complete absence from Golgotha forces me, again with the Jesus around whom my consciousness gyres, to the climax's second half. Having cried out his abandonment, Jesus then declared a final act of faith: *Yet into Your hands I commend my spirit.*[22] Unbeknownst to me for years, those words were also from a psalm (Psalm 31). All I knew was that they were, in my mind, joined always to the words that preceded them from the mouth of Jesus as he was dying. First abandonment, then trust. The power of Jesus' ultimate handing himself over depends on that penultimate forsakenness.

My knowledge of the literary sources of Jesus' last words, and my questions about their historicity, have not changed their meaning or their character as the ground of my faith. The cry of despair and the act of self-surrender, in fact, come from separate accounts of Jesus' death, yet they are recounted as instants in the one story. In their conjunction, these two anguished cries amount to the purest form of prayer, which is inevitably an affirmation of oppositions. Rage at the Father and trust in the Father in the same moment. In my experience, those words—accusation and commendation—are the only prayer, and they must be twinned. That such a contradiction is at the heart of this mystery can itself seem to be a source of shame, a violation of order, and the cause of an ultimate negation. Nihilism after all. But the contradiction exists, and in the dispensation of this faith, the contradiction evokes the primal vision, God looking upon such oppositions and saying simply, *This is good. This is very good.*

5. IN GOD WHO IS NOT THERE

If this is a book about being Catholic, it must be a book less about bishops and doctrines and nostalgia and theology and history—the *reconquista*, the so-called culture of death, an argument with modernism, a German pope who downplays the German crime, the hatred of sex, clerical defensiveness, sexual abuse—than about the simple moment when a human being's heart opens in the act of handing himself, and all that he cares for, over into the care of God—but the care of God who is not there. Catholicism is nothing if not a way of doing that.[23] Nothing, that is, if not a kind of worship at the altar of contradiction. It is impossible to account fully for human existence except by reference to something outside the human realm, but it is equally impossible to articulate what or who is being referred to. Prayer, therefore, is this book's deepest subject—the prayer of those who find prayer impossible.

The ultimate contradiction comes at the moment for which every prayer is an act of getting ready. As noted in the introduction, we Catholics easily describe ourselves as "practicing," which implies the hope of getting better. As a defining phrase, "practicing Catholic" thwarts the impulse to claim much in the way of holiness or gravitas, yet it implies a question. What, actually, are we practicing for? And the answer comes not easily but automatically, and it comes out of the depths. What we are practicing for is death.

To repeat what I was taught: there are two lives, and they are divided by the moment of death. Ordinarily, we think of the moment of dying as off in some undefined future, but the "practicing" to which we Catholics are called involves the recognition that every moment is the moment of death. That is literally true, as each instant yields to the next, with the past accumulating behind us like so much detritus. Memory is the faculty with which we not only retrieve what has been lost, but also, and more to the point, experience it as treasure instead of waste. We are back to Augustine, living life in anticipation, but understanding it in reminiscence, and the understanding is what promises the defeat of death. "Life is not ended," Catholics are told in every funeral liturgy, "but only changed."[24] Yet the change begins when we learn to think this way. The longed-for afterlife is already here.

Clearly, the mode of this reflection on the meaning of my Catholic faith is essentially an act of brooding memory, but that is because remembering is itself a refusal of death. Remembering is concerned less with the past, rendered present in memory, than with the future that memory's wisdom makes possible. The divided, and therefore always alienating, experience of threefold time (what drove Billy Pilgrim to Tralfamadore) collapses into the felt unity of an eternal present. Not collapses, but rather rises. For this enactment itself, in the light of faith, is a foretaste of resurrection.

The figure of "Christ Crucified," in St. Paul's phrase, has its roots deep in the Christian imagination. How could it be otherwise, given what Christians claim to believe? Creeds aside, however, the corpus of Jesus hung on a cross, as an object of art as much as of devotion, was conceived in the refusal to avert the eye from the worst fact of the human condition. The point of the story of the crucified God, after all, is that no one is exempt from the fate that defeats every hope, not even the One who made it so.

The Western imagination has been similarly branded by the implications of this object. As ancient Greek art defined itself around the voluptuous and athletic nude, one could argue, the art of Christendom, even into the Greece-worshiping Renaissance that marked its end, defined itself around the naked agony of the man on the cross. I myself am the measure of what such physicality does to the imagination, for, though I was taught from an early age to distrust the body as "an occasion of sin," I simultaneously understood that physical existence is what really matters.

When, at the age of five or six, I was set free to run in the woods, experiencing myself as fleet-footed, capable of great leaps, susceptible to shortness of breath, exhilarated by the simple movement of my legs—I was as in love with my body as any hedonist. When, eventually, physical self-awareness became a matter of sexual restlessness, I knew, too, that flesh had transcendent significance, the realm of salvation as much as damnation. My five senses—smell, sight, touch, hearing, taste—were canonized by my religion. Hence sacred associations, already noted, with the stink of the stockyards, the jangle of bells, the hissing of radiators. Smut and guilt were part of the story—girlie pictures. Or, say, the ambushing sight of a classmate's ankle below the hem of her plaid skirt. But so were sensations of delight and satiation—the blissful exhaustion of playing touch football into the twilight. That girl's eyes, when she caught me looking at her. Bodies mattered in this religion, and we saw that above every altar. The body of Jesus, that is, was posted in our world as an icon of sensuality, an inevitable invitation to attend to our own bodies, for better and for worse.

Though the image of the crucifixion, thus implanted in culture, lives on as the vertical-horizontal measure of a world religion, it is rarely seen in the fullness of its historic horror. The body of Jesus shows what can befall the body. Ironically, if the horror is lost, so is its transcendent meaning. The crucifix should console less than appall. I remember putting my hand in front of my face and imagining what a nail through its palm would feel like. Yet pain could be exquisite. That, too, is part of the story of this kind of sensuality.

Why has the agonized death of Jesus so preoccupied the Christian imagination? Or has it? Protestant Christianity defined its objection to Roman Catholicism by nothing more dramatic than the banishment of the corpus from the cross. In most Protestant churches there is no body, only the wood; the "remains" are gone.[25] This rejection of the vivid reproduction of Jesus' suffering was partly a matter of an iconoclastic repudiation of visual excess, but it was also a way of pointing toward the Resurrection. The empty cross evokes the empty tomb.

But the purging of the corpse also reflected an ancient uneasiness with the knotty center of the Christian story. The naked wood of the Protestant cross, by what it does not display, acknowledges, in effect, the catastrophe—and the catastrophic problem—on which Christian faith is based. Similarly, in the Eastern Orthodox tradition, little or no emphasis has ever been given to the cross, much less the crucifix. Instead of the corpus, in the East one sees the iconic face of the risen Christ; instead of the crucifixion, it is the Resurrection that unfetters the imagination; instead of misery, glory is rendered.

In the first three centuries after Christ, the cross was not a defining Christian symbol, the corpus even less so. On the walls of catacombs, one sees images of the fish, the cup, the loaf of bread—not the cross.[26] It was only with the early-fourth-century conversion of the emperor Constantine, after a vision of the cross in the sky, that this symbol (with the mythic resonance of its vertical-horizontal axis) seized the Christian imagination. Crucifixion had been eliminated as a means of capital punishment, and the many thousands of crucified victims of the empire began to fade from memory as the cross was associated exclusively with Jesus. And when the "true cross" was discovered by Constantine's mother, Helena, the responsibility for the crucifixion was decisively shifted from the Romans to the Jews. Even then, the cross was taken more as a token of resurrection than of brutal death.

It was only in the medieval period that the Latin Church began to put the violent death of Jesus at the center of faith, but that theology was tied to a broader societal obsession with death, related to plagues, millennialism, and the carnage of the Crusades. Grotesquely literal renditions of the crucifixion came into art when self-flagellation and other mortifications came into devotion. Indeed, the moment of the death of Jesus was then understood as marking the division in time between the old era (Old Testament) and the new (New Testament). The death of Jesus, that is (not the Resurrection or the content of his teaching or the example of his life), was understood as the saving event. Death became the center of the religion here.

The theology underwriting all of this was expressed in the eleventh-century treatise *Cur Deus Homo?* (Why Did God Become a Man?), written by St. Anselm, the first great theologian of the Middle Ages. The answer to the question was direct: God became a man because only the infinite sacrifice of a God-man could atone for the infinite offense God took from human sin, and the atonement could be accomplished only by the death of the God-man. Protestants and Catholics both interpreted this "atonement theology" to mean the infinite offense God took at the sin of human beings could be atoned for only by an infinite act of punishment. This theology was commonly read as positing a loving God who handed Jesus over to executioners out of infinite compassion for each sinner, yet it equally assumed a cruel Father who, for his own appeasement, required the extreme suffering and death of his only son, a divine scapegoat. This theology reflected the age, coinciding as it did (1098) with the First Crusade, a campaign of savage violence launched under the slogan "God wills it!" It was in this culture of sanctified suffering that artists began to sculpt figures of Jesus *agonistes.*[27]

But the corpus-on-the-cross struck a deep chord in the Christian psyche. After all, the Jesus movement evolved into "the Church" precisely by coming to terms with the great shock of the leader's death. Jesus himself was mistaken about his prospects, and his followers' hopes were crushed by his demise. Hopes for Israel, in particular. How could he and they have been so wrong? How could the horrors of Good Friday have come to pass? How could the Romans have been triumphant over Israel?

In answer to these questions, the bewildered and grief-struck Jesus people drew on a heretofore unemphasized Jewish tradition (seen in Isaiah and Psalms) that viewed suffering as a sign of God's election. The followers of Jesus invented an interpretation of his death (the Passion narratives of the Gospels) that reversed normal human expectation, turning defeat into a kind of victory. ("O death," St. Paul asks, "where is your sting?"[28]) Existential and ontological reversal became the Christian motif, with an exaltation of servanthood over lordship that was embodied by the Lord himself. Signs of "life to the full" were detected in the death of Christ, and that insight was given expression in the story of the Resurrection.

It was when Christians dared to see in Jesus an analogue of God that this cult of reversal took on transcendent meaning and boundless appeal, especially among the masses of subject peoples in the Roman Empire for whom such reversal represented the only imaginable hope. Paul began with the insight that God works the divine will in the world by using what the world holds in utter contempt: a crucified man. Soon that man was understood to have been—and still to be—God. A profound question about the injustice and perplexity of the human condition found its answer in the extraordinary assertion that God, too, is at the mercy of injustice and perplexity. It was impossible for this idea to remain at the level of abstraction; it had to be rendered imaginatively, physically. That is why, ultimately, the stunningly eloquent symbol of this mad hope became the body of the man who was taken to be God, at the moment when all of its divinity was gone. The moment, as Paul puts it, when God "emptied Himself."[29]

The Roman Catholic Church, unlike Orthodox Christianity and most Protestant churches, defines itself by the crucifix, and there are problems with that—not just the hint, or even the sanction, of sadomasochism. The *living* of the life of Jesus deserves as much emphasis as the ending of that life, and the light of Easter dawn should penetrate farther than the darkness of the Good Friday noon. But Catholics are attuned to the structure of the Gospel narrative, according to which the Resurrection is not the climax but the denouement. The moment that reverberates in the Catholic imagination, when God is simultaneously present and absent, is the moment of brute finality, which is the moment of final option. The option in favor of the harsh truth of God's absence, and in favor of an act of handing-over anyway. That the climax of the story of Jesus is such a double-barreled instant of dying—accusation and commendation both—gives shape less to our faith than to our way of understanding existence itself. Each present moment is practice, therefore, for the last. *Why have you abandoned me?* becomes *Into your hands.*

Each present moment *is* the last. And now we know. The claws that would drag us back down into the bog, and against which we have so passionately kicked our whole lives long, will not have their way with us in the end. Or, if they do, the bog will not be what we feared it was.

CHAPTER TWO

THE GOD OF MY YOUTH

1. THE PERFECT SOCIETY

THE TURNING POINT of my young life was not the decision to become a Catholic priest but the decision to become a particular kind of priest. We will see more of this later, but here it is important to note that my mature Catholicism follows from a vocational choice that, given my circumstances, I should never have made. Because, at the time of my deciding, I was a student at Georgetown, the Jesuit university in Washington, and because my father had himself been educated by Jesuits, at Loyola in Chicago, I might have been expected, if I was to be a priest, to become a Jesuit. Or, because I was mainly raised in the Washington area, and our family circle included influential members of the Washington clergy, I might typically have become a priest of the Archdiocese of Washington. As a "secular priest" I would have been able to follow my father into the Air Force, if as a chaplain. I had attended a Benedictine prep school in Washington, and was drawn, even as a boy, to the beauty, fraternity, and rigor of the monastic life. But I chose none of those paths. Instead I joined a small, relatively unknown religious order, the Paulist Fathers. I like to think my girlfriends were surprised that I felt called to be a priest, but the surprise for most others who knew me was what kind of priest.

The Paulists were a "modern" group operating under the slogan "missionaries to Main Street." They were known, if at all, for their publishing house, Paulist Press. Their flagship publication, the *Catholic World,* was an influential journal, but only in the relatively marginal world of highbrow Catholicism. The Paulists sponsored Catholic shows on radio and television, aiming to present the Church in its most ecumenical light to the wider culture, but the programs—test-pattern testimonials—were broadcast mostly in the hours when stations signed on and off the air. But if the order was obscure, that was surely because to America it was a bit too Catholic, while to Catholics it was a bit too American.

The Paulists had been founded in New York by an American convert from Protestantism in the middle of the nineteenth century, Isaac Hecker. An early intimate of Emerson and Thoreau, Hecker was a one-person bridge across the mid-nineteenth century's otherwise unpassable chasm between immigrant Catholicism and mainstream America, yet he was a man I had never heard of. My parents, pleased as they were to imagine me as a priest, were mystified by my choice of the Paulists, and, looking back on it, so am I.

Hecker turned out to be a transitional figure for Roman Catholicism, a pioneer in a new way of thinking of the Church, and his influence grew quietly across the century after his death. The Paulists themselves—there were fewer than three hundred of them when I joined, compared to something like thirty thousand Jesuits—were a kind of slow-rising yeast in American Catholicism, embodying insights of liberal democracy, respect for personal freedom, and belief in the primacy of the individual. These tenets, more Thoreau and Emerson than Ignatius and Benedict, led, at several points in their history, to their being looked at askance—if not suppressed by the Vatican. Hecker was nearly condemned as a heretic.

I was conscious of neither this history nor its implications for my future development as a certain kind of Catholic, but I must have been implicitly attuned to the undercurrent. Indeed, I was only accidentally drawn to the order, following an unplanned encounter with a Paulist recruiter at Georgetown during my freshman year, but I was instantly attracted to that spirit, even without being able yet to identify it for what it was. I remained a Paulist for a dozen years. It has been more than thirty-five years since I left the order, but the Paulist esprit, as I experienced it back then, still defines the kind of Catholic I am.

To fully appreciate what an astounding turn in my life story my choice of the Paulist Fathers was, and to appreciate what a turn in the story of Roman Catholicism the Paulists foreshadowed, it is necessary to go back to the beginning, to the Church in which I first became aware.

Catholics of a certain age remember the Church as a self-described "perfect society," a designation officially dating to Pope Leo XIII late in the nineteenth century.[1] In the twentieth century, a theology of the Church as the "Mystical Body of Christ" reinforced us in our conviction that, just as Jesus had all the attributes of a human yet was divine, so with the institution of which he was founder. The Catholic Church and its Lord were somehow identical, and claims made for one could be made for the other. This theology was given its ultimate expression in the encyclical *Mystici Corporis,* which was issued in 1943, six months after I was born.

We knew that the Church was all too human, with its "whiskey priests" and, during the corrupt Renaissance era, its hedonist popes. We took for granted that our nuns were irascible, that the young curate had a vain attachment to the part in his hair, and that the monsignor's brusqueness with the altar boys approached cruelty. We the Catholic people, well instructed by those selfsame nuns and clergy, were all too aware of our "fallenness," manifest at every Mass, when almost no one presumed to approach the Communion rail, where only those in the "state of grace" were welcome. That *Domine, non sum dignus* was the proclamation that kept the people in their pews at Communion time. Parochial school children, having been dutifully ushered to Confession on Saturday afternoon, were expected to climb over their rigid parents and other worshipers, whose adult venality—adultery?—was on full display in their immobility.

Yet such manifestations of the universality of sinfulness seemed oddly to confirm the large claim made for the Church as such, a community of the fallen that nevertheless understood itself as God's one true way of being present in the world. Abject awareness of moral servility, after all, was the purest form of virtue.

That paradox was captured in the Church's sense of itself as a sacrament of the Real Presence. If this claim seemed to contradict undisputed facts of history or undeniable foibles of the hierarchy, still the contradiction could be discounted because the sanctity of which we bragged was, well, mystical. It never occurred to us that the doctrinal phrase "Mystical Body" was really a contradiction in terms. What we knew was that membership in this holy, if all too human, Church (which membership involved the triune notes of Baptism, profession of the faith, and union with the pope) was enough to alter one's destiny forever. And the sacredness of such membership was not merely theoretical. There was a reassuring totality about our lives as Catholics; it enabled us to accommodate the nurtured sense of being fractured, that unworthiness.

Church was the center of life, and its rituals were soothingly predictable. All we ever heard from the pulpit was that we had better show up at Mass on Sundays or go straight to hell; that we owed absolute loyalty to the pope, the divine-right monarch of our truest realm; that the Blessed Virgin Mary was the avatar of the dutiful subservience to which all were called, especially women. It never seemed to matter that the priest's most passionate denunciations were aimed at those who were not present. That our chain-smoking, hard-drinking pastor was nothing like Bing Crosby did not stop us from believing that the movie priest Crosby portrayed was real.

The word "parish" comes from the Greek and means "near the house," and that's where we midcentury Catholics spent our lives. We had our parish schools, parish bazaars, parish picnics, and parish clubs. The parish church dependably located us in space. On our knees before the tabernacle, or before the bank of blue votive lights at Mary's feet, we knew exactly where we were and where we belonged. At times of deep significance—not just the life stages of birth, death, illness, marriage, and passage into adulthood, but also the mundane but pointed moments of failure and success—the parish, through its elegantly simple sacraments, assured us we were not alone. The taste of an unleavened wafer, the sound of a warbling soloist, the aromas of wax and incense, altar wine, the male odor of a priest's cassock, the scent of soap on Sister, the sight of Kleenex squares pinned to the heads of young women, the feel of dime-sized tiddlywinks with which we covered squares on bingo cards—it all meant home to us.

In addition to space, the parish located us in time, stamping the very year. Advent and Lent were the brackets of winter, Christmas was the solstice to us, light in the deepest dark. Holy Week and Easter were the spring festival of death and new life. The week was stamped similarly—especially by fish on Friday and Mass on Sunday. Midnight Friday was good news, because then you could put hamburger meat in the frying pan, but on Saturday, midnight was bad because then you had to begin the fast ahead of Holy Communion the next morning. We were Catholics by the day, the week, the month, and the year. Membership in the Church was a womb of place and time. We believed its practice was the same across the earth (hence the importance of Latin) and across the centuries (the importance of unchangeability), notes that themselves gave expression to the overriding theological claim.[2]

2. MARTYR OF CONSCIENCE

For Americans there was a special poignancy in the notion of the Church's perfection, for we felt the sting of an avowedly Protestant nation's denigration of, or at best condescension toward, pope-centered Catholicism. We emphasized that the word "catholic" meant universal, even as we downplayed the way that "Roman" marked us as an inevitably parochial people, defined by geographical and cultural particularity. Indeed, our parochial schools represented our greatest accomplishment. Never mind that for everyone else the word "parochial" was no compliment. To us, the cosmic and the parochial were not contradictory, any more than there was a conflict of loyalties between, as we put it, "God and country," however much we were accused of that very thing.

The saga of Alfred E. Smith, the unsuccessful Democratic nominee for president in 1928, loomed large in the midcentury Catholic imagination. Al Smith had been a four-term governor of New York, a champion of immigrants, especially the Irish, an early advocate of welfare programs, and a staunch ally of labor. But he was also a petty man who, in later losing out to his home-state rival, Franklin Delano Roosevelt, broke with the Democratic Party and became a fierce opponent of the New Deal. In 1928, the boom-time prosperity that followed the Great War had seemed permanent, and voters simply associated it with the Republicans, making Herbert Hoover practically unbeatable. Yet Catholics took Smith's defeat only as evidence of the religion-based hostility of the general population toward anyone who honored the Roman pontiff.[3]

I was born fifteen years after the Smith defeat, but I was brought up in its aura of lasting insult, proof of the injustice of anti-Catholic bigotry that was a presumed pillar of American culture. A pillar of the Catholic culture, meanwhile, was this nurtured sense of victimhood, with emphasis given, for example, to the fact that a resurgent Ku Klux

Klan, not only in the Deep South but in rural areas of states like Indiana and my own native Illinois, listed Catholics on their target roster with Jews and Negroes. The redneck complaint against Catholics was that we put loyalty to the pope over loyalty to the Constitution, and we could therefore never be real Americans. It was a charge we heartily rebutted, without actually considering that it was, in some inchoate way at least, true.

Our great political-religious hero, after all, was St. Thomas More. That he was the patron of the parish in which I was brought into my first awareness as a Catholic stamped me. Shortly after my birth in Chicago, my parents had joined the wartime exodus to Washington, D.C., and we settled in a garden-apartment complex in Arlington, Virginia. The bright new suburb had its bright new Catholic church, named for the English martyr. I am certain that my first glimpse of a great work of art was of the Hans Holbein portrait of More, a reproduction of which hung in the vestibule of the parish school.[4] What impressed me in the painting was the ladylike fur coat and the stout gold necklace that were part of his chancellor's rig. I was in kindergarten or first grade when, thinking of Thomas More, I asked the nun one day, "More than what?" Whatever Sister answered, I remember feeling rebuked, and I did not understand when, later, my question became one of my parents' amused anecdotes, often retold, with laughs at my expense.

Thomas More suffered a martyr's death—beheading!—rather than put the English king on a par with the Roman pontiff. It could seem no coincidence in the United States that the Counter-Reformation scholar was canonized only in 1935, a full—and exact—four centuries after his death. The Vatican may have found it useful to make a saint of More at that moment to send a signal of no-compromise against a new strain of political anticlericalism in Europe (the republicans in the Spanish Civil War would ferociously target priests and nuns, murdering hundreds of them). In the United States, though, More seemed the perfect patron for a Catholic subculture insisting that loyalty to Rome was only a version of loyalty to God.[5] And that subculture was just coming into its own.

More's arrival as a saint seemed perfectly timed in America, for many of the chipper new parishes in the wartime and postwar boom of suburban development jumped to take him as a patron, as our parish had. Unlike the canonized majority of mystic virgins or pious curates, Thomas More, the lawyer and statesman, had evident relevance to the large number of Catholic men who were even then able, because of the GI Bill, to join the ranks of the legal profession. My own father's extraordinary trajectory was launched from a night law school run by Jesuits, and, even as a Catholic lawyer who never actually practiced, Dad prized a faux-bronze bust of Thomas More, which I inherited and which sits on the table beside me as I write. Similarly, my family's progression was embodied in the move from stench-ridden Back of the Yards Chicago to that gleaming suburb of the nation's capital; the move from Little Company of Mary to St. Thomas More.

Conscience: it seemed to us an expressly Catholic faculty, and More was an emblem of it. So also reason and a broad humanism, which we could celebrate in More because we knew nothing of his early role as England's grand inquisitor.[6] As King Henry VIII's chancellor, when the anti-Luther Henry was still defending Catholic doctrine (for opposing Luther, the pope honored Henry with the title Defender of the Faith, which British monarchs still claim), More enforced a brutal Catholic orthodoxy against the Protestant heresy. That all changed, though, when King Henry's marital (and succession) troubles emerged as an issue of church and state, and the king's devoted servant Thomas More found himself on the spot.

We American Catholics emphasized More's steadfast protestations of loyalty to the king who was persecuting him, insisting that worldly good citizenship in no way contradicted holiness. But this was disingenuous. What we drew less attention to was the fact that More's insistence on his faithful subjugation to the king was false; he had been given a choice between one loyalty and another—on the scaffold, he declared himself "the King's good servant, but God's first"—and had made that choice. We who knew little else about Thomas More knew that, at the obese and gout-ridden king's order, More's severed head had been hoisted on a pike on the Tower Bridge.

Catholics in England, after the volcanic Reformation erupted on the island nation, may have pretended, as More had, to be good subjects of the Crown, but they were anything but. American Catholics of my time assumed that persecuted English Catholics of More's time and after were unfairly targeted, victims of a Klan-like bigotry. Taking a cue from that 1935 canonization (which was, perhaps, its point), we constructed a mythology around the story of Catholic persecution in England, one that meshed nicely with our Irish readiness to think ill of London. Taking further cues from the twentieth-century saint makers in Rome, we honored the memory of the "fugitive" English priests like Edmund Campion, who, in Evelyn Waugh's celebration, "came with gaiety among a people where hope was dead."

Living a generation after More, when Catholicism was illegal in England, Campion was a Jesuit who posed as a jewel merchant, traveling from city to city and seeking converts to the Church of Rome. In the book Waugh wrote about Campion, he celebrated such covert English Jesuits: they "brought with them, besides their priestly dignity and the ancient and indestructible creed, an entirely new spirit of which Campion is the type: the chivalry of Lepanto and the poetry of La Mancha, light, tender, generous and ardent . . . [They] followed holiness, though it led them through bitter ways to poverty, disgrace, exile, imprisonment, and death. [They] followed it gaily."[7]

But our perceptions of what in America defined *our* nation's primordial Catholic-Protestant conflict were partial; it's not too much to say they were ill informed. We knew, for example, that once Edmund Campion was captured, Queen Elizabeth ordered him executed, in 1581, but we knew nothing of the explicit command that Pope Pius V had given to English Catholics, in 1570, to work for Elizabeth's overthrow.[8] We thought the Jesuits were simply being hounded for their religious convictions, not understanding how those convictions defined the political conflict of the time. The pope was at war with London and would have blessed the queen's assassination. The Jesuits going about England in disguise, however gaily they followed holiness, were traitors.

London and Rome understood each other as mortal enemies. (Even today, British law forbids a Roman Catholic from ascending the throne, or anyone in the line of succession to the throne from even marrying a Catholic.[9] Tony Blair, whose role as prime minister included the responsibility to appoint the archbishop of Canterbury, had to wait until leaving office to fulfill a long-standing wish to become a Roman Catholic.[10]) The clarity of that sixteenth-century Protestant-Catholic conflict had been sharpened in Ireland in those very years when the age-old and universal war against serfs was given its profoundly denominational hue. Ireland became irretrievably Roman Catholic for a simple reason: the faith was the only and absolute source of dignity and hope for an otherwise savaged people. One could argue that Ireland was as roughly colonized by an imperial Rome as by London—even if the colonization was spiritual—but a better perception would be that the wily Irish peasantry simply found in the rituals of Catholicism a weapon worthy of its primal enemy, the Protestant English.

Given how the Irish put their stamp on Rome, once the religion and the people moved from the Auld Sod to America (a story we are tracking in this book), one could equally argue that having wielded their spacious religious imagination against the king of England, the Irish would wield it against the pope, too. (Subsequent chapters explain how.) The Irish trick, in each instance, was to make that spaciousness seem cramped, so that opponents, whether in London or in Rome, could be taken by surprise.

Their priests told the dispossessed Irish peasants that they were the treasure of heaven. The priests told the peasants that, in duplicating the dispossession of Jesus at Golgotha, they were his closest partners. Peasants had a way to think of themselves as superior. The Irish priests did this naturally, because before being priests, they were Irish. The intimacy of Confession, the sustenance of Communion, the regularity of the liturgical calendar, the alliance of the saints, the felt proximity of this "vale of tears" to the certain world beyond—these were the great counterweights to the whip of the foreman, the condescension of the great house's mistress, the pang of hunger, and the grief over children lost to disease or emigration. All suffering was political, as all relief was religious. The faith, that is, in giving the Irish a way to turn ferocious oppression against the oppressor, gave the Irish a sense of self-worth, a way to survive, and a way to imagine that someday the tables would turn.

Across the ocean, they did. American Catholicism (abstracting, for the present, from the Hispanic Catholicism that, after all, had preceded the Puritans in the New World) was a stream with several currents, notably German, Italian, and Slavic. But the Irish so dominated the immigrant ecclesiastical culture that the papacy's ancient argument with London (in 1215, Pope Innocent III had declared the Magna Carta null and void) and London's savage exploitation of peasant Ireland remained an undergirding for the mutual antagonism between American Protestants and U.S. Catholics of whatever ethnicity.

There is a direct, if not quite unbroken, line between Increase Mather's 1669 definition of Catholicism as the "Roman Anti-Christ" and John Greenleaf Whittier's 1851 dismissal of "Rome's harlot triple-crowned." John Adams contributed funds for the construction of a Catholic church in Boston, but that was when the bishop was a Frenchman named Cheverus, not an Irishman named O'Connell. When the Irish came to dominate the Catholic presence in America, subliminal prejudice broke into the black flower of the Know-Nothings, the nineteenth-century nativist movement (members of the anti-immigrant secret society were sworn to answer inquiries "I know nothing"). But even that essentially tribal conflict between "America" and "Rome" took its energy from the old one between London and Rome. I knew enough, even as a boy in my early teens in the mid-1950s, to take wicked pleasure when the irreverent Irish playwright Brendan Behan—"a drinker with a writing problem"—remarked offhandedly on *The Jack Paar Show* one night that, while the Catholic Church was founded on the rock of St. Peter, the Church of England was founded on the balls of Henry VIII.

3. NO SALVATION OUTSIDE THE CHURCH

One did not have to attend St. Thomas More parochial school to learn what, for Catholics, was the most important fact about the American Revolution—that the single resoundingly English principle the colonies had *not* broken with was contempt for Rome. But the standard of patriotic conformity was not the only one of which Catholics in America were deemed to fall short. In addition to the redneck bigotry of the Know-Nothings, there was the genteel prejudice of the economic and cultural elites, which found Catholics inherently wanting, on one side, in matters of taste (all those bathtub Virgins), and on the other, in intellectual heft. The Catholic Church, after all, in its contest with the Enlightenment, had formally condemned the writings of the founders of contemporary thought, from Descartes to Diderot to Dumas father and son. Thus anti-Catholicism was the antisemitism, as a midcentury saw went, of the intellectuals. In this respectable bigotry, in fact, Jews had one of their rare points of association with the WASP establishment.[11] Such prejudice mostly took the form of an exquisite condescension, to the vibrations of which we Catholics were closely attuned.

Thus, we perhaps overcelebrated the achievements of Catholic writers like Waugh, Graham Greene, G. K. Chesterton, and Barbara Ward, making little of the fact that they were English. We might have given more emphasis to celebrated American Catholic writers, like Mary McCarthy, F. Scott Fitzgerald, Theodore Dreiser, Jack Kerouac, John Dos Passos, and Eugene O'Neill, but they were known to have repudiated the faith, which could seem a precondition of their being broadly celebrated. Non-Catholics, who seemed to take no notice of the Catholic religious vows of obedience and poverty, were openly skeptical about the vowed chastity of the Catholic clergy. If we Catholics had our own doubts about our priests' ability to suppress every erotic impulse, we suppressed them under a kind of rebuttal contempt for non-Catholic sexual obsessiveness. The gutter gossip about secret tunnels between rectories and convents, or about priests plying altar boys with sacramental wine to have their way with them, seemed more perverse than the perversities being alleged (although, tragically, that gossip too would decades later be revealed as having been partly true).

Nevertheless, the condescension of the elites plucked a chord of our cultural insecurity, one we could only inadequately address. In 1955, it was one of the Church's own, the Catholic University historian Monsignor John Tracy Ellis, who blasted the intellectual mediocrity of American Catholicism. Catholic universities in America were more famous for football than for scholarship. Gifted Catholics might become lawyers or doctors, but almost none became academics. Those who did were not distinguished. It was not mere Protestant prejudice that kept Catholic scholars from holding even a single position of influence in the world of academia. What then?[12]

But the political accusation against us was more readily dealt with. In most major cities of the United States, Catholics held important public offices, and our active participation in the civic life of the nation went without saying. We readily denied any conflict between our national and religious identities (as John Kennedy would so famously do in 1960), but in fact the bigots who attacked "papists" on such grounds were like the pope himself in sensing something incompatible between Catholicism and Americanism. Indeed, "Americanism" had been condemned as a heresy (with the First Amendment of the Constitution especially indicted) by the same pope, Leo XIII, who had defined the Roman Catholic Church as "perfect."[13]

If American Protestantism defined itself in some essential way in opposition to pope-centered Catholicism, in other words, the reverse was equally true. The Church-dominated culture into which I was born had its roots in the Counter-Reformation, when all things reformed were repudiated. The Council of Trent, convened in three sessions between 1545 and 1563, was the Church's overdue response to the challenge from Luther. However anachronistic its provisions can seem in the twenty-first century, in the sixteenth its enactments amounted to a first serious attempt to correct the abuses Luther had decried. The hedonism of Renaissance popes was rejected, disciplines were imposed on the clergy, sacraments were regularized, and the spiritual content of Catholic life was emphasized. Trent established basic notes of the Catholic identity into which I was initiated at the church named for St. Thomas More: rules of fasting and abstinence, fish on Friday, Easter Duty, the requirement of Confession, a universal rubric of the Mass, with emphasis given more than ever to Latin, in reaction to the vernacularizing of Protestants. In rejecting the Lutheran slogan of *sola scriptura*, and its corollary that claims to truth were to be measured against the Bible, Trent gave unprecedented emphasis to the idea of (capital *T*) Tradition. Catholicism here affirmed that the long practice of the Church, as identified by those in charge of it, was like Scripture in constituting a mode of sacred revelation. Indeed, Scripture, in this view, was itself the product of Tradition: the Church had created the Bible, and not the other way around.[14]

But in one thing above all Trent stamped the consciousness of Roman Catholicism, and that was in its militant reiteration of "No salvation outside the Church," an idea dating to the 1302 papal bull of Boniface VIII, *Unam Sanctam*. The notion that firm loyalty not only to the Catholic Church but to its head, the pope, was a prerequisite to admission to heaven had been articulated by the Church's greatest theologian only a few years before Boniface began his pontificate. That theologian's name was Thomas Aquinas (1225–1274), the Italian-born Dominican who trained in Cologne and came to prominence at Paris—a geographic expansiveness that had its equivalent in the expansiveness of his mind. Aquinas stamped the character of Catholicism with his various summaries (*Summae*) of thought and faith, for the High Middle Ages was a time when a thinker could presume to condense the totality of knowledge and belief, an intellectual totality that reflected the organizational totality of the Church.

Thomas Aquinas's masterwork consisted in his invention of decidedly Christian expressions of Aristotle's magnificent intellectual constructs, but the medieval theologian's social rendition of the Greek's philosophical "hierarchy of being" was profoundly culture-bound. Aquinas saw Christendom as the cosmos, and, reflecting the social order of his own thirteenth century, he saw the bishop of Rome as occupying the pinnacle of power that was both temporal and eternal.

Yet the concern of Aquinas, and those who followed him three centuries later at Trent, was not only chauvinistic. Salvation for them was not a private experience but a communal event, and it was inevitable that they conceive of it in terms of the one community they knew as authentic. The question of an *individual's* place in such an economy of salvation did not arise for Aquinas because consciousness of individual standing as a prime value had yet to emerge—although that would be at issue in the crisis facing the fathers of Trent. Aquinas was not the first to treat a contingent ontology as if it were God's truth revealed once and for all, nor would he be the last. But his rendition would be decisive for most of a millennium, and popes, beginning with Boniface VIII, would gratefully appeal to his authority.[15]

In his restrictive definition of what was required for salvation, Aquinas effectively wrote off the Eastern Orthodox Church, which had been out of communion with the pope for two hundred years at the time of his writing. Within Western Christendom, of course, there had been no "outside the Church" until Luther,[16] and at Trent this "no salvation" doctrine was fired at Luther's followers, as well as those of John Calvin and Henry VIII, like a lump of molten lead from a theological cannon. After all, in bygone eras the idea of salvation did the work that the idea of meaning does today. To be without salvation in the anticipated afterlife was to be without any coherence or significance, any value or happiness, in the present life. And that is precisely why this anathema about tomorrow would be wielded today. Fate there and then at the service of power here and now.

4. INFALLIBILITY

Shallower but equally solid roots of the Catholic culture into which I was born had been planted more recently, in the second half of the nineteenth century, during the long pontificate of Pius IX (1846–1878). Indeed, under Pio Nono, as he was affectionately known by some Catholics, the Counter-Reformation can be said to have morphed into the Counter-Enlightenment. Catholics of my time did not appreciate the most important legacy of that period, the time of our grandparents and great-grandparents—that Catholic notions of papalist spiritual power originated in a crisis of political power, when the pope lost what remained of his ancient temporal kingdom in Europe. We were taught, that is, that a relatively recent manifestation of Catholicism dated back not decades but millennia, to the time of the Apostles.

Pius IX was regarded as a goodhearted man, and he had begun, when first elected to the papacy in 1846, as something of a liberal. But when revolutions struck Rome early in his pontificate, he was traumatized. From then on, his bonhomie was reserved for the shrinking group that agreed with him, as he set himself against "modernism," by which he meant all that was then coming into flower in the United States. It wasn't just Protestantism that the Catholic Church opposed, but the entire political, economic, and social ideology that it had spawned, from individualism to nationalism to republicanism to capitalism. And then the Church opposed, equally, the ideological reaction to all this—socialism.

As the papacy had struggled to survive the various onslaughts that followed the French Revolution—the 1791 confiscation by the nascent French Republic of papal territories in France, including Avignon; the taking of Rome by French troops in 1798; the kidnapping to France of Pope Pius VI the same year—it understandably defined itself against the letter and spirit of the new age. But as the hierarchy of the Church, the First Estate, was lumped together with the nobility, the Second Estate, large majorities of the lower clergy, including most orders of nuns, at first associated themselves with "the people," as the so-called Third Estate now understood itself. Therefore the shift in power away from a medieval theocracy could seem to be no threat to the mass of Catholic people. They, too, had something to gain from the new order. This was true, early on, almost everywhere the revolutions struck.

But soon enough Catholicism itself was seen as the enemy of the new cult of human rights. For a time, the goddess Reason replaced the God of Christianity as the object of worship in the cathedral of Notre-Dame de Paris. The Catholic Church was deprived of most of its property, which meant that schools, hospitals, orphanages, and other refuges for the poor went the way of vast landholdings, abbeys, and episcopal palaces. All lost. Those Catholics who saw in liberty, equality, and fraternity core values of a Gospel faith became suspect to the revolution as well as to the rulers of the Church. Hundreds of members of the lower clergy, too, were sent to the guillotine. Events in France seemed a harbinger of what could come in other lands.

In 1832, Pope Gregory XVI had declared that it "is false and absurd, or rather mad, that we must secure and guarantee to each one liberty of conscience; this is one of the most contagious of errors . . . To this is attached liberty of press, the most dangerous liberty, an execrable liberty which can never inspire sufficient horror."[17] The horrors that followed from 1789, in the papal view, had been spawned by events in the United States dating to 1776.

From a detached perch in the twenty-first century, the antimodern anathemas of nineteenth-century popes can seem like irrational diatribes against all that became the conventional wisdom of liberal democracy—a Catholic embarrassment. The same Pope Gregory XVI who denounced freedom of the press, after all, banned railroads in the Papal States. But in condemning an American idea of freedom, Gregory also condemned slavery and the slave trade, well before Americans turned against them. In looking back, that is, one should not assume that virtue resided only on one side, or that there were not circumstances that made reaction necessary. Popes had exercised political autonomy over various domains since the fourth century, and from their point of view the inexorable loss of territories had to seem like the destruction of the Church itself. And that loss was tied to the new political ideal, which therefore had to be resisted. But more than mere worldly self-interest was at stake in this rejectionism. To Catholics, the spirit of liberal modernity increasingly seemed based on notions of the radically subjective individual as entirely cut off from structures of community—and so from any deep value beyond the solipsism of the self. The much-touted American ideal of the separation of church and state cut off the realm of personal morality from the common good—which suited the American slaveholder just fine. The slaveholder, like the railroad baron, for that matter, could seem to embody the modern ideal.

Indeed, events of the twentieth century would show that there was much to be wary of in nineteenth-century celebrations of the individual, and of the individual writ large, which would be the nation-state. When the fatherland replaced the Father, and the national anthem replaced the Lord's Prayer, even as a new industrialism reinvented the technical means of destruction wreaked in the name of the new movements, unprecedented catastrophe would follow. The extremes of the revolutionary era's violence—before he was himself guillotined in 1794, the Jacobin leader Maximilien Robespierre had sent tens of thousands to that death machine—would be recognized too late as a warning of the reign of terror to come.

The reactionary popes, in fact, gave Catholics worldwide a way of mitigating the deadly appeal of the cult of nationalism. But the Church's defensiveness could seem at the time to be little more than what American bigots said it was. In 1864, Pius IX condemned what he called, in his *Syllabus of Errors*, eighty "mistakes" of philosophy, theology, and politics to which he attached the anathema. Rejected in particular was any notion that "the Roman Pontiff can and ought to reconcile and align himself with progress, liberalism, and modern civilization."[18] And the pontiff increasingly came to be seen by Catholics everywhere as the symbol of a new resistance. An emotional attachment to the besieged cleric in Rome—ultramontanism, as it was called, fervent loyalty to the man "across the mountains"—became a social counterforce. The Holy Father became an antinational equivalent, for Catholics, of the nationalist heroes around whom state ideologies were jelling, from Garibaldi in Italy to Bismarck in Germany to Lincoln in the United States.

All that was being condemned seemed centered on a social philosophy that included the underpinnings of American democracy. The Catholic Church thus formally repudiated the separation of church and state, freedom of the press, what would later be called pluralism, a polity based on rights, and any idea that authority came from below instead of from above. In the United States, revolution had been romanticized, in part because the violence of the American Revolution had been relatively restrained and mainly limited to warring armies. (That would change when the Revolution's unpaid bill, slavery, came due eighty years later, with the Civil War.[19]) But in Europe the brutalities of revolution were manifold and manifest, from the guillotine madness of 1789 through periodic outbursts of mass murder that came every two or three decades for a century and a half, culminating in the October Revolution in Russia.

Not just the papacy but also the Catholic Church in Europe, perceived univocally as one of the "estates" of the *ancien régime,* was consistently targeted. Whenever and wherever the blood-red flags of the new order were raised, priests and bishops were murdered, Church properties were confiscated, Catholicism was demonized. In the last third of the nineteenth century, this assault reached a set of bloody climaxes across the continent. In Germany it was the *Kulturkampf* that exiled priests and imprisoned bishops. In France it was the Paris Commune that turned churches into stables and murdered the archbishop. In Italy it was nothing less than open warfare against the pope, culminating in the theft of the most cherished part of his temporal realm, not only the Papal States that cut a wide swath across the middle of the boot of Italy, but the city of Rome itself. All lost. Measured against such brutalities, there was no equivalent in America, although the rise of the anti-Catholic Know-Nothings in the previous decades was extreme enough.

In Europe, the Catholic Church was the self-anointed guardian of a last-ditch Christendom, a besieged culture that had come so wonderfully into flower in the high medieval period—"the chivalry of Lepanto, the poetry of La Mancha." Not to mention the cantos of Dante, the frescoes of Giotto, the thought of Thomas Aquinas, the soaring reach of the Gothic cathedral, the purity of St. Francis, the mystical bliss of Gregorian chant, the social unity of feudalism in which every person's place was defined, illuminations of the monastic ideal, humane inventions of economy and transportation, the recovery of classical philosophy, the roots of Renaissance, of science, of humanism itself. What sort of Enlightenment is it that assigns such wonders to an era dismissed as the Dark Ages? Having held out against the Puritan assaults of the Reformation, these golden achievements were threatened by the nineteenth century, which was as evil as the thirteenth was wondrous. And the names of the demons were well known: Darwin, whose theories undermined the all-controlling Creator; Nietzsche, with his hubristic assault on God; Marx, in whose name the social revolutions were destroying the structures of Europe; Garibaldi, who finally closed in on the pope in 1870, making him a prisoner in the Vatican.

In response to all of this, Roman Catholics affirmed their loyalty to the pope more absolutely than ever. Not incidentally, they were able to do this effectively because of new technologies, the telegraph and the (papally disapproved) railroad, which began to provide Rome with unmediated access to distant Church communities. Historians mark this as the start of "papal populism."[20] With ferocious energy, Catholics embraced a romantic ideal that was more nostalgia than recovery of classical values; a sham version of Gothic architecture; the scholasticism of a watered-down Thomas Aquinas; a cult of the Blessed Virgin that partook more of superstition than of authentic veneration—all of it centered on the Holy Father. If the forces of the Enlightenment—secularism, atheism, nationalism, capitalism—combined to emphasize the papacy's significance as a last symbol of all that remained to be overthrown, then Catholics would rally to the pope as never before. If the papacy was a world target, it could also be a historic bulwark. If the pope's temporal power was stripped from him by the enemy, his spiritual power would be given unprecedented emphasis by his coreligionists. This is why the near simultaneity of Garibaldi's successful assault and the declaration by the fathers of the Church council that was held at the Vatican is so emblematic—the formal casting in doctrine of papal infallibility.

The revolutionaries had encircled Rome by the early summer of 1870. On July 18, the Vatican Council promulgated *Pastor Aeternus,* the dogma that His Holiness, teaching *ex cathedra,* could not err in "matters of faith and morals." A long tradition that the Church was "inerrant" in its essential faithfulness to the Gospel was now narrowly applied to the pope himself, as "infallible."[21]

The council's declaration begins, "Seeing that the gates of hell, with daily increase of hatred, are gathering their strength on every side to upheave the foundation laid by God's own hand, and so, if that might be, to overthrow the Church, we therefore . . . [propose the doctrine] in which is found the strength and solidity of the entire Church." Anyone rejecting the teaching of the "eternal pastor's" moral and theological supremacy was condemned "with the loss of faith and of salvation." *No salvation outside loyalty to the infallible pope.*

Two months later, on September 20—gates of hell indeed—the revolutionaries took the city, the Franco-Prussian War broke out, and the Vatican Council was dispersed. The pope fled to the Vatican from his central-Rome palace, the Quirinale, which Garibaldi took for himself, and which remains to this day the residence of the Italian head of state.

So the Catholic bishops meeting in council responded to the destruction of the pope's political power by defining his spiritual power as more total than had ever been the case before. This required submission "not only in matters which belong to faith and morals, but also in those that appertain to the discipline and government of the

Church throughout the world . . . under one supreme pastor . . . the Roman Pontiff."[22] The Catholic Church's ultimate spiritual claim resulted from its ultimate temporal defeat. In the past, the doctrinal and institutional authority of Roman Catholicism had been more or less consistently—if, at times, contentiously—shared by bishops meeting in councils, with the pope operating within constraints established by those councils. At least since the fourteenth century, popes had been resisting conciliar notions of Church governance, but local churches had meanwhile accumulated considerable autonomy. Catholic laypeople had conscientious leeway. No more. From now on, the papacy would have unprecedented reach over the beliefs and practices of Roman Catholics, with, for example, the Church-defining power to choose and appoint bishops efficiently moving from regional Church bodies to a newly centralized governing structure in the Vatican. Papalism.

The more besieged Catholics felt in their far-flung parishes—from *Kulturkampf* Cologne to *No Irish Need Apply* Boston—the more they would lift up the unifying symbol of the papacy as the Catholic version of the nationalist hero around whom to rally—a holy man on horseback. By the middle of the next century—my time—we Catholics had forgotten that the pope-centeredness of our faith was a modern phenomenon, and that, as it was being promulgated in 1870, many Catholic leaders, including bishops and theologians at the Vatican Council itself, had firmly opposed the formulation as a violation of all that Jesus had taught. Instead, as forecast earlier, we Catholics came to believe, as I was taught, that infallibility, and the totalitarian claims made in its name, was a charism, an extraordinary power, bestowed on St. Peter and his successors by Jesus himself: "Thou art Peter, and upon this rock I will build my Church, and the gates of hell shall not prevail against it."[23]

5. AMERICANISM

Aware of all that set them apart from their non-Catholic neighbors, American Catholics were less conscious of how different they had also become from their coreligionists in the old country. The experience of emigration, indelibly marking most American Catholics to the third and fourth generation, gave them a set of references of which relatives who remained behind knew nothing. In Europe, the borders drawn by the Peace of Westphalia, which ended the Thirty Years' War in 1648, were expressly intended to keep warring religious groups apart. The old-country kinsmen of American immigrants simply did not rub elbows with those who believed differently. In the United States, elbows were rubbed raw.

As we have seen, the trauma of emigration consisted, for Catholics, of dislocation followed by denigration. The more the prevailing Protestant culture of the United States took the inferiority of newcomer Catholics for granted, the more Irish, Italian, German, Polish, and other groups asserted their one claim to real distinction, which was nothing less than God's sure—and exclusive—favor. Right through the twentieth century, American Catholicism would be marked by the loyal conformity of almost all bishops to the Vatican (we will note one exception) as well as by the fierce, if less doctrinally conformist, attachment of the laity to their parishes. This pattern would hold throughout an era in which postmodern Catholic ties in Europe, even in Ireland, would be growing ever slacker. (The period's story of priests and nuns, as opposed to bishops and laity, is more complex, as we'll see.) But the social context, more than religious devotedness, may explain this difference between America and Europe.

In the United States, beginning in the nineteenth century, certitude about the superiority—no, supremacy—of their religion braced the identities of otherwise uncertain immigrant populations. While their religion made them feel individually unworthy (*Domine, non sum dignus*), it made them feel communally superior (*Extra Ecclesiam nulla salus*). In Europe, cultural identity was a matter of a whole complex of associations (social class, trade, merchant guild, farm collective, etc.) of which religion was only one. The cluster of such character-defining notes, including religion, was inherited. In the New World, identity was chosen. Religion in America was understood to be voluntary in ways that were unthinkable in the villages and cities—parishes—from which immigrants came. That resulted in the peculiarly American phenomenon among most Christian denominations of active proselytizing, which put the choice of religious identity at the center of freedom. At its most passionate, such convert-making spawned the revivalism that became a mark of Protestantism in the United States. Catholicism was not immune to such spirit, and a kind of defensive search for converts found a place on the immigrant Church's agenda. Ironically, in the open market of religious give-and-take Catholics could join with confidence—not because they took their own faith convictions less seriously than European Catholics, but because they were certain of their possession of God's truth, and could expect to win the competition.[24]

In the new realms of urban anonymity and prairie isolation, voluntary religious association defined city neighborhoods and rural communities both. Across the young nation, in a variety of settings, immigrants and their children found their most important source of affiliation in places of worship. Far more than the deity was being served. In the United States, this was a Protestant and Jewish phenomenon as well as a Catholic one, and this particular, non-European function of religion as a source of identity in an otherwise deracinated world would be one important factor in the distinctive religiosity of American society long after secularism had eroded religious loyalties in Europe.

For immigrant Catholics in the nineteenth and early twentieth centuries, the subculture in which newcomers cherished and preserved customs, languages, and identities tied to the old country could seem to depend on expressly defined opposition to a broader Protestant culture that did not want them anyway. In such a context, the democratic pluralism of that culture, taking the leveling of assimilation for granted, could seem especially threatening, and many Catholics, led by their foreign-born priests, assumed the permanence of a certain ethnic separatism, ideologically defined around religion because socially defined around the parish. Insurance associations, professional guilds, fraternal orders, and eventually an entire system of education, from kindergarten to college, established a spacious bubble within which Catholics could breathe freely. Such a separatist spirit even marked communities where Catholic settlement had predated the nineteenth-century immigration influx, like Hispanic areas in the West, French in Louisiana, or Anglo in eastern Maryland, which was first colonized by fugitive English Catholics. (Charles Carroll of Carrollton was much celebrated as the only Catholic signer of the Declaration of Independence—celebrated by Catholics. In the American pantheon, he mostly remains unnoted.)

The threat to dignity wasn't only a question of religious or cultural abstractions. In the America in which my parents were born and raised, a majority of Catholics lived at or below subsistence (which, by the

Depression, was put at between $1,100 and $1,400 per year per family).[25] Rank poverty was taken for granted by most Catholics, certainly by my parents and their siblings. (My mother left school after the eighth grade, to add a wage to the family income.) Deprivation was the condition from which all other experience took its character. Despite habits of feigned gentility, instilled especially by the nuns of the parochial schools, the effects of poverty were psychologically corrosive. In such a situation, where the nun-commanded plaid skirts and navy-blue pants could be a Catholic child's only decent clothes, the Church could seem to be the only source of self-respect. Again, because immigrants to the New World were cut off from other means of cultural affirmation that were available to the parents, siblings, and neighbors they left behind in the Old World, this function of religion as a key, if not the sole, source of positive identity was a peculiarly American phenomenon.

Theological absolutism was the armor of an insecure people, and the artillery. Beginning around the turn of the twentieth century, that absolutism, launched from Rome, was aimed in a particular way at America. When the Spanish-American War broke out in 1898, the European Catholic memory associated it with the Spanish Armada—Spain's role, even back in 1588, as the point of the spear aimed at English Protestantism. Remote as such a reference would have been to Americans, Catholics in Europe—certainly those in Rome—had little trouble siding with Spain against a Protestant enemy. The United States claimed not to be an imperialist nation, yet look at what it was doing in Cuba, Puerto Rico, and the Philippines. However the Spanish-American War was perceived in Washington, from Rome it involved a decidedly religious aspect, as if the long-stewing cauldron had been abruptly brought to a boil again. That the war was quickly over, with the Spanish readily and shamefully dispatched—this time without the ocean storms that had sunk the Armada—only sharpened the hostility.

It was in the next year, 1899, that Pope Leo XIII issued an apostolic letter, called *Testem Benevolentiae Nostrae,* that expressly condemned as heresy what it called "Americanism," deemed nothing less than a cluster of Protestant ideas that, having been spawned in the New World, threatened the universal faith from within—even in Europe.[26] What motivated the Vatican was not mere antagonism toward the enemy across the ocean, but a growing dread that its heresies were subtly taking root in the whole of Catholicism. The purifying spirit of separatism, embodied in Europe's confessionally defined frontiers, had not been maintained in the New World, where the undefined frontier, forever beckoning, had proven to be an irresistible leveler. The papal war against modernism was one thing when waged against an enemy outside, but what if modernism was infecting the Church? And where else should such a thing have begun to happen but in the United States, where ideas had wings? Americanism was, in a phrase the next pope would use about modernism, "the synthesis of all heresies."[27]

Relativism, for example. A spirit of what might be called pragmatic relativism informed the thinking of important American figures like William James and John Dewey. The self, conceived in isolation from community—an abstraction that amounted, in the real world, to an impossibility—was taken to be the measure of meaning. Crudely understood, this radical subjectivity posited the individual's experience, not tradition and not institutional norms, as the starting point of reflection, and value. In America, religion itself, just then undergoing one of its periodic revivals, could seem to be self-obsessed. The self was the American absolute. Not merely aggrandized, the American self was nothing less than a creator in the process of its own creation.

There were relativist streams in Europe as well, with Nietzsche, say, leading the antifoundationalist charge against ideas of universal truth, and with Marx challenging the pie-in-the-sky postponement of hope, but the Continental relativism of "God is dead! Religion is opium!" was making a frontal assault on religious tradition. By contrast, the threat from American philosophical recasting, with its evangelical aspect and claims to rational piety, could seem more insidious because more indirect. America, from across the ocean, could be seen as a repudiation of tradition as such, with the very landscape, forever beckoning from an unapproachable horizon, making the future far more important than the past. Indeed, as Europe was defined by its past, so was America defined by its future—which is why all those immigrants, just by the fact of arrival, could claim to be Americans, a form of national appropriation that was inconceivable in Europe.

And so American relativism, having upended the meaning of place, in a landscape that itself altered the relationship between self and community, reversed the meaning of time, a second revolution. This was so because American relativism located the absolute not in the past but in the future. And what in the world was an absolute that had yet to come into existence? American pragmatism, ironically, could seem impossibly abstract. This was deism's appeal as the implicit American theology, with an indeterminate God ("In God we trust") superseding both the Yahweh of the Bible and the Trinitarian Father of the Nicene Creed. And if such a God was detached from history, those who located the definitions of revelation in time—whether the past (Tradition) or the present (the Church)—were left high and dry.

Roman Catholicism's argument with America was thus only superficially denominational. That a kind of Protestantism thrived here reinforced a suspicion that went to the core of the national idea. The Union, that is, could seem essentially Unitarian, which was a foretaste of a greater problem, as Unitarianism came to seem, from the point of view of every religion of revelation, like the start of secularism.

But from Rome, it looked as if certain Catholics in America, against the prevailing immigrant ethos, were a bit too intent upon assimilating into this deracinated culture. That the culture was Protestant did not define the entire problem, for Protestantism in the United States contained currents that Rome did not find in Europe—or find nearly as threatening. Chief among these was the emphasis on freedom that followed logically from the separation of church and state, for the removal of coercion from the realm of belief meant that personal choice defined religious affiliation.

Coercion by the state in defense of a univocal orthodoxy, after all, had been as much a Protestant impulse as a Catholic one—with reformers like Ulrich Zwingli defending his theocracy in sixteenth-century Zurich by sending magistrates to smash statues and destroy altars. Oliver Cromwell's England brought the use of force in defense of state-defined religion to a new intensity—which drove the Puritans to the New World in the first place. Protestant sectarianism led to ferocious intolerance among Protestants, and the low point of such religiously licensed violence in Protestant Europe—and America—came with the witch-hunt frenzy that cost untold numbers of women their lives. This worst outbreak of Protestant violence had little or nothing to do with Catholicism.

So infamies of the Inquisition are only part of the coercion story. In theory, Catholicism always assumed personal and internal assent in matters of faith, and by the nineteenth century the Catholic Church had mostly renounced overt forms of state coercion in enforcing orthodoxy. But that did not mean anything like an unmediated freedom to choose when it came to religion. In this, the view from Rome was exactly like the view from Geneva or London or Leipzig or Stockholm, where confessional states—and received, not chosen, religious identities—were still taken for granted. The freedom that Americans were so wont to go on about did indeed define a national characteristic, and U.S. Catholics, too, were getting drawn into it. The political had become the theological.[28]

Hence that condemnation of the new heresy of Americanism. The imagined Americans who were most worrisome to Rome were not Emerson, Thoreau, James, and Dewey, but Roman Catholics in the thrall of such thinkers. Such Catholics were leaving their ethnic communities behind. They were attending public schools. They took for granted the separation of church and state. They believed in the dominance of the individual. They affirmed freedom of speech and ideas, to the point of claiming the right to read whatever they wanted. They thought they could contribute to the "development of doctrine," the idea that basic tenets of Catholic faith could change over time, a kind of theological equivalent of Darwinian evolution theory.[29] That such imagined Americans existed in low numbers, and that some of the ideas attached to their image belonged as much to Europeans—like the English prelate John Henry Newman, who coined the phrase "development of doctrine," or the German Jesuit Johann Joseph Ignaz von Döllinger, who decried the authoritarian reach of the Vatican—counted for less than the ease with which the dangerous thinking could be so neatly labeled, and condemned.[30] Americanism: *anathema sit!*

6. ISAAC HECKER AND THE PAULISTS

On early-Renaissance maps of the world, the landmass of the Western Hemisphere was designated Terra Incognita. At the Vatican, where such maps are on display to this day, that perception (or lack thereof) held. Pope Leo XIII had come to his agitated conclusions about Catholic life in America through European impressions of it, especially those attached to a French translation of an English-language biography of the American Catholic priest Isaac Hecker.[31] His story is not well known even by Catholics, yet it is central to the narrative unfolding here, and, as indicated earlier, Hecker's life became unexpectedly key to my own.

Hecker was born and bred in New York, where his family's business had prospered as one of the nation's early enterprises to adopt methods of mass marketing; their product was flour. In 1858, Hecker established, in New York, the first Catholic order of priests to be founded in the United States. They took St. Paul as their patron, and called themselves the Paulist Fathers. They would be a small group, never numbering more than a few hundred. But their influence would vastly surpass their size, and the character of that influence would be fateful. The Paulists defined their order as a bridge between the Catholic Church and American culture, a bridge on which traffic would run in both directions.

Isaac Hecker had begun as a Protestant, baptized as a Lutheran like his near contemporaries Karl Marx and Friedrich Nietzsche. Though he was the son of German immigrants, Hecker was so self-consciously American that, as a young man, he attached himself to the New England transcendentalists, establishing intimate bonds with, among others, Emerson, Thoreau, and Orestes Brownson—themselves a kind of trinity of the new American religion. That the movement's pieties would immediately influence James Russell Lowell, Margaret Fuller, Herman Melville, Louisa May Alcott, the Peabody sisters, Nathaniel Hawthorne, and, ultimately, Walt Whitman shows its importance to the national character. Yet that their innovation called itself transcendentalism embodied the problem that eventually undercut it. For if you level the hierarchy of being, as the radical religious democrats aimed to do (indeed, as New England's Unitarians had done in rejecting the hierarchy of the Trinity in the Godhead), is human access to the transcendent itself not undermined? Doesn't transcendence assume hierarchy? And what is a democrat to do with that?

The transcendentalists were not mere theorizers. In 1841, they established a utopian commune on two hundred acres of farmland on the edge of Boston, with members committed to share equally in labor and income. This was Brook Farm. Agricultural work, but also educational and spiritual endeavors, defined the life. The Brook Farm roster included names that would live on in America: Alcott, Channing, Dana, Emerson, Fuller, Parker, Brownson, and Hawthorne. (Hawthorne's 1852 novel *The Blithesdale Romance* is set there.) Young Isaac Hecker was one of the most enthusiastic members of the Brook

Farm experiment. The good-natured sobriquet "seeker" was applied to him by his fellows at the farm, and Hecker sparked to the coming American idea.

Among the transcendentalists, Calvinist notions of the depravity of human nature were as scorned as the Calvinist ideal of private judgment was elevated. The rational was taken to be an opening to divinity, even as the skepticism that followed from rational religion was overcome by spiritual ecstasy—"experience"—as the true measure of the soul. Individualism, primacy of the inner voice of conscience, freedom from the corruptions of Old World institutions, a belief in the perfectibility of the person, faith in God's unmediated accessibility to the willfully devoted person—these became Hecker's defining notions. As such, they survived the relatively quick collapse, in 1847, of Brook Farm. Like the other residents, Hecker moved on.

But the idealistic commune so stamped him as an Emersonian that he brought its spirit with him when he subsequently—still the seeker—went back to New York. The bustle of that booming metropolis stood in marked contrast to the agrarian tranquillity of Brook Farm, but as others, including Walt Whitman, were discovering, the city had its own peculiarly American appeal. Hecker's return to the place and culture of his origins opened him freshly to the spiritual quest, and, perhaps to his surprise, in immigrant-rich New York he encountered a vigorous strain of Roman Catholicism. New York was the original and quintessential melting pot, and immigrant religion gave the stew its flavor, even as it was becoming something else.

That something else amounted to a nascent intellectual and spiritual movement that Hecker quickly embraced. Ironically, he showed what an Emersonian individualist he had, in fact, become by what he did then: he became a Roman Catholic, and a priest. Ten years after the demise of Brook Farm, Hecker established the Paulist Fathers, his own attempt to realize the American utopian dream in a Catholic context.

By the start of the twentieth century, suspicions of things American had reached a high pitch in the Vatican, which since 1870, as we saw, doubled as the pope's prison. By 1900, Hecker was remembered as a priest who had brought the suspect new ideas into Catholicism, although as an authentic disciple of Emerson's, he had imported more of a vision than a theology. The order of priests he founded—cheerfully plunging into free-market religious competition as "missionaries to Main Street"—was known more for intellectual energy than for theological acuity. Religion to Hecker had been more metaphor than dogma, which meant that the Vatican was right to be wary of his influence. A champion, for example, of preaching to immigrant Catholic communities not in their native languages (German, Italian, Polish) but in good American English, Hecker had effectively been an advocate of assimilation at a time when Catholicism was still insisting on protecting immigrants from mainstream society. This dispute about language was alone enough to make his memory suspect in Italy, where the word for translator overlapped with the word for traitor.

In true American fashion, Hecker had defined his central idea for the Paulist Fathers by expressing a preference for, as he put it, the excesses of freedom over the abuses of tyranny. The first generation of Paulists, only a dozen or so men, had gathered in New York, where Hecker's merchant family subsidized them. They were all native-born Americans, and all were converts to Catholicism. They assumed that their native land would, like themselves, eventually grasp the irresistible truth of Roman Catholicism, even as the Church recognized the American milieu as one in which it could thrive. The Paulists, that is, were as determined as Hecker to bring American ideas to the Church, and vice versa. This spirit was manifest in things large and small. For example, instead of living by a "Rule," the universal discipline of Catholic religious orders, they made a point to adopt a "constitution." If Hecker was their leader, or "Superior General," it was because the members had elected him, not because the Vatican had appointed him. Instead of an organization based on power, this religious order was based on honor, a distinction that led the Paulists to reject the idea of binding themselves by solemn vows.

Such oaths, a vestige of the feudal system, had become sacred in Roman Catholicism, defining all orders in the Church. To be "professed" as a religious was to kneel before the superior exactly as the knight had knelt before his liege lord. Thus for the Paulists to repudiate the sworn vow was an implicit attack on the very structure of hierarchy. Paulists, to be sure, accepted the traditional disciplines of poverty, chastity, and obedience, but instead of swearing vows to live by such norms, they took, as they said, mere "promises." The point was that the Paulists' freely given word did not need to be reinforced with the mortal sanctions of an oath. In emphasizing the freely given word of honor, Hecker was affirming the American principle of freedom.

In the basic American idea, Hecker saw not a contradiction but a fulfillment of Roman Catholic aspiration. The theological language he used to express this compatibility was centered on the Holy Spirit. But in this Hecker seemed to owe more of a debt to Emerson's "Over-Soul" than to St. Augustine's "indwelling." ("You shall find God in the unchanged essence of the universe, the air, the river, the leaf," Emerson said in 1865, ". . . and in the subjective unfolding of your nature.") Whatever its provenance, Hecker was explicit in affirming the idea that God resides in the soul of each individual as much as in the hierarchical institution of the Church. There were many justifications in the tradition for such an assertion ("For behold," Jesus said, "the Kingdom of God is within you"[32]), but in the modern context, as seen from the Vatican, the emphasis on such interiority could only evoke concerns about a coming religious democracy.[33]

These notions were reflected in the pastoral work to which Paulists were drawn, especially in preaching and in the printed word. They saw themselves as preachers to America, but that meant breaking out of the Catholic subculture when others in the Church wanted to reinforce it. In effect, they were missionaries as much to their Church as to their nation, preachers within Catholicism of the American esprit. For example, while the Jesuits were establishing their system of denominationally defined colleges and universities (numbering twenty-eight today), the Paulists were inventing a Catholic campus ministry, sending priests to, as they were called, "non-Catholic" colleges and universities. Especially following the land grant legislation of the late nineteenth century, institutions of public and private higher education had mushroomed, and suddenly there was a sizable population of university students across the country. The Catholics to whom Paulists ministered at non-Catholic schools, according to norms set by the reactionary Catholicism of Rome, were not even supposed to be in those places.

The first campus ministry center in the United States was established at the University of California at Berkeley in the first decade of the twentieth century, with the Paulists as directors. They called it the Newman Club, in honor of John Henry Newman, the great English prelate, himself a convert, a founder of University College Dublin, and the author of a seminal treatise on education, *The Idea of a University.*

But Newman had opposed the doctrine of papal infallibility at the Vatican Council. And, as we saw, he was guilty of a religious echo of Darwin, insisting, against the Council of Trent's notion of unchanging dogma, that doctrine could "develop." Newman's position here would define one side of the Catholic Church's twentieth-century argument with itself,[34] and the Paulists had yoked him to the American vision.

Decades after the Paulists started their movement, the conservative American priest Leonard Feeney denounced it. "[Newman Club] members are those tragically misplaced persons, Catholic students at non-Catholic colleges. And their very name, Newman, gives them away." Feeney attributed Newman's malign influence to his supposed Jewish background, and he defined the Newman Club as an "excuse for the presence, the sinful presence of Catholic students at secular universities founded and fostered by Masons, and, lately, indoctrinated by Jews."[35] Newman Clubs, whatever the likes of Feeney made of them, would be at the center of Paulist ministry, and would be adopted by the Catholic Church after the Second Vatican Council in the 1960s. By the twenty-first century, nearly every "non-Catholic" institution of higher learning in the United States would have one.

Pope Leo's 1899 condemnation of Americanism, expressly tied to the French translation of *The Life of Father Hecker* by one of the early Paulists, was a trauma for the order. Hecker narrowly escaped being personally, if posthumously, condemned for heresy, and the Paulist Fathers just escaped being suppressed, but the officially rejected ideas would be permanently associated with him and the order. A few years later, the related heresy of modernism was formally condemned by the Vatican, and among those tarred by the controversy were several Paulists and the Paulist journal, the *Catholic World*. At least one member of the order was effectively forced to leave the Church.[36] The Paulists were shaken by all of this, and they would spend much of the subsequent decades downplaying their particularly American character. Like liberals surviving in periods of reaction, they would keep their heads low.

Yet the Paulists maintained enough of their distinctive character that by the early 1960s, even a conventionally minded Catholic like me would be drawn to the order as something fresh. Georgetown, where I was a student, was begun in 1789, the year of the French Revolution.

The college had served sons of the Catholic aristocracy in Maryland, boys who were not welcome at Jefferson's university in Charlottesville or at Princeton or Harvard. I had enrolled at Georgetown because thoughts of entering a non-Catholic school had no more crossed my mind than they had the minds of my parents. We were aware, though, that Georgetown's founder was the Jesuit John Carroll, a cousin of the Declaration signer Charles Carroll. John Carroll went on to become the first Catholic bishop of the United States. Perhaps unconsciously, our ambition was satisfied by the mere association with a branch of the Carroll family that had not been poor. To us, Georgetown was arrival enough.

But then I had an accidental encounter with a visiting Paulist priest, and the ground shifted under me. Coming as I did from the Irish-American center of Council-of-Trent Catholicism, I glimpsed in the Paulists a way of being Catholic that I had never imagined. The priest I met at Georgetown, it turned out, was a recruiter for the order—the "vocation director." What struck me most about him was his breezy informality, a dramatic contrast to the Jesuits against whose sternness I was braced.

Here is where I saw it: the Paulist priest wore penny loafers just like mine, and the sight of those shoes on a priest was an epiphany. Loafers were the style of young people, decidedly opposed to our fathers' wingtips and the dull cap-toed shoes that were as much a part of priestly garb as shiny-kneed black trousers. Shoes without laces meant, subliminally, life without strictures. Slip-ons . . . slip off. Such shoes were also decidedly American, striking a postwar note of sartorial contrariness that set our masculinity apart from that of a still bridled European manhood. James Dean wore loafers. Loafers went with Levi's. Loafers worn with a black clerical suit made an even more pointed declaration. A declaration of independence.

For years afterward, I joked that I made the defining choice of my life because of penny loafers, but it was no joke. The shoes embodied something intangible, an esprit I was unconsciously searching for. My life as a Catholic, and as an American, was marked forever when I chose to become a Paulist, a son of Hecker, and eventually a Newman chaplain.

CHAPTER THREE

COMING OF AGE

1. RICHARD CUSHING

THE FALL OF my freshman year at Georgetown was the season of John Kennedy's election. I used to walk the few blocks from campus to the president-elect's house on N Street, to stand on the sidewalk and watch as Pierre Salinger came to the door each afternoon to brief the dozen or so assembled reporters. A few times I saw Kennedy's brothers coming and going, and once I saw Jackie Kennedy, even more glamorous in person than she was in pictures. By being in accidental proximity to Kennedy as he set out to "get the country moving again," I was permanently recruited to be part of my country's ongoing reinvention.

But I first took up that role from within the Church, for that was also the season in which I met that loafer-wearing Paulist. If I were a couple of years younger, perhaps my idealism and simple wish to help would have led me to join the Peace Corps, but Catholicism was crossing its own new frontier just then, and I picked up its spirit as I began to consider entering the Paulist seminary. Politics and religion had never seemed more attuned, with Pope John XXIII, although old enough to be the young president's grandfather, seeming like his soul brother. In a similar way, the new pope was setting things moving in the Church, using the word *aggiornamento* to define his agenda—"bringing things up to date." Elected to the papacy in 1958 as a compromise candidate, the elderly Angelo Roncalli had been expected only to keep the chair of Peter warm for a few years. Instead he took the Catholic old guard, centered in the Curia, the Vatican bureaucracy, by surprise when he called for an ecumenical council, a rare gathering of the world's bishops. It would take place in Rome in three sessions, between 1962 and 1965, and would be known as Vatican II. Recall that Vatican I was the 1870 council that had defined papal infallibility as doctrine. What Vatican II would define, among so much else, was nothing less than my entire life as a Catholic.

I did not know it then, but there was someone who made the link between John Kennedy and Pope John XXIII more than metaphorical. He was Richard Cushing, the archbishop of Boston, who was perhaps the only person in the world who was a friend of both the new president and the new pope. Not well remembered now, and not well understood at the time, Cushing played a pivotal role in the astonishing innovations accomplished by both men. And, as it happened, he would play a pivotal role in my life once I was a priest.

Richard Cushing, born in 1895, was the son of a blacksmith from Cork. Cushing was from the gritty edge of South Boston, a street of three-decker tenements that bordered a tank farm that was being constructed between the neighborhood and the waterfront. To feed the growing number of automobiles and furnaces, oil tankers would dock nearby and offload their fuel in the huge storage tanks. The stink of petroleum hung in the air, an ominous presence for blacksmiths like Richard's father. The steady roar of oil delivery trucks began to define O Street, on which Cushing grew up. He was a tall, gangly lad, a ballplayer and trickster. He ran errands for longshoremen, but also sneaked onto freighters and climbed into the dockside corrals for the hell of it. No mama's boy, still he often played with his sister Dolly and loved to tag along with her to Southie's Carson Beach. He also helped his father hammer out horseshoes at the trolley yards, but made it clear he would never be a blacksmith himself; he knew what the tank farm signified.

Dick Cushing went to the local public school, but in South Boston that was still within reach of the local nuns, who took note of his sharp intelligence and buoyant personality. As they did with the brightest boys and girls, the nuns slid Cushing onto the rails of their own purposes, arranging for him to attend the Jesuit-run Boston College High School. From there he went as a commuter to Boston College, where he became active in political clubs. During election campaigns, he made his mark as an amusing, if rough-hewn, public speaker. His irresistible personality, more than eloquence or grace, was what impressed. He crisscrossed the city on horse wagons, giving speeches for party candidates, one of whom was the young James Michael Curley, who would dominate Boston politics for the next half century.

In those years, exceptional Irish boys went into politics, but the extremely exceptional, once put on the rails by the nuns, were channeled toward the priesthood, and Dick Cushing was one of those. The nuns' impulse touched something in the lad. For all of his rambunctious extroversion, he felt most himself, by his own account, when quietly attending early morning Mass in the Jesuit chapel. After graduating from Boston College, he entered the seminary.

Despite his rough edges, Cushing was tapped for the North American College in Rome, which had recently become the Church's answer to Americanism, a place for schooling the most promising U.S. seminarians in the Vatican-centered doctrines of antimodernism and papal supremacy. But World War I was on, and because of U-boat dangers to transatlantic travel, no American Catholic seminarians were being sent to Rome, which meant Cushing did not receive his inoculation—or his domestication. Had he been molded in Rome, the particularities of his personality, what his critics would regard as his eccentricities, would never have followed him into the priesthood. Nor would he have been capable of what would turn out to be an open-armed, large-hearted embrace of American culture. He was ordained to the priesthood in 1921.[1]

During World War II, while still relatively young at forty-nine, Cushing was named archbishop of Boston. His fast-track ecclesiastical career was something of a fluke, for upon his ordination he had wanted only to join the foreign missions. That was the era of Albert Schweitzer's Christ-inspired—and broadly inspiring—medical mission in Africa, and a burst of magnanimous longing to spread the love of God overseas had likewise gripped American Catholicism. Bringing the Gospel, and also medicine, schools, sanitation, and food, to the poorest of the poor in remote sections of the globe had been Cushing's first ambition. He imagined a hard life for himself, something to match his upbringing.

But Cardinal William O'Connell, the princely archbishop of Boston, seeing in the irresistible South Boston extrovert what, say, James Michael Curley had seen, had assigned young Father Cushing not to the missions but to the task of raising money for them. Because he passionately believed in the cause, Cushing threw himself into fundraising, and he was great at it. Soon he was in charge of the Boston office of the Society for the Propagation of the Faith, a position from which, as the donations came in, he was noticed.

Even as archbishop—he succeeded the polished O'Connell in 1944—Cushing remained as rough-hewn as the old neighborhood. He never forgot where he came from, though he had moved into the Italianate palazzo that his predecessor had built in Brighton, near fashionable Chestnut Hill.[2] For more than four decades, O'Connell had so embodied the Romanist spirit that its continuance was assumed, even under the very different man who succeeded him, but when showing people around his mansion, Cushing would gruffly say, "Get a load of this place."[3]

With a granite-like profile to match the gravelly voice that emphasized his Boston accent (reciting the daily rosary on the radio, his nasal intonation, "Haaa-iiil Mary," became his much-imitated hallmark), Cushing soon epitomized an Irish-American Everyman who made good. Where O'Connell had been feared, Cushing became widely beloved in his hometown, especially for his open-mindedness toward Protestants and Jews. In fact, as an omnidirectional fundraiser for whom wealth had long before become nearly as important a point of character as religious affiliation, he had slid easily into an ecumenical mindset, and it stuck.

There was an irresistible contrast between the warmth of Cushing's craggy face and the iconic sternness of the biretta he wore in the cathedral. Given to sporting outlandish hats with his clerical garb—a fireman's helmet one day, a baseball cap at Fenway Park the next, a yarmulke before Jewish groups—he took delight in sending up the stereotyped image of the Catholic hierarch. Visiting the nuns, he always brought bags of Hershey's Kisses for them, for the sake of the punch line "These are the only kisses you and me will ever get!"

Cushing was—in style and, as events would show, in substance—the opposite of his near contemporary and counterpart in New York, Cardinal Francis Spellman. Both men had started out as priests of Boston, and they became rivals. Spellman molded himself after the princely O'Connell. He disapproved of Cushing's common-man image and used his own considerable influence with the aristocratic Pius XII to keep Cushing from being named a cardinal. That did not happen until 1958, a full twelve years after Spellman was so elevated. Cushing received the red hat only when Pius was succeeded by the peasant pope John XXIII, who saw in Boston's down-to-earth archbishop a version of himself. In a slap at Spellman, Cushing's promotion was one of the first things the new pope did. In fact, something had happened to give that elevation a special significance as a sign of Pope John's own agenda.[4]

2. LEONARD FEENEY, S.J.

In the late 1940s and early 1950s a Boston Jesuit, head of a religious institute near Harvard University, became notorious for an aggressive program of street-corner preaching. His message was "No salvation outside the Church," which he often took into the public square, with groups of supporters—and bodyguards—who handed out leaflets inviting conversion to the One True Faith. The priest was Father Leonard Feeney, the Newman Club critic, and his favorite venue was the Boston Common, the park that had begun as the Pilgrims' common grazing area.

The Feeney controversy went back to that avatar of Catholic resistance St. Thomas More. A year after the English martyr's canonization in 1935, a group of Catholics founded a bookstore in Harvard Square, naming it in More's honor. Many years later, I would haunt the Thomas More bookstore myself, but by then it was very different. In the beginning the shop was a center for young Catholics at Harvard and Radcliffe who were being thrown on the defensive by their decidedly non-Catholic professors and fellow students. From one side, disciples of Sigmund Freud attacked Catholicism as a primitive neurosis, and from the other, sympathizers with Spanish republicanism attacked it as fascist. More disturbing to the bookstore clique was the spirit of indifferentism that seemed to mark many of their fellow Catholics at Harvard.

One of the Thomas More Catholics was a young Harvard Law School student, Avery Dulles. His father, John Foster Dulles, was already a prominent Wall Street lawyer and would serve as Dwight Eisenhower's secretary of state, an office that had been held by his grandfather and by his uncle. The Dulleses were Presbyterian, and when Avery converted to Catholicism in 1940, it was treated like a scandal. This was a time when well-connected converts to Catholicism, like the writer, politician, and socialite Clare Boothe Luce, were big news.[5] To midcentury American Catholics, such conversions were the religious equivalent of anti-Communist defections. Avery Dulles would become a Jesuit and a famous Catholic theologian whose conservatism would earn him an appointment, in 2001, by Pope John Paul II to the College of Cardinals.[6]

But in 1940, Dulles was one of the avidly assertive Catholics at Harvard. He had a fresh convert's enthusiasm for the One True Church, and with a few others he established a storefront meeting place for study and mutual reinforcement. Called the St. Benedict Center, it evolved into an educational institution specializing in a reactionary Catholic apologetics, with an emphasis on rejection of the secularism of Harvard and, even more, of the creeping relativism that was showing itself within the Church. The St. Benedict Center was, in effect, a self-appointed bastion against the heresy of Americanism.

In 1945, Father Feeney, with the permission of his Jesuit superiors, was named the chaplain and, soon after, director of the center. Feeney, then forty-eight years old, had studied literature at Oxford and had been serving as an English professor at Boston College. He had made a name for himself as a writer of devotional poetry and popular religious essays. His directorship came at the time the center qualified as an educational institution for federal funding through the GI Bill. Its publication, *From the Housetops,* quickly found a wide circulation, and in the years after World War II, large numbers of Catholics were drawn to the movement. Feeney's book *Fish on Fridays* was in Catholic households all over America, including mine. I remember its cover, and its title struck an early note of my own awareness.

Feeney's genius lay in identifying the single issue in terms of which worried Catholics could articulate their campaign: *Extra Ecclesiam nulla salus*—"No salvation outside the Church." That battle slogan was aimed as much at liberals inside the Church—"Americanists" who were embarrassed by a forthright proclamation of strict Catholic doctrine—as it was at enemies outside it. Those drawn to the St. Benedict Center thought of themselves as defenders of the One True Faith, a unique manifestation of Catholic restoration, but in fact "Feeneyism," as it was soon known, was a Catholic version of the religious revivalism that was a mark of both post–World War II existential anxiety and early Cold War hysteria. Billy Graham's contemporaneous—and much larger—"crusade" movement, emphasizing the necessity of being "born again" to be saved, was a Protestant equivalent. (The percentage of self-identified churchgoers in the United States went from less than fifty percent in 1940 to more than sixty percent in 1955.)[7]

This emphasis on salvation as a consequence of faith brought with it an obsession with the opposite of being saved, which was, of course, damnation. Hell was near at hand. At various periods in history, Christians had been overcome with a vivid sense of dread about the afterlife, usually in times of plague or other kinds of threatening upheaval. Preoccupation with imminent doom was a symptom of millennial fever, and indeed, the first great theological expression of the inner workings of salvation had come in the first millennium, at the same time as the First Crusade. The genesis of Graham's own crusade offers a clue to what underlay the fresh urgency of this theology in the early 1950s. Graham's first great revival, in Los Angeles, took place in 1949, shortly after the Soviet Union exploded its first atomic bomb. The felt imminence of a world-ending Armageddon spawned the anguish that expressed itself religiously in this preoccupation with being saved. "The end of the world is nigh" was no longer a crackpot warning.

While Graham invited the public inside his revival tent, ignoring those who chose not to come, Feeney's delight was to go outside the church, outside the tent, to harangue passersby with threats and ultimatums. The more offensive his preaching was taken to be, the more he featured offensive elements. His theme was less the good news of salvation than the bad news of eternal doom, and he emphasized the special jeopardy of "perfidious" Jews. Feeney's offensive harangues walked the thin line between the Church's traditional anti-Judaism and its modern offshoot, racial antisemitism. The stereotyped slur became one of Feeney's rhetorical staples. Here is a typical example from 1953: "The Jews control the book publishing industry . . . They control the press, they control the news agencies. Witness their vicious propaganda campaign against Catholic Franco and for the Communists during the Spanish Civil War."[8] Even after revelations of the death camps in Europe, Feeney could declare that Jews were the particular enemy of the Catholic Church and that the Church's survival required their defeat once and for all.

The Jews of Boston objected, and so did others. Feeney became controversial. "I am not over-tactful," he bragged, "in taking into account what non-Catholics will think."[9] Archbishop Cushing was embarrassed, but it wasn't clear what he could do. Feeney's publicly proclaimed message of *nulla salus* may have been exceptionally uncivil, but it fell well within the bounds of traditional Catholic teaching. Strictly speaking, there *was* no salvation outside the Church—a tradition, as we saw, that went back to Pope Boniface VIII, and before him, to Aquinas. Not only Trent had reinforced the anathema for non-Catholics; so had popes of the Counter-Enlightenment within living memory of many. The doctrine had its roots in the sacred realm of Tradition, which Trent had emphasized as a form of revelation. If this solemnly reiterated teaching could change, what else could?

It was true that in recent years, out of some problematic regard for the "invincibly ignorant," the doctrine had been downplayed, and not only by Americanist liberals. The 1943 encyclical *Mystici Corporis,* which gave new emphasis to the mystical character of the Church, held out the possibility that non-Catholics could be attached to the One True Church "by some kind of unconscious desire and longing." That, however, was not an established countercurrent to a dogma of the still flowing mainstream.

The more Cushing was confronted with Feeney's bald iteration of *Extra Ecclesiam nulla salus,* the more it made the archbishop squirm. For Cushing, the question was intensely personal. His sister Dolly, who worked as a token taker on the Metropolitan Transit Authority, was married to a fellow named Dick Pearlstein. That Dolly married a Jew outside the Church had been a blow to the whole Cushing family. But a nephew of Dick Pearlstein's told me that, as a young priest, Cushing himself had quietly blessed his sister's marriage.[10] Beginning with those childhood forays down to Carson Beach in Southie, Cushing worshiped his sister and over the years had been drawn into the love she had for her husband.

Dick Pearlstein was of the family that ran Louis, a men's clothing store a few blocks up Boylston Street from the Common. The Pearlstein brothers liked to walk in the park during their lunch break, and they regularly encountered Feeney's claque. The archbishop often visited Dolly on Sunday afternoons, where he heard what Feeney was saying about the Jews—"horrid, degenerate, hook-nosed perverts."[11]

While listening to these reports, Cushing could not bear to meet his sister's eyes.

Soteriology, the theology of salvation, was not the archbishop's strong suit, but he was a good judge of character. Having found a large place in his heart for Dick Pearlstein, Cushing could not believe that there was no place for him in God's heart. And for others like him. Cushing saw up close the pain inflicted by mean-spirited ideas whose time, whatever their validity in bygone eras, was long past. Wasn't it true that nothing was impossible for God? And wasn't it true that God was all-loving? Who was to say, finally, who was worthy of salvation and who was deserving of damnation? Weren't we all poor banished children of Eve, dependent on the Lord's mercy? The archbishop asked Father Feeney to come to his office.

Feeney obeyed the summons. They recognized each other as cut from the same cloth. Feeney started out a Mick from Lynn, a blue-collar Irish enclave just north of Boston, but with his Oxford pretensions and literary ways he would have disdained the still unpolished archbishop. Cushing, for his part, knew who was in charge. He nicely asked the Jesuit to stop preaching "No salvation outside the Church." Feeney rebuffed him with references to Church councils and papal pronouncements going back a thousand years. Hadn't Jesus himself decreed that "no one comes to the Father except through me"?[12] How could one come authentically to Jesus except through Baptism, which in its Protestant form was null and void? Pope-centered Catholicism was the one true way. And as for Jews, it wasn't Feeney who called them "children of Satan," but the Lord himself, in the Gospel of John.[13] As the priest fired off his citations from encyclicals and verses of Scripture, Cushing knew he was getting his own version of the Boston Common harangue. It was ugly.

Over many months, the archbishop tried everything he could think of to get the firebrand Jesuit to temper his message. Cushing asked Rome for a clarification of Church teaching, but the question remained murky. Feeney's superiors in the Society of Jesus reassigned him to the College of the Holy Cross in Worcester, but Feeney refused to leave the St. Benedict Center. He became more strident than ever, and others picked up his theme. They ignored the ways theologians in recent years had tried to reconcile the tradition of Catholic absolutism with a growing respect for the consciences of others.

"No salvation outside the Church" didn't necessarily mean what it seemed to say. We saw this in reference to the narrow doctrinal opening provided by *Mystici Corporis*, and by now some theologians were pushing through that opening to talk of a "Baptism of desire." If the Church can be understood mystically, why not the qualifying sacrament? Through this kind of Baptism, someone who was not Catholic, but who genuinely desired to carry out God's will, could be counted as a member of the One True Church—even if he did not know it, even if he wanted nothing to do with it. That definition fit Dick Pearlstein to a T, though Cushing understood that his brother-in-law would not be flattered to have it applied to him.[14] Equally so for the other Jews, Protestants, and even atheists whom Cushing had befriended. In his opinion, what the mysteries of God's ways of dealing with non-Catholics needed was a good leaving alone.

To Archbishop Cushing, the thing was simpler than theology. Feeney's self-proclaimed orthodoxy, as it fell on the ears of Boston, was a sin against charity and it had to stop. Cushing gave the order. Feeney disobeyed. Cushing silenced him altogether with a formal interdiction. Still Feeney disobeyed. *No salvation outside the Church!* Years later, when I myself was one of Cushing's priests, I often heard the story recounted of what had happened then. Boston's priests universally mimicked Cushing, and his own version of the event was endlessly repeated, Southie accent and all. Cushing threatened Father Feeney with excommunication, but the priest seemed to welcome it. In fact, in one of their last encounters, Feeney pronounced Cushing himself a heretic. As Cushing told the story, just as he was about to inform Feeney of his excommunication, the priest said to the archbishop, "In the name of the Blessed Virgin Mary, I excommunicate you!"

"What could I do?" Cushing said with a twinkle in his eye. "He beat me to the draw." The line always got a good laugh. But Feeney was out.

At the time, the Feeney matter was dead serious. The reactionary priest had forced the issue, and now the Vatican, bound by its own solemn teachings going back to the thirteenth century, would have to confirm or deny what Cushing had done. To the amazement of Catholics everywhere, Rome upheld Archbishop Cushing's disciplining of Father Feeney. The priest's defenders always insisted that the excommunication was not a repudiation of the doctrinal content of Feeney's preaching, and indeed the Vatican decree was explicit in disciplining him "for grave disobedience toward Church authority," not for heresy.

In this the Vatican was like the U.S. Supreme Court, settling a case on narrow procedural grounds that don't address the basic issue.

The Vatican was careful to reaffirm the Tradition (capital *T*) of *nulla salus,* but, in explanation of its objection to Feeney, changed the definition of what constituted membership in the Church. In other words, the Vatican followed the lead of the liberalizing theologians. One could be a Catholic *in re,* which meant a real Catholic—which is what most people meant by membership. Or one could be a Catholic *in voto,* "in will," or "by desire"—a membership that is invisible to everyone but God, including to the "member" himself. This was casuistry of the highest order—Feeney's point exactly—and it reduced the doctrine to the absurd, but the distinction served the twin purpose of affirming the Tradition while breaking away from it.

Such convoluted reasoning was the only way in which an institution that claimed to be unchanging could change. This, of course, is the great Catholic problem, and the hierarchy's inability to take up the question directly—how does a church that claims to be unchanging change?—continues to define the issue even of this book. One result of obfuscation on the question of who is saved is that the doctrinaire exclusivity of Trent can periodically make a comeback in Catholicism.

Decades after Feeney, for example, the actor and filmmaker Mel Gibson, in discussions prompted by the release of his *The Passion of the Christ,* would assert that his wife, an Episcopalian, would regrettably be damned to a lake of hellfire forever because she was not a member of the One True Church.[15] Gibson's film would be approved by Vatican officials, and his *nulla salus* would seem to be affirmed by Joseph Ratzinger, speaking both as prefect of the Congregation for the Doctrine of the Faith and as Pope Benedict XVI.[16] But such triumphalism would strike most twenty-first-century people, especially Catholics, as bizarre.

With Feeney's excommunication, no matter what hairsplitting explanations accompanied it, the long-settled doctrine of *Extra Ecclesiam nulla salus* was undercut, though not quite overturned. Theologians would continue to struggle to reconcile a necessary new ecumenism with the triumphalist claims of old. "Baptism of desire" would morph into a theology of the "anonymous Christian,"[17] but no one would be able to pretend a radical change had not already taken place in the very self-understanding of the immutable institution.

What began here would be completed a decade later, as we will see, at a new council in Rome.

Feeney's excommunication, coming in 1953, occurred when I was ten years old. I remember it well, a subject obsessively discussed, though we were far from Boston, in my Alexandria, Virginia, parochial school and at home. I had no way to understand the larger implications of the dispute—how it grew out of the way the American context had only recently been transformed for the children and grandchildren of Catholic immigrants. My parents were typical, their situation and prospects having been changed utterly by the great societal leveling of World War II. Indeed, the exact decade since their move from Chicago to Washington (and, as it happens, since my birth) had been the decisive period. If the gates of a once hostile society had been unexpectedly opened—my blue-collar father amazed to be a senior figure in the national security establishment; my dropout mother stunned to be a part of the Washington social set; both of them newly initiated members of a formerly excluding Old South country club in Alexandria; my brothers and I proudly mustered in a Boy Scout troop that met in a Protestant church into which we had been previously instructed never to set foot—then an existential question was unavoidable: If "they" are no longer excluding us in *this* world, why should we go on excluding "them" in the next?

I now recognize the Feeney controversy as the occasion of my first foray into theology. Like many Catholic children of my generation, I was inculcated with a vivid sense of God's nearness. I made room in the seat of my small desk for my guardian angel. I knew that God was watching me, which was intimidating, and watching over me, which was a consolation. As I was brought into the mystery of death, I felt the open-ended anguish of an undefined afterlife, and the prospect of an eternity without God seemed real. When I heard discussions of salvation, usually involving its impossibility for non-Catholics, I was also aware of the thin grasp we Catholics had on our own prospects for being saved. That *Domine, non sum dignus* had already seared my consciousness, and I was alert to the implication of our obsessive prayers for the "grace of a happy death," by which we meant dying in the presence of a priest. A priest could, by the wave of his hand, absolve the sins that would otherwise send us straight to hell. When I received the sacrament of Confirmation around that time, the gift I got was a wallet, and with it a wallet card that said, "I am a Catholic. In case of an accident, please call a priest." Only that absolution at the final moment guaranteed entrance into heaven, even for us.

Thus, the furious discussion of the eternal fate of Protestants and Jews and atheists was, at bottom, a discussion about what was waiting for us all. By emphasizing the advantage that we Catholics had over the others, or so it seemed to me, we had been trying to overcome an inbred uncertainty about our own destinies. But wait a minute! Now the nuns and priests were saying that our advantage was not what we'd been told? No matter how I tried, I could not parse the contradiction, as befuddled Sister Miriam Theresa and equally hapless Monsignor Stevens explained Father Feeney's excommunication to us in religion class.

Finally, I brought my simple question to my mother: "But I thought 'No salvation outside the Church' was what we believed."

"It was," she replied.

"What do we believe now?"

And with exquisite theological nuance, she answered simply, "Live and let live, and leave the rest to God." My mother was an Americanist.

3. EXPERIENCE OVER DOCTRINE

In the story of Cushing and Feeney we have a parable of how change in the Church actually occurs. Of old, it was thought that theological insight into the nature and being of God was the basis of morality. God is good, and therefore humans are called to be good, too. Humans are born with a constitutional depravity (in the Catholic tradition, Original Sin; in Luther, the desire to rely on "works"), and only knowledge of God (Baptism, faith) enables them to overcome it. In God, humans are capable of goodness. Understanding God in heaven, humans can draw conclusions about the moral life on earth. Morality follows theology.

But what Cushing did reversed this. He had an ethical insight that came to him not from theology but from an experience at his sister's dinner table. His theology, as accurately—if rigidly—asserted by Father Feeney, told Cushing that his brother-in-law Dick Pearlstein was cursed by God, but the archbishop himself felt only love for the man. Cushing's own experience of love—a moral insight—opened into an intuition about God's capacity for love—a theological insight. The starting point was not God, but Cushing's own experience.

Cushing himself, while almost certainly aware that he was elevating *something* above dogma, might have described what he was doing as putting the pastoral before the doctrinal. I remember this distinction being made when I was in the seminary. By labeling an otherwise forbidden course of action "pastoral," our moral-theology professor was offering us a way of applying common sense to an impossible human situation. In the name of a pastoral, as opposed to a doctrinal, response, we might be taught, say, that it was all right to encourage a battered wife to leave her abusive husband. The pastoral advice to a sickly woman with nine children might consist of telling her it was okay to take the birth control pill. The point was, a pastoral exception left the contradictory doctrine intact. It met the particular human need without suggesting that Church teaching should change.

Whether he would have acknowledged it or not, what Cushing did went further than this. He may not have explicitly argued that all Jews had to be brought into the dispensation of Christian salvation, but he was certainly rejecting the proposition that his brother-in-law was *ipso facto* damned for being a Jew. Without knowing it, Cushing was repeating the essential revolution that began when a Polish cleric named Nicolaus Copernicus, reversing Ptolemy, theorized that the earth revolved around the sun, and when Galileo Galilei later proved the theory with his telescope. Religion's problem here was not only with what was being observed (a heliocentric universe, not a geocentric one, as in the Bible[18]), but also with the experimental mode of knowing. The scientific method prizes experience (investigation and observation) over ideology, reason over faith. That reversal is the challenge that science puts to religion.

Here in a nutshell is what this reversal does to traditional assertions of belief. The starting point of experience is not God's existence ("In the beginning God") but the person's ("I think, therefore I am"). How do I know I exist? Not because God tells me ("God said . . .") but because I can experience myself asking the question. The self-awareness of the thinking being is the primal source of knowledge, which is why close attention to such awareness (observation, investigation, experimentation) is the absolute value of science. Science, as we understand it, began with Copernicus and Galileo. The self is the center of awareness, not a revealing deity. The irony here is exquisite, because Copernicus, by removing the earth—and therefore humanity—from the center of the cosmos, was understood to be removing humanity from the pinnacle of creation, a radical devaluation. He was doing that, but he was also making vastly larger claims for the knowing individual than had ever been made before.

When the Enlightenment, expanding broadly on the insight of scientists, thus gave primacy to the experience of the individual, the Church correctly understood that claims for its own primacy and that of the pope—not to mention God—were under assault. But what if the revolution in human thinking that was initiated by the age of science involves a simultaneous and intrinsic revolution in ethical reasoning? What if the scientific method is a moral method? In that case, certitudes in the realm of religion would be overthrown every bit as much as those in the realm of science. The Church therefore launched its battery of antimodern anathemas, as if reason *were* the enemy of faith. So the Church's response was, in its own terms, reasonable.

When science triumphed anyway, religion settled for a separate realm in which the scientific method (the primacy of experience) would not apply. Science, for the sake of its independence, accepted the dichotomy. The result, however, was a disaster for both. Religion, speaking generally, remained hostage to primitive thinking. The Roman Catholic tradition, which, with Augustine, Aquinas, and Copernicus himself, had enshrined reason, leading to science, would join fundamentalists in the elevation of belief above critical thought. Science, for its part, mostly shirked its responsibility to confront the moral implications that are intrinsic to all learning. Scientists and pastors were usually content to leave each other alone.

Yet when Archbishop Richard Cushing was faced, however inchoately, with a conflict between reason and faith, he changed the faith. Instead of pretending there was no conflict—as Church figures did who preferred to say Feeney's offense was disobedience, not heresy, or who would have solved the dilemma with a merely pastoral dodge —Cushing forced the doctrinal issue in a way that Rome would have to take a position in response. *If this message offends charity, how can it be orthodox?* Cushing took his own experience of love for Dick Pearlstein, and his thinking about it, as a higher value than that of the clear meaning of a thousand-year-old tradition of the Roman Catholic

Church. Cushing, that is, did what Galileo did, even if, this time, the Vatican's response was very different.

And this process of change was only getting started.

The great question that modernity put to faith was, Can religion change as human beings change? As Newman put it, Can doctrine develop? Or, to put the question in more loaded language, Can religion evolve? The Catholic Church's first answer to that question, symbolized by Pius IX's proclamation of the doctrine of the Immaculate Conception in 1854, just as Charles Darwin was preparing to publish *On the Origin of Species by Means of Natural Selection,* was a resounding No! The Immaculate Conception is commonly misunderstood to refer to the miracle of Mary's virginal conception of Jesus, but it actually refers to the idea that Mary, in order to be pure enough to bring God into the world, was herself conceived without Original Sin. God shaped Mary, the pope declared in effect, as God had shaped Adam and Eve. The idea that God directly intervenes in the conception of a human person is incompatible with evolution's corollary that God's intervention, if such occurs at all, is bound by the laws of time and nature.

To promulgate as the Church's official teaching an assertion about the moral significance of the egg and sperm in the womb of Mary's mother, joined to a cult of Marian miracles typified by hysterias attached to Our Lady of Lourdes, whose "apparitions" soon began, was as complete a repudiation of scientific thinking as the Church could muster at that moment. The repudiation lives on in a fierce attachment to crude notions of the miraculous. The Catholic Church officially recognizes fifty-eight "healings" as having been accomplished by the intervention of Mary at Lourdes, most recently in 1999.[19]

Ironically, from another point of view the Immaculate Conception itself shows the inevitably evolving character of doctrine. Even though this belief about Mary is said to be entirely consistent with Tradition, there was nothing driving it inexorably toward such formal proclamation. Pope Pius IX's definition of the Immaculate Conception as an article of faith was, in fact, the first time a pope had ever presumed to make a declaration of dogma apart from his fellow bishops meeting in general council. As such, the pronouncement was widely seen as Pius's *a priori* invocation of infallibility (which was not defined, as we saw, until 1870). Nor was there any real precedent for such an elevation from popular piety to formal dogma of beliefs about the mother of Jesus. Mariology *evolves!*

The oversimplifications of the Vatican's panicked—not so much irrational as antirational—reaction to the challenge put by new knowledge, a reaction reflected in a whole host of late-nineteenth-century pronouncements, were not worthy of religion's deep and complex past, or its future.[20] Religion began, after all, not long after *Homo sapiens* began, when religion was, with toolmaking, a main realm of *sapiens—a first mode of thinking.* Religion formally established itself during the Iron Age (around 1500 B.C.E.) and reached a transforming climax in the next millennium (from around 900 to 200 B.C.E.). Around the globe in this period, religious genius was manifest in multiple forms, from Confucianism, Buddhism, and Hinduism to the monotheism of the Hebrews.[21]

Whatever their affirmations, all of these religions share elements of denigration of the value of this world, and that is part of what is reflected in religion's instinctive hostility toward a scientific view that gives primacy to the *experience* of this world. But another part of such skepticism toward the new vision has to do with the time-bound character of belief as such. The worldviews of the era when the great religions jelled, apparent in foundational texts, myths, and cults, continue to inform many religious assumptions today, certainly in the traditions derived from Hebrew religion. There is God in heaven intervening in nature, hurling thunderbolts and sending rain. While nature, by not being God, is essentially devalued, "Man" is still the pinnacle of creation, and man's planet is the center of the universe.

But what happens when the worldview of the Iron Age bumps up against the scientific age? The issue is even more pointed in our so-called information age. All of human history is a record of growth—evolution—in human knowing, and information technologies, as culminations of scientific invention, are bringing about essential changes in the meaning of that knowing. Especially in the West, religion spawned philosophy, as astrology spawned astronomy. Down the millennia, truths grasped through tested experience constantly challenged early religious expression, a process that became explosive in the past three hundred years, when science and discovery accomplished what amounts to a massive mutation in thought.[22]

The Renaissance and the Enlightenment, in combination and progression, while removing "Man" from the center of the cosmos, brought about a far more optimistic appraisal of earthly life. "Nature" is its own realm, and it does not need to be interrupted by "supernature" to be completed. Or, to put it another way, miracles are unnecessary. The whole cosmic business is miraculous. The age of miracles, that is, is past. Can religion, which began as the very fount of thought, keep pace, or must it at last be seen as opposed to thought, and therefore relegated to the nursery? That question hung between Cushing and Feeney.

Cushing assumed the Enlightenment progression from self and experience to others and learning, just as he assumed what the Enlightenment never affirmed—that ultimately that progression leads to faith and God. No doubt miracles remained live possibilities for Cushing, but there was nevertheless a profoundly modern assumption at the root of what he accomplished in that movement from self to other. This equals movement not from theology to ethics (one must know God to be good), but from moral insight to a conclusion about God. One's own empathetic experience of the neighbor means God loves that neighbor, too; ultimately God loves everyone. And God loves creatures not because they are baptized or have faith or accomplish "works," but because God created the creatures in the first place. Creation is an overflowing of love. If salvation consists in being beloved of God, all are *ipso facto*—or, better, *in esse*—saved. Or, as Mom put it to me, "Live and let live, and leave the rest to God."

Cushing's act was classic Americanism, rooted as it was in an experience of culture that especially (if not quite uniquely) belonged to the United States. This is not to argue that the affirmation of God's unconditional love, to use a contemporary phrase, for God's creation *simply because it exists as God's creation* is unknown in the Christian tradition. But when salvation became the main meaning of Christ's coming, with the human condition (after the Fall) defined as inherently damnable, such an essentially positive and open reading of the faith became a minor note. Nevertheless, it was struck repeatedly through the ages, by mystics like St. Teresa of Ávila in the Renaissance and Thomas Merton in our time, who found God in their interiority as much as in Church membership; by thinkers like Abelard in early-medieval Paris and Döllinger in Enlightenment Germany, for both of whom Jesus was less Savior than Revealer—revealing that we are all *already* saved simply by virtue of existing. For that matter, such affirmation of the human was made by the author of the Gospel of John, who defined creation as the *logos* of God.[23] Creation itself is sacramental.

These and similar assertions that human experience as such is an opening to the presence of God were authoritatively labeled "wild readings" and "evil interpretations" of the Gospel as early as the second century. "If spiritual understanding may arise from human experience"—here is how one scholar characterized the reservations—"doesn't this mean that it is nothing but human invention, and therefore false?"[24] Interiority is an unreliable measure of meaning, spiritual or material, and faith in the "human" can be drastically misplaced.

But suspicion of such optimistic faith experience, as opposed to authoritatively defined "revelation," was rooted even more in an organizational mandate, for the label of "heresy" was being applied to such readings by Church figures whose concern was to gain control of the dispersed and diverse understandings of the meaning of Jesus. "Mysticism begins in the mist," as one summary of the rejection goes, "is built around the 'I,' and ends in schism."[25] Drawing boundaries around the Jesus fellowship and its ideas was the purpose of this condemnation, and an ultimate denigration (damnation) of those outside the boundaries followed. This was probably an inevitable development in the way a new and vulnerable and widely scattered network of communities understood itself, even though such organizational pressures effectively contradicted key elements of Jesus' own teaching.

Ordering (read "ordaining") for the sake of orthodoxy ("right thinking") was perhaps a natural part of a movement's evolution into a church, and it reached a climax in the fourth century when, after Emperor Constantine became a Christian, the ordering was done with the power of the state. Mystics, Gnostics, Arians, heretics of various kinds—all who represented a preference for the intuitive and the interior over the hierarchical—were targeted. Although it violates the heroic narrative of steadfast believers thrown to the lions in the Colosseum to say so, more Christian "martyrs" died at the hands of the Christian emperors than had been killed by pagan emperors. But despite all this, the Christian tradition never fully let go of the innately positive impulse to see human life itself—and not only a strictly defined membership organization—as a way to God.[26]

In the United States, perhaps because of its essentially positive esprit, and surely because of its homegrown, if accidental, inclusiveness, these more open-minded minority impulses of the Christian tradition began to be retrieved even by Catholics, whose *nulla salus* ideology had become so excluding. This was as simple as demographics, geography, the pull of the West, the steady influx into cities, and the consequent refusal of the newcomers' close-knit neighborhood to stay, well, closed for more than a generation. Born in an immigrant enclave, Archbishop Cushing—and, more to the point, his sister Dolly—was drawn out of it. In America, Jews, Protestants, and Catholics, sooner *and* later, encountered each other as neighbors (as, eventually, would Confucianists, Hindus, Buddhists, Muslims—and atheists). In the Cushing case, they encountered each other as spouses.

To return to a point made earlier: in the Old World, boundaries defined experience. Across generations, Jews lived in ghettos, Christians lived in confessional states. Encounters of like with unlike were the exception. In the New World, boundaries—the very frontier—existed to be crossed. Immigrants often settled with fellows from the old country, but those arrangements in the New World were temporary and fluid. In the United States, plurality was literally a source of union. *E pluribus unum.* Rubbing elbows with neighbors, and finding more commonality than divergence, meant that the absolutes of the enclave were constantly in question. In America, that occurred even within the religion that understood itself as more absolute than any, Roman Catholicism.

4. JOHN COURTNEY MURRAY, S.J.

Just when Archbishop Cushing was having his own experience of dissolving boundaries with Dick Pearlstein, his near contemporary the American Jesuit John Courtney Murray was giving it explicit articulation. Murray was a shy theology professor working in a backwoods seminary in Maryland, but his writing was explosive. Once the idea of neighbors living together, each with his or her own separate religious understanding and commitment, was affirmed as a good thing, it followed that the imposition of absolute claims by one religion on another was a violation of neighborliness. In the period after World War II, as American Catholics (like my parents) were increasingly drawn into the national consensus, Murray argued that the American system of protecting religious freedom, through the separation of church and state, instead of contradicting Catholic assumptions, fulfilled them. That was because the separation, far from being hostile to religion, was acting in its service. By removing state power from creedal affirmation, the conscientious creedal affirmation of each citizen was being protected.

After all, the newly articulated idea, brought to a head by the Feeney controversy, that the workings of conscience, even in non-Catholics—"Baptism of desire"—were the main mode of salvation meant that conscience itself had primacy over any institutional formality. To fully appreciate what a revolutionary idea this was in Roman Catholicism, it helps to recall that, before the social transformations of World War II, the innovative Murray himself had been arguing for a strict reading of "No salvation outside the Church." His theology, too, was changed by the broader shift.

Implicit in this elevation of conscience over express institutional affiliation was a distinction between private and public morality—a distinction that would generate Murray's "reflections," as he called his push into a new theology of church and state, and bedevil many who tried to apply it to troubling cases of moral and civil law. If overt membership in the Roman Catholic Church was not the ultimate value, then the individual's self-defined pursuit of the truth had to be. We will see that over time Murray moved from docilely bowing before Church authority to an affirmation of individual religious freedom. In hindsight it seems obvious that his asking how the Church should respect the conscience of non-Catholics would lead to his asking how it should respect the conscience of Catholics. The point here, however, is that Murray's reflections on the separation of church and state at least implicitly raised the question of the separation of church and church member. And for Catholics that separation, especially since the condemnations of modernism, had been as inconceivable as a separation between a lever and its fulcrum. The magisterial Church, aiming to preserve conformity among the teaching, the teacher, and the taught, was right to warn against such American ideas.

Yet despite how the American proposition was caricatured by its critics, especially in Rome, the American pursuit of truth, like the pursuit of happiness, was no mere adventure of narcissistic solipsism. True, the individualism of the Calvinist ideal could and did underwrite socially irresponsible tendencies to reward the achievers and punish those left behind. The separation of public and private morality had been an implicit pillar of slavery, since slaves were private property, and no public institution (for example, the federal government) could challenge it. But as the carefully arrived at conventions of this social polity showed, especially including the eventual high-cost abolition of slavery, American constitutional democracy was an enterprise of regulated mutuality. That mutuality implied communal self-criticism and change. Hence the Emancipation Proclamation.

Despite a general impression to the contrary, Calvinism was the opposite of rank individualism. After all, the dominant image of God in Calvinist theology (as in Jewish theology) was as the covenant maker. John Calvin (1509–1564), a Frenchman who spent most of his life in Geneva, was trained as a lawyer, and that shows in the emphasis he brought to the Protestant Reformation. His establishing a theocracy in Geneva was consistent with his theology. Calvin's God is one who enters into a binding agreement with the chosen people. Agreements assume not individuals but parties. Parties to agreements may not be equal, but each has responsibilities and privileges that flow from the covenant. Such theology has immediate consequences for social organization, for politics.

But the Calvinist God as covenant maker stands in marked contrast to the dominant image of God in Roman Catholic theology—the image of a damning judge. That, at least, was the divine figure that gripped the mind of the Latin Church in the Middle Ages. Martin Luther, for all he changed, carried this image over wholesale into his reform, and it shows in his doom-laden theology. If God is a damning judge, then religion is mainly a matter of sin and guilt, and then, after penitence and punishment, of salvation. Salvation has thus been a Catholic (and Lutheran) preoccupation in ways it simply has not been for the Protestants in train with Calvin (and for Jews). This, too, is manifest in the Catholic encounter with America, whose covenant-based politics expressly derives from Calvinist theology, not Lutheran. Indeed, the word "federal" has roots in the Greek word for covenant.[27]

If God is a covenant maker, religion is a matter of solemn promises between people, an idea that eventually takes form in the U.S. Constitution, a secular covenant that protects the individual *through the community.* Its checks and balances include checks on the individual as well as on the community, and the entire system includes principles of its own self-criticism. American constitutional democracy involves, therefore, a profoundly communal aspect, realized in the protections of the nation's social compact—its covenant.[28]

The primacy of conscience, Murray argued, could be affirmed not against the community, as Catholic anathemas had warned for a century, but within the community. Exactly in that tension—*e pluribus unum* indeed—resided the genius of the United States. Religious liberty, to put it most simply, was consistent with Catholic teaching. The Americanist strain in Murray's position was reflected in his readiness to take nothing less than religious instruction from the Constitution and the Declaration of Independence—*instruction for the Church.* Thomas Jefferson, at last, was being taken as a teacher of Catholics, too. Murray's most famous book would be called *We Hold These Truths.*[29]

Feeney would have argued that Murray's was just the kind of heretical thinking that followed from the refusal to uphold the doctrine of *Extra Ecclesiam nulla salus.* Feeney was trying to protect the Church's great insight that salvation was not a private experience, as if a person's fate could be cut off from a neighbor's, but a communal event. This important point of the Catholic substance, essential to the argument against the Protestant principle, was lost, however, in Feeney's chauvinism and in his tendency to oversimplify what American individualism actually entailed.

Yet if the Vatican was prepared to reject the crudity of Feeney's position, it was not yet ready to affirm the subtlety of Murray's. His position, too, raised problems. After all, Jefferson's line "We hold these truths to be self-evident," the boldest of American assertions, epitomized an Enlightenment confidence in the new method of knowing—that truth is not revealed by God but discovered by the self ("I think, therefore I am"). But wasn't Descartes, with his false elevation of thinking over being, the author of the great modern divide between the self and society, between science and reason, between spirit and matter—and didn't those regrettable dichotomies underwrite Jefferson's "wall of separation" between church and state? By the middle of the twentieth century, the French philosopher's smug declaration could be recognized as a prime instance of the hubris of materialistic modernity, the "self-evident" certitudes of which collapsed in the moral chaos of two world wars and multiple genocides. In 1954, the year after it supported Cushing in silencing Feeney, the Vatican silenced Murray. Unlike Feeney, Murray obeyed. But the Church was in conflict with itself.

5. CATHOLIC CAMELOT

All of these issues might have remained abstract, with their significance never being brought fully into cultural consciousness. The forces of reaction within the Catholic Church, like the habit of discrimination in the United States, might have rallied in time to push a pair of thumbs in the one dike before the wave of massive change broke. But that did not happen, in Catholicism or in America, and it was because of the epic narrative that was unfolding just then, a story embodying all of these dynamics while simultaneously bringing them to climax. Indeed, this story functioned, in the realms of church and state both, as a transforming myth worthy of Homer. And wasn't Richard Cushing central to this tale, too?

On a crisp and windy day in September 1953, 750 of the very best people squeezed into St. Mary's Church in Newport, Rhode Island, for a nuptial Mass over which Archbishop Cushing presided. The gathering was an anomaly, for that quaint church in the center of the town existed for the use of servants who worked in the magnificent Cliff Walk "cottages" and on the "saltwater farms" of the social elites of Newport. Yet that day, the thirty-six-year-old groom and the twenty-four-year-old bride were a golden couple. Servants were not in attendance. Held in the very heart of the upper-class establishment, the matrimonial festivities, complete with a tenor's rendition of the *Ave Maria* and the archbishop's promulgation of a papal blessing, were a triumphant assertion of Roman Catholic arrival.

The Catholic bride was no Bridgit, though. Jacqueline Lee Bouvier's mother had divorced her father and married a divorced man—the patrician and Protestant Hugh Auchincloss. His standing at the pinnacle of the Newport social set was the reason the wedding was held in this tony resort community, if not in this particular church. Auchincloss walked his stepdaughter Jacqueline down the aisle in place of her rakish father, John "Black Jack" Bouvier, who had turned up at the church too inebriated to give his daughter away. Protestants and drunks, take your pick. After the nuptial Mass, the party adjourned to Hammersmith Farm, the Auchincloss oceanside estate, where another thousand VIPs joined the swells coming from St. Mary's.

Aware of her own besmirched status in the Church—a "bad marriage"—the bride's mother, Janet Auchincloss, had wanted to downplay the Catholic aspect of the wedding, but the groom's family would not hear of that. They were Kennedys, and downplayed nothing. Hence the Irish archbishop brought down from Boston, papal blessing and all. Joe Kennedy knew that he and his kind would not have been admitted to the clubs of Newport, which was why he wanted nothing less than a full damn display of the thing that most disqualified him.

John Fitzgerald Kennedy was a Protestant's idea of a good Catholic. But to the likes of Avery Dulles, who was his 1940 classmate at Harvard, Kennedy could only have represented the rot of indifferentism that had taken hold in the Church. In Cambridge, young Jack Kennedy would never have heard of the Thomas More bookstore, much less the St. Benedict Center, or, if he had, would never have crossed the threshold of either. And now, as a politician, Senator Kennedy was famously a Mass-goer, but he had barely disguised his philandering. His most serious commitment was to his own advancement. Such open disregard of the moral norms of the faith could only offend the converted son of a Presbyterian elder. What might have prompted the Dulles family to indulge the visceral anti-Catholicism of their kind was precisely what drove the young convert Avery toward a purifying Catholic reform.

The wedding was taking place seven months after Father Feeney's formal excommunication, which had made Archbishop Cushing a national figure—an unexpected avatar of a new Catholic liberalism. His very presence here was of a piece with all that a Catholic of the Council of Trent might object to. But Catholics who welcomed a chance to enter the mainstream of American life had to see it differently. Cushing's highly publicized standoff with Feeney, and the Vatican's surprising support of the archbishop against the priest, marked a watershed moment, and people saw it even then. Catholics who were rubbing elbows with non-Catholics no longer had to squirm with embarrassment at the uncivil dogmatic pronouncement that such coworkers, friends, neighbors, and, increasingly, spouses and in-laws were doomed to float forever in the lake of hellfire. What good is your yacht there?

Concerning this transformation, I have vivid memories of my own. At age ten, I felt an intense relief to be able to assure my chums and fellow Boy Scouts—Protestant Dickie Boris, Jewish Peter Seligman—that as far as I was concerned they were fine with God. That assurance of mine, I understood, was a precondition of my being fine with them. How could I not have been relieved to hear a Gospel preached at church in which the great commandment was that I should love them, my neighbors, as I loved myself, and so be released from the doomsday conviction that the boys I thought of as best friends were lost forever? And if they weren't lost—here was my secret relief, secret because it showed my lack of faith—perhaps I wasn't either.

It would not have seemed incidental to those at the Kennedy wedding celebration, but this shift in the basic Catholic assumption about non-Catholics nicely served the purposes of a politician poised to spring from his mostly Irish-Catholic constituency in Massachusetts onto the larger stage of national politics. It would not do to go around telling the voters that they were damned. Kennedy did not have to be the cause of a new Catholic ecumenism to be its first beneficiary. Whether he wanted to be or not, politics made him its first missionary.

In the national memory, it is well understood how his arrival changed the state. What needs to be emphasized here is how, beginning with that wedding, when a Protestant actively took part in a Catholic sacrament to give away his Catholic stepdaughter, Kennedy's arrival changed the Church.

If there was a certain, undenied playboy aspect to Kennedy's image, well, that too could seem a relief to a pinched, Jansenist community. If its new motto was to be "Live and let live," why not retrieve the Lord's promise of "life, life to the full"? Why couldn't "Live and let live," that is, open into "Live it up"? Or, as the new Mrs. Kennedy might have put it, "*Joie de vivre!*" Glamour, fun, sexiness, affluence, intellectual achievement, happiness, pure delight—yes, *class!* Who said Catholicism had to be forever sunk in the bog of Irish melancholy? Hadn't God looked down at the earth and pronounced it good? Before the Fall, that is, wasn't there beatific bliss? Not even Genesis defined Original Sin as the original condition. Who said, therefore, that the gloom of guilt and self-denial was necessarily the main note of religious faith?

The new affirmation that salvation was available to those who desired it, even if they were not members of the One True Church, was a liberation as much for us Catholics as for the non-Catholics at whom it was directed. Desire, too, could be a virtue. And if God turned his face in mercy toward non-Catholics, was it (to repeat) too much to think he did so toward us Catholics, too? A break from the obsessiveness about salvation that had spawned those wallet cards came with a self-mocking joke that circulated around that time, a new kind of wallet card: "I am an important Catholic. In case of an accident, please call a bishop."

Kennedys were important Catholics, and by God they had their bishop. But the point about Cushing was that he belonged to all of us. The Kennedys could have had Cardinal Spellman of New York. (Recall that Cushing was not a cardinal because Spellman blocked it. And the Kennedys were by then more New York than Boston.) Indeed, Spellman, in his bearing and famous connections at the Vatican, was a true prince of the Church, and Newport was his kind of place. But instead the Kennedys wanted Cushing, the Catholic Everyman. We could look at the glamorous Hammersmith Farm wedding party and, as had never before been possible, see a promise addressed to all of us. The servants' entrance no more. Postwar America was poised on the edge of an unprecedented boom, and Catholics could enjoy it. This spirit was unprecedented, too, and it found its embodiment in Kennedy's arrival, which came perfectly timed to match the social and economic transformations that, for an immigrant subculture, were about to change everything. As a disapproving Avery Dulles might have been the first to grasp, John Kennedy was soon the meaning by which to measure the new American Catholicism.

Cushing was central enough to the Kennedy agenda—willy-nilly, an agenda for church and state both—that some (like the *Boston Globe*) had detected Kennedy political machinations even behind the archbishop's challenge to Feeney. Cushing had been appointed archbishop of Boston in the first place, as we saw, because of his prowess as a fundraiser for the foreign missions and other Catholic charities, and Joseph Kennedy had been one of his most reliable benefactors. Their partnership was so storied that, as Joe Kennedy began to openly promote his son for the nation's highest office, an effort that involved the dispensing of thousands of dollars in "campaign contributions" to political hacks and kingmakers across the country, rumor had it that Cushing was a source of cash. On Sunday evenings, it was said, the hundreds of thousands of dollars that had that morning been put into collection baskets in Catholic churches around Boston were delivered to Joe Kennedy, who wrote out a check to the archdiocese to cover the sum, plus, say, ten percent more. Kennedy could take a tax deduction for the entire amount, and he would have a slush fund that was untraceable.[30]

If Cushing was a suspect figure in Rome, a bit too associated with the Americanist impulse that was detected in the now silenced John Courtney Murray, that was dispelled in 1958 when the newly elected Pope John XXIII elevated Boston's archbishop to the College of Cardinals. The red hat came back to Boston, a sure signal that, with Pius XII gone, Cardinal Spellman's influence would wane. By then, Cushing was quietly rooting for John Kennedy, who was already well into his campaign for the Democratic nomination for president.

Kennedy's religion was an unavoidable issue, and not only for Protestant bigots. Catholic bishops, including Spellman (who would openly support Richard Nixon in 1960), were not at all sure about his detached brand of Catholicism, and soon their suspicions were proven apt. One of the staples of Kennedy's foreign policy speeches, for example, was his standard reference, when discussing problems of underdeveloped nations, to the "population explosion." But in 1959, the Catholic bishops, through their organization in Washington, condemned that term as "a recently coined terror technique phrase."

Birth control was the point of contention. The Catholic hierarchy had steadily used its influence to oppose any relaxation of the general prohibition of contraception that still held sway in many states, and it fought against every attempt to use federal funds for birth control programs in poorer countries. In Massachusetts, Cushing himself had been a champion of such opposition. In 1948, for example, Planned Parenthood had sponsored a bill in the state legislature to allow doctors to prescribe birth control to married women for whom pregnancy posed health risks. Cushing's campaign against that legislation culminated in a massive rally built around a Catholic Youth Organization parade in downtown Boston. Tens of thousands of young Catholics marched, and many thousands more Catholics cheered from the sidewalks. Rarely had a political bloc demonstrated such clout. Cushing said, "Human life was never held in greater contempt than it is now . . . [by] the birth-controllers, the abortionists, and the mercy killers." The bill was defeated.[31]

But now, a decade later, as Kennedy's strong defender, Cushing was not so absolute. When Kennedy refused to support reducing aid to developing nations that used public money for birth control, Catholic bishops saw a signal of his rebelliousness. Still Cushing defended him. Kennedy's position, though, was not enough to mollify his Protestant critics, who took for granted his subservience to the Catholic hierarchy in Rome. Kennedy was getting it from both sides. The issue came to a head when the candidate was invited to address the Houston Ministerial Association, to be introduced by Norman Vincent Peale, who opposed Kennedy on religious grounds. These ministers, who were upset about the possibility of a religious entity interjecting itself into American politics, did not hesitate, as just such an entity, to do the very thing themselves. The speech Kennedy delivered there on September 12, 1960 (his seventh wedding anniversary), addressed the question head-on.

"Whatever issue may come before me as President," Kennedy said, "if I should be elected—on birth control, divorce . . . I will make my decision in accordance . . . with what my conscience tells me to be in the national interest, and without regard to outside religious pressure or dictate. And no power or threat of punishment could cause me to do otherwise." This clear assertion of individual conscience over "religious pressure or dictate" was decidedly not in accord with Catholic norms, yet it was precisely what the nation needed to hear. "But if the time should ever come," Kennedy went on, "when my office would require me to either violate my conscience, or violate the national interest, then I would resign the office."[32]

Even Kennedy's imagined conflict was couched in terms not of his Church's instruction but of his own conscience. Note that he did not say "either violate my Church's teaching, or violate the national interest." Conscience, not doctrine, had never been more steadfastly affirmed. In reading press accounts of the speech at the time, I was struck that, in the question-and-answer session following it, Kennedy declared that as president he could attend Protestant church services—for example, funerals. Was that true? I had been firmly told otherwise by the priests and nuns. Kennedy was breaking ground.

On what authority? Far from a freelancing Catholic who was making up his own rules, Kennedy—and his speech writer Theodore Sorensen—had carefully consulted Cardinal Cushing before the Houston speech. Sorensen had had the text vetted by none other than John Courtney Murray, discreetly reading it over the phone to him.[33] Not that Cushing and Murray offered an imprimatur that conservatives in the hierarchy would accept. But in Houston, the direction set by the Feeney affair was continued. With the Jesuit Feeney excommunicated and the Jesuit Murray silenced, it fell to this Catholic layman to articulate the nascent shift that was occurring in theology. John Kennedy, in effect, offered a public forecast of the thinking of John Courtney Murray on the knotty questions of Church authority in tension with the enshrined American respect for individual conscience, of the distinction between public and private morality, of the wall of separation between church and state.

Pope John XXIII, it would soon be apparent, was more in line with the new than the old. As we will see, his Vatican Council would bring these trends to completion, with Murray being summoned out of exile to a triumphant arrival in Rome. There, as an officially credentialed Vatican Council *peritus,* or expert, he would shape, with Cushing's support, the council's breathtaking affirmation of all that had been condemned, sixty years before, as the heresy of Americanism.[34]

On January 20, 1961, Cardinal Cushing went to the podium on the top step of the U.S. Capitol. As he prayed his lengthy invocation, a short circuit in the amplification wiring sent smoke curling up from the lectern into his face. Yet he prayed on, as if aware only of the importance of what he was doing. Cushing's invocation, on behalf of a man who had begun his day by attending Mass at Holy Trinity Catholic Church in Georgetown, was a defining moment for the nation and for the Catholic Church. When John F. Kennedy, as the thirty-fifth president of the United States, followed Cushing to the podium, he delivered his inaugural address. I was standing in the crowd, and recognized the moment as a defining one for me as well. I was that Georgetown freshman who had haunted the Kennedy townhouse on N Street. I had worked with the Young Democrats for Kennedy's election, and now, looking up at him from amid the huge throng, I recognized in him an image of the man I hoped to be. Kennedy's eloquent call to service would mesh with the impulse that, at Georgetown, brought me in to see that visiting Paulist priest. Kennedy's address, too, marked a before-and-after of my life.

Its last line was itself an encoded affirmation of the Americanist idea. I did not yet know enough to grasp that implication, or to understand why it moved me so, but Kennedy's peroration was my conscription—a first, but also final, summons to my lifelong vocation. "With a good conscience our only sure reward, with history the final judge of our deeds, let us go forth to lead the land we love, asking His blessing and His help, but knowing that here on earth God's work must truly be our own."

CHAPTER FOUR

THE COUNCIL

1. POPE JOHN XXIII

I HAVE SPENT my adult life trying to understand why John XXIII had such an impact on me. Angelo Giuseppe Roncalli is affectionately remembered as the roly-poly peasant pope whose evident goodwill transcended the sectarian antagonisms of the past. Even non-Catholics took to retelling the anecdotes that demonstrated his warmth and humanity. Encountering a woman whose ample bosom was set off by a crucifix, for example, Roncalli exclaimed, "What a calvary!"[1] His myth is irresistible, an old man (turning seventy-seven soon after becoming pope in 1958) elected to be a caretaker pontiff who then shocked the world by convening an ecumenical council, a gathering of bishops from around the globe, to take up great questions of Church governance and doctrine. Such events had occurred on average, as we noted, only once a century, going back to the Council of Nicea in 325, but what made this convocation a greater surprise was the assumption that, since the First Vatican Council had defined the pope's infallibility as the Church's supreme and complete teaching authority, no future councils would be necessary. None had occurred since that 1870 gathering of bishops, and none was supposed to. Bishops, as mere agents of papal rule, were no longer seen as having such coresponsibility for the Church. The age-old tension between papacy and council had been at last resolved in favor of the papacy. Hadn't it?

But the new pope said early on that he would never teach infallibly, and when he declared that we are not meant to be "museum-keepers, but to cultivate a flourishing garden of life,"[2] he was laying bare a truth about what a lifeless institution the Church had become: a forbidding fortress, a lighthouse with its crystal lamp shrouded, a sacristy to which laypeople were admitted only as servers. Pope John compared the Church to a dark and stuffy house whose windows needed to be thrown open. It was as if the emperor himself had pointed out that his courtiers wore no clothes—all were naked, pretending ("the perfect society") to be richly dressed.

In calling for *aggiornamento* (updating), Pope John was saying how outdated the Counter-Reformation and Counter-Enlightenment struggles had left the Church. If anyone else had said this, the Catholic people would have become defensive. The instant the pope said so, Catholics could admit it was true. The announcement of a coming council was itself treated like a wonder. Non-Catholics, meanwhile, were astounded by the pontiff's joyfully offered act of simple self-criticism.

As a high school senior, I met Pope John. Because of my father's rank—stationed in Germany, he was the senior Catholic officer in the Air Force in Europe—my family was granted a papal audience in 1959.[3] My parents, brothers, and I were ushered into his private library in the Vatican's Apostolic Palace. A monsignor lined us up, and when the pope swept into the room, he threw his arms up in delight, congratulating my parents for having such a big Catholic family. He greeted us each in turn. When His Holiness came to me, I towered over him. He pulled me down into his embrace. He whispered something into my ear. I did not know what he said—it could have been Italian, it could have been Latin—nor did I appreciate what he was already doing for Catholicism. But I felt the irresistible pull of his personality. The absolute affirmation of his presence, as vivid to me as the feel of his whisker stubble against my cheek, the aroma of soap pouring off his skin, laid the foundation of what I would eventually claim as my own vocation in the Church. I could not know it in 1959, but I was to develop a deep affinity with this free-spirited man. My mother had bounced me on her knee to the lyrics of that song that celebrated Jim for being out of step. If John XXIII was out of step with almost all the prelates of his generation, so, in a different way, would I be out of step as a Catholic. When I later understood more fully what was at stake in the initiatives he took, I would look back on that meeting as my personal commission into Pope John's work, a commission to which I still aim to be faithful.

What made John XXIII different? That one of his first acts as pope was the promotion of Archbishop Richard Cushing of Boston to the rank of cardinal is a clue. We have already seen how Cushing represented the reversal of the usual order, his movement from ethics to theology—from ethical insight, that is, to theological change. It was implicitly a modernist dynamic to go from experience to theory instead of the other way around. Angelo Roncalli, while not consciously a modernist himself, had made an equivalent move in his own life, even more momentously.

Before being named the patriarch of Venice in 1953, the post from which he was elected pope, Roncalli had been an intimate witness of the century's agonies. He served as a hospital orderly during World War I. Beginning in 1934, he served as a papal diplomat in Bulgaria, Turkey, and France. Those were the years of the coming of fascism and Nazism, the devastation of Europe. Before, during, and after World War II, he was in the thick of one crisis after another. As nuncio in German-occupied Sofia and Istanbul, Roncalli was the rare Catholic prelate to actively resist the Holocaust when it was under way, providing hundreds, perhaps thousands, of fleeing Jews with counterfeit baptismal certificates to enable their escape. Some of his fellow (do-nothing) prelates objected: Wasn't this lying? Do the ends justify the means? Roncalli brushed them aside, another reversal: if the ends don't justify the means, nothing does.

Late in the war, he was transferred to Paris, arriving after the liberation. As papal delegate there, he had to deal with Catholic bishops who had collaborated with the Vichy government. His investigations made him one of the first to confront both what had happened to the Jews of France and the Church's complicity in their fate. He moved at once to enable the return of Jewish children to their own relatives or to other Jewish families—children who had been hidden with Catholic families. Many of those children had been baptized, but Roncalli ruled that such baptisms, whatever their theological meaning, were no justification for refusing to return the little ones to Jewish families. In this Roncalli was overruled by Pope Pius XII.[4]

The record of Pius XII's failure actively to oppose the Holocaust became a controversial issue when Roncalli was pope, with the sensational play *The Deputy* by Rolf Hochhuth. The drama portrayed Pius XII as far more concerned with opposing communism than Nazism; as well aware of the fate of Europe's Jews, but indifferent to it; as too cowardly, in any case, to challenge Hitler. The play swept Europe and was a hit in New York. One reliable report had it that when Pope John was asked what to do against the play and its devastating portrait of his predecessor, he replied, "Do against it? What can you do against the truth?"[5]

Roncalli saw that the Church's entanglement in what happened to the Jewish people was more than a matter of individual malevolence or failure of nerve. The entire culture of Catholic belief and practice was suddenly at issue. Once he became pope, he publicly welcomed to his library—the very place where I met him—Jewish scholars and historians who made the connection between Christian traditions, including the Gospel slanders of Jews, and antisemitism.[6] The "replacement" theology according to which Jews and Judaism, after the triumph of the Church, no longer had a religious reason to exist was as firmly set as any doctrine in Christianity, but Roncalli learned to take the events of the Holocaust themselves as an indictment of that theology. No religious reason to exist had morphed, under Nazism, into no reason *whatsoever* to exist.

When, as pope, Roncalli defined the Church as a dark and musty house in need of fresh air, he was thinking most of all about what had just unfolded in the shadows of that house. *Ethical insight required theological change.* Thus, on his own authority, the new pope ordered the elimination from the Good Friday liturgy of the ancient modifiers "faithless" and "perfidious" as applied to Jews. An apparently minor adjustment of language, yet in this change Pope John was implicitly affirming the ongoing faithfulness of the covenant people. Then, in summoning the world's bishops to the ecumenical council, he ordered them to take up as a matter of urgency the Church's relationship to Jews and Judaism.

What could the pope be thinking? conservative Catholics wondered. What was there to take up about Judaism? But the pope knew. He had seen where nearly two thousand years of contemptuous Christian teaching about Jews had led, and he was calling for change. One of his firmest allies in that, as we will see, would be the freshly elevated Boston cardinal whose sister was married to a Jew. When Cardinal Spellman of New York issued a knee-jerk condemnation of *The Deputy*, Cardinal Cushing was asked by a reporter what he thought. He replied that Spellman should not have condemned a play he had not seen.[7]

2. ENTERING THE NOVITIATE

As a young man of nineteen, I arrived at the Paulist Fathers' novitiate in September 1962. A cross between a monastery and a spiritual boot camp, Mount Paul was a remote retreat in the Picatinny Mountains of New Jersey, about an hour west of New York City. In the center of a thousand acres of forest, at the end of a mile-long winding road, the novitiate building sat beside a man-made lake. The Paulists had acquired the place decades earlier from a wealthy New Yorker who, stocking the lake, had used the mountain lair as a hunting and fishing retreat. In season, the woods still boomed with gunfire.

Paulist novices had been housed in the converted hunting lodge, but to accommodate a steadily growing recruitment pool, that timbered structure had recently been replaced by the bright new edifice that awaited us as first occupants. An architectural cliché, the novitiate building was a version of the pale brick dormitories that were springing up on college campuses across the country. A distinct wing with an upward-jutting roofline that resembled a squared-off silo included a chapel, from which a slender cross reached skyward. Already afraid of having buried myself in a Gothic past, I liked the contemporary feel of the place at once.

The arriving class of novices consisted of about twenty-eight men, of whom I was one of the youngest. I would learn that, to enlist in the Paulist Fathers, about half had interrupted their college careers, as I did, and that the others were college graduates, leaving behind real jobs in what we would soon be calling "the world." A stockbroker, a salesman, a former naval officer, a potato farmer, a tailor, a lounge singer, a law school dropout. The oldest of us was in his mid-thirties. No sooner had we offloaded our suitcases and trunks and bidden our families farewell than we were ordered by the novice master to show up in the chapel wearing the black cassocks that would be our uniforms from then on.

I remember how pleasantly surprised I had been that the arriving group of my fellow novices appeared to be, for the most part, college

Joes, normal-looking guys with "Ivy League" haircuts, chinos, button-down shirts, and loafers. Their raucous laughter had been, to me, as nervous as it was welcome. But I also remember how instantly transformed we all were then, a somber brigade filing into the chapel in floor-length black robes that, devoid of the shaping Roman collar, made us look like either overgrown altar boys or half-sworn clergy. We did not know it, but such ambiguity—were we children or adults?—was essential to our new status as men of the Church.

The novitiate in this remote retreat was to be the first year of a seven-year training program, with the following six years to take place at the Paulist seminary near Catholic University in Washington. After that we would be ordained to the priesthood, and our devoted lives would unfold from there. But here was where it began, a yearlong ("a year and a day," in the precise formulation of canon law) exercise in reclusive spirituality, a learning the ropes of prayer, fasting, mortification, meditation, poverty, chastity, and obedience. There would be Bible study and spiritual reading, instruction in Latin and in the classics of Catholic contemplative literature—St. John of the Cross, *Dark Night of the Soul;* St. Teresa of Ávila, *Interior Castle*—all of it pointing toward the ecstasy of mystical union. But the locating center of all our study would be the conferences led by visiting Paulist priests, focused on the defining figure of the order's founder, Isaac Hecker, the "seeker" with whom we were expected to identify.

The system of "formation" was meant to inculcate in us a dual sense of our priestly responsibility—familiarity with, in the argot, "the two poles of Paulist spirituality." We were to be "contemplatives," and we were to be "activists." It seemed an impossible ambition, of course, yet over the years of training, that contradiction came to seem more like a paradox. In my case, the training took. An easy familiarity with silence and solitude would become a lifelong character trait, but so would a readiness to throw myself into programs and obligations.

Even though the Paulists were noted for a spirit of relative freedom and independence, they were required to shape the training of new members according to norms set by the Vatican, or rather, set by the Council of Trent in the sixteenth century. In this way, the seminary intended to make us docile and obedient, but the rules could seem so arbitrary, and the priests in charge could seem so petty in trying to enforce them, that they became easy to disobey. "Keep the Rule," went a slogan, "and the Rule will keep you." But the main function of the

Rule, as it turned out, was to give us a foil against which to define ourselves. Like many of my fellows, I became adept at sneaking cigarettes, at leaving the seminary grounds without permission, at acquiring forbidden books, like the works of Jean Paul Sartre. The further along I went in the years of training, the less conflicted I felt about making my own choices, even in defiance of my superiors. Those superiors, too, were less than committed to the system, and an early preoccupation with not getting caught evolved into a subtle strategy of not embarrassing the boss by making him enforce regulations no one believed in. Ironically, resistance would prove to be a more effective part of my formation than submission. I would not see it until years later, but the men I found most congenial were like me in this, and it is no surprise that few of them—including Paulists who had been in charge—are still in the priesthood.

But all of that came later. I arrived at the novitiate at the mercy of an anguish I could not name. The impulse to become a priest, in my case, had its roots in my having been singled out by nuns in grade school and in all but overt messages I had received from my parents. I was surely like my fellow novices in that. A Catholic boy of my generation, if he showed any sparkle at all, was bound to be channeled toward the Church. *Many are called, but few are chosen.* It was as if we had such slogans stamped on our foreheads. *I will make you fishers of men.* The nuns handed us off to parish priests and, when we went to Catholic colleges, to our clerical professors. *Lord, what wilt thou have me to do?* This traditional scaffolding of the religious vocation would not, however, have been enough to make me climb in. I had been a life-loving, girl-chasing high school kid, and despite my encounter with Pope John XXIII in Rome, the sex-hating regime of celibacy was more than enough to turn me away. *It is not good for man*—so ran my rebuttal from Genesis—*to be alone.*

But then, at Georgetown, in those first Kennedy years, I was ambushed by an existential dread, a collision of public and personal insecurities that shook me to the core. Wholly identified with my Air Force father, I had fully intended to follow him into military service. ROTC was my major interest in college. But that identification with Dad carried another implication. In his office at the Pentagon, where he was director of the Defense Intelligence Agency, he was one of the high priests of the nuclear holy of holies. Ever since we had been stationed at an air base in Germany during my high school years, I had been acutely aware of my father's role as one of the Knights Templar fending off the coming war with the Soviet Union. And then, during the Berlin crisis in the summer of 1961, when President Kennedy ordered Americans to build fallout shelters, I caught from my father the fever of a transcendent worry. In the season that included the provocative building of the Berlin Wall, Dad warned me that he might not come home one night; in that case, I would have to take his place with my mother and brothers.[8]

The war scare passed, but I could not climb out of the pit of fear into which it dropped me. Beginning with Berlin, I heard nothing, it seemed, but the ticking of the coming bomb. I did not know what to do with the feeling, except turn to God. I began to haunt the Dahlgren Chapel at Georgetown, staring at the flickering of the sanctuary lamp, especially at night. That flame was supposed to point beyond itself to the Real Presence of the Lord, but the flame and the shadows it cast were presence enough for me. I returned to the place most mornings for Mass, hoping my jovial friends would not notice. I became a boy apart, unable to describe my experience to any of my chums, to any girl. To my great surprise, solitude had become its own consolation.

There is a canal beside the Potomac River, running from Georgetown to Great Falls, about fifteen miles away in Maryland. I spent hours on the dusty footpath. "*Did you see my little Jimmy marching?*" A primordial affirmation underwrote what thin capacity I had to confront those feelings of isolation. "*Were you there, and tell me, did you notice? They were all out of step but Jim.*" Regarding my friends, and every social group to which I was connected, I was profoundly out of step. In ROTC, at the drill sergeant's order, "Change step, *harch!*," I had mastered the ability to keep in step on the parade ground, but not on the canal. Ordering myself to stop brooding, I could not obey. I was engaged in an endless conversation, though I was alone. Worry, I found, discharged itself in words. My stream of consciousness was its own canal, and it carried me along. Soon I began to realize that I was not, as I feared at first, talking to myself. I knew already that Freud would call what I was doing "projection," but I called it God, the hell with Freud. Such visceral expression itself assumed that the one to whom it was instinctively offered was real. I was talking to God, though God was nowhere to be seen. I had made the leap of faith, a "Change step, *harch!*" of my own.

The absence of God had become a presence, and I experienced an encounter. Such was the intensity of the longing I felt that it became its own assurance that the object of longing can be taken for granted. I had entered a relationship. The experience had nothing to do with the rote recitations that had, until then, defined my idea of the devotional life. Yet I knew to call this prayer. I had discovered that prayer came as naturally to me as breathing—or rather, breathing was how I prayed. I had moved into an entirely different realm from the one over which Bing Crosby and the priests of Hollywood loomed as images of the religious man. I told my father one night that instead of the Air Force, I wanted to devote my life to, as I put it, "the things that last." He nodded, which was all I needed. That was what took me to my appointment with the loafer-shod Paulist priest who happened to be visiting Georgetown.

I brought the knot of existential anxiety with me to Mount Paul, and I would be astounded to find it directly addressed by the intellectual and spiritual language in which I was then instructed. This, for example, from perhaps the first volume of "spiritual reading" to which I turned, *The Waters of Siloe* by Thomas Merton: "What is the use of living for things that you cannot hold on to, values that crumble in your hands as soon as you possess them, pleasures that turn sour before you have begun to taste them, and a peace that is constantly turning into war?"[9]

I had never been much of a reader, and attuned silence did not come naturally to me. But that would change. The shape of my life as a novice would come from words and from the absence of words—to both of which I attended as never before. My naïve notions of God's nearness, learned on that Potomac River canal, would be stripped away from me, and then a chastened naïveté would return. Amazingly, I would find the long sessions of meditation with which each day began and ended to be both the most difficult and most consoling periods of all. I realized that the unspeakable feelings I carried within had, in fact, been carried by others before me, and had, in fact, been spoken of. Once the human imagination grasps that the future itself is mortal, that there will come a time when all that is simply ceases to be, then the wonder is that things exist right now. That wonder is what we mean by holiness, and it is timeless. Mystics from the Middle Ages, writing of the "Last Things," Kierkegaard of "fear and trembling," Hopkins of "shook foil," Tillich of "contingency," Bonhoeffer of "God's powerlessness," and Jesus himself, for that matter, foreseeing the destruction of Jerusalem—many had known exactly what it felt like, even absent the prospect of radioactive fallout, to be alive in the last half of the twentieth century. What drastic relief, as my puerile assumptions of the uniqueness of the nuclear age were shattered, to have such anguish shared.

At Mount Paul, the esoteric disciplines would be balanced by a daily regime of manual labor—tending the grounds, mangling sheets, cleaning the chicken coop, waxing the floors, working in the kitchen with Karl, the irascible cook whose cigarette ash forever hung from his pouty lips above the pan of corn bread. In the autumn, we novices would rake leaves and slaughter the chickens. In winter, we would remove ice from the gutters and shovel snow off the frozen lake for a hockey rink. In spring, we would deliberately set the grassy hill afire, to nurture the soil with carbon, and clear the woods of the winterkill. In summer, we would weed the vegetable garden and rebuild the sheds. Season in and season out, the coveted job would be driver, because that meant taking the pickup truck down the mountain twice a week to fetch milk cans from the dairy farm. Otherwise, novices were hardly ever permitted to leave the place.

The truth is, I would love it. My fellow novices were an extraordinary group of men, smart, experienced, kind, determined to do something important with their lives. With relief, I would recognize in them the same esprit that, among my mates at Georgetown, I had thought was more or less unique to me—a mix of out-of-fashion Catholic devotedness and up-to-date Kennedy-inspired idealism. My peculiar nuclear dread would remain mine, a kind of patrimony, but in this company it would seem less troubling, even if I could still not speak of it. At recreation, the hi-fi would more likely blast show tunes or Bach cantatas than Chubby Checker or the Beatles, but these future Paulists would seem surprisingly hip to me. On the football field, they would be aggressive athletes. In choir, they would readily harmonize. In the reading seminars and conferences, they would say things I'd never thought of. They would be mimics and nicknamers—wise guys. I would be proud to be among them, and before long I would make the first real friendships of my life.

It was an odd time to enter the Church. American Catholicism was in its heyday, with seminaries all over the country filled with young men like us (by 1960, there were more than 50,000 priests in the United States, and nearly 40,000 seminarians in more than 500 seminaries), a vocation boom that had begun after the war, running in flood tide all through the fifties, when Bishop Fulton J. Sheen, host of a prime-time weekly television show called *Life Is Worth Living,* got consistently higher ratings than Milton Berle on Tuesday nights. Politics reflected this phenomenon, with the Catholic hysteric Senator Joe McCarthy dominating the national obsession with Reds and the Church itself emerging as an anti-Communist bastion. The militant and triumphant Catholic culture, based on the absolutes of the Council of Trent and defined against the Protestant mainstream at home and atheistic Marxism abroad, seemed vindicated by the Church's midcentury arrival.

We Catholics sensed that air of cultural triumph in the books we were reading, especially those by the Trappist monk Thomas Merton, whose best-selling autobiography *The Seven Storey Mountain* had made him a national celebrity in the years after World War II. Merton had been born in France of an American mother and a New Zealander father. Orphaned at sixteen, he was sent by relatives to school in England. At Cambridge University he made a girl pregnant, which prompted his grandparents to bring him back to New York. He enrolled at Columbia University and became a protégé of Mark van Doren, the leading intellectual of the time. Merton's progress from atheist bohemian and certified Manhattan hipster to his startling reinvention as an otherworldly contemplative at Our Lady of Gethsemani Abbey in rural Kentucky—where, imposed silence notwithstanding, he continued to write best-selling books about the search for God—was a defining tale of religious vindication.

Thousands of young Catholic men, especially including war veterans, had carried Merton's books with them (*The Sign of Jonas, Seeds of Contemplation, The Waters of Siloe*) as they showed up at monasteries and seminaries, all in search of answers to the subliminal question that the century had churned up. Merton was their Camus, their Sartre, eventually their Bob Dylan, their Ingmar Bergman. "Now my whole life is this," he wrote. "To keep unencumbered. The wind owns the fields where I walk and I own nothing and am owned by nothing and I shall never even be forgotten because no one will ever discover me. This is to me a source of immense confidence. My Mass this morning was transfigured by this independence."[10]

My novice-mates and I were in the wave that followed Merton into that sea of independence, although we could not know we were on the swelling edge of it. We were the largest group of novices the Paulists had ever recruited (hence the new building), and our number would not be matched again. The wave was already breaking. We were among the last of the Merton men. Nor did we know that the first to repudiate his cult of arch-Catholicism would be Merton himself.

To us, the election of Kennedy seemed naturally tied to the intensity of our religious certitude. The Catholic president's arrival seemed the fulfillment of a promise that had been made long before. As fully contemporary as Kennedy was, we sensed in his larger significance something timeless, the confirmation of an ancient wisdom long denied, but around which we were constructing an identity. The discipline by which we novices measured our lives now—the hours of our day, the content of our prayers, our mode of dress, the Latin salutations with which we awoke in the morning and went to sleep at night—*Benedicamus Domino! Deo gratias!*—had all been set four hundred years before in the post-Luther purifying of clerical life. The novitiate itself was Trent alive, but alive as a petrified monument to the Counter-Reformation.

And yet, at the time of our initiation, although we did not see it, all of that was ending. Before the year was out, Latin lessons would be dropped. The world that we novices intended to make our own, and to which I had already responded as a consoling source of significance, was about to be upended. What made the change unpredicted and unpredictable was that, unlike all others, this was a revolution from above. Barely a month after our novitiate year began, the rule that forbade us television, that ultimate emblem of "the world," was suspended by the novice master. He ordered an old Philco hauled into the common room so we could watch the opening ceremonies of the Second Vatican Council. It was October 11, 1962.

3. REFORM AND REUNION

We took our instruction in the meaning of the council from the same man who instructed Pope John himself, a young Swiss theologian named Hans Küng. His book *The Council, Reform and Reunion* had just been published in English.[11] The novitiate library was stocked with copies, and we read Küng as if he were Ian Fleming. Küng had been trained at the Gregorian University in Rome and the Sorbonne. He was only in his early thirties, so we could almost think of him as a peer, but his book's authority came from the fact that the pope had appointed Küng his special theological adviser ahead of the council. The book laid out a program that was presented as the pope's own. No work of theology had ever been published to more effect.[12]

And what a program! The words "reform and reunion" in the title were the hint of a startling prospect, for what Küng declared was nothing less than the long-overdue end of the Counter-Reformation. "Reform" had been a disdained word in Catholic circles, forever associated with the Protestant enemy. Even modernists had spoken instead of renewal, or, lately with Pope John, *aggiornamento.* But Küng put reform in the center of the council's purpose, recalling that the Latin *reformare* means "to shape something according to its own essential being." Indeed, the word "reform" did not originate with Luther but with a previous Church council, at Constance in 1414, which called for "reform in faith and practice, in head and members." *Ecclesia semper reformanda* was the Protestant watchword, but it captured an ancient Catholic impulse toward permanent reform, and Küng boldly recast it as *Ecclesia catholica semper in reformatione.*[13]

But the reform he proposed was only the means to a real and complete reversal of the Reformation, which was the meaning of that word "reunion." In the past Catholics had envisioned not the reunion of the Christian denominations but the penitential return of the apostate denominations to the One True Church. Küng spoke instead of "the ecumenical task" of the Catholic Church, which was to purify itself of the things that had driven the reformers away, so that "separated Christians" would recognize the Roman Church as having returned, in effect, to them. Reunion assumed a mutual purification. The enmity of Protestantism, which had defined the Catholic sensibility even in America, even over much of my own life until then, was simply no longer to be assumed. Pope John himself, reflecting Küng's hope, spoke of the spiritual renewal of "the whole flock of Christ."[14]

That is what Pope John launched in the second week of October, and we saw it. As new Paulists, we were already being instructed in the significance of these developments for our order. Though then consisting of only about 250 priests and operating almost exclusively in the United States, the order was one of the few Catholic organizations that had any history of respectful outreach to non-Catholics. That

Paulist tradition, having been pursued quietly in university Newman Clubs, at downtown "information centers" that sponsored "dialogues," and in publications of the Paulist Press, was suddenly in vogue as "ecumenism." The Paulist bridge between American Protestantism and Roman Catholicism had sharp relevance for the whole Church.

Not only were the anathemas that had brought Isaac Hecker under a cloud of Vatican disapproval early in the twentieth century—Americanism—already being revisited by the Church as it prepared for the council, but one of the key figures operating behind the scenes of the conciliar organization in Rome was a Paulist priest who embodied the spirit of Hecker. His name was Father Thomas Stransky, a stocky Polish American and, like Küng, in his early thirties. Stransky had a fullback's bulk, but his amiable wit and ready smile set him apart from other Vatican functionaries.

True to their mission—representing America to the Church and the Church to America—the Paulists had long manned the American Church in Rome, a parish to which visitors, diplomats, and expatriates from the United States belonged. Not incidentally, the American Church's titular supervisor was Cardinal Cushing of Boston. From that Paulist outpost in Rome, while working on his doctorate at the Pontifical Gregorian University, Stransky had become a theologian on the staff of Cardinal Augustin Bea, a German Jesuit and one of the biblical scholars who had been pressing for liberalization of Catholic attitudes toward Scripture. Anticipating the council, Pope John had established the Secretariat for Promoting Christian Unity and appointed Bea its head. The cardinal, in turn, tapped Stransky for the secretariat because of his Paulist connections to ecumenism. If reunion was to be a main purpose of the Vatican Council, Bea and, by extension, Stransky were going to be key players. Soon the Paulist Fathers would begin to see an unexpected vindication, as the radical impulses of the Paulist founder, and the necessarily implicit convictions of the order ever since, were affirmed by the highest teaching authority in the Roman Catholic Church. By the time I was ordained to the priesthood, Stransky would be president of the Paulist Fathers.

It is now widely agreed that Vatican II was the most important religious event of the twentieth century. "We can't possibly get a council ready by 1963," Vatican bureaucrats had told the new pope. In reply, he told them, in that case, to have it ready by 1962.[15] And here it was.

More than 2,500 Catholic bishops were seated on raised platforms in the nave of St. Peter's Basilica. At their sides, or just behind them, were theological advisers (*periti*) as well as invited observers, including Protestant, Orthodox, and Jewish religious leaders. Their presence alone was a signal of what would make this council different. We novices sat around the Philco watching the opening ceremonies as if they were the World Series. We hadn't a clue what was coming, but we knew it was momentous. A hush filled the common room. We in our black cassocks were like a youthful version of the bishops in theirs—since their red soutanes came across on the screen in black and white.

In his opening speech the pope chided the "prophets of gloom" who were already warning against the dangers of the reform movement he was initiating. Shockingly, John denounced those who saw in the modern era "nothing but betrayal and ruination . . . forever forecasting calamity."[16] This was shocking, of course, because it was his predecessors, dating back a century, who had consistently spoken of the contemporary world in just that way. (Recall that Pius IX's *Syllabus of Errors* condemned the proposition that "the Roman Pontiff can and ought to reconcile and align himself with progress, liberalism, and modern civilization.") Neither we novices nor the pope himself could miss the implications of what he was announcing, but neither we nor he could have understood the resistance he was about to encounter.

Ahead of the council, numerous schemata, or outlines, were prepared by officials of the Roman Curia, the conservative Vatican bureaucracy that was determined to thwart change. These documents reiterated the traditional positions on revelation, morality, family life, chastity, the liturgy, and the exalted place of Mary. The Curia proposed a set of conciliar commissions that would take up the far from radical questions implied in these schemata, and it presumed even to nominate the men who would chair the commissions. It was a wily formula for control of the council. Some bishops grumbled when presented with such *faits accomplis,* and many suspected that the Curia was acting not only without the pope's approval but against his wishes. The bureaucrats, though, had the advantage of being insiders who knew how to quietly invoke obscure procedures and rules—*Romanità.*

The conservatives' trump card, to be played as a way of inhibiting the bishops, was the Curia-imposed requirement that all proceedings of the council take place in Latin. Few of the council fathers were as fluent in the language as they felt obliged to be, with the Italians having an edge over the others because they could slide between a faux Latin and their native tongue. But what non-Italian bishop would publicly hint at his ignorance by challenging the Latin requirement?

Well, at the outset one maverick did. Perhaps it is no surprise that he was Cardinal Richard Cushing, who openly complained, as the first session began, of not understanding what was being said. "I didn't know," he later said, "if it was Chinese or Eskimo."[17] Cushing offered to fund the cost of a United Nations–style simultaneous-translation system, but the organizing committee, depending on the mass of bishops to pretend to Latin fluency, overruled him. "I represent the Church of silence," he later said.[18] Cushing would not be alone in depending on his *peritum* to steadily whisper translations in his ear. He was only alone in having acknowledged the truth.

Compared to such efficiently enforced *Romanità*, the esprit of the reformers, not to mention the influence of the Holy Spirit, counted for little, and the pope was necessarily aloof. For one thing, the bureaucracy was skilled at marginalizing even its purported head. "*Sono nel sacco qui*," Pope John confided to Cardinal Cushing, describing the Curia's power. Cushing later loved to tell the story, with the pope's own translation as the punch line: "I'm in a bag here."[19] But it wasn't only that. What no one knew on October 11 was that two weeks before, Pope John's doctors had discovered that he was suffering from a fatal stomach cancer. "At least I have launched this big ship," the pope confided to a friend after the opening ceremonies. "Another will have the task of taking it out to sea."[20]

Within the first few days, the Curia's organizing committee presented the council with a document on the liturgy. The leader of the conservative bureaucracy was Cardinal Alfredo Ottaviani, the head of the Holy Office, the Inquisition-style watchdog of doctrinal purity. After the pope, Ottaviani was the most powerful figure in the Vatican. It was he who had silenced the American Jesuit John Courtney Murray, and who had made certain that Murray was not called to the council as an advising theologian. The Ottaviani-inspired decree on the liturgy was immediately put before the bishops as a final draft, ready to be voted upon. A pious encomium of divine activity in the sacraments, it proposed no change.

For years, liturgical reform had been one of the most pressing questions before the Church. Pressure had been building to move away from Latin as the exclusive language of Catholic ritual. This had been at the explosive center of the Reformation, and it was when Protestants embraced the vernacular, not only in liturgy but in Scripture, that the authority of laypeople began to compete with that of the clerical elite. In reaction, Roman Catholicism had renewed its emphasis on Latin. The esoteric language was, above all, what empowered the priesthood and kept average Catholics on the margin of Church power. Thus enormous social and political implications were embedded in the debate over the use of the vernacular at Mass.

So it was with other liturgical questions. Was the Eucharist a sacrifice, enacted on an altar by the *alter Christus,* the priest, with the laity present as mere spectators? Or was it a meal, like the Last Supper, to be shared in by all? In that case, the altar would properly be refashioned as a banquet table and moved away from the far wall of the church, into the center of the community—"facing the people," as the slogan had it. The Mass would be celebrated not by one man but by the whole congregation. Here, too, great questions were at stake. Could anything in Catholic life or belief change, or was the Church changeless? Newman's old question of "development of doctrine" had resurfaced, centered on the trappings of the Mass. Historical consciousness itself was at issue. It was as if Jesus were remembered by conservatives as speaking Latin, when of course he spoke Aramaic; as if Jesus conducted the Last Supper as a priest celebrating Mass, wearing ornately embroidered fiddleback vestments instead of the simple garb of a Galilean peasant.

Should the Communion bread continue to be placed on the outstretched tongues of kneeling laypeople, as if they were not worthy to touch it with their fingers, as if they were children to be fed? Or should communicants stand upright like adults and take the sacred food into their hands, worthily, to feed themselves? Indeed, should the bread *be* bread, or should it continue to be the insipid wafers that were stamped out of a press, resembling nothing so much as coins? Should the laity be offered the cup as well? Should they be allowed to enter the sanctuary as readers of Scripture, as lectors? Would they ever join the priest in distributing Communion? Such impulses reversed the "Lord, I am not worthy" self-denigration of Catholics that I had found so unsettling as a child. Child indeed: suddenly the hitherto most sacred liturgical traditions of Catholicism were exposed as a way of infantilizing parishioners before a dominant clergy. Novice though I was, and devotee of those very traditions, I instinctively grasped what was at stake in the Church's argument with itself.

The entire meaning of the reform project, in other words, was tied to symbolic and real consequences of the council's declaration on the liturgy. The Curia, understanding this, had made its preemptive strike. Its change-nothing decree on the liturgy—with sacramental use of the vernacular decisively repudiated—was the first proposed council pronouncement to be circulated. Progressives among the bishops, and what might be called the Hans Küng faction among the *periti,* were blindsided by this move of the conservatives. Off balance and apparently in the minority, progressives saw their hopes for the reform council about to be squelched.

Tradition prohibited any public display of discord in such a setting as the council. The Catholic world, after all, was under the impression that Church deliberations did not descend to anything so mundane (from the Latin for "worldly") as liberal-conservative disputes. That the *other*worldly Church was guided by the Holy Spirit, not politics, meant that open proceedings in St. Peter's would be marked by concord and amity. Otherwise the Catholic people would be scandalized. The broad assumption, therefore, was that the bishops would dutifully vote to approve what was put before them. But if they did, the "reform and reunion" council would be over before it started.

4. THE CUBAN MISSILE CRISIS

That might have been what happened, except for the other world-historic event that began to unfold just then. On October 15, four days after the council opened, aerial photographs of the Cuban countryside were laid before Secretary of Defense Robert McNamara as he attended a dinner party at the home of General Maxwell Taylor, the chairman of the Joint Chiefs of Staff. The next morning, McNamara laid them before President Kennedy. The photos showed that the Soviet Union had begun construction of missile launch pads. The Cuban Missile Crisis had begun. That was Tuesday. At first, the facts were kept secret, but by the weekend, nervous rumors were sweeping the world. Then on Monday, October 22, the president went on television to address the nation. At Mount Paul, we novices crowded around the old Philco in the common room again.

The president's speech stunned America, no one more than me. Kennedy drew a line in the sand that night, declaring American readiness to go to war rather than allow Moscow's missile preparations to proceed. He ordered nuclear-laden B-52 bombers into the air. One hundred thousand U.S. troops were sent to Florida, a Cuban invasion force. Most provocatively, Kennedy declared a quarantine of the island nation, ordering the Navy to attack any Soviet ship that attempted to approach Cuba. There were numerous Soviet freighters en route, and if they declined to turn back, there would be war. "We will not prematurely or unnecessarily risk the costs of worldwide nuclear war in which even the fruits of victory would be ashes in our mouth," the young president declared, "but neither will we shrink from that risk at any time it must be faced."[21]

The ashes were in my mouth. I did not know it that night, but the crisis had begun when my father, as director of the Defense Intelligence Agency, brought the crucial photographs to General Taylor's house, a dinner party to which he and my mother had expected to be mere guests. But DIA analysts had discovered the missile evidence in the photos that afternoon, and Dad simply brought them with him to the party. As my mother later told me, he, Taylor, and McNamara disappeared into a room off the parlor and did not appear again at the dinner. My mother did not see my father for the next two weeks.

For all of the significance of the Cuban Missile Crisis as a turning point in the Cold War, it also marked the confluence of disparate currents of my own life. I had embraced the Church in pursuit of "things that last," not appreciating how that set me apart from my peers. I had shared in the widespread idealism and optimism generated by the arrival of Kennedy, but I had also been in the grip of an existential foreboding. Unlike my fellow novices, I had embraced my vocation more out of alienation from my previous desire to join the military than out of longing to join a religious community. Mine had been a rather different mood, but all at once that changed. My mood was suddenly not so different. Never had the transience of "things that do not last" been made so palpable to so many. My decision now seemed to be confirmed by all that had occurred during those unbelievable days in October.

Few noticed at the time, but the near catastrophe had deep significance, in a particular way, for the Catholic Church—both because of what had started to unfold at the Vatican Council and because of Pope John XXIII's unprecedented, and still underappreciated, role in bringing the standoff to a peaceful resolution. Meanwhile, the two brackets of my own life at last snapped together. The nuclear dread that I had already begun to feel became a public obsession that week, with millions of people around the globe at the mercy of a transcendent fear. The end of the world, in an anticipated flash, had shown itself—finally, not just to me. News photos displayed a line of penitents at New York's St. Patrick's Cathedral stretched out onto Fifth Avenue. In Times Square a stunned throng began a vigil below the flashing ticker-tape banner, taking the news in moment by moment. The crowd would be there throughout the fateful thirteen days.

The reaction was not mere hysteria. Though he called it a quarantine, what Kennedy had thrown around Cuba was a blockade, traditionally defined as an act of war. Soviet ships continued to steam toward Cuba, with U.S. ships arrayed to stop them. A confrontation at sea might spark a nuclear holocaust. On October 24, the first Soviet vessel to arrive at the U.S. line seemed about to challenge it, but then, with the globe watching, the ship turned back. Other vessels did as well.

The next day, Ambassador Adlai Stevenson rudely chastised the Soviet ambassador at the United Nations, and two days after that, an American reconnaissance plane was shot down over Cuba, the pilot killed. At that point, it would later be learned, Kennedy's advisers were unanimous in urging an invasion of the island. Still later it would be learned that had that invasion occurred, Soviet commanders in Cuba would have used the tactical nuclear weapons that they had already smuggled onto the island. The nuclear conflagration would have followed.

It turned out that Kennedy and Soviet leader Nikita Khrushchev were alike in standing less against each other than against their own hawkish advisers. Neither wanted war, but neither could be seen as backing down. That is where Pope John came in. By his offering a face-saving way out of this dead end, the two leaders found in him an unexpected ally. Having secretly consulted both Moscow and Washington ahead of time, the pope acted, an exercise of what he called "diplomacy of conscience."[22] On October 25, Vatican Radio carried an unprecedented broadcast, the pope's own voice addressing a personal plea for peace equally to President Kennedy and Chairman Khrushchev, each of whom needed to be seen as responsive to a broad human anguish that transcended national politics. The pope was the only figure who could have given expression to such a sentiment.

The next day, the Soviet leader made certain that *Pravda,* the official Soviet newspaper, carried as its front-page headline the words from the Vatican: "We beg all rulers not to be deaf to the cry of humanity!" Khrushchev made a point of appearing to take the initiative in responding to this plea. On October 28, he announced that the missiles would be removed from Cuba, claiming the moral high ground. "What the pope has done for peace," Khrushchev said, "will go down in history."[23] In Washington, the Catholic president had to be more reticent about the papal role, but he would later award the pope the Medal of Freedom.

The pope's role in helping to end the standoff peacefully was little noted by the world press at the time, although his biographers, as well as historians who later dissected the Cuban Missile Crisis, would emphasize it.[24] But the fathers of the Vatican Council were quite aware of what he did. This unmistakable manifestation of John XXIII's historic significance came at a crucial moment in the council, bracing those bishops who wanted to realize his vision of "reform and reunion" and giving those who opposed his plans a new reason to take him seriously. The Cuban crisis seemed to amplify what the stakes were in the pope's call to confront "the signs of the times." The world urgently needed a relevant and magnanimous Catholic Church, renewed in the image that its leader was then making so dramatic.

Even more significant, what was about to unfold at the Vatican Council would be the clearest instance yet of the revolutionary dynamic we have already noted, the move from ethics to theology. The recognition of the world's new plight in the nuclear age led to the unprecedented religious reform that aimed to be nothing less than the Catholic Church's response to the extreme jeopardy of the new human condition.

5. *NOSTRA AETATE:* JESUS, A JEW

On October 22, the day of John Kennedy's televised address in which he drew the line against Moscow, the Curia-prepared document on the liturgy was put before the council fathers. Over the next three days, while the world teetered on the edge of the nuclear abyss, the progressive bishops found their voice. How could they not have at such a moment? They dared to break with the traditional decorum that Cardinal Ottaviani was counting on, and in council deliberations inside St. Peter's and at the coffee bars in the ornate corridors where the world press was gathered, they went public with their dissent. The vast middle group of bishops who might ordinarily have refused to be drawn into the dispute also began to speak up. The conflict came to a head more rapidly than anyone imagined was possible, until, in the formal setting of St. Peter's, one bishop dared to move the question, calling for a vote. This was the context within which Pope John's desperate plea for peace in Cuba was heard. I firmly believe that it was no accident that that was the moment the bishops voted overwhelmingly to reject the Curia's declaration on the liturgy.

An enraged Cardinal Ottaviani took the microphone at the speaker's lectern. He denounced the revolutionary impulses of the council fathers and played the conservatives' trump card, warning of the "scandal" such unseemly divisiveness would cause the Catholic laity. While the human race was glimpsing, like lightning bolts in the distance, flashes of its worst nightmare, the prefect of the Holy Office chastised the bishops of the Catholic Church as if they were altar boys.

But the man who had sought to use procedural maneuvers to protect the status quo made a mistake: his furious speech ran over the set time limit. The presiding bishop indicated that Ottaviani should stop. When the cardinal ignored the request, his microphone was cut off. At that, the bishops spontaneously broke into thunderous applause. That simply, the die was cast. When, weeks later, a new document on the liturgy proposed radical changes, which included the approval of the use of the vernacular and the restoration to local bishops of long-lost authority over sacramental disciplines, the vote in favor was 1,922 to 11. One theologian said, "This day will go down in history as the end of the Counter-Reformation." The pope, watching the proceedings in his apartment on closed-circuit television, said, "Now begins my Council."[25]

The Second Vatican Council met in four sessions between 1962 and 1965. It issued sixteen declarations of varied solemnity and on various topics. But one had importance above all others. What Pope John had begun long before in relation to the Jewish people was continued in the declaration *Nostra Aetate* (from its opening words, "In our time"), which repudiated the Christ killer charge against Jews and affirmed the ongoing validity of the Jewish religion.

The declaration represented a reversal of the most ancient Christian assertions. The charge that the Jews murdered Christ, after all, was first lodged not by the gutter anti-Semites of history, but by the Gospels themselves. The council fathers nevertheless rejected it, leaving for later the loaded question of how Christians were now to read the anti-Jewish texts of the New Testament. When *Nostra Aetate* defined the Jews as *still* the chosen people of God (the document uses the Latin word *electione*, which carries more weight than the usual English translation, "most dear"), it was throwing out nearly two thousand years of Church teaching.

These two reversals are incomprehensible apart from what prompted them, which was, of course, the awareness in the conscience of those bishops of what Christian anti-Judaism had finally produced in Europe. *Nostra Aetate*, that is, amounts to the ultimate instance, after the Holocaust, of theology following ethics. As for the larger project of Church reform in other realms, here is the question that *Nostra Aetate* raised: If the Catholic Church could change what it taught about the Jews and their religion, going back to the New Testament—"replacement theology" itself being replaced—then what could it not change?

I was typical of a young Catholic cohort who through this debate gained a new awareness of the centrality of Judaism to the meaning of Christianity, both negatively, by reckoning with antisemitism and its genocidal consequences, and positively, by understanding the permanently Jewish character of Christian belief. And not only that: understanding the permanent character of Judaism itself, with its vital rabbinic tradition that had long since moved on from the religion of the Old Testament. In other words, the Jewish religion, *as practiced today*, was sacred.

For me, as for the Church, the question of the Jews was the wedge. In late winter 1965, while the council was still in session, I was part of a round-the-clock interfaith vigil in Washington, standing with Protestant and Jewish seminarians across from the Lincoln Memorial in support of the Voting Rights Bill. We were determined to remain there, in shifts of three, until Congress passed the bill. One night, when I was standing with two others in the wee hours, a big car suddenly pulled up and a strange-looking figure got out. He wore a military-style tan shirt, a Sam Browne belt crossing his chest, and a swastika armband. We recognized him at once as the notorious American Nazi George Lincoln Rockwell. He snarled "kike" at us, but we three understood he was speaking to the Jewish seminarian beside me. Then he took up a position across from us—a counter-vigil to oppose the Voting Rights Bill. I felt both fear in being identified with my Jewish colleague and shame because I recognized where, in part at least, Rockwell's hatred came from. By the time dawn came, and the next team of seminarians arrived to relieve us, Rockwell was gone, but so was my easy assumption that Nazi hatred of Jews sprang whole out of the Teutonic forest, a purely pagan phenomenon. Hitler, I learned for the first time, had died in official good standing as a Catholic.

Once I understood that Jesus was fully and completely Jewish, right to the end of his life, preaching only the God of Israel, my most basic assumptions about faith changed. In Jesus, I, the descendant of far northern Celts, was brought into the covenant that the One God had made with Israel—the covenant that held. And "One God" was the point. No longer was a "New Testament" God of mercy set against an "Old Testament" God of judgment, a Christian God of love against a Jewish God of vengeance. As this old-new contrast showed, the very structure of Christian thought was a denigration—and at last I saw it. That structure, that theology, had to change. My seminary reading, discussions in class and in the recreation room, and an ongoing crisis of conscience as I confronted my own previously unexamined antisemitism formed the core of the religious and personal transformation I underwent during the years of the council. By their end, my vocation, which already had the issue of peace as one pole, would have the issue of Christian-Jewish reconciliation as the other.

It is noteworthy that Cardinal Cushing, the brother-in-law of a Jew, made one of his two formal "interventions" at the council (apart from his complaint about Latin) to speak in favor of *Nostra Aetate,* which its critics were attempting to water down.[26] Cushing was in favor of a full-blown act of Catholic repentance for the long history of anti-Judaism, something beyond what the council would do. Jews, Cushing said, no doubt thinking of Dick Pearlstein, "are the blood brothers of Christ." And then he went on with real passion—and scarcely veiled criticism of the Church: "I ask myself, Venerable Brothers, whether we should not humbly acknowledge before the whole world that, toward their Jewish brethren, Christians have all too often not shown themselves as true Christians, as faithful followers of Christ. How many Jews have suffered in our own time? How many died because Christians were indifferent and kept silent? . . . If in recent years, not many Christian voices were raised against those injustices, at least let ours now be heard in humility."[27]

6. RELIGIOUS LIBERTY

Cushing's second intervention came when he spoke in favor of a proposed decree on religious liberty. This was the issue that had first made him famous beyond Boston, in the dispute with Father Feeney a decade earlier. Already the council fathers had approved a "Dogmatic Constitution on the Church," *Lumen Gentium.* Instead of as an institution or hierarchy, the Church was defined as a people; instead of as a "perfect society," it was described as "always in need of purification"; instead of as the center of all truths, the Church was called a pilgrim people en route to the truth but not yet in full possession of it.

The implication of change that had been brought out by the Feeney affair was now made explicit—an unambiguous repudiation at last of *Extra Ecclesiam nulla salus.* Of non-Catholic Christians *Lumen Gentium* declared, "We can say that in some real way (*in re*) they are joined with us in the Holy Spirit, for to them too He gives His gifts and graces whereby He is operative among them with His sanctifying power." Of non-Christians, including atheists and agnostics, the constitution says, "Nor is God far distant from those who in shadows and images seek the unknown God, for it is He who gives to all men life and breath and all things, and as savior wills that all men be saved. Those also can attain to salvation who through no fault of their own do not know the Gospel of Christ or His Church, yet sincerely seek God and moved by grace strive by their deeds to do His will as it is known to them through dictates of conscience."[28]

Conscience: at last the Roman Catholic Church was prepared to affirm the primacy of conscience. Indeed, the council fathers, having originally intended to address the issue as part of *Lumen Gentium,* decided the subject of religious liberty deserved its own standalone decree. The poet laureate of conscience, among Catholics, was the silenced Jesuit John Courtney Murray, and once Cardinal Ottaviani was turned aside by the council fathers, Murray was invited to come to Rome. In one of the great reversals in Catholic history, the former misfit was given primary responsibility for the redrafting of a major statement on religious freedom, which would appear in 1965 as *Dignitatis Humanae* (On the Dignity of the Human Person). Murray's partner in that work was Thomas Stransky, the Paulist priest and my fellow son of Isaac Hecker.

Here was the end of the story that had begun with the Vatican's condemnation of Americanism in the early twentieth century. The Catholic Church, as Hecker had insisted it would, had finally drawn lessons from the American experience. Religious pluralism was affirmed instead of condemned. The language of "rights" was invoked instead of bemoaned. Themes from foundational American texts, including Jefferson's word "endowed" (as in "endowed by their Creator with certain unalienable Rights"), were explicitly repeated. The "dignity of the human person," of the individual, was defined as the ground of religious freedom, and every government was called to protect that freedom—even, as was the case in Spain and certain nations of Latin America, from the Catholic Church.

When Cardinal Cushing rose from his chair in St. Peter's Basilica to speak in favor of *Dignitatis Humanae,* the world's bishops became acutely attentive. Cushing was known as the man who had brought this issue to a head a decade before. He was Murray's advocate, and his association with John Kennedy's affirmation of a particularly Catholic conscience also marked him. What Cushing asked for was not merely that the Church move to a position of tolerance, but that, as he put it, the Catholic Church become "the *champion* of liberty, of human liberty, and of civil liberty, especially in the matter of religion." When Cushing finished, the bishops, who had sheepishly refused to support him on language, roundly applauded.[29]

As our novitiate year drew to a close, we novices were herded into the common room to watch television again, this time, in June 1963, for the funeral of Pope John XXIII. One had to think of other great figures whose time had been cut short. Lincoln's assassination had made him a martyr. Had he lived, he might have been given a more mixed appraisal, yet he would have had an opportunity to influence the era of Reconstruction, which, without him, was a disaster. What would have followed for the Catholic Church if John XXIII had been given another handful of years? Would the reactionary countermovement have arisen so quickly?

It was not a question we could ask yet. The stomach cancer had at last taken our beloved pope, but not before one more singular accomplishment. Pope John had published that spring what was read as his last will and testament, *Pacem in Terris* (Peace on Earth). It was one of the greatest papal encyclicals of all time; certainly it was the most widely read. The statement was composed in response to the Cuban Missile Crisis and raised the forbidden question of the nuclear age: Could war any longer be conceived as serving a just purpose? Pope John's final act, in effect, was to enlist the Catholic Church decisively on the side of peace, a long-overdue renunciation of the cry issued by Pope Urban II as the call to the First Crusade in 1095: "God wills it!"

7. THOMAS MERTON AND PEACE

The question of war and peace would cut to the center of Catholic identity, especially in America. My own life, given my Air Force father's status as a leading cold warrior, would be upended by it. The figure of Thomas Merton, around whom we novices had begun to construct identities of otherworldly detachment, would be transformed when the hermit monk entered the fray of political dispute over the war in Vietnam. He had already written to a friend in Latin America, on November 20, 1961, "Pray for us. We are starting an American Christian peace movement. It will be very difficult. We are, alas, very late."[30]

While I was embracing a life of obedience, with only the sneaking of cigarettes as an emblem of freedom, Merton was starting to resist at a loftier level. In a 1960 letter to the great French Catholic philosopher Jacques Maritain, he described how his order forbade his collaboration with a Zen master—prohibiting *communicatio cum infidele*, communication with the infidel. His father general, Merton wrote, "objected to this kind of dialogue between a member of the Order and Buddhists, Protestants, Jews and so forth." In a follow-up letter to Maritain, Merton added, about the father general, "He does not think, apparently, that I have sufficiently the mind of the Church to be able to engage safely in a dialogue of this kind."[31]

"The mind of the Church": for tens of thousands of us, that is exactly what Thomas Merton embodied. He was our second Scripture. And when he changed, how could we not? In our own quest for "religious liberty," we would go from cigarettes to civil disobedience. Merton had led us into the "perfect society" of the Church. An alternative world. And an alternative *to* the world. But then he led us into a human church very much *of* the world. This was, of course, a journey mapped by Pope John XXIII and then charted by the fathers of the Second Vatican Council. But for Merton the pressure point apparently was no theological category and no religious imperative. Instead, it was overwhelmingly the question of war and peace. This was especially true of nuclear war, which, he wrote in 1961, "is glorified as Christian sacrifice, as a crusade, as the way of obedience. So much so that now there are many who insist that one is not a good Christian unless he offers a blind and unresisting obedience to every behest of Caesar."[32]

In 1961, I was one of those blind Christians. As an ROTC cadet at Georgetown, I had won a prize, a model B-52 bomber, and I had been proud to bring it with me to the seminary. That gleaming stainless-steel warplane sat on my bureau like a relic of something holy. Merton continued, thinking of the likes of me: "This is for me a complete nightmare and I realize that I have to be very careful how I protest. Otherwise, I will be silenced." But protest he did.

In 1965, a number of people came to Gethsemani Abbey for a retreat with him, on the theme "The Roots of Protest." Attended by, among others, James Forest, A. J. Muste, and the Berrigan brothers, Philip and Daniel, that meeting would be regarded as the birth of the Catholic wing of the anti–Vietnam War movement. Merton would be frightened and conflicted about the course they embarked upon, opposing, for example, Daniel Berrigan's refusal to condemn as mere suicide the self-immolation of the young Catholic Worker Roger LaPorte at the United Nations later the same year. That refusal was the beginning of Berrigan's trouble with Cardinal Spellman, who expelled him from New York. And it was the beginning of his prominence as a leader of the antiwar movement. But Berrigan had learned, as I and so many others would, to listen to Merton. Even when they disagreed—especially then. About Merton, Berrigan would write, "Still my friend suffered and did what he could. Kept messages coming.

Stuffing them in bottles and casting them on the tide. His was, I think, the purest kind of truth telling. The kind that endures even in the empire of the deaf."[33]

The challenge of the Vietnam War was one noise that would drag me out of my *magnum silentium*, my great silence. The other, already referred to, was the play *The Deputy*, which broke over us seminarians in that period like a crushing tidal wave. Its charges against Pius XII called into question the ground of our faith in the Church, in its essential sinlessness. We Catholics prized the image of the Church as Hitler's mortal enemy, a conviction into which I had been initiated as a teenager in Germany. To have the illusion of the Church's heroism questioned, if not ripped away, was traumatic. As I would soon understand, part of what motivated Philip and Daniel Berrigan and others in their resistance to the war in Vietnam was the determination not to repeat the scandal of the Church's standing by while the Nazi death machine moved into gear.

And so too with Merton. Not for nothing was his shocking book of 1965 called *Conjectures of a Guilty Bystander*. Before that, Merton had written about *The Deputy*, properly rejecting its slanderous characterization of Pius XII as supportive of Hitler's anti-Jewish genocide, but also accepting the play's challenge to what Merton called "the magic image of Church innocence." Merton left no doubt that he found the silence of Church leaders, from the pope down, to be shameful, a jolt to his own identity. In *Conjectures* and in his other book of 1965, also shocking, *Raids on the Unspeakable*, Merton put the trial of Adolf Eichmann at the center of his meditation. And reflecting on Hannah Arendt's controversial account of the trial, Merton wrote in *Conjectures* that the Holocaust requires "a sordid examination of the conscience of the entire West." He began that examination with his own life, and he certainly extended it to the Church.

We needn't sentimentalize Merton or remember him apart from the context in which he lived. Much of what I take for granted would no doubt strike him as wrongheaded. He complained about what he called "extreme progressives." Merton loved to see himself, in good Catholic fashion, as a man of the reasonable middle. But he also railed against U.S. militarism, much as the radicals were doing. His writing about war was especially crucial, transforming the situation of many young Catholic men through the 1960s. The great Thomas Merton could serve as an authoritative rebuttal to draft boards that did not recognize claims to conscientious objector status based on appeals to Catholic theology, which, after all, had enshrined the concept of just war in the Western mind. But in this Merton was following in the footsteps of John XXIII. The pope was the one to put peace at the center of a new Catholic identity.

Here is the bottom line on Merton, at least for Catholics of my generation. Having led us into the true glories of the great Catholic Church, a greatness we will always honor, he led us to see the ways in which the Church also stands greatly in need of reform. And having learned the hard way, he offered such witness, at least toward the end, with the full knowledge that he was standing against the sanctified authorities of the Church, to whom he had once believed he owed absolute obedience. Merton showed us how to dissent from Catholic teaching while still being authentically Catholic. And even in this, he would have explained, he was following John XXIII. Indeed, Thomas Merton was that pope's masterpiece.

8. THE DEATH OF JOHN F. KENNEDY

Pope John's death in June 1963 was tied, with mythic power, to the death several months later of John F. Kennedy. He, too, having learned from the Cuban Missile Crisis, had moved boldly to affirm the primacy of peace. On June 10, one week after Pope John's death, Kennedy delivered his greatest speech, at American University in Washington—a resounding repudiation of his own fevered Cold War rhetoric. Kennedy, the "Americanist" Catholic, spoke that day of what he had learned not only in his political struggles but in his religious ones: "And if we cannot end now our differences, at least we can help make the world safe for diversity. For in the final analysis, our most basic common link is that we all inhabit this small planet. We all breathe the same air. We all cherish our children's future. And we are all mortal."[34]

Pope John and President Kennedy were alike in the way their own mortality sealed them forever in the bond of the world's affection. Certainly in mine. Again, as with Lincoln, it is impossible not to ask how history might have been different had Kennedy lived. The question, still, only adds to the grief. By November 22, 1963, my classmates and I, novices no more, were full-fledged Paulist seminarians in Washington. Kennedy's funeral, the most widely watched television broadcast in history up until then, instructed the nation in the power of Catholic ritual. The sacrament is a source of healing, and not just for those who believe it. And on television, we saw it. *Here! Here was what we would be ordained to do!* Heartbroken, yet we were firmer in our sense of vocation than ever. The death of Kennedy also laid to rest any question of whether a Catholic could fully participate in the American consensus. How were we to know that that consensus itself was about to break, with Catholic iconoclasts joining in the smashing? How could we know, for that matter, that the secrets of Kennedy's sexual restlessness, when they came to be exposed, would themselves point to a grave, and as yet unaddressed, Catholic pathology?

Cardinal Cushing was never more himself, nor more our surrogate, than when he put his hand on the coffin at the Cathedral of St. Matthew the Apostle and said, through his tears, "Dear Jack." The cardinal would wear the symbol of his office, the pectoral cross, less and less, but he would from then on wear John Kennedy's dog tag inside his shirt, a gift from Jackie.[35] Cushing was sixty-eight years old. He looked ancient to us. He seemed defeated by this loss, but he was not. His strong interventions at the Vatican Council were ahead of him, and so were unexpected acts of boldness, including one in defense of the president's young widow. But to us, with the liberalizing council under way, the Paulists soon to be vindicated, and the significance of what we had set for ourselves assured, even the grief we felt was like fuel for the torch that had just been passed to us. In watching our president being laid to rest, we new Paulists heard the call to complete the work we had been commissioned to do by our two beloved Johns.

CHAPTER FIVE

A NEW LANGUAGE

1. END OF LATIN

MOST CATHOLICS HAD a thin grasp of the Vatican Council as it was unfolding. The American press reported the proceedings energetically, but more as a political convention than as an ecclesiastical gathering. Gossip, rumors, factional disputes, backroom dealings, and memorable characters marked the coverage.[1] The theologians and bishops were grappling with questions of Church administration (Should local episcopal conferences share in the pope's governance? What is the proper role of the laity?); of Catholic relations with other religions (Are Protestants in the Church? Does Judaism have any validity after Jesus?); of Church relations with the larger world (How is the Church to relate to the state? Is war justified in the nuclear age?). Sixteen council documents would be published, an extraordinary record of the bishops' wide-ranging agenda. But in truth, especially in the early days of the council, it confronted only one question in which the Catholic people at large had a stake: Would the Mass be said in a language they understood?

The question of whether to use the vernacular in the liturgy might seem trivial compared to all those others, yet the common intuition of the people was right. They were like Cardinal Cushing, with his proposal at the council's opening session that its Latin proceedings be translated. And they were like the vast majority of council fathers, who trumped the reactionaries with that first vote on liturgical reform. Language was the fundamental issue, and it had been from the Church's earliest times. Below questions of rational understanding were questions of power within the Church. Even more basic, language, once attention was drawn to it, opened into the very meaning of revelation, the way humans relate to the *unspeakably* transcendent, and the way the transcendent, in an overflowing of expression, relates to creation—which is that expression.

Because language is so fundamental to human experience, and therefore to the religious questions that this book raises, it is necessary to take something of a detour from the more or less chronological narrative of twentieth-century Catholicism. The midcentury flowering of Catholicism involved a reckoning with the deepest questions of meaning and expression, going back to the very beginning of the Church. The Second Vatican Council initiated an era of biblical and theological innovation among scholars and, in direct consequence, of biblical and theological literacy among the Catholic people. But that presumed a revolution in the way the texts of Scripture and the Tradition were regarded.

The most exciting chapter in human life is the one in which we come to language, but we don't understand the glories or difficulties of that adventure until we can look back on it. That is true, too, of the glories and difficulties of the process by which Catholics came to the new language of their renewed religion. That process involved, above all, a confrontation with Latin, the ingenious Roman tongue that had, across the centuries, rendered the people mute.

"*Ad Deum qui laetificat juventutem meam,*" I used to say with a proud flourish. Here is where, in memory, this abstract issue gets personal. As an altar boy, it was my sacred privilege to recite such antiphons in response to the priest. "I will go unto the altar of God," he would have said in Latin, the opening phrase of the Catholic Mass. My reply translates "To God who gives joy to my youth." But fifty-some years ago, when I enacted this ritual, translation was unthinkable.

To exchange the meticulously memorized verses with the priest was indeed a joy to my youth, involving prideful satisfaction in a first intellectual achievement. For us altar boys, as for all Catholics, Latin provided a structure of meaning that was untouched by the fact that the verses themselves were meaningless. Legions of people came to live secure in the love of God because of that ritual. Latin may have been a dead language, but it was the living symbol of all that we were taught to value about our faith: its unchangeability (Latin dated to the birth of the Church), its hierarchy (Latin was the language of those to whom God gave power), its order (Latin's rigid conjugations diagrammed the absolute truth), its universality (the Mass was equally incomprehensible everywhere). The note of unchangeability loomed above all, which is why early rumblings about Mass in the vernacular were rudely dismissed by every monsignor to whom I ever handed cruets. If the Latin Mass was good enough for Jesus, it was good enough for us.

Marshall McLuhan, the twentieth-century media theorist, once observed that what doomed Latin as a liturgical language was the invention of the microphone.[2] McLuhan loved to tease readers with examples of the ways machines dominated machine makers, and his point here can be overdrawn. But the mystical aura of Virgil's tongue was indeed dispelled once congregants were able actually to hear the mumbo-jumbo of the priest, stooped over the distant altar. From the garbled cadence of his recitation, now rumbling through the whole church, it was clear that the words were nonsense as much to him as to them. In McLuhan's view, the technology of amplification, as much as any shift in ideology, made the move away from Latin inevitable. I would argue that technology facilitated a process that was already under way, much as the invention of movable type by Johannes Gutenberg around 1440 aided and abetted the already unfolding Renaissance celebration of individual intelligence.

And once Catholics entered into the mystery of the Mass as literate participants instead of as passive spectators, an unprecedented renewal took hold—and my own steadfast devotion to Mass attendance until now is a measure of it. The vitality and warmth of today's typical Catholic liturgy, involving intelligible encounters with sacred texts, has American Catholic parishes surprisingly full, even in a time of widespread disillusionment with clerical leadership. The order that was embodied in the old tradition, and its language, turned out to be a dead letter in comparison to the meaning and nourishment that now regularly draw Catholics to the Eucharistic meal.

It should be no surprise that, early in his pontificate, Pope Benedict XVI escalated his long campaign against the reforming spirit of Vatican II—when he used the word "reform," he put it in quotes—by authorizing, in 2007, the return of the Mass in Latin. The language question went to the heart of the reform question—indeed, to the heart of the power question. That had long been the case, which is why the Vatican II battle over what language to use at Mass was, as I only slowly realized, a replay of an earlier battle over what language to read the Bible in.

I was in the seminary when these questions first arose. The arrival of English in the liturgy, and the resulting transformation of my own experience of worship, was the precondition of my changed understanding of what had been at stake in the Church's argument with Protestants. There, too, as with electronic amplification in our time, technology had played its role. It wasn't so much the Renaissance, perhaps, that the new printing process enabled as the Reformation, which consisted, at bottom, of the demand by laypeople for the Bible in a comprehensible language.[3]

Jesus had been nothing if not accessible. He spoke Aramaic, the vernacular of first-century Palestinian Jews. In all likelihood, he was himself illiterate.[4] But his literate disciples wrote in Greek, the lingua franca of the Roman Empire, making that the foundational language of Christian Scripture. Hebrew was the language of Jewish Scripture, of course, although a Greek translation of the Jewish texts (the Septuagint, named for the seventy translators to whom it was attributed) was in wide circulation in the ancient world, and was, in fact, taken over by Christians for their so-called Old Testament.

It is important to understand that the Church came to its "Bible" only gradually, and by a process filled with contingency, accident, and contention. In the first centuries after Jesus, "Christianity" consisted of many diverse and widely dispersed communities around the Mediterranean world, and many of these communities regarded locally composed writings about Jesus—compilations of sayings or parables, for example—as sacred texts. We will see more of this later. Suffice to note here that as the Church, in the period of unifying control exerted after the conversion of Constantine in 312, emphasized one orthodox understanding of Jesus, dozens of regional texts that did not mesh with that understanding were cast aside. The approval of orthodox texts, simultaneous with the approval of an orthodox creed, came with the establishment of the canon, the official list of the books of the Bible. This process took place over the century after Constantine, culminating in 397 at the Council of Carthage, which formally set the canon.[5] At about the same time, an ascetic scholar based in Bethlehem, named Jerome, completed the work of putting the Greek and Hebrew texts of the Bible into Latin, by then the vernacular, or vulgate, of the Roman Empire. Jerome's is the Vulgate Bible.

But when Rome fell Latin calcified, and over time it became the language of clerks and clerics. For an increasingly illiterate laity, the Bible was reduced to simple stories, a paucity of melodramas (Adam, Eve, and the serpent; Noah and the flood; Jonah and the leviathan) that were rendered in stained-glass windows or summarized in homilies. Instead of being based on the words and example of Jesus, Catholic faith was soon centered on cults of saints, with relics and rites that had little or nothing to do with Bible narratives. The purpose of preaching was not the reasoned elucidation of Scripture, but an emotional exhortation to pieties rooted in accretions of Tradition, the most notorious of which, by Martin Luther's time, involved the granting of indulgences. That quantification and commercialization of the afterlife, the spark of Luther's revolt in 1517, could seem a logical outcome of a system of religious excess that had been cut loose from the religion's origins. But when Protestant reformers challenged the clerical establishment of the Catholic Church in the sixteenth century, their first treason was translation.

2. THE BIBLE TOLD THEM SO

By the time of the Reformation, more than a thousand years after Jerome's Vulgate Bible, most "vulgar," or common, Christians had little access to biblical literature, and little capacity, therefore, to measure their devotedness against the Gospels. That was the first battle the reformers fought. With the help of the printing press, they put Scripture into the hands of non-ordained believers—first the elites, ultimately the masses—undercutting the proprietary power of the clergy. The cry "Scripture alone!" involved a rite of purification, an abandonment of the pieties and cults that could not find precedent in the Gospels of Jesus or the New Testament letters (Epistles) written about Jesus.

The reformers' clearest and quickest repudiation involved the seven sacraments. Since only two, in any reading of the Gospels, could be attributed to Jesus himself—the Eucharist and Baptism—the other five were jettisoned, along with clerical celibacy and other practices not found in Scripture. These abrupt changes amounted to a shocking mutation that the mass of soon-to-be-called Protestant Christians could accept only because they could read the change-sanctioning Bible for themselves. Luther published a New Testament in German in 1522, only five years after nailing his Ninety-five Theses to the cathedral door in Wittenberg. In those five years, hundreds of thousands of copies of his own works in German were sold, and his German New Testament followed suit.[6]

The prophet of English translation was a priest named William Tyndale, whose version of the New Testament appeared in 1526. A decade later, for producing this translation, he was burned as a heretic (having been denounced by my own St./Sir Thomas More), but the English people hungrily consumed Tyndale's outlawed verses, as readers and as hearers, transforming not only the faith but the nascent language. The majesty of Tyndale's work in English stands as a cultural milestone. When the King James Version of the Bible was published most of a century later, in 1611, fully eighty-five percent of its New Testament was taken directly from Tyndale. The English of William Shakespeare was Tyndale's English. The thrill of language, and the play of the mind that freed language set loose, is reflected in the fact that during Shakespeare's lifetime, 211 separate editions of the English Bible were published, selling hundreds of thousands of copies in a British population of only six million.[7]

The Protestants left the rigidity of dead Latin behind, and also of a univocal reading of texts. Their translations, and their emphasis on Scripture as the self-authenticating source of Christian faith, led to a flourishing of exegesis, a new emphasis on the sources of Scripture, and the study of historical contexts within which the texts were composed. Biblical scholarship would be a permanent hallmark of Protestant Christianity.

The Roman hierarchy, meanwhile, reemphasized Latin, putting the Bible farther out of reach than ever. Indeed, the Council of Trent, convened to rebut Luther and the others, while defining the Gospel as "the source of all saving truth and rule of conduct," also said that the Gospel is to be found "in the written and unwritten traditions which have come down to us . . . preserved in continuous succession in the Catholic Church."[8] The Church, not the Bible, is supreme. After Trent, theology became ever more rigid, with even Catholic scholars losing touch with the subtleties of traditional ways of reading the Bible. There would be no vernacular Bible for the laity, but preachers, too, would leave Scripture aside in favor of sermons based on the lives of saints and their "spiritual writing." Such preaching often wandered across a firmly nonbiblical geography of the afterlife, with heaven, hell, purgatory, and limbo conjured in details that owed as much to pagan myth as Holy Writ.[9] Affective responses—docility, repentance, edification, remorse—were the goal. Biblical ignorance became a mark of Catholicism.

3. COPERNICUS, GALILEO, AND DARWIN

Compared to the way Scripture had long been read in the Church, the Catholic approach to Scripture after the Reformation—that is, during the Counter-Reformation—was fundamentalist. The older tradition had accommodated complexities and even contradictions. Origen, a Church father of the third century, for example, had included the allegorical and analogical in his biblical interpretation. Jerusalem was less the city where Jews lived in the past than it was the Church of the present and the heavenly city of the future. St. Augustine, in the fourth century, and St. Thomas Aquinas, in the thirteenth, had in similar ways accommodated metaphorical readings.[10]

But the Reformation had made Scripture and its *literal* authority a loaded issue. Although emphasizing Tradition over Scripture, Rome could not be seen to be backing away from such literal-minded authority when Protestants were emphasizing it. This double bind caused the Church serious trouble in the aftermath of the Reformation, most notably in the case of Galileo Galilei. His observations of celestial bodies, published in 1610, bore out the heliocentric theory of Nicolaus Copernicus, who had published *On the Revolutions of Heavenly Spheres* in 1543. Today the Copernicus-Galileo conflict with the Catholic Church is a shorthand symbol of the "unbridgeable gulf" between religion and science, a characterization that fails to credit religion and the Church as the very fount of science. After all, Copernicus was the dean of the cathedral in Kraków and carried out his speculations as a faithful son of the Church. Galileo was a layman, but he was a devoted Catholic, and his sponsors included princes of the Church. The modern science of astronomy, Galileo's enterprise, had begun when cathedrals were laid out with exquisite precision for the purpose of tracking the movement of the sun so that the liturgical calendar, and in particular the date of Easter, could be calculated accurately.[11]

What defined the crisis between Galileo and the Inquisition was the fact that Galileo's assertions contradicted literal readings of verses of Scripture. Once again, technological change was a precondition of ideological change. Copernicus did not draw the Church's fire as Galileo did after him because Galileo's telescope, invented in 1606, moved the argument about the movement of the earth around the sun from the realm of hypothetical abstraction to that of proven fact.

Earlier, we saw a revolution catalyzed when Archbishop Cushing went from an experience (his loving regard for his Jewish brother-in-law) to a doctrinal change (Dick Pearlstein's eligibility for salvation despite not being Catholic). We argued that this primacy of experience over doctrine is characteristically modern. But here we add nuance to the assertion, for experience is not enough, and the Copernicus story demonstrates that. After all, his thesis that the earth revolves around the sun, and not vice versa, contradicts the ordinary experience of the untutored eye. The sun *can be seen* to be moving across the sky. The assertions of Copernicus by themselves approached the threshold of modernity, but the crossing of that threshold came with Galileo, when the new, contradictory experience *could be tested.* And the test could be repeated and verified. The scientific age begins, that is, when primacy is given to knowledge that can be tested. The test is the key, which is why the defining moment in the Galileo case comes when he aims the telescope, an instrument he first used to search the horizon for arriving ships, up to the sky. And once experience passes the test, no countervailing doctrine can stand—not even one standing on the ground of Scripture.

After the traumas of the Reformation, especially as they had involved Protestant assertions of the Catholic Church's disregard of Scripture, the Inquisition pounced, in 1615, on Galileo's claim, made in his *Three Letters on Solar Spots,* that the earth revolves around the sun. It was not only, or perhaps even mainly, that Ptolemy's geocentric schema of the universe had been the accepted scientific paradigm since the year 150, but that the Ptolemy paradigm[12] was explicitly backed up by biblical texts—which Church authorities of the Counter-Reformation felt bound to take literally.

"The world is firmly established and it cannot move," reads Psalm 93. "The Lord set the Earth on its foundations, and it cannot be moved," reads Psalm 104. The Book of Joshua assumes a moving sun when it describes that motion stopped: "And the sun stood still, and the moon stayed, until the people had avenged themselves upon their enemies . . . So the sun stood still in the midst of heaven, and hastened not to go down about a whole day."[13] Thus, Galileo was charged by the Inquisition with claiming "that the language of the Holy Scripture does not mean what it seems to mean."

Galileo replied, "There are in Scripture words which taken in their strict literal meaning, look as if they differ from the truth."[14] The point was not to take them literally. Some Church authorities, perhaps aware of the precedents of Augustine and Aquinas, agreed with Galileo that if what would later be called hard data contradicted Scripture, then the sacred texts must be reinterpreted. But even such enlightened prelates were forced by pressures of the age to go along with the inquisitors who required Galileo's recantation. "To affirm that the Sun, in its very truth, is at the center of the universe . . . is a very dangerous attitude," Cardinal Robert Bellarmine, a chief investigator, declared, "and one calculated not only to arouse all Scholastic philosophers and theologians, but also to injure our faith by contradicting the Scriptures."[15]

At his heresy trial in 1633, Galileo renounced his firm intellectual conviction that the earth moves around the sun, but then, according to a well-known legend, followed his renunciation with a muttered "*E pur si muove.*" And yet it moves.[16]

What is the Bible? Christianity, like Judaism and Islam, is defined as a religion of the Book. But how is that Book read? Who wrote it? Tradition says that the Bible is "inspired" by God. How so? A revolution in thought occurs when the question moves from "What is the meaning of the text?" to "What are its *meanings?*" What did it mean to those who actually put words to paper (or papyrus or vellum)? What did it mean to those who later decided that this text, and not that one, was to be included in the "book," the word that, in Greek, is "bible." What do Scripture's methods of composition and canonization mean to those for whom the myth of supernatural interventions in history is broken?

Almost fifty years after the trial of Galileo, in 1678, a French Catholic priest named Richard Simon, working in Paris, published a history of the Old Testament. As a faithful Catholic, he was attempting to show that a critical and historical reading of Scripture, revealing its inconsistencies and internal contradictions, undermines the Protestant claim that "Scripture alone" is a sufficient guide to faith. The Catholic reliance on Tradition was necessary. But Simon's line of reasoning was fraught in that contentious era. From his close reading of the texts, he concluded that the first five books of the Hebrew Scripture, the Pentateuch, were compositions written in different times and places. Those books were attributed to Moses by Jews and Christians alike, yet it was inconceivable to Simon that they were written by a single author, be it Moses or any other writer. But multiple authorship of the Pentateuch contradicted the literal word of the texts and the ancient tradition honoring Moses as sole author, and Simon's work was immediately condemned by Bishop Jacques-Bénigne Bossuet, an influential member of the French court and the leading Catholic theologian in France.

Simon's book was, in Bossuet's phrase, "a mass of impieties and a rampart of freethinking." Using his influence with the king, Bossuet saw to it that almost all copies of Simon's history of the Old Testament were burned, and Rome affirmed this censorship. Simon was driven in disgrace from his religious order, and Roman Catholic Scripture scholarship was stunted by his fate. Contrary to Simon's instinct that historical criticism could be used against the Protestants, their regard for Scripture by now included a determination, in some circles at least, to understand its origins and contexts. It was they who carried on the work of such "scientific" exploration into the sources and forms of the Bible.

Through the nineteenth century, as we saw, the Catholic Church fought a rear-guard action against modernism—a whole host of ideas following from the so-called Enlightenment that could only be taken to undermine the basic assumptions of religion. The philosophical challenge (Descartes, Kant, Nietzsche) to classical metaphysics (Aristotle, Thomas Aquinas) had its equivalent in the scientific revolution that, having begun with Copernicus and Galileo, rolled on to Newton and Darwin, each of whom proved in his sphere that "it moves." The heretofore absolute conviction that the ground of being is stable was overturned: *all is flux.* Ironically, the Church, a self-appointed defender of mystery, reversed roles with science, the discipline of precision and fact. For as scientists, moving from telescopes to microscopes—both of which opened into infinite worlds—were confronting the irreducible impossibility of ever eliminating the ambiguous from their perceptions, the Vatican was declaring war on ambiguity, insisting on a univocal notion of truth that was hostile to mystery. In other words, the Church, in its war against modernism, had become one of modernism's great manifestations.

The 1899 condemnation of Americanism by Pope Leo XIII, a decree that had almost named Isaac Hecker as a heretic, was a volley fired in this battle, but Pope Pius X, as we saw, fired the heavy artillery when he condemned modernism in 1907, issuing both a decree (*Lamentabili Sane*) and an encyclical (*Pascendi Dominici Gregis*). Part of what drew this fire was the special alarm felt by the Church establishment at a return by Catholic biblical scholars to the scientific method, and it was happening far more in Europe than in suspect America. The ghost of Richard Simon was returning to haunt the Church, but the Church was striking back. Against any reading of the Bible that took cues from the so-called liberal Protestants, in whose disciplines, for example, the search for the historical Jesus was well under way, the authorities in Rome once more affirmed the ahistorical literalness of sacred texts. The words of the Bible mean exactly what they seem to mean, and never mind internal contradiction and inconsistency.

Those Catholic scholars whose work called that literalness into question were condemned by name. Alfred Loisy, a leading French scholar, was excommunicated in 1908, a punishment so extreme among intellectuals whose inquiry was defined by devotedness that it chilled the entire discipline of Scripture studies among Catholics for generations. It was not until 1943, with Pope Pius XII's *Divino Afflante Spiritu*, that a thaw began to set in. That encyclical, showing a glimmer of what Protestant scholars had been suggesting for a century, said that the human dimension of Scripture must be understood. Texts must be read, the encyclical declared, with an eye to "the form of expression and the type of literature" if "true and genuine interpretation" is to be arrived at.[17] So-called form criticism was all right. This simple affirmation served as an opening to a new and more liberal way of reading the Bible.

For most mid-twentieth-century Catholics, the question had long boiled down to Charles Darwin. His 1859 work, *On the Origin of Species by Means of Natural Selection*, had made the question of how the Bible is to be read a public sensation. Then came his *Descent of Man*, published in the traumatic year of 1871. The Catholic Church was already reeling. In that period, the archbishop of Paris was murdered by the revolutionaries of the Paris Commune,[18] and the pope himself, confronted with Italian revolutionaries, had been made a "prisoner in the Vatican." Revolutionaries pressed in on every side —even in the abstractions of the sciences, which were turning out to be the most dangerous of all. Galileo had said that the earth moves. Now Darwin was saying that man moves, too: humans *evolve.* Because the Catholic Church was in retreat on so many fronts, the challenge from Darwin, which most of Protestantism took as a life-threatening blow, seemed like only one more jolt. Rome's sweeping condemnations of modernism included rejections of various assumptions of Darwin,[19] but the British scientist was an enemy far removed from Rome. In England and the United States, his notoriety was monumental.

Darwin represented four challenges to traditional religion: the world had not been created all at once, but had evolved; the earth was millions of years old, not a few thousand; human beings are not unique, but share an origin with all other life forms; the means by which all of this occurs, natural selection, is not ordered but random. The last two ideas attacked foundational principles of every traditional religion, yet only the first two were taken by most Christians to be a frontal assault on the faith. And on the Bible. It was simply impossible to credit both Darwin and any kind of literal reading of the opening chapters of Genesis, and in Protestant America, especially, the battle was joined.

Yet to Catholics, the rejection of evolution by Bible belt fundamentalists,[20] famously embodied in the Scopes monkey trial of 1925, seemed somewhat frenzied. John Scopes, defended by Clarence Darrow and prosecuted by William Jennings Bryan, was convicted of violating the Butler Act, a Tennessee law forbidding the teaching of evolution, a law that was not repealed until 1967. Average Catholics were no more inclined to see humans and monkeys as cousins than others were, but the foolish extremes of fundamentalist rejectionism ("God put fossils in the cliffs to test our faith") helped them come to their own commonsense conclusions about evolution, even before they were doctrinally instructed.

Catholic Scripture scholars, after the Vatican's early-twentieth-century condemnations of modernism, were lying low, but as the century wore on, they could not ignore the vitality of the Protestant version of their discipline. In 1921, the German scholar Rudolf Bultmann, for example, published *The History of the Synoptic Tradition*, a seminal work that began to show how Gospel texts were composed, drawing on oral tradition and the collected sayings of Jesus. The study of the forms of the texts (story, parable, saying, etc.) was key. Bultmann stimulated an entire school of Scripture scholarship—the "form criticism" to which I referred earlier—that would flourish throughout the century. Catholics, too, were drawn into it, and eventually the Vatican came to understand that something vital for the faith was at stake in the new disciplines.

That is the background of Pope Pius XII's surprising 1943 encyclical *Divino Afflante Spiritu*. It proposed in general terms a new approach to Catholic biblical studies, but questions tossed into the air by the Scopes trial lent the document a particular relevance in the United States. In the common discourse of average Catholics, the pressing issue was what to make of the opening chapters of Genesis. Promulgated in the year of my birth, the encyclical gave Catholic teachers the leeway to assert, as I was told by nuns as a child, that since God's "day" may last for thousands or millions of years, there was no contradiction between Genesis and evolution. The metaphoric reading of Scripture that was denied to Galileo was permitted to me, though no one drew attention to the change. Yet the very thing that worried Cardinal Bellarmine and others who'd condemned Galileo began to happen. The slope started to slip. If, in loosening its definition of time, the story of the creation was not to be taken literally, what about the parting of the Red Sea? What about the Three Kings? What, for that matter, about the Resurrection of Jesus? What parts of the Bible were to be taken as invented metaphor and what parts as "fact"?

4. LEARNING TO READ

As it happened, I was initiated into Catholic biblical scholarship as all of these forces converged. In 1964, my third year in the seminary, I began my first serious course of Scripture studies, and it was then that the Vatican issued its first truly liberal instruction on the subject.

Vatican II was having its liberating effect here, too. The wedge issue in biblical studies, as it turned out, was not the creation account in Genesis but the Church's relationship with the Jewish people, starting with the anti-Jewish texts of the four Gospels, the Acts of the Apostles, and the commonly understood anti-Judaism of St. Paul's Epistles. A group identified as "the Jews" are portrayed throughout the New Testament as the enemies of Jesus, a conflict that builds, in the dramatic narrative of the Passion, to the explicit charge that the Jews, not the relatively more benign Romans, were guilty of the murder of Jesus.

As Cardinal Cushing had moved from ethics to theology, going from his certitude that Father Feeney's contempt for Jews, including Cushing's brother-in-law, did not square with an all-loving Father in heaven, so the fathers of the Vatican Council, concluding after the Holocaust that the Christ killer charge had prepared the way for lethal Nazi antisemitism, went from an ethical insight to a theological change. The leader in this, again, was Pope John XXIII, who had required the council fathers to take up the question of the Church's relationship with the Jewish people. After his experience in the years of the Holocaust, he had seen that as *the* crucial issue. No question at the council was debated with more anguish, and finally the fathers issued their milestone declaration. Contradicting nearly two thousand years of Church teaching, *Nostra Aetate* proclaimed that Jews as a people were not guilty of the murder of Jesus. "What happened in His passion cannot be blamed upon all Jews then living, without distinction, nor against the Jews of today."[21]

But this immediately posed a problem, because the Gospels are rife with the charge that the Jews bore exactly such guilt. The Gospel of John, for example:

> Pilate said to them, "Take him yourselves and crucify him, for I find no crime in him."
>
> The Jews answered him, "We have a law, and by that law he ought to die, because he has made himself the Son of God . . ."
>
> He [Pilate] said to the Jews, "Here is your king!"
>
> They cried out, "Away with him, away with him, crucify him!"[22]

How is such a text to be read? More to the point, if it and other Gospel accounts that explicitly blame the Jews for the death of Jesus are not true to what happened, as *Nostra Aetate* suggests, how did they come to be written? Does the inspired Word of God lie? Such questions fired our classroom work. The enemies of Jesus, as the New Testament tells the story, were not the Romans but the Jews: "His own received him not."[23] If that was not true, what was? Was this foundational element of Christian belief a fiction? Even more disturbing, if the Jews were innocent of the murder of Jesus, were the Gospel writers guilty of a slander? A slander that led, ultimately, to genocide?

In the classroom, we began to understand that Christian faith had begun not with some glad intervention in history by God, but rather with a series of unexpected disappointments that crushed the first believers again and again, generating stories that evolved into oral traditions, which eventually sent chroniclers and scribes to their desks. First there was the ignominious death of Jesus, which violated every hope of that small band of Galileans who loved him. There was, in the decades after Jesus, just as his stories were being written down, the devastating victory of Rome over God's reign, a savage war in which a million of their fellow Jews were slaughtered—and in which the center of Jewish Christianity was itself obliterated. There was the failure of Jesus, now believed to be the apocalyptic Lord, to return in glory as he had promised. And as if all of this were not enough, there was the profoundly unsettling insult when the large majority of their fellow Jews began to spit out the Jewish followers of Jesus as heretics and idolaters.

Each of these traumas, unfolding between the death of Jesus and the destruction of Jerusalem a hundred years later, played its decisive role in how the first records of Christian life were set down—Epistles, Gospels, Acts, and Revelation. And it was these crises, involving conflicts between the followers of Jesus and those Jews who disputed their claims, that generated the anti-Jewish slant of those texts. A later hatred, that is, was rendered as hatred dating back to Jesus, not because the Gospel writers were liars, but because they saw the past through the lens of what they were experiencing in the present. As humans always do.

The texts of the New Testament were not divine books, we seminarians began to see, but human documents, mementos of tragedy and magnificent adaptation. We took to reading and studying them with committed urgency. Our times, too, were traumatic. We were hardly able to articulate the way that, in this esoteric pursuit, the entire house of our faith was at stake. Was it a house of cards? Having just followed the Protestants into the realm of vernacular worship, we Catholics, suddenly able to draw on a century's worth of liberal Protestant scholarship, were about to get intellectually and religiously serious about the Bible. The result would be explosive. And wonderful.

"The Catholic exegete, under the guidance of the Church," the 1964

Vatican instruction said, "must make skillful use of the new aids to exegesis, especially those which the historical method, taken in its widest sense, has provided; that method, namely, which minutely investigates sources, determining their nature and bearing, and availing itself of the findings of textual criticism, literary criticism, and linguistic studies."[24] For more than a hundred years, scholars in various fields had been making discoveries about the origins of the Bible that now came at us in a rush.

Cultural anthropologists provide contexts that complicate and alter various simplistic notions. My earlier assertion that Jesus was most likely illiterate, for example, contradicts the pious image of him as a multifaceted genius, but is based on the finding that ninety-seven percent of the Jewish population in Palestine at the time was illiterate, including groups associated with the carpentry trade.[25] Therefore, Gospel verses showing the young Jesus impressively reading Scripture must be looked at skeptically. To take another example, anthropology reveals that divine-origin stories, like those told of Jesus (virgin birth, celestial phenomena, visiting Magi), were common in the ancient world and were a natural way for Jesus' followers to make such a claim for him as a way of asserting their faith in his divinity, arrived at years later.

For a century, archeologists (with assists from shepherds and nomads) had been turning up ancient manuscripts and papyrus scrolls in clay jars in caves and excavations from Egypt to Israel to Iraq to Turkey: "The Teaching" (in Greek, *Didache*) was the rule of a first-century Christian community, discovered in 1873 in a monastery in Istanbul; independent second- and third-century texts, such as the Gospel of Peter, the Gospel of Mary, and the Gospel of Thomas, were found in Egypt in the late 1800s; the Nag Hammadi codices, fourth-century Gnostic texts, were discovered in Egypt in 1945; and the Dead Sea Scrolls, elaborate records of a Jewish sect dating to the time of Jesus, were uncovered at Qumran beginning in 1947.[26] Texts like these enabled Christian scholars to examine the New Testament as it had never been before, like the written score of a symphony that had been read on the page but never played, never heard.

The "new aids to exegesis" included form criticism, which shows what the original genres of the texts were; source criticism, which shows what documents derived from earlier documents; redaction criticism, which shows how copying alters texts over time; and tradition criticism, which shows how meanings develop through time. All such criticism enabled the opening up of layers of the Gospel, revealing how Matthew and Luke derive from Mark; how John derives from all three; how all four depend on a long-lost source, known as Q (from the German word *Quelle*, for source); how the slant of each text reflects the time and place in which it was composed.[27]

To know the actual time of composition is one of the most revealing new aids of all. Taken as "gospel," the Gospels are most often read as eyewitness accounts of what they report. They are anything but. Jesus died around the year 30. The Gospels were not written down until many decades later: Mark in about 70, Matthew and Luke between 75 and 90, John in about 100. They are wartime literature,[28] written in the traumatic days of Rome's savage war against the Jews, and their inciting incident was the destruction of the Temple in Jerusalem in 70. The Temple was the center of Jewish religious identity, and every Jew, including at that point nearly every follower of Jesus, was thrown into a profound crisis by its abrupt disappearance. What is it to be a Jew without the Temple? Some Jews answered: To be a Jew now is to be more dedicated than ever to Torah, the study of the Law. This response evolved into rabbinic Judaism. Other Jews answered: To be a Jew now is to be centered on Jesus, the New Temple. This response, obviously, evolved into Christianity. The point is that, with the destruction of the Temple, two new religious entities (if not new religions) came into being. They were rivals.

When the Gospels have Jesus "predicting" the destruction of the Temple and identifying himself as its replacement,[29] they are describing an after-the-fact adaptation that Jesus' followers made to what the Romans had already done. Writing in 80 or 100 a story that claims to be happening in 30, they bring into that story, as prophecy, the decisive destruction of the Temple in 70. The Temple *will be* destroyed, Jesus says, because the Jews are rejecting him. But the rejection in question is experienced not by Jesus in 30, but by Jesus' followers in 80 or 90 or 100, after the Temple *has been* destroyed. The later the Gospel, the more distance there is between Jesus' followers and the Jews who disagree with them, and therefore, in the Gospel, between Jesus and the Jews with whom he is portrayed to be in conflict. The last Gospel, John, is by far the most anti-Jewish, using the loaded phrase "the Jews" seventy-one times, compared to the sixteen times it appears in Matthew, Mark, and Luke combined.[30] The polemical phrase "the Jews," since it is still being used by Jews, refers not to the Jewish people as a whole, but only to those Jews who reject the claims made for Jesus. This is a fact that will become impossible for mostly Gentile Christians to grasp. They will think of Jesus as one of them—not really Jewish at all. The anti-Jewish polemic of the Gospels that played out to such lethal effect across the centuries, that is, was rooted not in any conflict Jesus himself had with his own people in the year 30 (he lived and died a faithful Jew, proclaiming nothing but the God of Israel), but in the intra-Jewish argument between the two traumatized groups of Jews who disagreed, fifty years later, on what Jewishness meant without the Temple. The Gospels are the record of that argument (or rather, one half of that argument, since the other side, the Jesus-rejecting Jews, left a partial record at best of the dispute). Critically unpacking the layers of the Gospels like this is essential to unpacking —and defusing—their otherwise self-perpetuating anti-Jewish meaning. Biblical criticism, as history has shown, is now a matter of life and death.

5. THE MARY CODE

So what is it like to actually read the Bible critically? Let's stay a bit longer with our detour from a chronological history of Catholicism and look at a case study, to see what critical reading entails and to learn how revolutionary such reading can be for both doctrine and practice.

I have indicated what such reading can mean for Church attitudes toward Jews, and during my first foray into Scripture studies that question was central. But at about the same time, debates over the place of women in the Church began, and the Scriptures were, and still are, invoked to justify what has been increasingly recognized as clergy-sponsored discrimination by gender. What was the place of women in the circle of Jesus' first followers, and then in the first generations of the community that took his name? For this question, the "new aids to exegesis" that came into play during and after Vatican II were quickly seen to have sharp relevance. Nothing makes this clearer than a fresh reading, in light of those aids, of the story of Mary Magdalen, in relation both to Jesus and to the power structure of the early Church.

Mary Magdalen is the avatar of the woman of the Church, but she is more. The whole history of Western civilization is epitomized in her cult. For many centuries the most obsessively revered of saints, this woman became the soul of Christian piety, defined as repentance. Yet she was only elusively identified in Scripture and has thus been endlessly held up as the scrim onto which a succession of fantasies has been projected. In one age after another, her image was reinvented, from princess to prostitute to sibyl to Venus to mystic to celibate nun to passive helpmeet to feminist icon to the matriarch of divinity's secret dynasty. How foundational texts are read, how the past is remembered, how sexual desire is domesticated, how men and women negotiate their separate impulses, how power inevitably seeks sanctification, how tradition becomes authoritative, how revolutions are co-opted, how fallibility is reckoned with, how sweet devotion can be made to serve violent domination—all such modes of acculturation show up in the way the story is told of the woman who befriended Jesus of Nazareth. But what does the Bible really tell us about her?

Who was she? From New Testament texts, one can minimally conclude that Mary of Magdala (a name referring to her hometown, a village on the Sea of Galilee[31]) was a leading figure in the circle of those attracted to Jesus. When the men in that company abandoned Jesus at the hour of mortal danger, Mary of Magdala was one of the women who stayed with him, even to Golgotha.[32] She was the first person to whom Jesus appeared after his resurrection[33] and the first to preach the "good news" of that miracle.[34]

These are the only specific assertions made about Mary Magdalen in the Gospels. From other foundational texts of the early Christian era, it seems that her status as an apostle, in the years after Jesus' death, rivaled even that of Peter.[35] This prominence derived from the well-known intimacy of her relationship with Jesus, which, according to some accounts, had a physical aspect that included frequent kissing.[36] Beginning with the threads of these few statements in the earliest records of Christian memory, dating to the first and second centuries, an elaborate tapestry was woven, leading to the creation of a portrait of St. Mary Magdalen, the most consequential note of which is almost certainly untrue—that she was a repentant prostitute.[37] On that false note hangs the dual use to which her legend has been put ever since: discrediting sexuality in general and disempowering women in particular.

Confusions attached to Mary Magdalen's character were compounded over the centuries, as her image was conscripted into one power struggle after another and twisted accordingly. Attitudes toward the material world, focused on sexuality; the authority of an all-male clergy; the coming of celibacy; the branding of theological diversity as heresy, and then its obliteration; the political uses of sin obsession; the sublimations of courtly love; the prurience of a masochistic self-denial; the unleashing of "chivalrous" violence; the marketing of sainthood, whether in the time of Constantine, the Counter-Reformation, the Romantic era, or the industrial age—through all of this the reinventions of Mary Magdalen played their role. Her reemergence in the popular imagination, in the hugely popular novel *The Da Vinci Code* (2003), as the secret wife of Jesus and the mother of his fate-burdened child, source of his biological line, shows that the conscripting and twisting are still going on. This woman's appeal remains enormous.

But the confusion starts with the Gospels themselves, where several women come into the story of Jesus with great energy, including the energy of erotic implication. There are several Marys—not least, Mary the mother of Jesus. There is Mary of Bethany, whose sister is Martha and whose brother is Lazarus.[38] There is Mary "the mother of James and Joseph,"[39] and Mary "the wife of Clopas."[40] Equally important, there are three unnamed women who are expressly identified as sexual sinners: the woman with a "bad name" who wipes Jesus' feet with ointment as a signal of repentance,[41] a Samaritan woman whom Jesus meets at a well,[42] and an adulteress whom Pharisees haul before Jesus to see if he will condemn her.[43] The first thing to do in unraveling the mysterious tapestry of Mary Magdalen is to tease out the threads that properly belong to these other women, but that is complicated by the fact that some of the threads were quite knotted in the first place.

It will help to remember how their multifaceted picture was composed, how the story that includes them all came to be written. To repeat a point made earlier, the four Gospels are not eyewitness accounts.[44] They were written four to seven decades after the death of Jesus, a jelling of separate oral traditions that had taken form in dispersed Christian communities. Again, the basic chronology: Jesus died in about 30. Matthew, Mark, and Luke date to between about 70 and 90, and have sources and themes in common. The Gospel of John was composed later, around 100, and is distinct.

It is important to remember these facts of composition, because when we read about Mary Magdalen in each of the Gospels, as when we read about Jesus, what we are getting is not history but memory—memory shaped by time, by shades of emphasis, by accidents of circumstance, including the separate preoccupations of widely dispersed communities, and by efforts to make distinct theological points. And even in that early period, as is evident when the varied accounts are measured against each other, the memory is blurred.

Regarding Mary of Magdala, the confusion begins in the eighth chapter of Luke. "Now after this he made his way through towns and villages preaching and proclaiming the Good News of the kingdom of God. With him went the Twelve, as well as certain women who had been cured of evil spirits and ailments: Mary surnamed the Magdalen, from whom seven demons had gone out, Joanna the wife of Herod's steward Chuza, Susanna and several others who provided for them out of their own resources."[45]

Two things of note are implied in this passage. First, these women "provided" for Jesus and the Twelve, which suggests they were well-to-do, respectable figures. (It is possible this was a reading back into Jesus' time a role of prosperous women some years later.) Second, they had all been cured of something, including Mary Magdalen. The expression "seven demons," as applied to her, indicates an ailment (not necessarily "possession") of a certain severity. In time, as the blurring work of memory continued, and as the written Gospel was read by Gentiles unfamiliar with such coded language, those "demons" would be taken as a signal—not necessarily intended in the text—of a moral infirmity.

This otherwise innocuous reference to Mary Magdalen at the start of the eighth chapter of Luke takes on a kind of radioactive narrative energy because of its juxtaposition to what precedes it at the end of the seventh chapter,[46] an anecdote of stupendous power and one that would eventually overwhelm the Mary Magdalen reference:

> One of the Pharisees invited him to a meal. When he arrived at the Pharisee's house and took his place at table, a woman came in who had a bad name in the town. She had heard he was dining with the Pharisee and had brought with her an alabaster jar of ointment.

> She waited behind him at his feet, weeping, and her tears fell on his feet, and she wiped them away with her hair; then she covered his feet with kisses and anointed them with ointment.
>
> When the Pharisee who had invited him saw this, he said to himself, "If this man were a prophet, he would know who this woman is that is touching him and what a bad name she has."

But Jesus refuses to condemn her or even deflect her gesture. Instead he recognizes it as a signal that "her many sins must have been forgiven her, or she would not have shown such great love . . . 'Your faith has saved you,'" Jesus tells her. "'Go in peace.'"[47]

This story of the woman with the bad name, the alabaster jar, the loose hair, the "many sins," the stricken conscience, the ointment, the rubbing of feet, the kissing, became the dramatic high point of the story of Mary Magdalen. The scene, expressly attached to her, would be rendered again and again by the greatest Christian artists. But even a casual reading of this text, however laden its juxtaposition with the subsequent verses, suggests that the two women have nothing to do with each other, that the weeping anointer is no more connected to Mary of Magdala than she is to Joanna or Susanna.

And other verses in other Gospels add to the complexity. Matthew gives an account of the same incident, but to make a different point and with a crucial detail added:

> Jesus was at Bethany in the house of Simon the leper, when a woman came to him with an alabaster jar of the most expensive ointment, and poured it on his head as he was at table. When they saw this, the disciples were indignant; "Why this waste?" they said. "This could have been sold at a high price and the money given to the poor." Jesus noticed this. "Why are you upsetting the woman?" he said to them . . . "When she poured this ointment on my body, she did it to prepare me for burial. I tell you solemnly, wherever in all the world this Good News is proclaimed, what she has done will be told also, in remembrance of her."[48]

This passage shows what Scripture scholars commonly call the "telephone game" aspect of the oral tradition from which the Gospels grew.[49] Instead of Luke's "Simon the Pharisee," we find here "Simon the Leper." Most tellingly, this anointing, unlike the first one we saw, is specifically referred to as the traditional rubbing of a corpse with oil, so the act is an explicit foreshadowing of the death of Jesus. The story of the "unnamed woman" in Mark[50] takes on added power because that evangelist sees the anointing woman's acceptance of the coming death of Jesus in glorious contrast to the (male) disciples, who refuse to take seriously Jesus' own predictions of his death.[51] Mary Magdalen, in other passages,[52] is remembered *by name* as having attended to the corpse of Jesus, which helps explain why it was easy to associate this anonymous anointing with her.

Indeed, with this incident Matthew's narrative begins the move toward the climax of Golgotha because the offense the disciples are here seen taking at the waste of money motivates one of them, "the man called Judas," to go, in the very next verse,[53] to the chief priests to betray Jesus.

In both anointing passages the woman is identified by the same alabaster jar, but in Luke, with no reference to the death ritual, there are clear erotic overtones to the anointing. Perfumed oil was, as it still is, an aid to sexual intercourse, and it was therefore one of the tools in a prostitute's kit. So too with the woman's loosened hair, which a man was meant to see only in the intimacy of the bedroom. Such associations are implied in the offense taken by witnesses in Luke, which are related to sex, while in Matthew the offense concerns money. And in Luke (not Matthew) the woman's tears, together with the words of Jesus, define the encounter as one of abject repentance.

But the complications mount. Matthew says the anointing incident occurred at Bethany, a detail that sends the reader leaping, trapeze-like, across the pages to the Gospel of John, which has yet another Mary, the sister of Martha and Lazarus, and yet another anointing story:

> Six days before the Passover, Jesus went to Bethany, where Lazarus was, whom he had raised from the dead. They gave a dinner for him there; Martha waited on them, and Lazarus was among those at table. Mary brought in a pound of very costly ointment, pure nard, and with it anointed the feet of Jesus, wiping them with her hair.

Again Judas objects in the name of the poor, and once more Jesus is shown defending the woman. "'Leave her alone; she had to keep this scent for the day of my burial. You have the poor with you always, you will not always have me.'"[54]

As before, the anointing foreshadows the death, which follows quickly in John. And there is also resentment at the waste of a luxury good, so death and money define the content of the encounter. But the erotic is implied as well, for there is the loose hair, a wanton gesture of intimacy.

The most emotionally expressive event in Jesus' life, leading to his greatest miracle, the raising of Lazarus from the dead, takes place in relation to this same Mary, the sister of Lazarus. Weeping is again a feature of the story. It occurs not long after her brother has died. Jesus approaches Bethany. "Mary went to Jesus, and as soon as she saw him she threw herself at his feet, saying, 'Lord, if you had been here, my brother would not have died.'" Jesus responds by weeping himself, and accomplishes the miracle—an event his enemies take as a reason to move against him.[55]

The death of Jesus on Golgotha, where, as we saw, Mary Magdalen is identified as one of the women who refused to leave him, leads to what is by far the most important affirmation about her. All four Gospels, and other first- or second-century texts like the Gospel of Peter,[56] name her as present at the tomb, a first witness to the Resurrection of Jesus. This—not repentance, not sexual renunciation—is her greatest claim. Unlike the men who scattered and ran, who lost faith, who betrayed Jesus, the women stayed. (Although Christian memory glorifies this act, its historical context may have been less noble: the men in Jesus' company were far more likely to have been arrested than the women.[57]) And chief among them was Mary Magdalen. The Gospel of John puts the story poignantly:

> It was very early on the first day of the week and still dark, when Mary of Magdala came to the tomb. She saw that the stone had been moved away from the tomb, and came running to Simon Peter and the other disciple, the one whom Jesus loved. "They have taken the Lord out of the tomb," she said, "and we don't know where they have put him."

Peter and the others rush to the tomb to see for themselves, then disperse again.

> Meanwhile, Mary stayed outside the tomb, weeping. Then, still weeping, she stooped to look inside and saw two angels in white sitting where the body of Jesus had been, one at the head, the other

at the feet. They said, "Woman, why are you weeping?" "They have taken my Lord away," she replied, "and I don't know where they have put him." As she said this, she turned round and saw Jesus standing there, though she did not recognize him. Jesus said, "Woman, why are you weeping? Who are you looking for?" Supposing him to be the gardener, she said, "Sir, if you have taken him away, tell me where you have put him, and I will go and remove him." Jesus said, "Mary!" She knew him then and said to him in Hebrew, "Rabbuni!"—which means Master. Jesus said to her, "Do not cling to me because I have not yet ascended to my Father and your Father, to my God and your God." So Mary of Magdala went and told the disciples that she had seen the Lord and that he had said these things to her.[58]

As the story of Jesus was told and told again in those first decades, narrative adjustments in event and character were inevitable, and confusion of one with the other was a mark of the way the Gospels were handed on, not only before the texts were written down, but afterward, too. Recall that most Christians (like most people) were illiterate. Women in the community are understood by scholars to have emphasized lament, and men to have emphasized exegesis, the critical explanation of present experience in the light of inherited traditions.[59] It was this complex work of memory and interpretation, not history as we think of it, that led, eventually, to texts.[60]

Once the sacred texts were authoritatively set, exegetes could make careful distinctions, keeping the roster of women separate, but common preachers were less careful—because less capable. The telling of anecdotes was essential to them, and so too, therefore, were alterations. The multiplicity of the Marys by itself was enough to mix things up.[61] So also with the separate accounts of the feminine anointing, which in one place is the act of a loose-haired prostitute, in another of a modest stranger preparing for the tomb, and in yet another of a beloved friend named Mary. Women who weep, albeit in a range of circumstances, emerged as a motif. As with every narrative, erotic details loomed large, especially because the attitude of Jesus toward women with sexual histories was one of the things that set him apart from other teachers of the time. Not only was Jesus remembered as treating women with respect, as equals in his circle; not only did he refuse to reduce them to their sexuality; Jesus was portrayed as a man who loved women, and whom women loved.

The climax of that theme takes place in the garden of the tombs, with that one word of address, "Mary!" It was enough to make her recognize him, and her response is clear from what he says then: "Do not cling to me."[62] Whatever it was before, bodily expression between Jesus and Mary of Magdala must be different now.

Out of these disparate threads—the various female figures, the ointment, the hair, the weeping, the unparalleled intimacy at the tomb—a new character, despite exegetes, was created for Mary Magdalen. Deciphering what might be called "the Mary code" can illuminate the process by which the Christian memory and its texts took form. Perhaps, for example, the emphasis on Mary's lamenting character reflected the preoccupation, early and late, of female members of the Jesus movement.[63]

Out of the threads, that is, a rope was woven, a single narrative line defined, far more than the Gospels are, by an economy of character-in-action. Over time, this Mary went from being mainly an important disciple whose superior status depended on the confidence Jesus himself had invested in her, to being primarily a repentant whore whose status depended on the erotic charge of her history and the misery of her stricken conscience. In part this development arose out of a natural impulse to see the fragments of Scripture whole, to make a disjointed narrative adhere, with separate choices and consequences being tied to each other along that rope, in one drama. It is as if Aristotle's dramatic unities, given in the *Poetics,* were imposed, after the fact, on the foundational texts of Christianity.

Thus, for example, out of discrete episodes in the Gospel narratives, unauthorized readers would create a far more satisfying legend—because more unified—according to which Mary of Magdala was the unnamed woman being married at Cana, where Jesus turned water into wine. Her spouse, in this telling, was John, whom Jesus immediately recruited to be one of the Twelve. When John went off from Cana with the Lord, leaving his new wife behind, Mary collapsed in a fit of loneliness and jealousy, and began to sell herself to other men. She next appeared in the story as the by then notorious adulteress whom the Pharisees thrust before Jesus. When Jesus refused to condemn her, she saw the error of her ways. Afterward, she got her precious ointment, a tool of her trade, and spread it on his feet, weeping in sorrow. From then on, in chastity and devotion, she followed him, her love forever unconsummated—"Do not cling to me"—and more intense for being so.[64]

Such a woman lives on as Mary Magdalen in the religious imagination of Western Christianity (and the secular imagination of Western civilization), down, say, to the late-twentieth-century rock opera *Jesus Christ Superstar*, in which Mary Magdalen sings, "I don't know how to love him . . . He's just a man, and I've had so many men before . . . I want him so." The story has its timeless appeal, first, because that problem of "how"—whether love should be eros or agape, sensual or spiritual, a matter of longing or consummation—defines the human condition. What makes the conflict universal is the double experience of sex—the necessary means of reproduction and the ecstasy of passionate encounter. Can the spouse and the lover be one? In women, once the progression of generation begins, the maternal can seem to be at odds with the erotic, a tension that can be reduced in male desire to the well-known opposite fantasies of the madonna and the whore. I write as a man, yet it seems to me that the much-noted ambivalence of male attitudes toward women has its counterpart (if not equivalent) in female attitudes less toward men than toward femaleness itself. The divide between the erotic and the reproductive can represent a threat at worst, but even at best it poses a dilemma. The image of Mary Magdalen gives expression to such tensions, and draws power from them, especially when it is twinned with that of the other Mary, the greater one.

Christians may venerate the Blessed Virgin, but it is Magdalen with whom they identify. What makes her compelling is that she is not merely the whore against whom the mother of Jesus is madonna, but that Mary Magdalen combines both figures in herself. Pure by virtue of her repentance, she nevertheless remains a woman with a past. Her conversion, instead of removing her erotic allure, heightens it. She makes conversion seem romantic. The misery of self-accusation, known in one way or another to everyone, finds release in a figure whose abject penitence is the condition of recovery. That what she is sorry for—the willful life of a sex object—is inevitably of interest only makes her more attractive as what might be called a repentance object.

So the invention of the character of Mary Magdalen as repentant whore can be understood as having come about because of pressures inhering in the narrative form—Aristotle's unities—and in the urge to give expression to the inevitable tensions of sexual restlessness. But neither of these was the main factor in the conversion of Mary Magdalen's image, the woman who went from being a Jesus-empowered challenge to the misogynist assumptions of men to being a confirmation of those same assumptions. The main factor in that transformation was the defensive manipulation of her image by those very men, ultimately including the exegetes who had started out protecting her. The mutation took a long time to accomplish—fully the first six hundred years of the Christian era.

6. THE GOSPEL OF WOMEN

As we understood the evolution of the anti-Jewish element in Christianity by focusing on the chronology of its development, it helps to have a chronology in mind to understand the evolution of the place of women in the Jesus movement, with Mary as the key. Phase one (around the year 30) is the time of Jesus himself, and there is every reason to believe that, according to his teaching and in his circle, women were empowered as full equals. In phase two, when the norms and assumptions of the Jesus community are being written down, the ongoing equal status of women is reflected in the letters of St. Paul (c. 60), who names women as full partners—*his* partners—in the Christian project,[65] and in the Gospel accounts that give evidence of Jesus' own attitudes, and highlight the importance of women, whose courage and fidelity stand in marked contrast to the cowardly men.

But the Gospels themselves, emphasizing the authority of "the Twelve," who are all males, hint that by the time of their composition, two generations after Jesus (70–100), his unusual rejection of the dominant patriarchal modes of the prevailing culture (Jewish and Hellenistic alike) was being eroded within the Christian community. (The all-male character of the Twelve is used today by the Vatican to exclude women from ordination.[66]) The intra-Christian argument over the place of women in the community is implicit in the books of the New Testament, but it becomes explicit when we read other sacred texts of that early period—call it phase three (after the Gospels are written, but before the New Testament is defined as such). Not surprisingly, perhaps, the figure who most embodies the imaginative and theological conflict over the place of women in the Church, as it now calls itself, is Mary Magdalen.

I have been emphasizing the importance of understanding how the New Testament texts came to be composed. It is equally important to recall how those texts came to be selected as forming a sacred literature. The common assumption is that the Epistles of Paul, Peter, Jude, John, and James and the four Gospels, together with Acts and the Book of Revelation, were pretty much what the early-Christian community had by way of foundational writings. These texts, "inspired by the Holy Spirit," are regarded as having somehow been conveyed by God to the Church, and joined to the previously "inspired" and selected books of the Old Testament to form "the Bible." But the process by which the holy book of Christianity (and of Judaism, for that matter) was established was far more complicated (and human) than that.

The explosive spread of the Good News of Jesus around the Mediterranean world meant that distinct communities sprang up all over the place—Rome in Italy, Alexandria in Egypt, Corinth in Greece, Antioch in Syria, Lyons in France, Hippo in Algeria, Caesarea in Palestine, and so on. The geographic diversity was matched by a lively diversity of belief and practice, often identified with the memory of particular Apostles, whether they had actually been instrumental in establishing such communities or not. That diversity was reflected in the oral traditions and, later, in texts to which the dispersed communities had reference. The texts were sometimes attributed to the locally revered Apostles, so we find Gospels named for Peter, Thomas, and others. No one knows now how many such texts were created, but there were probably hundreds, and they were all regarded as holy. From these many dozens, a relatively few—twenty-seven—survived the winnowing down of canonization.

It was not until the end of the second century or the early third century that the list of canonized books we now know as the New Testament first began to surface in any kind of transregional consensus. As we saw, that selection of texts was not doctrinally defined until the Council of Carthage in 397. Those books were to be read *over against* the books soon to be designated, in a denigration, as the *Old* Testament. This amounted to a milestone on the road toward the Church's definition of itself in opposition to Jews. At the same time, and more subtly, the Church, in its power structure, was on the way to an understanding of itself against women. Recall that after Constantine, the Church was moving in conjunction with the recently Christianized Roman state toward a system of total political and religious control. With the emperor's support, Church authorities began to enforce both the orthodoxy of its doctrinally defined creed (after the Council of Nicea in 326) and the canonization of its sacred texts. The many dozens of rejected texts (and sometimes the people who prized them, also known as heretics) were destroyed.

In the mid- to late fourth century, just before the defining Council of Carthage, as we saw, the powerful bishop of Alexandria, Athanasius, affirmed the twenty-seven selected books and ordered the burning of all the others. The texts that were found in the late nineteenth and twentieth centuries in caves and buried jars from Turkey to Egypt, whether by shepherds, nomads, or archeologists, were presumably preserved and hidden by members of pressured Christian communities who regarded the suppression of, and threat to, their sacred books with horror.[67]

Such contention was partly a matter of theological dispute (If Jesus was divine, how? Who had authority over the faith?) but also of boundary-drawing against Judaism, paganism, and Christian sects deemed heretical, like Arians. But a philosophical inquiry inhered in all of this, as Christians, like their pagan contemporaries, sought to define the relationship between spirit and matter. Among Christians, the main code for that argument would soon be sexuality (within a generation of Athanasius came Augustine and his implication of the sex act in Original Sin). But the real battleground would be the existential tension between male and female.

When the sacred books were canonized, what texts were excluded, and why? This is the long way around, but we are back to our subject, because one of the most important Christian texts to be found outside the New Testament canon is the so-called Gospel of Mary, a telling of the Jesus-movement story that featured Mary Magdalen (decidedly not the woman of the alabaster jar) as one of the Church's most powerful leaders.

Having been lost in the early period, whether through outright suppression or mere neglect, the Gospel of Mary reappeared in the nineteenth century, one of those paradigm-shifting archeological finds referred to earlier. A well-preserved, if incomplete, fourth-century copy of a much earlier document, dating to about 150,[68] written on papyrus, mysteriously showed up for sale in Cairo in 1896. Other fragments of this text were found. Only slowly, through the twentieth century, did scholars appreciate what the rediscovered Gospel revealed, a process that culminated in the publication in 2003 of *The Gospel of Mary of Magdala: Jesus and the First Woman Apostle* by Karen L. King. It tells us a lot about what happened when "Mary's" text disappeared that it occurred when the real Mary Magdalen was beginning to disappear into the writhing misery of a penitent whore, which was happening in the time of the disappearance from the Church's inner circle of women themselves.

In sum, Jesus rejected patriarchy, as symbolized in his commissioning of Mary Magdalen. But gradually patriarchy made a powerful comeback within the Jesus movement. In order for that to happen, however, Jesus' own commissioning of Mary Magdalen had to be reinvented. One sees this very thing under way in the Gospel of Mary.

For example, Peter, whose preeminence is elsewhere taken for granted (in Mark[69] he is one of those who is dismissive of Mary's report of the Resurrection), is here seen deferring to her:

> Peter said to Mary, "Sister, we know that the Savior loved you more than all other women. Tell us the words of the Savior that you remember, the things which you know that we don't because we haven't heard them."
>
> Mary responded, "I will teach you about what is hidden from you." And she began to speak these words to them.[70]

Mary reports the content of her vision, a kind of esoteric description of the "ascent of the soul." The male disciples are disturbed—not by what she says, but by how she knows it. And now it is a jealous Peter who complains to his fellows, "Did [Jesus] choose her over us?" This draws a sharp rebuke from another apostle, Levi, who says, "If the Savior considered her to be worthy, who are you to disregard her?"[71]

That was the question, not only about Mary Magdalen but about women generally. It should be no surprise, given how successfully the excluding dominance of males established itself in the Church of the "fathers," that the Gospel of Mary was one of the texts shunted aside in the late second century. As that text shows, the early image of this Mary as a trusted apostle of Jesus, reflected even in the canonical Gospel texts, proved to be a major obstacle to establishing that dominance, which is why that image itself had to be reinvented as an icon of subservience.

Simultaneously, the "patristic" emphasis on sexuality as the root of all evil, typified by Augustine, served to do something similar to all women.[72] The ancient Roman world was rife with flesh-hating spiritualities (what we designate as Gnosticism, Manichaeism, neo-Platonism), and they influenced Christian thinking just as it was jelling into doctrine. Thus, the need to disempower the figure of Mary Magdalen (even when it was rediscovered, her Gospel would be dismissed by contemporary scholars as Gnostic[73]), so that her succeeding sisters in the Church would not compete with men for power, meshed with the impulse to discredit women generally. This was most efficiently done by reducing them to their sexuality, even as sexuality was reduced to the realm of temptation, the source of human unworthiness—"concupiscence." All of this—from the sexualizing of Mary Magdalen, to the virginizing of Mary the mother of Jesus, to the embrace of celibacy as a clerical ideal, to the marginalizing of female devotion, to the asceticizing of Christian piety, particularly through penitential cults—came to a kind of defining climax at the end of the sixth century. It was then that all the philosophical, theological, and ecclesiastical impulses curved back to Scripture, seeking an ultimate imprimatur for what by then was a firm cultural prejudice. At last the exegetes joined in, which was when the rails along which the Church—and the Western imagination—would run were laid down.

7. FAITH OF THE FATHERS

Pope Gregory I (540–604) had been born an aristocrat, the son of a senator, and had been himself the prefect of the city of Rome. After his father's death he had given everything away and turned his palatial Roman home into a monastery, where he had become a lowly monk. It was a time of plague, and the previous pope himself had died of it. When the saintly Gregory was elected to replace him, he at once emphasized penitential liturgies as a way of warding off the disease. His pontificate marked a solidifying of discipline and thought, a time of reform and invention both. But, as in the Thebes of Sophocles, it all occurred against the backdrop of the plague, a doom-laden circumstance in which the abjectly repentant Mary Magdalen, warding off the spiritual plague of damnation, could come into her own. With Gregory's help, she did.

Known as Gregory the Great, he was one of the most influential figures ever to serve as pope, and in a famous series of sermons on Mary Magdalen, given in Rome in about the year 591, he put the seal on what until then had been a common but unsanctioned reading of her story. With that, the conflicted image of the saint was set, as it were, in the stone of the statue we all know so well.[74]

It all went back to those Gospel texts. Cutting through the exegetical distinctions—the various Marys, the sinful women—that had up to then made a bald combining of the figures difficult to sustain, Gregory, standing on his own authority, offered his decoding of the relevant Gospel texts. The Mary code again. Gregory established the context within which its meaning was measured from then on: "She whom Luke calls the sinful woman, whom John calls Mary, we believe to be the Mary from whom seven devils were ejected according to Mark. And what did these seven devils signify, if not all the vices?"

There it was, the woman of the alabaster jar named by the pope as Mary of Magdala. He defined her:

> It is clear, brothers, that the woman previously used the unguent to perfume her flesh in forbidden acts. What she therefore displayed more scandalously, she was now offering to God in a more praiseworthy manner. She had coveted with earthly eyes, but now through penitence these are consumed with tears. She displayed her hair to set off her face, but now her hair dries her tears. She had spoken proud things with her mouth, but in kissing the Lord's feet, she now planted her mouth on the Redeemer's feet. For every delight, therefore, she had had in herself, she now immolated herself. She turned the mass of her crimes to virtues, in order to serve God entirely in penance.[75]

The address "brothers" is the clue. Through the Middle Ages and the Counter-Reformation, into the modern period and against the Enlightenment, monks and priests would read Gregory's words, and through those words as a distorting lens, they would read the Gospel texts themselves. Chivalrous knights, nuns establishing houses for unwed mothers, courtly lovers, desperate sinners, frustrated celibates, and an endless succession of preachers would treat Gregory's reading as the Gospel truth. Holy Writ, having recast what had actually taken place in the lifetime of Jesus, was itself recast.

The men of the Church who benefited from the recasting, forever spared the presence of females in their sanctuaries, would not know that this was what had happened. Having created a myth, they would not remember that it was mythical. Their Mary Magdalen was no fiction, no composite, no betrayal of a once revered woman. Rather, she was the only Mary Magdalen—not that mattered, but that existed.

This once-and-for-all obliteration of the textual distinctions of which we have already taken note was accomplished at the service of evoking an ideal of virtue that drew its heat from being a celibate's vision, conjured for celibates. Gregory the Great's overly particular interest in the fallen woman's past—what that oil had been used for, how that hair had been displayed, that mouth—brought into the center of Church piety (especially male piety) a vaguely prurient energy that would thrive under the licensing sponsorship of one of the Church's most revered reforming popes. Eventually, Magdalen, as a denuded object of Renaissance and Baroque painterly preoccupation, became a figure of nothing less than holy pornography, guaranteeing the ever-lustful harlot—if lustful now for the ecstasy of holiness—a permanent place in the Catholic imagination.

It was in this way that Mary of Magdala, who began as a powerful woman at the side of Jesus, "became," in the scholar Susan Haskins's summary, "the redeemed whore and Christianity's model of repentance, a manageable, controllable figure, and effective weapon and instrument of propaganda against her own sex."[76] There were reasons of narrative form for which this happened—those dramatic unities. There was a harnessing of sexual energy to this image. There was the humane appeal of a story that emphasized the possibility of forgiveness and redemption. But mostly, what drove the antisexual sexualizing of Mary Magdalen was the male need to dominate women. The canonized sacred texts reflect that need, as do the ways in which they have been read down through the centuries. That they are still being read by Catholic authorities—no women at the altar!—in a way that clearly violates the original will of Jesus shows the importance of the critical counterreading that what the Vatican called "new aids to exegesis" at last make possible.

From the Vulgate to the vulgar, from the Word of God to the words of humans, from the abuses of power to the retrievals of criticism, from Jews to women, from religious illiteracy to spiritual competence —all of this testifies to the importance of the Testaments. Reading the Bible can amount to the farthest thing from mere piety. It can be the ground of true revolution. The Church's big mistake, as events began to show, was to teach us this.

CHAPTER SIX

SEX AND POWER

1. UNNATURAL LAW

By the mid-1960s, the momentum of Catholic reform was running strong. Even what had been regarded as pillars of belief were shifting where they stood: the religion of Jews is no longer to be regarded as superseded by the Church, but has its own ongoing integrity; the texts of the New Testament are not to be read as fact-defined documentations of history, but as conditioned statements of faith; salvation is available to non-Catholics, non-Christians, even nonbelievers; the conscience of the individual has primacy over the authority of the hierarchy; sacred liturgy is the action not of the priest alone but of the whole community; the Church is not a "perfect society" in sole possession of the truth but a pilgrim people always in need of reform; women are equal to men. The dismantling of the battlements of the Counter-Reformation was fully under way, and the ground on which I would stand—do stand today—was being cleared.

To be a seminarian at this time was a thrilling experience. Our daily class work included taking in the astounding bulletins from Rome, as one council decree after another was openly debated and then published. In short order, our chapel Masses went from being stilted rites in Latin plainsong to rambunctious celebrations, complete with guitars and the music of Bob Dylan; our monastic isolation gave way to highly charged "encounters" with seminarians from Protestant, Jewish, and "ethical humanist" institutions; otherworldly detachment was replaced by fieldwork in inner-city parishes, which soon had us on civil rights picket lines. Our professors, centered on the faculty of the previously inhibited Catholic University of America, in northeast Washington, were infused with the new spirit of free inquiry. Formerly censored and censured scholars were all at once the darlings of Catholic thought—many of them, like John Courtney Murray and Karl Rahner, serving as experts at the Vatican Council itself. Theology and the religious life alike were set loose from their rigid moorings, and our delight as students was to sail with the wind, the fresh air that had blown into the Church when John XXIII had thrown open its windows.

I noted earlier that Pope John had been diagnosed with stomach cancer just as his council began. His illness had been kept quiet, but in April 1963 he had said, "That which happens to all men perhaps will happen soon to the Pope who speaks to you today." On June 3, to the distress of people around the world, he succumbed to the cancer. He was eighty-one years old and had served as pope for a mere four and a half years. Yet he had probably changed the Church more than any of his predecessors.

John XXIII was replaced in 1963 by Pope Paul VI, a very different figure. Giovanni Montini had been archbishop of Milan, and before that a protégé of Pius XII. Paul VI was an aristocrat where John had been a peasant, a man of the Church bureaucracy where John had been an outsider, a conservative by temperament where John had emerged as a bold innovator; nevertheless, Paul kept the council's groundbreaking energy moving forward. That a man of such differing character had done so showed how deeply into the soul of the Church the braces of reform had sunk.

But then, late in 1964, like a dark line appearing on the blue horizon, a message came from the pope's palace to the bishops gathered in St. Peter's. They were debating elements of the so-called Schema 13, which would eventually be published as *Gaudium et Spes*, "Pastoral Constitution on the Church in the Modern World." Deliberations were to include a section on married life and "responsible parenthood," and loaded questions had already been put on the table. One cardinal had asked in the open session if the injunction in Genesis to "increase and multiply" had been emphasized by the Church to the detriment of the Genesis mandate that "they will be two in one flesh." The traditional Catholic prohibition of "unnatural" contraception had rested on assumptions about "nature," but council discussion had entertained the possibility that static notions of nature should be nuanced by evolutionary philosophy, the idea that change is built into the nature of things. Bishops, too, had noticed how the intellectual ground was shifting under ethical theory.

But suddenly the pope's unforeseen "intervention" ordered the council not to take up the question of artificial contraception. Schema 13 and, ultimately, *Gaudium et Spes* were not to touch on the subject, and the fathers were no longer to discuss it. Any teaching on birth control, thus "removed from the competence of the Council," would be handled by the pope alone. Even abstracting from the potentially controversial character of the birth control question, and the ominous signal that it was somehow beyond debate, this intervention was a rank violation of the principle of collegiality—the bishops sharing in authority with the pope—that had guided the council from the start.

The conservative minority of the fathers welcomed this abrupt manifestation of papal power, but most bishops were deeply unsettled by it, and Catholics around the world took note of what happened next. Here was the moment for which open press coverage of the council's proceedings had prepared: the bishops themselves could be seen responding to an authoritarian mandate by debate rather than by instant submission. The bishops, that is, spontaneously demonstrated a new model (new in the modern era) of Catholic behavior. Of all the revolutionary initiatives taken by the council, none was more transformative than this reaction by the bishops to the pope, especially since it was not deliberative, but visceral.

In response to the papal order, episcopal protests were openly lodged in the nave of the great basilica. These mitered men knew better than anyone what was at stake, both in the pope's violation of the implicit contract of coresponsibility and in the now proscribed issue itself. Significantly, the sharpest challenge to Paul VI came from one of the four moderators, or chairmen, of the council and one of the most respected prelates in the Church, Cardinal Léon-Joseph Suenens of Belgium. He responded to the pope's unilateral removal of birth control from the agenda by rising immediately with a warning: "I beg you, my brother bishops, let us avoid a new 'Galileo affair.' One is enough for the Church."[1]

It was a prescient statement. The Galileo affair, as we saw, had raised the foundational question of whether the earth "moves," a powerful symbol of whether the Church could adjust imaginative structures of the mind to include the developmental, historical, and therefore relative character of all human knowing. Birth control raised equally large questions. Folk remedies and primitive methods (coitus interruptus) had long been associated with the human wish to avoid conception, but true contraception was a technique of modernity. (The first sheep's gut condom had been invented in Galileo's time; the reliable latex rubber condom and the latex diaphragm were not invented until the 1920s, after refined vulcanization had multiplied the uses of rubber.)[2]

Beyond questions of technique, contraception was made a pressing question in the twentieth century. More was at stake than the preferences of coupling individuals. Their preferences, in fact, arose from conditions of which individuals could be only vaguely aware. A dramatic change in human population requirements resulted from shifts from agrarian to industrial economies, which made large families more a burden on wealth and well-being than a producer of them. Concomitant improvements in nutrition, health care, and life expectancy removed the need for multiple pregnancies from the age-old project of bringing a single healthy child to adulthood. Such social change inevitably sparked change in the roles of men and women. (The so-called first stage of feminism in the early twentieth century focused on women's suffrage, but also, with Margaret Sanger, on free access to birth control.[3]) Ultimately, demographics would undergird technological and social revolutions in everything from methods of reproduction to the very meaning of sexuality.

The Galileo dispute had involved the Church's attempt, however conditioned by traumas tied to the Reformation and new discoveries in science, to defend its method of reading Scripture. Any contemplated change in the Church's teaching on birth control, by contrast, raised issues of previous papal teaching, but did not involve the Bible. To take another example, the Church's rejection of divorce and remarriage was rooted in Jesus' own affirmation of the indissolubility of marriage, but again, the prohibition against birth control had no such provenance. Yet given what had been claimed since the nineteenth century (recall that papal infallibility had been decreed only in 1870; the pope had been absolutizing his internal Church authority ever since), the challenge to authority was taken to be just as grave. And, in a way, it was.

A contraception-condemning encyclical issued by Pope Pius XI in

1930, *Casti Connubii,* was his successors' big problem. Without ambiguity, the 1930 teaching had tied sexual intercourse to a "primary aim," the generation of new life. Violating its own logic, the encyclical had also allowed "natural reasons of time," taken to be the infertile period in the female menstrual cycle, to be used to avoid conception.[4] Pope Pius XII reiterated *Casti Connubii* in the early 1950s.

Paul VI, and those whose advice he depended on, apparently took this declaration as definitive, but it was difficult to see it as belonging to the "deposit of faith," to unbroken Tradition, since the question of artificial contraception as a practical matter (involving more than sheep's gut or primitive rubber) was less than a century old. Yet the pope's defenders, perhaps hoping to dig a moat around his authority, dug just a hole. Their claim that the prohibition of birth control was the Church's "constant teaching" was, on the face of it, absurd, since there was no constant teaching on a subject that had become relevant only in modern times. Alas, that was not how several generations of Catholic men and women (including my parents, who had five sons and more pregnancies) had been instructed. An eternal claim had been made against the condom, even though the condom, in anything approaching reliability, was new.

The issue, in other words, was not birth control but papal authority, and even there the teaching was not "constant," but modern. Ongoing Catholic defensiveness in relation to Protestantism was part of the story, too. The year of *Casti Connubii,* 1930, was also the year that the Lambeth Conference, the worldwide Anglican governing body meeting at Lambeth Palace in London, passed a resolution *in favor* of birth control. Acting sooner or later (the Lutherans, for example, only in the 1950s), Protestant denominations followed suit, leaving the Catholic Church alone in its opposition. Could the Protestants have been right?

Impossible. Birth control became a point of institutional loyalty, like devotion to the Blessed Virgin Mary. Indeed, St. Mary's lifelong sexual abstinence, like her husband's supernaturally patient chastity, took on new gravitas as a point of Catholic identification. The pope's real problem lay in the fact that, on his predecessors' decree, the faithful had been threatened with hell over using birth control, and, as higher Catholic birthrates in Europe and the United States showed, they had obeyed.

The Vatican's agenda, ever since the pope's temporal authority had been stripped from him by nationalist forces in Italy, had been to extend the pontiff's spiritual authority—his control, that is, over the interior lives of the faithful. Whether pursued consciously or not, the dynamic, when applied to sex, was ingenious, as Catholic couples found themselves with a third party in bed with them—not the Holy Spirit but the pope. What the condemnation of modernism had done to corral the Catholic clergy, the condemnation of birth control had done to rein in the Catholic laity. Because such anathemas were attached to this teaching, the idea of changing it would call into question the very premise of Catholic hierarchical authority—authority that extended to the life hereafter. If birth control were all at once to be permitted, what about those for whom it had involved grave sin, and who had already been damned?

The pope's resistance to liberal expectations of change in the teaching on birth control, in other words, was entirely predictable. Yet when that resistance was mounted by Paul VI, with his intervention raised as a bulwark against the winds of change, we seminarians—unlike our contemporaries at Berkeley, say, or those on Freedom Rides in the South—were not the ones to fight back. Perhaps, as young celibates, or as clergy in training who were not yet actually counseling married couples, birth control was too abstract for us. Perhaps we were too freshly vowed to obedience to resist. Whatever the reason, we young Catholics were mere witnesses to it when the council fathers—the Church's very hierarchy—at first refused to bow. A few months after removing birth control from the council's "competence," the increasingly anxious Paul VI instructed the bishops, in 1965, to reaffirm *Casti Connubii* in their upcoming declaration *Gaudium et Spes.* He seemed to have realized that to ignore Pius XI's encyclical would undercut its authority almost as much as contradicting it. Nevertheless, numerous bishops openly argued against any mention of *Casti Connubii.* In a liberal-conservative compromise, yielding to the letter of the pope's mandate yet effectively mocking it, *Gaudium et Spes,* as finally voted, did refer to the 1930 encyclical, but only in an obscure footnote.[5]

2. PERSONALLY OPPOSED

At that time, 1965, Catholics in the United States were given an unexpected example of how to regard—or disregard—the Church's authority on the question of birth control. In Massachusetts, legislators were considering a proposed law that would repeal the commonwealth's ban on contraceptives. (It was only in that year that the Supreme Court struck down a Connecticut law forbidding the sale of contraceptives, establishing the privacy rights of couples, and of patients with their doctors.[6]) The Roman Catholic Church could be expected to oppose any such repeal, but that is not what happened, and once more the figure manifesting a new Catholicism was Cardinal Richard Cushing.

Such was the political power of the Church in Massachusetts that a word of opposition from the archbishop of Boston on almost any proposal would have ensured its defeat on Beacon Hill. We saw this earlier—how in 1948 Cushing had rallied Catholics in parade. "Human life was never held in greater contempt than it is now," Cushing said then, and went on to condemn "the birth-controllers." The bill was soundly defeated.

But in 1965, as legislators considered the question again, Cushing struck a very different note. He told a radio interviewer that, as a Catholic, he was convinced that artificial birth control was immoral, but then he went on: "I am also convinced that I should not impose my position upon those of other faiths." Cushing was here drawing on advice he had just received from Father John Courtney Murray, who was riding high as the main author of *Dignitatis Humanae*, the decree on religious liberty that would soon be promulgated by the Vatican Council.[7] Following Murray, Cushing's advice to Catholic legislators was explicit: "If your constituents want this legislation, vote for it. You represent them. You don't represent the Catholic Church." The contraception ban was repealed.[8]

Equally significant for future political debates on moral questions, especially abortion, Catholic politicians had their "personally opposed but publicly positive" rationale for votes in favor of policies known to be condemned by the Catholic hierarchy. And they had it originally from this man of the hierarchy himself. Conservative critics have denounced this rationale as morally incoherent, and they are correct. It also smacks of dishonesty. When someone, whether archbishop or politician, says "I personally oppose but publicly enable," it is reasonable to ask if the opposition is genuine.

The question becomes pointed in relation to abortion. If abortion is in every case murder, as the Catholic Church teaches, then how can any Catholic who affirms the Church's position acquiesce in any way to abortion? Such a Catholic can't. Catholics who claim to be privately convinced of Church teaching on the question while voting to make abortions possible are not credible. If they thought abortion was murder, they would not support abortion rights. The truth is, they do not believe what their Church teaches.

And that was the lesson we took from Cushing about birth control. We understood that a cardinal of the Church could not openly defy the pope by contradicting him on the matter, but we also understood that behind his rhetoric about not imposing Catholic morality on others was an essential rejection of that morality. Cushing, and the politicians who follow his lead to this day,[9] may not have penetrated to the full truth of what his position meant, but it *was* Galileo again: the public act of saying something he did not believe.

Paul VI's panic about what the council fathers were up to was made still more manifest when, in October 1965, he intervened for the second time, to forbid any discussion of priestly celibacy. "It is not opportune to debate publicly this topic which requires the greatest prudence, and is so important."[10]

What birth control was to the laity, celibacy was to priests and nuns. A discipline of the Latin Church officially dating to the twelfth century (the Second Lateran Council, 1139), celibacy had been imposed on priests mainly for the most worldly of reasons: to correct abuses tied to family inheritance of Church property. In the world of lords and vassals, property was power, and the Church's power was continually undermined by the claimant heirs of abbots and bishops. Celibacy solved that material problem, but because of the extreme sacrifice it required, it could never be spoken of in material terms. So it was that sexual abstinence came to be justified spiritually, as a mode of drawing close to God.

Soon celibacy emerged as its own source of power—the hierarchy's power over the interior lives of its clergy. The way to maintain control over subjects is to force compliance at this, the deepest level of personality. There were ancient habits of Catholic repugnance toward sexuality, most notably articulated by St. Augustine, whose neo-Platonism, as we saw, led him to disdain physical experience generally. And what was more physical than the erotic urge? French and Irish Jansenism[11] completed the work of the early Manichaeans, snapping a lock on the sexual imaginations of Catholics, especially in northern Europe and the United States.

Yet as the birth control and clerical celibacy debates surfaced in the Church, the cutting issue was not sex but power. Or rather, by making the issue sex, and requiring absolute subservience in matters sexual, power was being exercised absolutely.

3. CELIBACY AS CONTROL

As men en route to lifelong vows of sexual abstinence, we seminarians took note of this removal from the council's competence of the question we ourselves had only begun to imagine might be reconsidered. I was twenty-two years old. I had been a typical American boy, with girlfriends and a roving eye, always alert to breasts beneath sweaters, waistlines in summer dresses, the turn of ankles, the flash of tongues. Sex in the pre-1960s culture was both denied and exploited, with television, for example, combining prudishness (even married couples in twin beds) and titillation (every woman in a push-up bra). In prime time every week, Americans were treated to the outlandish behavior of the pianist Liberace without ever having to openly confront his flamboyant homosexuality. On Tuesdays, Milton Berle began every show as a transvestite, and no one thought it odd. We were a people in the grip of sex-obsessive denial.

The trick for a confused lad like me had been to play off sexual restlessness against puritanical repression through high school and into college, and I had more or less managed. The vivid nearness of hell—infinite anguish experienced with infinite sensitivity—had stamped my early adolescence, although that particular fear had faded. The evisceration of Catholic dread of eternal damnation had been one of the Vatican Council's most immediate and transforming consequences, a precondition of the other liberations that followed. Still, sex remained the measure of guilt. Entering the seminary had marked the start of a ruthless new self-discipline, and repression had taken the upper hand, even as I learned, in a first brush with Freud, to call it sublimation.

Across Fourth Street from the Paulist seminary was Trinity College, a Catholic women's college run by a high-class order of nuns, the Sisters of Notre Dame. The priests on our faculty took turns going to Trinity to celebrate early morning Mass for a large student congregation in the striking Byzantine chapel, with its soaring arches, mosaic icons, and marble Communion rail. Seminarians could volunteer for the role of altar boy at Trinity, and I signed up as often as I could, knowing exactly why. My chaste version of cheap thrills was to hold the gold paten under the chins of those pious coeds as they tilted their mouths up, eyes closed, tongues out to receive the consecrated wafer (one of them was a girl named Nancy D'Alesandro, known later as Nancy Pelosi). The hollows of throats, the sparkle of saliva, the occasional glimpse of merely hinted at cleavage—*Body of Christ. Body of Christ. Christ, what a body!*

Only years later would I realize what an impoverishment it was to have my relations with women reduced to the realm of puerile fantasy. My objects of desire were not real people but figments. There is nothing like the male renunciation of sex to reduce all females to sex objects. And, of course, in a sex-obsessed culture, such male renunciation is itself a kind of come-on, an almost explicit invitation to take the sexual measure of the one presenting himself as celibate, which in turn becomes a further source of titillation for all concerned. I was not above imagining those Trinity girls imagining *me.* I was quite aware of my *imagined* physical appeal. Not only the girls were fantasies; I became a fantasy to myself. Serving Mass at Trinity College—strutting about the sanctuary with my hands held just so, the part in my hair sharp enough to focus a camera on, the studied grace of my genuflections, the swish of my robes, the strict custody of my eyes—was such a construction of vanity as to be, in the argot, its own "occasion of sin," if forever unrecognized as such.

Having left my college friends behind, I no longer knew any real people who were women. Since I had so little idea—an early-sixties college boy's idea—of what sexual intimacy actually involved, what could it mean when I imagined my life without it? Even as I did that, I so idealized sexual intimacy that, in my dream of it, the fulfilled ecstasy I would never know became a kind of absolute. What I was instructed to regard as the spiritualizing effect of celibacy was, in fact, infantilizing. Yet apart from panicked moments in the middle of the night, I more or less convinced myself that it was possible to live that way. This sacrifice seemed the precondition of the growing sense I had of God's nearness, and that made it right. I had not made a final commitment, yet expected I would, and celibacy was a given. Oddly, I had not imagined that the Church might change its requirement, permitting priests to marry, until Pope Paul VI said the question must not be discussed. At that, I remember thinking, *Holy cow—celibacy is on the table, too.*

The council fathers submitted to this mandate without complaint, which was, of course, its point. Again, mandates about sex were really about power. But even so, the command called to mind the thing that was not to be brought to mind. *Right, Your Holiness, celibacy will never change.* I, for one, and for the first time, found myself repeating what I would come to think of as that Galileo moment. Right. No change. No movement. *But it moves.*

What is striking in hindsight is how subservient Catholic clergy were on the question that involved their own sex lives while becoming increasingly, even stridently, rebellious on the question of the sex lives of lay men and women—birth control. The pope's removal of celibacy from the council's agenda was a clear signal that there would be no change in the birth control teaching simply because there was no way the Church could ease up on the sexual demand it imposed on clergy while refusing to ease up on the demand imposed on laypeople. The Church's discipline on celibacy was inextricably tied to its teaching on birth control, and the two linked issues amounted to one strong message coming from the Vatican: *it does not move.*

4. WOMEN'S LIBERATION

Why, then, had so many Catholics, apparently including Cardinal Cushing on one side and defensive Vatican figures on the other, come to regard the building pressures for change in the Church's teaching as almost irresistible? Two things had happened in the early 1960s to make that so. The first was the dramatic launching of what has been dubbed "second-stage feminism," symbolized by the 1963 publication of Betty Friedan's *The Feminine Mystique.* That book was a cultural milestone because women from every corner of the United States recognized it as speaking out of their own situation—conditions of profound dissatisfaction.

The loosening of gender roles that had marked World War II, with millions of women recruited by the war emergency into the workforce, had been swiftly reversed. The suburbanization of America amounted to a massive, if often genteel, incarceration of women. Homemaking and housework were the brackets within which female creativity was expected to be expressed. Legions of mothers and wives dutifully spent their lives making peanut-butter-and-jelly sandwiches for children and fish-stick dinners for their husbands. They were chauffeurs and floor polishers. They were den mothers and bosses' wives. They wore white gloves, hair that did not move, and smiles that masked, in Friedan's phrase, the "problem that had no name." When I read the descriptions of frustration, depression, and loneliness that Friedan insisted were the lot of even privileged American women, I thought of my mother, and for the first time understood her periodic outbursts of anger, her splitting headaches, her vacant looks when she thought she was alone.

In the same year, 1963, the presidentially appointed Commission on the Status of Women issued a report that denounced the second-class status of women in the United States. The vibrant civil rights movement was a ready-made model, and three years later the National Organization for Women was established, a self-conscious emulation of the advocacy groups that were already leading the racial revolution. Gender, too, could be a question of justice.

Lest such feminist manifestoes be dismissed as the rants of the unchurched, Pope John XXIII's encyclical *Pacem in Terris,* also of 1963, lifted up the women's movement as one of three positive "signs of the times"—an approbation as extraordinary as it was unexpected. The pope praised women for demanding "rights befitting a human person both in domestic and public life."[12] Pope John did not mention birth control, but it could not be separated from second-stage feminism, and it was clearly on his mind. Around the time of *Pacem in Terris,* he appointed a commission to take up the question, especially in the context of world population. The Papal Commission on Population, the Family, and Natality consisted of six people, three of whom were laypeople. Why would the pope appoint such a body if change in Church teaching was out of the question?

Change in the meaning of birth control was occurring whether anyone wanted it or not—the second precondition of raised expectations among Catholics of a coming doctrinal adjustment. In 1960, the U.S. Food and Drug Administration approved a new form of contraception, "the pill." Developed by a Harvard obstetrician and gynecologist named John Rock, this oral contraceptive affected hormones present in the woman's body in such a way as to convince the brain that she was already pregnant, which resulted in the shutting down of ovulation. As long as the woman took the pill as prescribed, she would not conceive. Because this method was simpler and much more reliable than other methods, it quickly became the most widespread form of birth control. Women had never had such control over their reproductive lives.

Dr. Rock became a national figure; his picture was on the cover of *Newsweek.* Much was made of the fact that he was a devoted Catholic, attending Mass and receiving Communion every day. As a doctor based in Boston, he was a friend of Cardinal Cushing's. There can be no doubt that Rock contributed to Cushing's own evolution on the question. When Rome denounced Rock, Cushing said to him, "My God, Johnny, you've got the whole Vatican pregnant."[13] But Rock was outspoken in insisting that the pill, making use of the female body's own natural characteristics, was not in violation of the Church's condemnation of artificial contraception.

In 1963, which in this narrative emerges as a watershed year, Rock published *The Time Has Come: A Catholic Doctor's Proposals to End the Battle over Birth Control.* Rock thought his invention offered the Church a way out of its self-created dead end because, since 1957, the pill had been expressly allowed by Church authorities as a way to "regularize" an erratic menstrual cycle, for the sake of a more reliable use of the doctrinally permitted "rhythm method" of avoiding conception. Use of the pill, that is, was already approved by the Church.

Expectations tied to the pill, and the more open climate of the time, were precisely what prompted Pope Paul VI, in 1964, to withdraw contraception from the competence of the council, a signal of his strong disinclination to change the teaching. But he was still saddled with the Population, Family, and Natality Commission that John XXIII had appointed. Pope Paul moved to neutralize this half-lay body by expanding its membership from six to, eventually, seventy-two. The larger group was dominated by priests and theologians, and its power shifted to a new executive committee consisting of nine bishops and seven cardinals. There were only five women members in total, and they were chosen more for their Catholic devotedness than any competence. The commission would report in strict secrecy only to the pope. Its new president was the archconservative Cardinal Ottaviani, whom we saw earlier trying to thwart the move away from Latin. (And hadn't events shown him to have been right, that rebellion having led to all the others?) From Ottaviani's group no change could reasonably be expected to come.

The commission submitted its report to the pope in 1966, in secret. But the following year, an upstart Catholic weekly based in Kansas City, Missouri, the *National Catholic Reporter,* dropped a bombshell by publishing the commission's findings.[14] To the amazement of Catholics and the rest of the world, given the commission's makeup, its report went beyond the opening Dr. Rock had offered, declaring that there was nothing "intrinsically evil" about artificial methods of contraception. The papal commission was clear in its firm recommendation: the decision of whether to use birth control, and what kind, should be left to married couples. The Catholic prohibition should simply be lifted.

To be sure, the commission included members who rejected this majority conclusion, and though there was no official minority report, their dissent was duly noted. Of the seventy-two members, six were in opposition, and they included two bishops and one cardinal—Ottaviani. Once again, he had been swept aside, even by his own kind. The call for reform of the defining Catholic doctrine of the modern era had come from within the Church's own establishment. If this was not a sign of the Holy Spirit alive in the Church, then Bob Dylan was not our troubadour. "The times they are a changin'," we sang in the chapel.

5. 1968: HOWL

Nineteen sixty-eight was the year of student unrest in Europe and racial rebellion in America, the year the peace movement entered mainstream politics, the year of assassinations. Not a week went by, it seemed, without some public event shaking assumptions, and in an intensely personal way 1968 remains the defining year of my life.

Most momentously for me, the Vietnam War was destroying my relationship with my father. As the director of the Defense Intelligence Agency, he was responsible for tracking the progress of the war. The Tet Offensive of January 1968, when North Vietnamese and Vietcong fighters overwhelmed American and South Vietnamese forces throughout the country, if only for a time, showed that any vaunted "progress" against the Communists was an illusion. My father's failure, like the Pentagon's, was on display. That year broke him—and it broke our bond. Americans realized that there would be no victory in

Vietnam. In abject personal defeat—and in an act of authentic moral reckoning—Lyndon Johnson declined to run for reelection. He was an American Oedipus, mutilating his destiny in recognition of the plague he had caused.

Such grim events, of which we will see more in the next chapter, were only half the story. By the start of 1968, I had come firmly and contentedly into what I thought of as religious maturity. It was my last year of seminary. In June, I would be ordained to the diaconate, swearing a lifelong vow of celibacy. At the end of the year, I would be ordained to the priesthood. I had mostly resolved my inbred ambivalence about these steps. Indeed, my sense of vocation had only sharpened. The inventions of the Vatican Council had reinvented me as a believer, and I foresaw a ministry of enabling other Catholics to experience a like awakening to the acute relevance of the faith.

In the seminary's music room, the one homey space in an otherwise impersonal building, we Paulist members of the self-styled "new breed" could sit for hours and debate fine points of theology as if they carried all the weight of the future. In the background Miles Davis and Gerry Mulligan records subtly offered instruction in how to move freely within boundaries, or how to cross them, as the passionate improvisation of ideas taught us the free play of the mind, a Catholic skill that had been lost in the Counter-Reformation. In the endless seminar that was the seminary, I had a first experience of intellectual intimacy, the bond that brings the mind into lively communion with other minds. I also discovered that disagreement can be the source of new awareness—the precondition of it. I had learned to learn.

Central to that was my having claimed an unexpected identity as a reader, having found that books (Pierre Teilhard de Chardin, Albert Camus, Nikos Kazantzakis, Paul Tillich, T. S. Eliot, Herman Melville, Hannah Arendt, John Updike) can change everything. As the Vatican Council debated what would eventually be published as *Dignitatis Humanae,* the declaration on religious liberty that finally gave a Catholic affirmation of conscience, I learned more about conscience from reading, say, *The Adventures of Huckleberry Finn* than the *Summa Theologiae.* Like all schoolboys, I thought I knew Mark Twain, but his genius opened to me in the context of my search for the meaning of faith. Twain reversed it. Huck's decision to accept everlasting fire—"All right, then! I'll go to hell!"—for breaking the law to help a slave escape was my first real lesson in the potential heroism of disobedience.[15] In America, disobedience could seem a virtue, and I was learning that its Scripture was literature.

The thesis I wrote for my master's in theology, obtained in 1968, compared the theological implications of the Word (St. Augustine) with the poetics of mere words (Samuel Taylor Coleridge)—a foray into literature as a mode of revelation. The aesthetic imagination, Coleridge said, is the repetition in human beings of the creative "I AM" of God, a notion that undergirded my nascent impulse to link the vocations of priest and poet. But more, a sense of the "I AM" of God infusing all that exists—"I AM WHO CAUSES ALL THAT IS TO BE"[16]—was a first hint of a coming transformation, and literature was my clue. I studied writing, I wrote, and I began going everywhere with a pencil poised for a poem of my own. The Jesuit writer Daniel Berrigan, designated heir to Gerard Manley Hopkins and self-described protégé of Thomas Merton, became my personal ideal.[17]

Merton, as already noted, was our steady resource. In his *The Waters of Siloe,* I had found that first articulation of my question: "What is the use of living for things that you cannot hold on to . . . a peace that is constantly turning into war?" His *Seeds of Contemplation* had taught us piety as novices, but later, his *Conjectures of a Guilty Bystander* taught us protest. How could we ignore it when, in his own quest, Merton moved on from the fathers of the Church to the Beats and to Zen Buddhists? Because the Trappist monk did so, we studied wildly irreverent writers like Lawrence Ferlinghetti and Jack Kerouac, both of whom had Catholic roots. The Catholic imagination itself—from Dante and Michelangelo to Walker Percy and Flannery O'Connor—turned out to be far more expansive than we had thought. Once we actually encountered it, Catholicism's rambunctious aesthetic tradition rescued us from the narrowness of the Vatican-imposed repressiveness of the antimodern era. Repressiveness, that is, was not the only legacy we could claim. Merton, more than anyone, gave us the permission we needed to make the outrageous assertion that our rebellion was rooted in a deeper obedience. Merton, it would turn out, was no more immune to the anarchic consequences of such an assertion than we were, but we could not know that yet.

My reading as a seminarian did more than alter the content of my imagination. It changed the very way my imagination worked, especially in relation to "the God question." God was wholly other, no?

God was distant and unavailable. A voguish debate of the mid-1960s asserted that God was dead. That was a facile discussion, much noted in the popular press, but I knew exactly what problem had prompted it. The dichotomy between profane and sacred had long defined the limits within which I understood everything. There were the things that pass away and, as I had put it to my father in announcing my vocation, the things that last. There was nature and there was the supernatural. There was flesh and there was spirit. There was body and there was soul. There was time and there was eternity. There was the world and there was the Church. My purpose on earth (and surely in the seminary) was simply to align myself with the right side of the great existential divide. There was sin and there was holiness. But then, to cite only the most dramatic example of my awakening, I read "Howl" by Allen Ginsberg.

Howl and Other Poems had been printed in England (commissioned by Ferlinghetti's City Lights Books in San Francisco) in 1956, but the U.S. government had tried to block its entry into America because Ginsberg's work was regarded as obscene. The extended litigation made the book notorious, and by the mid-1960s it was a symbol of liberation and rebellion. Thomas Merton, from his Trappist sinecure, was one of Ginsberg's staunch defenders, which made the Beat poet must reading for us.[18] Who could resist the opening line of "Howl": "I saw the best minds of my generation destroyed by madness, starving hysterical naked"? Ginsberg was a self-described Buddhist-Jew, but his work struck an unexpected spiritual chord in me. The poem's profanity was mainly a matter of over-the-top sexual references, some of which pierced my naïveté: "who howled on their knees in the subway and were dragged off the roof waving genitals and manuscripts, / who let themselves be fucked in the ass by saintly motorcyclists, and screamed with joy, / who blew and were blown by those human seraphim, the sailors . . ." In truth, I didn't know what being fucked in the ass was, and had only a vague notion of what it was to be blown. Eventually I would understand more fully what explosive and destructive forces can be unleashed in the name of erotic liberation, and I would have to face the clerical version of such a tragic outcome. Sex is about love, yes, but also about narcissism, power, possession, and dominance—madness. But that knowledge would come later.

Despite the court case's notoriety, I experienced "Howl" at the time as having little to do with sex and everything to do with the mostly unaddressed anguish that underlay the nuclear age—anguish to which I was exquisitely attuned ("who disappeared into the volcanoes of Mexico leaving behind nothing but the shadow of dungarees and the lava and ash of poetry scattered in fireplace Chicago"). It did not take me many readings of "Howl" to feel not only addressed but spoken for.

The poem uses the word "who" as a constant point of punctuation; like the line just cited, dozens of others begin with it. As the poem strikes the ear, "who" becomes the sound of the "howl," a voice hurling itself against the age. But then, in the climactic transformation that devastated me when I finally got it, the "howl" of the poem becomes, in its last stanzas, the word "holy." The ancient Hebrew refrain, which, as the *Sanctus, sanctus, sanctus,* is the anchor of the Mass, landed in Ginsberg's poem as the anchor of its affirmation. "Holy! Holy! Holy!" is what the people cried out as Jesus made his way into Jerusalem. "Holy! Holy! Holy! Lord God of Hosts. Heaven and Earth are full of your glory! Blessed is He who comes in the name of the Lord! Hosanna in the Highest."

In *King Lear,* the word "howl" is hurled *against* heaven, but not here. The most pointed stage direction in all of Shakespeare reads, "Enter Lear, with Cordelia in his arms."[19] And then the old king pronounces the great lament: "Howl! Howl! Howl! Howl! O, you are men of stones: Had I your tongues and eyes, I'd use them so heaven's vault should crack. She's gone forever." But for Ginsberg, the vault of heaven was already cracked, and all that makes for howling was its revelation. Even death. After reading the poem, I heard something new in the liturgical refrain: "heaven *and* earth," not heaven *against* earth. Earth, too, is full of God's glory. Holy! Holy! Holy!

The first line of the section of the poem called "Footnote to Howl" simply repeats the word "holy" fifteen times. And then one reads, "The world is holy! The soul is holy! The skin is holy! The nose is holy! The tongue and cock and hand and asshole holy! / Everything is holy! Everybody's holy! Everywhere is holy! Everyday is in eternity! Everyman's an angel!"

There it was—a life-changing moment in which the dichotomy between sacred and profane was obliterated, the gulf between God and human beings. "Beat," Jack Kerouac said, means "beatific."[20] I vividly remember sitting in the crooked root of a tree on a ledge over Lake George, New York, the Paulist retreat where we seminarians rendezvoused in summers, looking up from Ginsberg's pages and getting it. *Getting it!* All that exists exults in the cry "I AM!" And in that cry, the "I AM God" is present. As present in the things of the world as in any heaven. As present in sexual desire as in holy renunciation. As present in cocks and balls as in the bread and wine. *This* is what it meant that, at the end of each day of creation, God looked at what he had done and said, "This is good," until finally saying, "This is very good." If Genesis then recounts a story of the Fall, it was not a story of a sudden vast distance between Creator and creation, but only the story of the abrupt—and mistaken—human perception of that distance. Jesus did not come to bridge the infinite gulf between God and humankind, I understood at once, but only to show us that no such gulf exists.

"The typewriter is holy the poem is holy the voice is holy the hearers are holy the ecstasy is holy . . . Holy my mother in the insane asylum! Holy the cocks of the grandfathers of Kansas!"[21] Here was the answer to my own Irish forebears' conviction that they were unworthy. *Domine, non sum dignus!* The answer to my own unworthiness. All wrong. "Holy forgiveness! mercy! faith! Holy! Ours! bodies! suffering! magnanimity! / Holy the supernatural extra brilliant intelligent kindness of the soul!" Worthiness, not fallenness, defined the human condition.

The obliteration of the gulf between God and humans was the central affirmation of a new religiousness that had caught the public imagination in the mid-sixties. The movement sounded the death knell of the idea that access to God depended exclusively on religious institutions. This was the end of "No salvation outside the Church," and more: "No salvation outside religion." Religion was not about salvation but about revelation—revelation that we are all already saved. Religion is not necessary; God loves us not because we "do" or because we believe, but because we are. Not faith, not works—simply *being*.

"Religionless Christianity" is a phrase of the anti-Nazi martyr Dietrich Bonhoeffer, and it was widely appropriated now. Bonhoeffer's call, issued from a Nazi prison not long before he was hanged, was for a religion freed of metaphysical supernaturalism and institutional corruption. The "Secular City" theologians advanced the idea that God is as present to mundane experience as to sacred.[22] The misunderstood, but effective, code for all of this was "God is dead." It was not God who died in the 1960s, but the deity so small as to be held in check by a church. And what a magnificent Church—ours!—that was prepared to announce this.

What I did not appreciate at the time was the way in which the 1960s spiritual revival, which was simultaneously anti-institutional and instinctively sacramental, finding everyday experience itself as a path to God, was a twentieth-century echo of the transcendental revival that had first inspired Isaac Hecker, founder of the Paulists. His Thomas Merton was George Ripley at Brook Farm, and his Allen Ginsberg was Ralph Waldo Emerson.[23] The Paulists were both a monument to Hecker's spiritual quest and a mode of continuing it. In taking the latest American manifestation of religious hunger as a countercurrent to the satiated triumphalism of European Catholicism, we Paulists were only being true to our tradition. "Happiness," Erasmus had taught me, "is the wish to be what you are." As the year of my ordination began, I was on fire with the desire to preach what I had learned, to be who I had become. And I finally understood why they call it Good News.

6. CATHOLIC RADICAL

Washington, D.C., was the vital center of the nation's political and social tumult, which made us Paulists feel like witnesses to history, and at times even participants. We could walk from Catholic University to the White House in less than an hour, and we did it often. When priests and ministers marched on Selma, Alabama, we seminarians threw up sympathetic picket lines on Pennsylvania Avenue. When Norman Mailer, Robert Lowell, and William Sloane Coffin, Jr., led marchers to the Pentagon, we were there. Out-of-town demonstrators from colleges where Paulist priests were chaplains brought their sleeping bags to the basement rooms of our college. When civil rights legislation was being debated in Congress, we donned our black suits to stand vigil at the Lincoln Memorial.

My seminary fieldwork, at Sacred Heart Parish in the heart of the capital's black community, gave me entree into the lives of African-American families. Out of Sacred Heart, I took a volunteer position with the Poor People's Campaign, the antipoverty movement started by Martin Luther King, Jr. Working out of offices in a Fourteenth Street storefront, we began organizing neighborhood groups to get ready for the expected influx of demonstrators from all over the country. The team of which I was a member consisted of young Afro-headed men from the neighborhood, some of whom were on probation, a few of whom should have been. For certain streetwise operators I worked with, the Poor People's Campaign was in part an opportunity for a hustle; I visited more than one in jail. But the young people I knew overwhelmingly embodied the spirit of what Dr. King promised. I felt a kind of giddiness to be thrown in with those kids—the operators as well as the idealists. In the rattletrap van of a neighborhood Pentecostal church, we traveled the city, and then the suburbs, drumming up support for the campaign. It was to culminate in the summer of 1968 with a massive march on Washington and the occupation of the National Mall, to be called Resurrection City. We believed in it.

And we believed in it *as Catholics.* The Church had been regarded as the most socially conservative of institutions, yet the council years had turned that upside down, too. Where once strident and simplistic anticommunism had dominated ecclesiastical thinking, now the Church, especially after Pope Paul VI's 1967 encyclical *Populorum Progressio* (The Progressive Development of Peoples), was firmly on record as a critic of free-market capitalism. "The hungry nations of the world cry out to the people blessed with abundance. And the Church, cut to the quick by this cry, asks each and every man to hear his brother's plea and answer it lovingly."[24] Answer it not with charity but with justice. Economic and social structures were at issue, and the voice of Catholicism was being raised in favor of fundamental, if not quite revolutionary, change in those structures. At the 1968 meeting of the Conference of Latin American Bishops, in Medellín, Colombia, the Catholic establishment, allied until then with the oligarchs, declared its "preferential option for the poor." A new direction was set, and in North America, the land of abundance, Catholics began to hear such calls as addressed to them. Certainly seminarians like me did.

And here was the real wonder: such activism, as it was called, was the meaning by which I had learned to measure the person of Jesus. He had become a real figure in my life, and precisely as one who commissioned me into his legion of prophets. Mine would be a timid participation, but as direct as I could make it. The religious ideal of solitary interiority, grounding an otherworldly holiness, was no longer enough. If you want to find God, we heard Jesus saying, don't go looking in the shadowy corners of Church sacristies, or even monasteries. Find God in the streets, in the jails, in the antiwar movement, in the struggle for justice. Learn to read the life of Jesus in a new way.

Ironically, after the fieldwork sessions were over, the visiting protesters gone, the black kids on their own, I returned to my contemplative seminary life, which enabled me to reconnect to the One around whom our world turned. Long hours of meditation in the chapel, the reading of the Gospels and the Psalms, the routine of daily Mass, the solitude of walks through the stations of the cross on the seminary grounds—in these things I found an equilibrium that balanced the painful transition I was making from conservative son of a military man to Catholic radical.

Catholic radical? It was an identity I had never imagined for myself; it was an identity that only a few years earlier would have made no sense to me. But the prime sponsor of it was not the student movement or civil rights or anguish tied to my father's war. If I embraced a new understanding of what my Catholic faith required, an understanding that remains the polestar of my belief today, it came to me from my first complete encounter with Jesus of Nazareth. That was by far the most important and lasting experience of my religious education in the seminary. I embarked on my own version of the quest for the historical Jesus, and gradually, without any dramatic epiphany, I found I had a relationship with a person who was totally real to me.

Reversing how the faith had developed through the first generations of the Jesus movement (a progression reflected in the evolution of written texts we tracked in the previous chapter), I stepped back from the emphasis on Jesus as God, back through a sense of him as the Jewish Messiah, understanding his permanent Jewishness for the first time, to a vivid discovery of a good man in the crosshairs of political, religious, and social dispute. His responses to that condition had transcendent significance, which his followers recognized, and which they articulated in the language, first, of Messiahship, then of divinity. But Jesus had never made such a claim for himself, which soon seemed to define the only kind of God he could have been. No uppercase *h* for him.

Though not a democrat, in any anachronistic way, Jesus was an egalitarian. The way he treated people defined his message. Human relationships were his opening to the divine. Eating with others was his religious method. Mundane experience was sacred. Women, as we saw earlier, were his friends. A man of the lower class, he rejected class as a mark of identity. His miracles were less acts of magic than transformations in the meaning of harsh experience. I learned to distinguish "curing" from "healing," for example, and now understood that to heal a man born blind by enabling a change in attitude about blindness could be more momentous than the biological wonder of restoring actual sight.[25] His firm rejection of brutal political authority (Rome), together with his faithfully Jewish critique of a collaborationist religious establishment (the high priests), made Jesus come alive in the context of the world I lived in. Wait a minute—government could be wrong! A religious hierarchy could be corrupt!

And then there was violence. Raised on Air Force bases, I had been taught to regard pacifism as an immoral shirking of the responsibility to resist evil. "Peace is our profession" was stenciled on the bombers commanded by my family's neighbor General Curtis LeMay. But now I saw in Jesus' rejection of force ("Put up your sword, Peter. He who lives by the sword, dies by the sword"[26]) the crucial lesson that the only way to real peace is through love, not violence. Love, for Jesus, implied not the warm bath of sentimentality but the stern work of justice. Military victory never establishes justice, Jesus taught, but only the conditions of the next outbreak of violence. This was why he defined his brave and aggressive resistance to Rome as nonviolent. The kingdom he preached (and to which I was aiming to devote my life) was not some impossibly ideal realm off in an undetermined future, but a way of living in the here and now.

The afterlife, whatever else it was, was not the point. It was Jesus, more than anyone, who invited me and my kind to stop worrying about hell ("Neither do I condemn you," he said to the adulterer[27]) and stop waiting for heaven. If Jesus was God come to earth, and I still believed (and believe) he was, it is because earth matters so much.

Poverty, chastity, and obedience became, in the light of Jesus' own example, not sacrificial disciplines but signals of a life built on availability and service. That such a life got him in trouble, cost him his reputation, made him a friend mainly to outcasts—all this became a source of my first real identification with Jesus. I stopped thinking of him as an object of worship and experienced him as my companion (from the Latin for "sharing bread") in the worship of the One he called Father. As I contemplated acts of disobedience (religious and civil) after the events of 1968, I recognized Jesus as my coconspirator (from the Latin for "breathing together"). You see, even Latin was working for me, finally.

With my fellow Paulists ("We few, we happy few, we band of brothers"), I had embraced a vocation to continue with the reform of the Church, for the sake of the world. My boyhood dream of the priesthood had become a manly ambition, rooted in a clear sense of God's presence, through Jesus, in my life.

7. MARTIN AND BOBBY

Lyndon Johnson's double announcement that he would seek neither victory in Vietnam nor reelection as president was the high point of the year. Bombing would stop. Peace was possible. The United States had at last renounced violence in favor of dialogue. The despised antiwar demonstrations had transformed politics. Because Johnson made his announcement on the evening of March 31, we read of it in newspapers on April 1, and some swore it was an April Fool's Day joke. But it was instead a tremendous vindication of the idealists, whose calls for negotiations with the enemy had until then been dismissed. The so-called realists, whose every response to the war's deadlock had been escalation, were discredited.

Our jubilation lasted exactly four days.

Then Martin Luther King was shot. The young black men whom I had befriended as partners in the Poor People's Campaign were among those who took to the streets in rage. Sacred Heart Parish went up in flames that night, fires set by the parishioners themselves—or, rather, by their sons. I went the next morning to the storefront where for months I had been working. Up and down Fourteenth Street, thin trails of smoke rose from still smoldering fires, and the wet stench of ash was in the air. On some buildings, the words "Soul Brother" had been scrawled. As I approached the storefront, I saw that the plate-glass windows on which "PPC," for Poor People's Campaign, had been neatly stenciled in Day-Glo paint were smashed. My young friends were clustered on the glass-strewn sidewalk. When one of them saw me coming, I raised my hand to wave, feeling relieved. But he hurled something at me, a stone I think. He and the others began to shout and curse in my direction, and the one word I heard most clearly was "honkie." They were telling me to get out of their neighborhood, and I did.

The feeling was that I began running that morning, and kept on running for a long time. Martin Luther King's death at the hands of a white man broke the dream of the 1960s into splinters. For a time that spring, Bobby Kennedy, whose authenticity as a grief-struck man enabled his unique identification with African-American suffering, seemed able to resurrect the dream. He was himself reborn in suffering, and when he shared Holy Communion with, say, the fasting César Chávez, leader of migrant Latino laborers, Bobby's newfound radicalism—his opposition to the war, his advocacy for the poor, his alliance with unions and workers—was seen as real because it was recognized as deeply rooted in a Catholic sensibility. Kennedy alone in American politics crossed boundaries of race, ethnicity, and class. He was our tribune of justice and peace, pure and simple.

At the beginning of June, my Paulist classmates and I were ordained to the diaconate. This was the penultimate step toward priesthood, and the ceremony was like a dress rehearsal for that solemn consecration, which would take place half a year later. It was during the diaconate ritual that we were required to take a lifelong vow of celibacy, making the ceremony the vocational equivalent of the Rubicon. I crossed it almost without hesitation, already anticipating the new power the ordination would give me. As a deacon, I was sacramentally charged to preach the Word. I had worked for weeks on what was to be the first official sermon of my life, and was scheduled to preach it at the Paulist community Mass the next day. I can't remember what that sermon aimed to be because, before we woke up the next morning, Bobby Kennedy was shot in California. Of the six people wounded in the attack, he alone died. Reports had it that his last words, concerning the others, were "Is everybody all right?"

At Mass, when it came time for my sermon, I found myself with nothing to say. I discarded the notes I had so carefully prepared, an exemplary exegesis of the day's assigned scriptural reading, no doubt.

I have a clear memory of standing at the lectern, looking out at the faces of my fellow Paulists. I had no way to articulate what I thought and felt. The second Kennedy assassination, coming so soon after King's, sparked a particularly American fear, the dread that our nation had tumbled over the edge of a political and moral abyss. It was as if, with the murder of John F. Kennedy nearly five years earlier, we ourselves had stopped breathing. Mundane experience had reasserted itself, and we forgot at what point of mortal extremity we had begun to live. Urban riots, racial hatred, what was taken to be a nihilist cult of rebellion among the young, and the insane escalations of the war in Vietnam all loomed as symptoms of a larger breakdown, but we had found it possible to deflect our gaze and ignore our own choking lack of oxygen. We were suffocating. America was lost. Something horrible and wicked was set loose among us, and within us.

Martin Luther King's murder was a moment of recognition, and now so was Robert Kennedy's. It felt like the end of a world, a last judgment, a day of doom. I had spent most of a decade constructing a faith in the redemptive power of suffering and death. John Kennedy's assassination had been paired in the minds of many Catholics like myself with the death of John XXIII, and the sentimental portrait of the two of them walking away from us across a tilled field, each one dropping a cone of seeds behind him, embodied our fantastic hope. The two Johns, even in their premature departures, had seemed to generate movements of social improvement—religious renewal, the civil rights crusade, and the determined idealism of the young. Traumatic as John Kennedy's murder had been, it had been taken as the initiating event of a hopeful new era.

But the subsequent assassinations had targeted not just individuals but the very movements that had come to define that hope. Suffering and death as avenues of salvation? Not this time. After King's death, the racial divide reopened, and after Bobby Kennedy's the war party rode high again. Vietnam would last another six years. So why should our souls not have been sorely troubled? I found no redemption in what had happened to Martin or Bobby. Each man qualified, as much as any saint in the litany, for the status of martyr, yet their murders seemed only wasteful and absurd. I saw no meaning that morning, no hope, which is what disqualified me from preaching. I must have spoken, however. If I had simply stood there with the truth of my silence, I would surely remember it. To do as much—or little—would have taken a courage I did not have. Whatever I said, it is right and just to have been forgotten. My first sermon, I am sure, was lies.

8. *HUMANAE VITAE*

The weeks after Bobby Kennedy's death are, in memory, blank, as if that trauma were followed by a lull, in expectation of a next one. And, for the likes of me, didn't it come? On July 25, Pope Paul VI issued *Humanae Vitae*, the long-awaited encyclical on birth control. For Catholics, this was one more upheaval in that earthquake of a year. "The Church," *Humanae Vitae* said quite plainly, "calling human beings back to the observance of the norms of natural law, as interpreted by her constant doctrine, teaches that each and every marriage act must remain open to the transmission of life."[28]

Having unambiguously affirmed this bedrock principle, the encyclical went on to contradict it by reaffirming the rhythm method—the Catholic roulette that aimed at closing off "marriage acts" from the transmission of life. The pope explained that he could not accept the overwhelming recommendation of his own commission, the call for change the text of which the whole world had read in 1967, because it "departed from the moral teaching on marriage proposed with constant firmness by the teaching authority of the Church." But on modern questions of contraception, as we saw, there was no "constant firmness" precisely because they were modern. The firmness dated to 1930. *Jesus!* I thought. *Jesus!*

Astoundingly, it was the teaching authority of the Church that rebutted this teaching, nowhere more powerfully than at my own Catholic University. The instant reaction to the pope's decree, that is, was a greater shock than the encyclical itself—but a happy one. On the day the encyclical was promulgated, a group of CU theologians called a press conference. *Humanae Vitae,* they said, was "based on an inadequate concept of natural law [and on] . . . a static world view which downplays the historical and evolutionary character of humanity in its finite existence."[29] A cardinal at the Vatican Council had invoked the Galileo affair as a warning, and here it was: an argument over whether human nature "moves." The debate over basic assumptions—static worldview (Aristotle, Aquinas) versus process philosophy (Alfred North Whitehead)—was a replay of the conflict over modernity's paradigm shift. Eighteenth- and nineteenth-century suspicion of Enlightenment values was still determining Vatican reactions, even after the council had made its peace with precisely those values.

The dissenting theologians were led by Father Charles Curran, whose lectures I had often attended and whose books I had been required to read. Curran was a lean, bespectacled figure, held in wide esteem on the campus as an exemplar of the vigor of Vatican II thinking. He was a witty and incisive scholar, and his classes were always full, yet he was not an intimidating figure. I had regularly seen him crossing the university's central quadrangle, kicking up the fluttering hem of his cassock. I had eaten meals at tables adjoining his in the cafeteria. He never knew my name, but he often waved to me as if he did. Such familiarity had only made his teaching more compelling. Father Curran, more than any other figure, had given shape to my moral theology. And now, unlike the cowed Galileo, he was refusing to bow before a Church decree, to say "It does not move." Instead Curran and the others contradicted the pope, declaring, "Spouses may responsibly decide according to their conscience that artificial contraception in some circumstances is permissible and indeed necessary to preserve and foster the values and sacredness of marriage."[30]

Eight other CU theologians were first signers of Curran's statement. It was a shot heard round the ecclesiastical world. Within days, hundreds of other theologians and Church officials joined them, including some of the most admired scholars in all of Catholicism, like Karl Rahner, Hans Küng, and Bernard Häring. Most of the Paulist priests who had been my professors over the previous six years affirmed the Curran position. Very quickly, Canadian and European bishops' conferences issued statements saying that Catholics should consider contraception a matter of conscience. Most American bishops were silent, which was taken to be the silence of dissent.

To my surprise, I was unhesitating in my reaction. It was a measure of how much I had changed in those years that the solemn promulgation of authority could land on me with so little weight. Before my ordination to the priesthood, I was being instructed in one-on-one sessions in how to hear confessions. I told the priest in charge of teaching me that I would never enforce *Humanae Vitae* in the confessional. Instead of rebuking me or encouraging me to dissemble, he told me that neither would he.[31] As far as I knew, not one of my classmates accepted the encyclical, and not one of our professors indicated that we should. No sooner had the encyclical been issued than vast numbers of Catholics instinctively understood that they could reject it without thereby becoming bad Catholics. This became an essential part of Catholic self-understanding, though bishops would rail against it for the next generation.[32]

Hell was no longer at issue. The link between sex and power was at last broken. This time it was left to the Vatican to mutter under its breath. *L'Osservatore Romano,* the pope's official newspaper, decreed that anyone who did not accept the teaching should just leave the Church.[33] In that, too, the Vatican was ignored. *Humanae Vitae,* intended to be a bulwark of unchecked papal authority, destroyed it. Alas, it destroyed more than that, as became clear only later.

CHAPTER SEVEN

THOU ART A PRIEST

1. A MONK IN LOVE

FROM THE VANTAGE OF 1968, the road ahead was strewn with wreckage. Roman Catholicism was in a ferocious argument with itself. Pope Paul VI, known as "the Hamlet Pope," had panicked when he saw how deeply into the Catholic imagination the council's reforms had begun to penetrate. The Reformation might have triumphed after all. Maybe Martin Luther had had a point. If so, denominationalism need no longer be a defining mark of Christian identity. Protestants, too, have custody of sacred revelation. Jews could be seen as faithful to God's will, even in their Jewishness. Perhaps sexuality was finished as a realm of ethical absolutes. Truth might be understood as universally elusive, instead of as the divinely bestowed property of the Catholic Church. The sinless bride of Christ, as it turned out, might, like the women in the Bible who generate the symbol, also be a prostitute. Women, for that matter, might actually be equal to men, with inevitable consequences for the exercise of power—in the Church as much as society. Pope Pius XII, silent in the face of the Nazi onslaught, might have failed in the great moral test of his pontificate; perhaps other popes had misread the signs of *their* times. The Holy Spirit, therefore, could influence the Church as much from below as from above. God's will could be seen in the eyes of the people. Jesus was not a Roman Catholic—nor even a Christian. The Church was established by his followers, not him. And so the one institution that understood itself as changeless could change—change drastically. Indeed, through history, it already had. All of this defines my Catholic faith to this very day.

But no. No to all of it! In fact, Paul VI was right to suspect that the Vatican Council had initiated the most fundamental reordering of Church meanings and structures since the time of Constantine. What its advocates called reform the pope feared was self-destruction, and he had started to see Catholic liberalism as a runaway locomotive. His duty had become clear—to stop that movement in its tracks, which he meant to do by throwing *Humanae Vitae* onto the rails.

As a man about to be ordained, I already felt, after that encyclical, like the survivor of a train wreck, standing in the smoking ruins, unsure if I should walk away. I could sense the way in which, just as the outside world felt in disarray (with its August invasion of Prague, the Soviet Union crushed the "human face" of socialism; in November, the untrustworthy Richard Nixon was elected president of the United States; the 1968 Kerner Commission warned that America had become two societies, "one black, one white—separate and unequal"), the Catholic Church was disqualifying itself as a moral center. How in heaven, as they say, would I go forward in this world, wearing the collar of a priest while carrying on an argument with much of what that collar stood for? This problem drove me to take an extraordinary step not long after *Humanae Vitae* was promulgated that summer, one that eventually led to nothing less than a redefining of my vocation, if not an abandonment of it.

But for now, in the last half of that tumultuous year of 1968, I moved through the blocks and lines of my role like someone onstage, assuming that if I enacted devotedness, I would be devoted. The priest on the seminary faculty who served as my confessor told me that at the final faculty evaluation of my class, an objection to my candidacy for ordination had been raised. As one who had glided through the seminary with high marks and flawless evaluations, I was shocked. But also I felt seen through. My inner conflict was as crippling as it was secret, but at least one faculty member sensed my turmoil and found it disqualifying. His opinion did not carry. When it came to a vote, I was approved. But someone whose name I never learned had my number, though I had not quite counted that high yet.

"It was like waking from a dream of separateness, of spurious self-isolation in a special world, the world of renunciation and supposed holiness." This is Thomas Merton, in *Conjectures of a Guilty Bystander*, writing out of *his* confrontation with the 1960s. At first I had assumed

Merton's celebration of a worldview represented by Allen Ginsberg had involved no break with the continuity that Merton himself had championed. But what had been implicit in the 1950s had become explicit a decade later, and Merton was suddenly writing in a different key. Stunningly, his writing now, in *Conjectures* and elsewhere, was a radical questioning of ideas basic to monasticism.

Beginning six years before, I had crossed the threshold into my own manhood—and into my religious identity—with the Trappist monk as my mentor. Merton's early readiness to see a great divide between "the world" and the sacred realm "out of this world" to which we men of religion belonged informed my understanding of myself and my future. "In the world, but not of it." We religious men were set apart as God's own—a status essential to the poverty-chastity-obedience disciplines that otherwise made no sense. Yet here was Merton reversing all that: "The whole illusion of a separate holy existence is a dream. Not that I question the reality of my vocation—"[1] But that, I sensed, was exactly what Merton was doing.

In an echo of his admired Beats, he had begun the decade by pursuing a collaboration with a Zen master. In Merton's case, though, that would have been no faddish flirtation with spiritual exotica, as it mostly was for the City Lights crowd. On the contrary, Merton was dead serious about deepening, if not rescuing, his own sense of the monastic reality, and he viewed the East as a source of new vitality for the monastic tradition of the West. We saw earlier how his superiors had forbidden this as *communicatio cum infidele,* communication with the infidel. Did Merton have "sufficiently the mind of the Church"?[2] Yet in the sixties such interreligious dialogue became common in the Church, and Merton, too, was able to pursue it, if mainly through writing. But the question of the *communicatio*'s effect on his own mind, as the solitude and silence of Gethsemani gave way to voluminous correspondence and a steady flow of visitors, became one the monk himself was asking.

Merton became a recalcitrant monk, increasingly outspoken in his criticism of both American politics and the Church hierarchy. The authorities of his monastery were embarrassed by him. Their frustration had reached a point where they granted him permission to withdraw from the community, to live as a hermit in a small house in the woods, a mile away from the main monastery buildings. The cottage lacked plumbing, and Merton wrote of his early morning treks to the outhouse, where a king snake lived. He addressed the snake: "Are you in there, you bastard?"[3] To live in such solitude was a break with the communitarian monastic ideal, which did not go unnoticed. Merton's personal troubles, conveyed between the lines of his ever prolific writing, became a preoccupation for many.

Then came a 1966 trip to Louisville for medical treatment. He described the illumination it was to be in the big city. A first sight in years of a bustling crowd on the sidewalk filled him, he said, with awe. "I was suddenly overwhelmed with the realization that I loved all those people, that they were mine and I theirs, that we could not be alien to one another, even though we were total strangers."[4]

Was it a multitude of strangers whom Merton loved, or was it a woman? Rumors of Merton's vocational crisis were sweeping through the cloisters and refectories of religious institutions across America (seminaries, but also convents, monasteries, rectories, and inner-city parishes). In fact, as would become clear later, Merton, in waking from a dream of separateness, had fallen in love. Those first rumors suggested that the woman was a nun. Or a nurse. The woman was his publisher. The woman was—

It was impossible. I, for one, refused to credit the gossip. Merton had given the likes of me the language in terms of which we understood ourselves and explained ourselves. I returned to *The Seven Storey Mountain,* the anthem of spiritual living that he'd written twenty years before: "I belonged to God, not to myself: and to belong to Him is to be free, free of all the anxieties and worries and sorrows that belong to this earth, and the love of things that are in it. What was the difference between one place and another, one habit and another, if your life belonged to God, and if you placed yourself completely in His hands? The only thing that mattered was the fact of the sacrifice, the essential dedication of one's self, one's will. The rest was only accidental."[5] How long ago it seemed that he had written that; how long ago that I had first read it, taking it to heart.

In his journals, Merton now wrote freely of his love for a woman identified only as "M," but he dismissed none of his feelings for her. She was a nurse at the Louisville hospital where he went for treatment. He was fifty-one, she was half his age. He was smitten by her dark, curly hair. "This love of ours," he wrote, "—very joyous today, very sure of itself, triumphantly articulate, is still an immense reservoir of anguish . . . But I don't care. Now I can accept the anguish, the risk, the awful insecurity, even the guilt . . . We are far beyond the point where I used to get off the bus in my old love affairs. I am in much deeper than I ever was before."[6]

We did not yet have access to Merton's frankly written journals. Once published, the writings about the romance would make me, and I am sure others, cringe with embarrassment. The passionate sincerity of the monk's longings had a puppy-love quality, an unreality, a foolishness. Indeed, Merton's infatuation with his nurse was tied to the immaturity of imposed neurosis that had corrupted the culture of Catholic clericalism, although that corruption would not be seen for what it really was for some decades. Without knowing it, Merton was struggling against the pressures of sexuality used as a form of control—Church-imposed (as opposed to freely chosen) celibacy. Yet despite that nascent resistance, male celibates took for granted the prevailing norm of male dominance over women. Merton wrote, "In the light of M's love I realize for the first time how deeply I was loved back in those days by girls whose names I have even forgotten."[7]

That men should cavalierly forget the women with whom they were intimate suggests the larger problem, and that, too, was flagged for Catholics in 1968, with the publication of *The Church and the Second Sex*, by Mary Daly, a professor of theology at Boston College, the Jesuit university. The book repudiated the passive ideal of femininity attached to ideas, especially, of Mary the mother of Jesus. We saw some of this in an earlier chapter's discussion of Mary Magdalen's submersion in the hypermale tradition of Church power. Daly's rejection of male authority made her book a sensation in Church circles, a Catholic version of the Betty Friedan manifesto with which the decade had begun. Feminism would play its role as much within the Church as outside it, and it seemed fitting that this Catholic feminist manifesto should have come from yet another Mary.

Even men who struggled against the whole system of Catholic belief on matters of sexuality were slow to understand how women took the weight of that imposed system. *Humanae Vitae* was one case in point. To control access to contraception was, above all, a way to control women. But Merton's love affair (and those of countless celibates who consciously or unconsciously imitated him) was another: an uncritically celebrated embrace of romantic love could still keep women down. We Catholic males, from right to left, had a lot to learn.

Those of us who lived within the claustrophobic zone of Church teachings on sex were already feeling stresses of dishonesty and duplicity; we were dishonest and duplicitous, first and foremost, with ourselves. Catholic sexual neurosis was a ticking time bomb in the Church, although decades would pass before it would explode in the priest-pederast scandal. At the time of Merton's publicly noted personal crisis, however, no one who remotely shared his situation, as I surely did, read his account judgmentally or condescendingly. The journals suggest that he and "M" (not another Mary but a woman named Margie Smith) may never have consummated their love; he seems to have broken it off sometime in 1966 or 1967.[8] That painful renunciation—and our focus was always on Merton's pain, not his then anonymous partner's—did nothing to soothe his uneasiness with his sacred isolation at Gethsemani. Perhaps Merton was intending to leave the monastery or the monastic life altogether. Certainly the rumors suggested just such a prospect, and we Catholic men who had followed him into the religious life were braced for what would come next.

In September 1968, we read his "Circular Letter to Friends" that flashed through Catholic seminaries and monasteries, Merton's deliberately open announcement of a new stage in his life. This was before the Internet or the fax machine, but it seemed everyone had a copy. "Dear Friends," his letter began, and, citing "rumor," quickly came to the point: "I'd better make the whole thing clear. Otherwise gossip may completely distort the real picture—as has happened before. I have been asked to attend two meetings in Asia, one of them a meeting of the abbots of Catholic monastic orders in that area, the other an interfaith meeting with representatives of Asian religions . . . I ask your prayers for the success of this undertaking: and of course, please do not believe anything that rumor may add to this simple scenario."[9]

2. WILLIAM SLOANE COFFIN, JR.

Even without understanding in detail what his struggles entailed, it was clear that the great Thomas Merton had become an emblem of my own insecurities. As post–*Humanae Vitae* dissent came to dominate the public conversation about Church doctrine and practice, I had to ask, regardless of whether Merton or any of my fellow Paulists did: Who was I to stand against the pope? I could hear the question that my mother had routinely put to me when I displeased her:

"Who do you think you are?" Now it was Holy Mother the Church from whom I heard that snarl, addressed to everyone from whom I had learned. "Who do you *all* think you are?" Never mind that my rebellious teachers and comrades were unanimous in claiming to bow before higher authority, appealing against one pope (Paul VI) to another (John XXIII), defending disobedience in the name of truer obedience. As this had at first seemed a liberation, now it seem a subterfuge. What moral wilderness had we entered? And unsettled as I was, how in the world would I offer moral guidance to anyone else?

Humanae Vitae was promulgated in the summer of 1968. I was to be ordained in the coming winter. That fall, for reasons that will become clear later, I concentrated on writing. I was finding publishers for my poetry and had a short play produced on television. These writerly credentials prompted the Paulist priest who was in charge of the Los Angeles–based Paulist broadcast ministry to ask to have me assigned to work with him once I was a full-fledged priest. The work of Paulist Productions was highly regarded, and its director was known as "the Hollywood priest."

The Paulists sponsored the national syndication of a weekly TV show called *Insight*, but when I watched it with a freshly critical eye, the program seemed a tame propagation of Catholic irrelevancies, like the lives of saints or the moral lessons of clean living. As for the Hollywood priest, he seemed like a good guy, but much was made of his rugged good looks, a poster boy of the erotically unavailable. Adept at using the celebrity culture for his own (higher) purposes, he was never seen without the Roman collar, French cuffs, and a black sharkskin suit, while I was already imagining myself, à la Daniel Berrigan, in a turtleneck sweater and windbreaker. "Hollywood Junior," my classmates began to tease me, though with a hint of envy. My assignment to L.A. after ordination was taken for granted.

I myself could not imagine it, but after the traumas of war and assassination, followed by the bombshell of the birth control encyclical, neither could I see myself organizing sodality suppers in a suburban parish. What, look after altar boys?

It was around then that I encountered William Sloane Coffin, Jr., the Yale University chaplain. He had become a national figure in the sixties as one of the first white men to throw in with black civil rights protesters in the South and then as a leader of the antiwar movement.

Only somewhat younger than Merton, he arrived in my life as a kind of counterfigure.

Coffin, like Merton, had spent some of his youth in France, and he, too, had come of age in Morningside Heights, at Union Seminary instead of Columbia. Like Merton's, Coffin's was a conversion story, but instead of progress from bohemia into a monastery, his route was from the cloak-and-dagger world of the CIA (he had been part of the brutal repatriation of Soviet POWs after World War II) to the high-profile Protestant establishment (his father had been chairman of the board of the Metropolitan Museum of Art; his uncle had been president of Union Seminary). Instead of the aura of burdened sexuality, Coffin had the air of robust masculinity, an unapologetically sexual energy. He was then married to the first of his three wives, and a much-told story about their engagement captures Coffin's rambunctious spirit. Her father was the famous pianist Arthur Rubinstein, and when he was introduced to Coffin, he said, "I'm not sure how I feel about my daughter marrying a Billy Graham." To which Coffin reportedly replied, "I'm not sure how I feel about marrying the daughter of a Liberace."

Coffin was a preacher, not a writer. An activist, not a contemplative. Indicting the worst aspects of American life with a fierce moralism, he seemed entirely free of the interior anguish of which Merton had become our poet laureate. As noted earlier, I had been in the anonymous throngs of demonstrations in Washington where Coffin had been prominent. In October 1967, with four others, he had led a ceremony at a Boston church where young men turned in their draft cards, which Coffin then handed over to the government, saying, "You must arrest us, too." The government did, and his trial in Boston was one of the other high dramas of 1968. With his fellow defendants[10] he was convicted, and then their convictions were overturned.

Coffin carried on, as he said in a phrase of Robert Frost's, "a lover's quarrel" as much with his church as with America. I did not grasp the significance of his position as a man protesting from within, however, until I met him in person, when he came to our seminary to give a lecture. Later I would go to jail with him, would be sustained in the cellblock by his singing, would find the courage to stand erect in court by imitating him. Eventually I would become his friend. But he never made a more powerful impression than in that first encounter at the Paulist seminary, when he gave me an unexpected glimpse of a new kind of religious identity, one in which contradictions were not the problem but the solution.

For all his worldliness and savoir-faire, it was a religious identity that defined Coffin's ministry. It was a religious identity, I sensed at once, that could be mine—and then I realized, so could that ministry. A quarrel, yes. But a *lover's* quarrel! Claim the conflict, I heard from Coffin, but do not let them define it as betrayal. "My love for an institution," he declared, citing John Stuart Mill, "is in proportion to my desire to reform it."

The work boots, Levi's, and corduroy jacket were what struck me at first. We seminarians still wore long black robes, the Paulist habit that was our daily uniform. If some of us aspired to the countercloth of turtlenecks and windbreakers, it was still black. As he strode into the auditorium, Coffin seemed oblivious to the sartorial difference between him and us, as if clothing did not matter. I know now that it mattered a lot, and that his working-class get-up was an affectation designed to make a point. He carried himself like a prizefighter, yet he was a tender person with the warmest and broadest of smiles. Coffin was full of what I took to be revolutionary earnestness, but he made us laugh uproariously. Though it would take years for me to articulate what drew me to him, I grasped the essence of his appeal at once. He was open-minded enough to learn from the students in his charge at Yale, to celebrate the courage and prophetic witness that had put young people in the front ranks of the peace and civil rights movements. But he also knew that the young were hungry for the food that he had, and he did not hesitate to offer it to them. "Students tell me my faith in Jesus is a crutch," he said. "And I answer, 'Maybe so. But who tells you you're not limping?'"

I had never taken such instruction from a Protestant before. It was Coffin, that day in our seminary dining-room-turned-lecture-hall, who made me understand that the Reformation was over, period. *The Council, Reform and Reunion* had been the title of the Hans Küng book that started the revolution we Catholics had been living through. And now here was the manifestation, as it came to me at least, that the "reform and reunion" had been achieved. Simply put, William Sloane Coffin and I belonged to the same Church, the Church not of Rome but of Jesus Christ. With Jesus Christ we were against Rome, not the Rome of the popes but of the caesars. And who were their successors, Coffin asked, but the principalities and powers of war and racism?

Of course, Coffin knew what he was doing. After reciting the litany of Caesar's laws that required breaking, he moved seamlessly—and in that Catholic setting, impishly—from Martin Luther King to Martin Luther: "My conscience is captive to the Word of God," Coffin intoned. "To go against conscience is neither right nor safe. Here I stand. I can do no other. God help me."[11] And like that—snap!—Coffin made me see that Luther, in some way I had never glimpsed before or dared imagine, had been right. Now, instead of my mother's "Who do you think you are?" I heard her lilting celebration of Jimmy: "They were all out of step but Jim." That affirmation of a person standing alone and standing against had formed an unconscious cord in my spine, and Coffin plucked it.

"William Sloane Coffin Dies at 81; Fought for Civil Rights and Against a War," the *New York Times* headline read in 2006. A *Boston Globe* headline the same day read, "CIA Agent Became Beacon of Antiwar Movement." Coffin had been a white man standing with blacks. A patrician who was tribune of the nobodies. A patriot in disobedient dissent. A critical thinker with a simple faith. What made Bill Coffin famous, and what first attracted me to him, was his rhetorical flair. His genius for the energetic sound bite was the solution to every reporter's deadline problem. And it was the essence of his gift as a speechmaker and preacher. "It's not enough to pray for peace," he would say. "Work for justice!"

"War is a coward's escape from the problems of peace."

"We must be governed by the force of law, not by the law of force."

This is the rhetoric of irony, a bringing together of polarities to see how the tensions of life can be brought to resolution. Irony of this sort is the essence of humor, which is why laughter came so naturally to him, and from him. Irony depends on an exquisite balance of language and ideas, opposites held in tension, not to split them apart—that's sarcasm—but to promise a new kind of unity. Bill Coffin, in his biography, in the choices he made, in the language he used, and in the jokes he told, held up the possibility of hope. That was what I saw. Coffin was a man of paradox, whose contradictions were not the source of inner discord, as mine were, but of a strength-producing tension. Perhaps my contradictions, too, could be a source of something other than self-doubt. Coffin told us by his preaching and his living that the human heart is not doomed to break, however cracked it is by war, by injustice, or by the fearsome sorrows, say, of a soon-to-be-ordained priest torn between conscience and the Church. God help him.

After Bill Coffin died, the doors of memory opened, and I was freshly in touch with what he had done for me at a moment of crisis. The low point of my life had come in the spring of 1972 when, after breaking the law at an antiwar sit-in at the U.S. Capitol, I was arrested and locked up in a Washington jail. My parents lived in that city, and to have so defied everything I'd been raised to plunged me, during that night, into a pit of despair that meshed perfectly with the shit-smeared cell where I was held. Coffin had been a leader of that demonstration, and he was in the next cell. In the middle of the night, I heard him begin to quietly sing. *Comfort ye, my people.* Coffin's a cappella singing of Handel's *Messiah* was irresistible, and soon others up and down the cellblock joined in. *I know that my redeemer liveth.* And miracle of miracles, I, who did not sing, joined in. *But we shall all be changed in a moment, in the twinkling of an eye.*[12]

After Coffin's death, as if he were the hero whose abrupt departure left the townspeople wondering who that amazing man was, I realized that he had told me again and again who he was, beginning with that day in the late 1960s when he came to my seminary, citing Martin Luther. Coffin, the man of paradox and hope, was, above all, a man who had built his life around the figure of Jesus.

Peace and justice, yes. Conscience, certainly. Those were absolute values, and in that season of Vietnam and the War on Poverty, I had imagined building my priesthood around them. But by Coffin's own account, he had those values not from his privileged background, not from his beloved America which he had served in uniform, and not from Yale, whose high-toned Puritan ethos he embodied. To the mystification and even consternation of many, Bill Coffin defined himself by Jesus, and that was what had most powerfully struck me on the day he came to speak to us. He was a walking *Bartlett's,* and having cited John Stuart Mill, Karl Marx, Groucho Marx, Simone Weil, and Albert Camus, Coffin went on without embarrassment to talk of the Lord as his own. Jesus was Coffin's first and last point of reference. And now I understand why. What Coffin loved about Jesus was *his* paradox. The contradictions that added up to hope. Jesus, the peasant nobody who is Lord of the universe. Jesus, the victim who is victorious. Jesus, who can say "My God, my God, why have you abandoned me?" while also saying, "Into your hands . . ." With that habitual rhetorical flair of his, Coffin often said, "I don't know *what* is waiting for me after death, but I do know *who.*" And from the start, in saying such things, he spoke for me.

When word came one day, late that fall of 1968, of a job opening at the Catholic Student Center at Boston University, I applied for it at once. Campus ministry seemed a way of embracing the ideal I'd glimpsed in Coffin, and even more, as Coffin himself had, I wanted the chance to learn from young people. It was in Boston that Coffin had liturgically received their draft cards, in Boston where he had been tried and convicted. Such rebellion frightened me, which was what made me realize I had to join it, too. Whether BU students were limping or not, I was.

When the Hollywood priest in L.A. heard that I'd applied for the campus ministry job, rejecting the privileged opportunity to work in his broadcasting enterprise, he felt personally affronted and dropped his bid for me. The more I thought about Boston, the more it seemed a solution to my largest problem. At ordination, at the Paulist church in New York City, I was going to have to put the steeple of my hands into the enfolding hands of Cardinal Terence Cooke, the archbishop of New York. More to the point for an oedipally challenged soldier's son like me, he was the military ordinary, the bishop in charge of approving America's war in Vietnam. I had long since stopped discussing such things with my father the general, but I was not going to be able to avoid declaring myself with Cardinal Cooke. With my hands in his, according to the ordination ritual, he would ask, "Do you solemnly swear to show respect and obedience to your ordinary?" To my bishop, that is. If I went to Boston, my ordinary would be Cardinal Cushing, and by then he was one bishop, if there were any, to whom respect and obedience were patently due.

3. PUBLIC SINNER

I had first heard of Cushing during the Feeney affair, when I was ten years old. In that dispute, he sponsored the beginning of my religious education. More recently, I had associated him with all that was good about the Vatican Council, beginning with his prophetic call to translate the proceedings from Latin. I had taken note of his refusal to toe a hard line on birth control. But above all that, he had been a point of personal connection for every American Catholic with the Kennedys. His intimacy with them had been made dramatic again only months before, at Bobby's funeral, when he sobbed before the casket. And now, in the fall of 1968, Cushing's tie to the Kennedys was once more on display, this time as a source of controversy.

At the end of October, Jacqueline Kennedy married the Greek shipping tycoon Aristotle Onassis, a man whose foreignness and reputation for shady dealings seemed unworthy of the woman who embodied America's grief. Jackie was our Woman of Sorrows. But after the June assassination, Onassis's wealth and power offered a guarantee of safety to the twice-shaken widow, and much of the world's sympathy flowed toward her. Much, though not all. In the eyes of the Vatican, Onassis was a man bound by a previous marriage. His union with Mrs. Kennedy was illicit. "Bad marriage" was the operative phrase. *L'Osservatore Romano,* the official Vatican newspaper, lost no time in condemning Jacqueline Kennedy Onassis as a "public sinner."

The next time Cushing appeared in public, he was asked about the Vatican's condemnation. Cushing replied: "This idea of saying she's excommunicated, that she's a public sinner—what a lot of nonsense. Only God knows who is a sinner and who is not. Why can't she marry whomever she wants? This woman is entitled to get whatever happiness she can get."[13] An enraged Vatican immediately demanded that Cushing condemn the marriage. He refused, and instead submitted his resignation, saying of Rome, "If they don't understand me after thirty years, they'll never understand me."[14] The Vatican, suddenly alert to a public relations disaster, declined to accept the resignation.

Cushing was our prince of the Church. Within months of the Onassis flap, he was even offering public words of support for Father Charles Curran, the besieged leader of dissent on birth control.[15] With Cushing, the hopes for change remained alive. A new Church was being born. And yes, my love for the Church was my desire to help with its reform. When the Paulists nominated me for the position at Boston University, Cardinal Cushing appointed me. I was privileged to be on my way to work for him.

4. THE END OF THE BEGINNING

Two things occurred at the end of 1968, one a conclusion, the other a beginning, although we recognized neither as such. On December 10, twenty-seven years to the day after he entered the monastery, Thomas Merton died in Bangkok, Thailand. After delivering a lecture to the East-West Intermonastic Conference of monks and nuns, titled "Marxism and Monastic Perspectives," he returned to his room, where, during rest period, he was electrocuted by the wiring of a defective fan. No one ever knew exactly what happened. He was fifty-three years old. When I learned of Merton's death, and of the confused circumstances surrounding it—some of my assassination-traumatized classmates spoke of murder—my first thought was that he had killed himself. That I could even entertain such an idea, and somehow understand it, was a crushing revelation of how far I'd come from the innocence of my novitiate, where the mere mention of Merton's name had been enough to lift my heart with joy.

And then, unexpectedly, joy returned. It was Christmas Eve. The astronauts of *Apollo 8* had gone into low orbit over the moon. One of them snapped the famous photograph of the earth, the first picture of the home planet taken by a human being, a fragile blue sphere suspended in the void. Eventually that photograph would be recognized as the icon of a new consciousness: the world without borders, the razor-thin atmosphere at risk, the magnificent insignificance of an object on the edge of a huge constellation, a vast galaxy, an infinite universe. If human beings began to dream of a new way of living together on their island home—an end to war, a recognition of the universal fate of mortal creatures, a global ethos—it started with that image, the blue ball hanging in nothing, the lapis lazuli ornament of hope. Mother Earth, Gaia, the world itself a living organism. Galileo's vindication.

As their spacecraft hovered low over the rough surface of the moon, the American astronauts took turns reading the first ten verses of Genesis. From "In the beginning God" to "And God saw that it was good . . . very good," the words of Scripture had never come more fully to life than on that Christmas Eve. The ancient craters of the moon offered a glimpse of the barrenness out of which the wondrous garden of the earth had been drawn. Never had we beheld such beauty as when, once again, the blue planet rose over the moon's horizon. Earthrise. Never had we felt closer to creation; never closer to the Creator. The message could not have been simpler: God loves everything that God has made. (There is no question of needing to be saved.)

And why would a believing young man not rejoice to hand over his future to such a God on behalf of such a vision.[16]

The two events at the end of 1968, the two poles of my faith: *Why have you abandoned me?* and *Into your hands I commend my spirit.* At the beginning of 1969, I was ordained.

5. CATHOLIC CHAPLAIN

I had never loved a room before, but that changed at Boston University. The Catholic chapel was the converted first floor of an old Back Bay mansion, in the center of the urban campus. The room may once have been an oak-paneled salon or a glittering banquet room, but a generation before it had been turned into a small church, replicating as much as possible the look and feel of the ecclesiastical tradition. Several dozen pews were lined up in front of the altar, which stood against the far wall. There were statues of Mary and Joseph, each with its small bank of candles and coin receptacle. There was a portrait of St. Jerome, the Bible translator, who'd been deemed an appropriate patron for an academic community. Attached to the wall behind the altar was a tabernacle, the golden box in which the Blessed Sacrament was reserved. Next to it was a candle stand, the red glass sheath of which was always aglow—the sanctuary lamp. In a corner stood a small Hammond organ, which sounded tinny, but was properly of the church.

To me, the chapel was a spatial representation of all that was wrong with the pre–Vatican II Church—the rigid order of hierarchy, the priest on his platform, the laity on their knees, their eyes cast down, the worship of solitaries, the preference for kitsch, statues, candles, the money box. No. If Jesus was to be a "real presence" here, it had to be in the people's interactions with each other, in community, more than in any wafer, however much revered. The day I walked into the chapel, I said to myself, This has to change.

But first I had to reckon with another kind of change—in my new status. As a priest, even if a newly ordained one, I was the holder of authority, not the challenger of it. And the first thing I discovered about my young charges at the university was that they had identified with the Catholic community at BU because they liked it the way it was. Adjoining the chapel was Newman House, a converted row house holding my office, meeting rooms, a kitchen, and a dining area where a Catholic in-group gathered for spaghetti suppers. They did not know what to make of me.

I was equally confused. I did not wear a collar. I introduced myself as Jim. If I had unscheduled time, I spent it hanging out at the student union or in the lounges of dormitories. When antiwar protests or teach-ins were held, I went, content to hover noncommittally at the edge of the crowd. But such tame signals of contrast with the kindly older priest, my predecessor who would soon be transferred, were offputting to the Newman House clique. What they saw as a clubhouse, a refuge from the threatening larger world, I saw as a base from which to enter that world, engaging it and challenging it. My expectation was to spend as little time as possible at Newman House; my predecessor hardly ever left it. Supposedly "father," I was barely older than the grad students, and if they were reluctant to grant me a position of authority, I was not inclined to claim it. For a few weeks, over spaghetti dinners, on the prearranged ski trip, at book group discussions, at rap sessions, the Catholic kids and I sized each other up.

I had arrived at my new position with a fantasy of what America's young people had become, made up partly of televised images of students taking over buildings at Berkeley and Columbia University, and partly of William Sloane Coffin's descriptions of the hero-resisters who put their lives on the line for civil rights and peace. The year just past—the "Strawberry Statement" at Columbia, the takeover of a dean's office at Harvard, riots on Paris's Left Bank, and the defiance of Soviet tanks in Prague—had been an initiation into a new era of youthful revolution, an outrageous overturning of attitudes about everything from sex to politics. Or had it?

Newman House, as it turned out, was defined by kids who were as unsettled by the times as, presumably, their parents were. And not only the times, but the place. BU was a large and impersonal urban university. It had a vocal minority of radicals who styled the campus as "the Berkeley of the East." The traumas of the time—those assassinations, riots, the "generation gap," the "credibility gap," the general collapse of order—had scared the shit out of many more young people than they had inspired. The much-celebrated sexual revolution translated for many into alienating experiences, like having to listen to roommates copulate, or having to defend one's own reluctance to have sex with near strangers, or, perhaps more disturbing, having to reckon with one's status as an object of sexual interest to no one. That the Catholic Church, including its local manifestation at BU, was apolitical, socially conservative, and still restrictive about sex was, for many, the essence of its appeal.

Martin Luther King, Jr., was an alumnus of the university, but the Catholic students I encountered were lily white, and King's legacy, in that year after his murder, was more or less unnoted among them. If the Vietnam War was an issue for the young people whom I had been sent to serve, it was not as an occasion of protest but of a paralyzing ambivalence. If they felt passionately about the war, it was more likely in favor of it, since Newman House was one of the few places on campus that still openly welcomed ROTC cadets.

Before every Mass, time was customarily set aside when, as the priest, I would wait in the dark booth of the confessional. As one of the privileges of my new status, I heard the confessions of young people who presented themselves on the other side of the screen. I had rehearsed for this in seminary, but there can be no preparing for the actual experience of being taken into the complete confidence of strangers.

My hours in the confessional proved to be deeply moving and humbling, but what surprised me was how trivial were most of the matters of conscience with which I was entrusted. For most kids, the sacrament was merely a rote recitation of sins they'd learned to confess at parochial school ("I forgot to say my prayers. I got angry. I used bad language"). Not great issues of war and peace, not existential crises having to do with the absent God, not abortion. Sexual transgressions were confessed to me, but much of what I heard on that score did not seem sinful, and when I gently proposed that perhaps God was not so preoccupied with what happened in bedrooms or bathrooms, the penitents seemed not to know what I was talking about.

In one of my first sermons, I spoke against the war in what I thought was a measured and respectful way, only to be roundly rebuked by a faculty member in the congregation. She told me to keep my political views to myself, and, more to the point, to give the young people positive messages. "These kids don't need your negative energy, Father." I calmly told her I would think about what she said, but inwardly I was shaken. Was it true—my energy negative? Challenging a conservative authority structure was one thing—"Power to the people!" But what if the conservatives *were* the people?

Just in time, I recognized that my first impulse to simply change the chapel by fiat—those pews, the votive lights, the altar at the wall—was a repetition, albeit from the left, of the old authoritarian tradition. Such an act would define a priesthood-shaping mistake. Like some monsignor, I would be imposing my idea of how things were supposed to go on pliant laypeople who knew no better. My first lesson as a priest, that is, was in my own complicity in a system I had resolved to change. I checked my impulse to install a new regime, even if I didn't second-guess the need for it.

A group of girls, in imitation of a parish altar guild, had been responsible for caring for the chapel, its linens, flowers, and so on. I invited them to think of themselves as the nucleus of a new Liturgy Committee, the establishment of which was my first initiative. Soon a dozen young people were meeting with me in the chapel, discussing ways to update the liturgy and warm up the space itself. They got the picture, and before long we went to work.

Impersonal categories like "conservative" and "liberal" dropped away as we got to know each other. Simple ideas for a renewed liturgy took hold: language that connected, informality that let kids be themselves, a community instead of a hierarchy, a friendly meal instead of a stilted ritual. There could be a "kiss of peace" at which people actually kissed. The music that mattered so to young Americans could matter also in their prayer. We talked about these ideas. They did not seem so radical. Once a basic common sense was introduced into the heretofore sacred realm of the purely given, ideological categories seemed irrelevant. And what the commonsense principles—a meal, informality, youthfulness—meant for the rearrangement of the room soon became obvious. Out with the tinny organ. Out with the statues. Out with the kneelers. Then someone said, "Out with all the pews! We can sit on the floor!"

The thought hadn't occurred to me, but I saw it at once: an open space taking its definition from people, not things. We all agreed. One of the students found a used-furniture store that bought the pews and hauled them away, which gave us enough money to have a bright red wall-to-wall carpet installed. From now on, chapel seating would be on the floor. Girls brought in pillows covered in Marimekko prints. A couple of boys whose fathers had taught them carpentry built a simple table, which we put in the center of the room. Other students hemmed some burlap, which we used as a tablecloth. Brightly colored banners were stitched. Masses had been scheduled at traditional hours on Sunday mornings; I added a Mass at midnight every Saturday.

What made me love the room was what we did in it. I loved it when it was crowded and, surprisingly, when it was vacant. An unexpected place for quiet meditation, I often went there to sit on the floor, focused on the Book, or the burning candle, or the vase of flowers. Others joined me. Every day at noon, a handful gathered for the Mass. Over time, their number doubled and doubled again. After a lifetime of watching the priest at the altar, I was now watching the eyes of worshipers watching me. Not me, but what I represented. I welcomed the recognition that, as a priest, my own personality was secondary. Instead of standing in a pulpit, I stood among the students who sat cross-legged on the floor. Instead of preaching, I found myself repeating the anecdotes we found in the texts, then elaborating or sometimes dramatizing stories about Jesus and his friends.

"I know not the man," Peter said, denying him not once but three times. And then three times the risen Jesus asks him, "Simon Peter, do you love me? Do you love me? But do you really love me?" The Gospels tell a story that begins in disappointment and ends in hope. "Lord, you know everything. You know I love you."[17] The story is not about religion but life. Peter and Jesus were best friends, one of whom grievously let the other down. I invited the students to say what the readings meant to them, and, shyly at first, they did. Disappointment, yes. Hope, too: the bottomless capacity of the young to hope. "If you love me," Jesus told Peter, "then feed my sheep." For the first time, I heard Jesus telling that to me. And even if the last image I wanted to have applied to my congregation was sheep, was such feeding not exactly what I was doing? The Gospel, once I actually began to preach it, came alive in a new way, which changed my relationship to it forever. Changed me. The evident relevance to the human condition—our condition—of the Word of God was as much a surprise to me as it was to them.

The Bible stopped being my object of study and became my dear companion. I carried a small blue New Testament with me everywhere, never letting anyone see it, but turning to it often. And the Mass. The unexpected center of my life was the Mass. The elegant simplicity of the Eucharistic prayer, which amounted, in my admittedly unauthorized improvising, to little more than extended blessings over the bread and the wine, proved an unexpected opening into tranquillity. As I passed through the cluster of exquisitely attentive students, breaking off pieces of "Syrian bread" instead of dispensing wafers, I felt an unprecedented intimacy, even with strangers. I understood for the first time why they call it Communion.

The Mass rooted me, and even as I began to make forays into the wider world of radical politics at BU, joining more directly, for example, in organizing antiwar protests that occasionally took me to other cities, I grew to love the small community who gathered with me each day in the red-carpeted chapel. I formed ties with non-Catholic kids at BU, activists who tended to be Jewish or self-proclaimed agnostics. I rather liked my status in their company as the "radical priest." But Newman House students were not radicals, and in truth neither was I. A Catholic radical, perhaps, but on the larger scale of culture and politics, my being Catholic disqualified me from being radical in any real way. Eventually I would feel deeply bound to young people with whom I marched in protests, but that connection paled beside what I felt with kids sitting cross-legged on that red carpet, before that homemade altar.

When they let their eyes lock briefly on mine, as I gave them bread, I saw that they, unlike their supremely cool classmates who showed no need of such a ritual, were palpably "using religion as a crutch." That was what that faculty member had been trying to tell me, in chastising me for mixing politics and religion. Having taken the professor's point, I saw now that the mixing was not the problem, but a possible solution. Here was where Coffin's example was useful to me: *Of course it's a crutch, and we're all limping.* Avoiding politics was not the answer, any more than refusing the consolations of the faith was. My charges were younger than I, and my traumas were not theirs, but as the sixties had rocked my young adulthood, the same time period had framed their adolescence. Berlin, Cuba, the Bomb, the assassinations, the turmoil in cities, the war, the dread of a nation that feared for its soul, the feeling of being cut loose from the certainties of the past—all of that bound us together. If I had been forced to face the difference between my parents' experience and mine, becoming a man in the process, now I recognized that these boys and girls, on the way to becoming men and women, had their versions of the same struggle. That, of course, was the point of my being "father"—I could be the parent figure who helped them work through the struggle—and I stopped resisting the title.

My BU kids entrusted me with the way they felt like lost souls. But as the turmoil running up to my ordination had made clear to me, I was a lost soul, too. We were all lost souls. My faith in God, and in Jesus, was the one way I felt found. Jesus had set himself against what he called the dark powers of the world. Lo and behold, those powers were still at work, and somehow, as I firmly believed, so was he. My job—and my privilege—was to let that faith show so that others, being found, might find it too. At Newman House, and in the red sanctuary of our chapel, that happened.

6. CONSCIENTIOUS OBJECTORS

As it turned out, the mixing of politics and religion was not something about which I had any choice. By 1969, the futility of the war in Vietnam was broadly evident, even if relatively few of the Newman House students moralized about it. They had been raised to believe in the innate goodness of their country, to do as they were told, to accept the idea that if the call to service came, they would answer. In all of this they were like me. I was a soldier's son, and I let them know it. Yet they also knew, from the notices I put on the bulletin board and my steady endorsement of campus antiwar activity, that I opposed the war and encouraged their opposition. Especially as I became known in the wider circle of Boston University, young men began to force the issue on me, because it was being forced on them.

Not many months had gone by after my arrival when boys I'd never seen began showing up at my office. They approached me tentatively, having heard of my presence at protests or rallies, or perhaps having slipped into the back of one of the larger Sunday liturgies. Whether I preached about the war or not, I always made a point to pray about it. And that was what brought young men to me. Typically they were juniors or seniors who were within months of losing their student deferments, a prospect that, in many cases, meant a first confrontation with the dangers and moral complexities of actually going to war—this war.

I associated myself with other chaplains and with already established draft counseling facilities in Boston, particularly the American

Friends Service Committee. As I'd learned from Bill Coffin, helping young men cope with the draft had been a central function of campus ministry from the mid-sixties on, but as the escalations in Vietnam brought troop levels above half a million, pressures of the Selective Service System increased. Deferments of all kinds were harder to get, and many draft broads had become positively hostile to those applying for an exemption based on conscientious objection. That familiar phrase, of course, assumed an understanding of what was meant by conscience. Was it conscience that told a person that he simply did not want to do something? Or, in the case of military service, could that equally be cowardice? How are such questions sorted out, and with whom? Can it be cowardice, some would ask, *not* to raise an objection to this war? Soon enough, I understood why Catholics, and young men who had been raised as Catholics, had a special problem with such questions, which all at once gave me a special function.

The Selective Service law had been revised as recently as 1967, when the enormous escalation of troop levels in Vietnam had begun, with a concomitant growth in induction quotas demanded of local draft boards. The law had two provisions that posed particular challenges to the young men I met. The registrant applying for classification as a conscientious objector had to be, as the law said, "conscientiously opposed to participation in war in any form." The authors of the law clearly intended here to rule out what was called selective conscientious objection—objection to some wars as opposed to all wars. The law meant to recognize appeals to conscience based only on a position of absolute pacifism, and men from "peace churches" like the Quakers or Mennonites had no trouble obtaining CO status.

Would you use force to defend your sister from a rapist? What if Hitler's army invaded New England? Would you fight then? Such were the questions put to every draft-troubled young man. In my experience, those men put such questions to themselves. But again and again they came up against the unique horror of Vietnam. The massacre at My Lai (where, in 1968, about five hundred Vietnamese civilians were murdered in a ditch by U.S. soldiers) was an illumination for many. Who were the rapists there? Who the Nazis? And what about the generalized destruction of massive air bombardment? Of napalm? The photo of a napalmed girl running down a road would be for antiwar feeling what photos of lynched black men were for the civil rights movement.

Local draft boards were neither qualified nor authorized to engage draftees in debates about the morality of particular wars, and the law was mostly read as forbidding that. In 1968, the American people had effectively voted against the Vietnam War, forcing Lyndon Johnson to renounce the goal of victory, as well as his own career, and then forcing the war-party Democrats out of office. By 1969, the rank and file of the U.S. Army itself was in increasingly open revolt, with in-country soldiers defiantly turning to drugs and, at times, violence against their own superiors. "FTA" was commonly scrawled on helmets and fatigue hats—Fuck the Army. Many Americans had concluded that the war was misbegotten, wrong, futile, unwinnable, tragic—there were dozens of ways of saying "no." Hundreds of thousands of draft-eligible young men had come to a position of visceral rejection. Subsequent history has shown that that position was a profoundly moral one, even if those reaching it were unable to make their case in the language of ethics or religion.

"Conscientiously opposed to participation in war in any form." Some claimants, seizing on the law's ambiguous language, argued that the phrase "in any form" referred not to "war" but to "participation," as if the issue was the registrant's refusal to serve in the military even as a noncombatant, but courts had not upheld that. Of pressing relevance for me was the fact that the "war in any form" provision posed a nearly insurmountable problem for Catholics because the Roman Catholic theological tradition, more so than other Christian denominations, had consistently upheld the "just war" theory, beginning with St. Augustine, then St. Thomas Aquinas, and right down to Pope Pius XII. Many Protestants, by contrast, could appeal to the pacifist example of Jesus himself, or to the early Church's prohibition of Christian service in the Roman army (which had to do not with pacifism but with idolatry, since Roman soldiers had to participate in ceremonies honoring the emperor as divine). But Roman Catholic authority, as everyone knew, ran less to Jesus than to the magisterium of the Church. To participate in some wars, the Church explicitly taught, was not only permitted, but virtuous. Pius XII, in 1956, in an otherwise innocuous encyclical outlining civic duties, had said that Catholics are morally obligated to serve in the military.[18] As for Vietnam, the American Catholic hierarchy, having taken its cue from the jingoistic Cardinal Spellman, was the religious body known to be most vocally supportive of the war. For all of these reasons, almost every local draft board was prepared to greet any conscientious objector request from a Catholic registrant with skepticism.

That was because draft boards knew nothing about changes wrought by Vatican II. The second provision of the 1967 Selective Service law that had relevance for me and the young men I encountered required that an appeal for CO status had to be based "on religious training and belief [and not on] . . . essentially political, sociological, or philosophical views or a merely personal code."[19] Young men who'd attended parochial schools years before, and had then effectively dropped out of the Catholic Church, began showing up at my office, having learned from draft counselors at the AFSC or Mobilization Against the War that appeals, say, to the Eightfold Path of Siddhartha Gautama would get them nowhere. Personal code and philosophical position, however diligently arrived at or eloquently expressed, were useless. In their applications, they had to define a "religious source" for their opposition to war, and they had to explain how they were trained in it.[20]

They came to me, usually in despair, to ask if, in their Catholic background, however remote, there was such a source. It was my pleasure to answer yes, and then, if they wanted it, to offer them a crash course in the "religious training" that draft boards would require them to cite. From John XXIII's encyclical *Pacem in Terris* ("It is contrary to reason to hold that war can now be considered an instrument of justice"[21]) to the Vatican Council's declaration "On the Church in the Modern World" ("The horror and perversity of war is immensely magnified by the addition of scientific weapons . . . [which] compel us to undertake an evaluation of war with an entirely new attitude"[22]), the Catholic Church had entered a time of transition, amending the "just war" tradition and moving toward an affirmation of conscientious objection as a Catholic option.

In the United States, the bishops, at the end of 1968, declared that Catholic teaching supported both conscientious objection and selective conscientious objection, but almost no one knew that. That was because the bishops made their statement about war in a pastoral letter, "Human Life in Our Day," that was overwhelmingly given over to a defense of the birth-control-condemning *Humanae Vitae*. The American bishops, in the teeth of near-universal opposition from Catholic laypeople, were calling a halt to dissent and confusion on the question of contraception: the use of artificial birth control ("arti-fucking-ficial," as one BU kid put it) was forbidden under pain of mortal sin, forever. The Church has spoken. Period.

In a coda tacked on to the end of the pastoral letter, as if the bishops knew it was unseemly to completely ignore the question that was ripping America apart, the subject of Vietnam was addressed with such hand-wringing ambivalence—"While it would be beyond our competence to propose any technical formula for bringing the Vietnam War to an end . . ."[23]—that it was properly understood as a continuation of Roman Catholic support for the war. That was what drew notice. The letter did express a convoluted, if unprecedented, sympathy for conscientious objection, and that was useful to me and others who prepared Catholic boys for draft board hearings.

But even that timid coda included an outrage. The bishops' discussion of conscientious objection began by stating that many who seek to avoid military service do so out of "cowardice." I could not believe that Catholic bishops had seen fit to introduce that word into any discussion of the dilemma facing young American men. In all the years of counseling them on the draft, I saw fear in the eyes of many boys, but never cowardice. On the contrary, their effort to deal truthfully and directly with the American tragedy amounted to courage pure and simple.

I was not the only one to react angrily to the bishops' pastoral letter. It gave rise to a quip among liberal Catholics that if American B-52s were dropping condoms on Vietnam, the bishops would have condemned the war in no uncertain terms, but since the bombers were dropping napalm, the bishops (celibate, yet self-appointed experts on sex) found it beyond their moral competence.[24]

I realized that, week after week, I had a solemn obligation to address such questions in front of the young people who came to my Masses, because every one of the males in attendance, whether he knew it or not, had this issue ahead of him. But more than that, I had an obligation to let them know about the Catholic roots of the Vietnam War. (Ngo Dinh Diem, a former French colonial functionary and a pious Catholic, had been living in exile in a New York seminary when Cardinal Spellman sponsored his 1955 appointment as prime minister of South Vietnam. Diem's Inquisition-style war against Buddhists sparked U.S. involvement in 1963.) And I had an obligation to let them know about the Catholic opposition to the war. (At Newman House we staged a production of Daniel Berrigan's play *The Trial of the Catonsville Nine.*) Soon, despite that professor who'd warned me about my negative energy, I was obsessively preaching about war, understanding that, for some of the boys in front of me, it had become—talk about negative energy!—a matter of life and death.

Newman House became a draft counseling center, and we staffed an office with young experts in Selective Service law.[25] I began offering courses with titles like "The Catholic Tradition and War," to instruct men wrestling with the prospect of being drafted and to give them a setting in which to express themselves on the question, in discussions and in essays written for me. Pedagogy aside, this was partly a way of helping them satisfy yet another condition of the CO application: to show evidence that they had given "expression, publicly or privately, written or oral, to the views herein expressed. Give examples."[26] My classes at Newman House were those examples.

The CO application also asked for "references that would support your claim of conscientious objection," and that was what I became for one young man after another. "Sincerity" was explicitly required of the applicant, and I attested to that as well. Like each of them, I was subject to five years' imprisonment for making any false statement in this federal matter, and in truth I found myself making assertions about intimate knowledge of motive and conviction that often could not be justified. There was never any doubt in my mind or theirs what the exercise was all about—exploiting the law, manipulating the VFW types on the local boards, snowing them with theology and piety, all for the sake of helping a kid stay out of the hell of Vietnam.

Again and again, applications for exemption that I helped prepare were turned down. "Greetings," their return letters said, conscripting the young men into a moral—and mortal—abyss. In point of fact, local draft boards did not give a damn about *Pacem in Terris.* If Vietnam was good enough for Cardinal Spellman, his successor Cardinal Cooke, and the other American bishops, it was good enough for Tom, Dick, and Ringo, if that was his name. More than once, I helped boys flee to Canada, arranging rides for them and putting them in touch with a network of resistance supporters. More often than that, I visited friends in jail who'd refused induction. It drove me nuts that, because of confusion in the way confused Church teachings were promulgated, Catholic boys were more vulnerable to the war machine than any of their peers.

7. CARDINAL CUSHING'S LAST HURRAH

The Catholic campus ministers of the Archdiocese of Boston were a second community for me. As Bill Coffin had done, I was crossing the threshold into serious opposition to the war in company with young men who had no choice in the matter. My choice was simply to stand with them. Other campus chaplains were doing the same, and in their company, more than anywhere else in those years, I felt understood.

Boston was higher education's paradise. Assigned to a dozen or so colleges and universities (including Harvard, MIT, Tufts, Northeastern, Boston College, and Boston State), the chaplains were led by Father Robert Bullock, the Catholic chaplain at Brandeis University. Bullock, a Boston priest, had the looks of a movie star and affability to match. From Brandeis, the Jewish university, he was already a prophetic figure in the Church, aggressively advocating the contacts that would evolve into a highly productive Jewish-Catholic dialogue. But the war was as much an issue at Brandeis as it was at BU or any of the other schools by 1970. Bullock had his appointment as director of campus ministry from Cardinal Cushing, and word was that Cushing had confidence in him. Where was Cushing on the war?

Cushing was seriously ill with emphysema, and he was rarely seen in public. Demoralized by the controversies over birth control and his support for Jacqueline Kennedy Onassis, and by the ever-worsening pain from his ailments, he was often in his cups. And he could be irascible ("You don't have enough brains to lose your faith," he told one troubled priest. "Go back to your parish"[27]). But he trusted Bob Bullock. When we campus ministers compared notes and found how common it was that young Catholic men were being rebuffed at draft boards, where claims of Church support for conscientious objection were regularly contradicted, Bullock proposed an idea to Cushing. That led to my unforgettable meeting with him.

Before coming to Boston, I had assumed, foolishly, that Cushing and I would get to know each other. But the archbishop's residence on the far edge of the city was a world away from BU. Although, memorably, that gap was once bridged after a young graduate student came to me pleading for a loan to make a past-due tuition payment. I explained that I didn't have the money, that the Newman House budget was administered at the archdiocesan chancery. "What's that?" the student asked. "Cardinal Cushing's office," I answered, assuming I had of necessity shut the young man off. That was that, or so I thought. A week later, the student returned to thank me for sending him to Cushing, who had agreed to see him and given him the loan.

Bullock's meeting was in the early spring of 1970, a little more than a year since I had come to Boston. Two dozen priests and nuns convened in a meeting room at the cardinal's estate in Brighton. I had been in his presence half a dozen times, but this was the first time I actually met the cardinal. He was gaunt and hollow-eyed and taller than I remembered. He made clear as he entered the room there would be no kissing of the ring; we were his intimate circle. He greeted me warmly.

Cushing sat with us for what seemed a long time. Our chairs were arranged in a semicircle in front of him. He listened as we described what our young people were going through as a result of the war. We pleaded for a clear, strong statement affirming the right of a Catholic to conscientious objection, and we asked him—more difficult—for his personal statement of opposition to the war. If the cardinal archbishop of Boston were to actively encourage rejection of the war...

He did not take the hint. Instead of responding to our earnest entreaties, he drifted off into innocuous reminiscence. I may have it confused with imitations I was hearing from Boston priests, but I recall him falling into what was clearly an anecdotal routine—Cushing imitating his imitators—the story of Father Feeney beating him to the draw. He positively cackled to repeat the punch line, Feeney saying, "In the name of the Blessed Virgin Mary, I excommunicate you!" At the end of the evening, I was unsure what, if anything, had been accomplished. But I was certain that the ailing Cushing was near the end, and it made me sad.

Weeks later, on Easter Sunday, March 29, 1970, the cardinal published one of the most remarkable pastoral letters ever to come from a member of the American Catholic hierarchy. In it, he had unstinting praise for young Catholic men who, as conscientious objectors, put the question of the morality of the Vietnam War before the American people. "Would it be too much to suggest," Cushing proposed, "that we empty our jails of all the protesters—the guilty and the innocent—without judging them; call back from over the border, and around the world, the young men who are called 'deserters'; drop the cases that are still awaiting judgment on our own college youth."[28] All young Americans who were in trouble because of their antiwar dissent had an unexpected ally. My happiest act as a Catholic priest was to read that letter to my students at Boston University. It was, equally, my proudest moment. No religious figure, and no figure of power, had yet weighed in with such unambiguous and strong support for the young people who, more than anyone, had seen the truth of America's disastrous mistake in Vietnam. Among members of the establishment, no one ever would match him.

Cardinal Cushing had begun my theological education when I was ten years old. He continued it through the years of the Vatican Council. And now he brought it to completion, sealing my love for this Church—a peace community at last. Yes, last: the pastoral letter was the cardinal's last hurrah. Five months later, as he turned seventy-five, he retired, and three months after that, he died.

CHAPTER EIGHT

THE SCANDAL

1. HOW I LOVED IT

THE RED-FLOORED ROOM at BU enshrined everything I had come to love about being a priest. The Mass, its simple intimacy stretching from the crossed-legged circle all the way to God, was the heart of my life, and that place was my heart's cradle. Boston University, it turned out, was a gyre around which antiwar turmoil threatened to spin out of control. Demonstrations and protests attracted, in addition to large numbers of idealistic students, a fringe of misfits who loved to provoke cops into wielding their clubs ("Ho! Ho! Ho Chi Minh! NLF is gonna win!"). Between protests, they were given to mischief like setting off false fire alarms and committing acts of arson. Among other instances, the BU president's office, just down the street from Newman House, was set on fire. From the stresses of such conflict and the general social strife of the time, not to mention the mere loneliness of a man vowed to solitude, the chapel was a true sanctuary.

Passing my secretary's desk, I would joke that I was going fishing without a pole, which is how I defined the meditative time I spent in chapel. I learned to sit still, transfixed, waiting to obey anyone who stopped by. The obedience to which I was bound resided less in the various figures of authority above me—from the pastor of St. Ann's Parish two miles away from BU, where I lived with fellow Paulists, to the head of the Paulist order in New York, to the archdiocesan director of campus ministry, to the cardinal across Boston—than in the demand to pay attention to the young. In the hierarchical order there is obedience upward, but there is obedience downward, too. From that direction would come an eroding of the order itself, but I did not know that yet. I simply loved the red place for belonging as much to the students as to me.

One of them, in response to a Good Friday sermon I preached, had made a banner that we hung on the wall, and it became an object of my contemplation: "We are broken servants to a broken world." I never looked at it without an unwilled act of emotional assent. How broken we priestly servants were I would not fully realize until years later. Yet to live with my Paulist brothers at St. Ann's was to live within a warning of that brokenness. I have described my general appreciation of the Paulists, but here was a shadow side. There were eight of them, all considerably older than I. Apart from the pastor, they were curates, hospital chaplains, and parish missionaries. As they settled into the plush chairs of the rectory's common room after dinner each night, highball glasses in hand, staring with glazed eyes at the television, from early evening quiz shows to late night Johnny Carson, I would return to Newman House, in flight.

After imbibing the ideal of Paulist community life for most of a decade, I was disturbed to find an alcoholic haze hanging over the clerical fraternity into which I had been initiated by ordination. And I sensed that my fellow priests were drinking not for the pleasure of the buzz but to anesthetize themselves. Their years as preachers of the Word, anointers of the sick, consecrators of the chalice, and forgivers of sin had left my confreres reeking of stoic unhappiness. Each of them, like most priests, had his consolations and satisfactions, but at bottom his hopes and dreams had long since been hollowed out. I would learn that theirs was a way of life typical of more than a few American Catholic priests. Such well-meaning, large-hearted men—but their hearts were broken.

The theory that I had embraced before ordination was that the vows of poverty, chastity, and obedience were the ground of our full availability to the people we served as priests. Unfettered by worldly concerns or prior obligations of career and family, we were ready to respond to the needs of all. We were "men for others." Such heroic readiness was not what I saw in the emotionally throttled garrison of St. Ann's. Once, in the middle of a wintry night, a fellow BU chaplain, an Episcopalian, called the rectory. The "priest on duty," wakened out of his sleep, answered the phone. My BU colleague asked for me, explaining that the Boston police had launched a drug bust on one of the university's high-rise dormitories. To alert each other, so that they might flush their dope down the toilet or toss it out the window, kids had set off fire alarms, which escalated the emergency. There were a dozen fire trucks in the street, surrounded by a thousand freezing students in pajamas.

It was the kind of crisis college chaplains lived for, a rare occasion when they, more than any other figure in the university community, had instant relevance. The other BU chaplains, Protestant and Jewish, were rushing to the dorm to help. I was needed. But the duty priest of St. Ann's did not wake me up with this news. My fellow campus minister had bolted from bed, leaving his wife and small children to respond, but I, celibate and therefore "radically available for service," was not to have his sleep disturbed. When I found the priest's note on my bedroom door the next morning, explaining that he had spared me the trouble, I felt something turn cold in my chest. Seminary rhetoric about "community" had not prepared me for the actuality of the petrified clerical culture.

The campus Newman House was a locus of good feeling compared to St. Ann's Rectory. That was especially true of our renovated chapel, where at night, with candles flickering off the richly paneled walls, it seemed like the interior of a jewel box. In the morning it was an open treasure chest, and the sunbeams that filled the air seemed generated from inside the room, an effect of several stunning new stained-glass windows. Created by one of our young members, the leaded glass deliberately repeated the patterns of the street scene outside. The inherent beauty of the way the sun moved across the sky was enhanced in this light, as the sun's reflections moved across the lucent red carpet. Another art student had painted a mural of those gathered around the table, an abstracted mirror image of the group at worship. One figure in the painting's center, recognizably holding a cup, was inspired by me. That the artist rendered that priest with the pointed hat and diamond-patterned tunic of a clown I took as a great compliment.

In a compromise with the intimidating conventions of the confessional, I took to sitting on the floor in the far corner where the traditional booths had been before our renovation. My position there was private enough, and when I donned the slim purple stole to mark a sacramental moment before Mass, students who wanted to enact the ritual of penance could join me in the corner. Sometimes we knelt side by side, sometimes we sat cross-legged like meditators. We spoke in whispers. Soon, out from under the rote setting, the rote words fell away. The confidences given me concerned not bad temper or swears but questions of love, real love, not fantasy. Questions of longing and discouragement, of the fear that burned under the surface of all that was hip. I learned what my most important function was—to be a steady source of kindness. I could see hope come into the eyes of the young men and women in front of me. When I pronounced the formulaic absolution, I always cupped the student's head with my hand, fully aware that the affirmative power that I could feel flowing between us, nothing to do with me, was God's power with which I had been entrusted. I was a priest. How I loved it.

2. THIS FATHER CARROLL

Cardinal Cushing, instrument and embodiment of the Church's break with the past, would die in November 1970, but not before seeing himself replaced in October by a very different man. As a sixteen-year-old, Humberto Sousa Medeiros had come to America from the Portuguese Azores, the son of a debt-fleeing farmer. Humberto came of age in the hardscrabble coastal city of Fall River, Massachusetts, but there was nothing of the laborer about him, and he soon took refuge in the Church. He was short, corpulent, and thick-lipped. He carried his head at an angle, as if ever asking permission. His hands, too, seemed supplicant, always joined. He was the first non-Irish archbishop of Boston in more than a century, and supplication might have seemed the proper attitude. To the Irish, "Portogees" were a kind of "colored" people, and Boston was a racial cauldron, soon to boil over in the school busing crisis. At his installation ceremony, Medeiros said, "Personally, I feel too weak and too small for the task entrusted to me by the Holy Father."[1] It seemed true.

Medeiros had made his mark as the compassionate bishop of Brownsville, Texas, in the Rio Grande Valley, one of the poorest dioceses in the United States. He was loved by the Chicano farm workers of the Southwest, and though we did not see it at the time, his elevation to the very seat of Irish Catholicism forecast the ethnic and demographic changes that would reshape the American Catholic Church over the coming generation.[2]

Hispanic Catholicism had long been marked by its emphasis on emotive devotion—a consequence, perhaps, of Inquisition-sponsored skepticism toward the rational element of faith. Spanish inquisitors had driven thinkers out of Spain, if not out of the Church. In taking hold in Latin America, Catholicism had made more than its usual compromises with indigenous religions, and much that passed for piety was native superstition.[3] Vatican II, with its licensing of theological criticism and its new mode of ethical inquiry, was decidedly not a phenomenon of the Spanish Church. Cardinal Medeiros was a well-educated man, fluent in five languages, yet he seemed an example of the hyperemotional, anti-intellectual strain of faith that the council was an attempt to outgrow.

But Hispanic Catholicism in the postcolonial (and post-Franco) era was also generating a newly politicized reading of the Gospel, what came to be called liberation theology. The movement was centered in Latin America, where priests, nuns, and even some bishops had thrown in with campesinos against landowners and oligarchs. This Catholic demand for social justice had its U.S. manifestation in César Chávez's United Farm Workers, around which Catholics of all stripes rallied. Grape and lettuce boycotts were widely promoted even in suburban parishes across America, with the slogan *Viva la Causa!* a regular feature of otherwise mainstream Sunday bulletins. As it had in the first years of the labor movement, responding to its early-wave immigrant constituency, the Catholic Church once more firmly sided with workers against bosses and owners. In Texas, Medeiros had been slow to challenge the agribusiness interests or to weigh in on contract disputes, but he had been attentive to the pastoral needs of migrant workers, often going out into the fields himself to say Mass on makeshift altars. The affectionate esteem in which farm workers held him was the most notable feature of his story when he came to Boston.

It would soon be apparent, though, that Humberto Medeiros was defined by piety, not politics. For the likes of me, that would spell trouble. I was one of a small group of presumptuous priests who asked to meet with him as soon as he arrived. Responding to his reputation in Brownsville, we explained in a letter that we hoped he would dramatize his solidarity with the poor by moving from the palatial cardinal's residence in Brighton to the relatively modest rectory of Holy Cross Cathedral in Boston's inner city. The new archbishop declined to meet with us, and he never considered living anywhere but in the palace.

I eventually met with Medeiros on several occasions, all of them contentious. Once it was with that same group of presumptuous priests, this time to ask him to condemn the unending war in Vietnam. In rejecting our appeal, the cardinal told us how much he suffered under the burden of indecision, not knowing what to do or say about the war. A similar indecision, although exacerbated by Irish Boston's implicitly racist contempt for him, would keep Medeiros sidelined during the crucible of the busing controversy. "I didn't say I believed in forced busing or that I was against it," he would explain. "That's a means to an end. And how to plan the integration of the city, that's beyond me. I have no competence there."[4]

More than once, I was summoned to the archdiocesan chancery, with the warning that Cardinal Medeiros was angry at me. The first time I responded to such an order, I arrived at the chancellor's office properly chastened. Whatever impression the cardinal had of me, I was far from a cocksure rebel. I already knew to worry that much of what I was advocating for the Church would have unintended negative consequences. Promoting Vatican II reforms in the liturgy, for example, meant trading in Gregorian chant for the banalities of pop music (my liturgical musicians at BU loved to conclude the Mass with the peppy song *Leaving on a Jet Plane*). In encouraging my once scrupulous Catholic students to claim their own freedom of conscience, I was inadvertently abetting the American spirit of "anything goes." In emphasizing love as a primary ethical principle, I was taken to be sponsoring the amorality of the sexual revolution. What I had most loved about the Church as a young man—the high culture of medieval Catholicism, exemplified by Gerard Manley Hopkins, G. K. Chesterton, Graham Greene, and others—I was helping to destroy. On such questions, I was my own harshest critic.

Arriving at the chancery, I was relieved that the cardinal himself was not going to see me. His crimson-sashed stand-in got right to the point by quoting Medeiros: "This Father Carroll," he said, half imitating the Portuguese prelate, "peeses me off." I heard the mocking of an immigrant accent as racist, but laughed anyway. The monsignor raised his hand to silence me. Not funny.

I was aware that any one of a dozen things could have pissed off His Eminence. The archdiocesan factotum explained that it had been brought to the cardinal's attention that I was guilty of a grave moral infraction. And then, as if rendering a verdict, he declared that I had encouraged students at BU to use contraception. I asked if he was asking me to discuss what I did in the private forum of the confessional. He pushed a letter across his desk at me, saying that the cardinal had the complaint from a student's parents. A quick look at the letter told me that it had not, in fact, been addressed to Medeiros but to the president of Boston University. Since the university, Methodist in its origins, had no connection with the Catholic Church, such a complaint should never have found its way to the archdiocese, but BU's president was a figure with whom I had publicly clashed over antiwar politics. Obviously, he had forwarded the oddball letter knowing it would get me in trouble.

"His Eminence should know," I said, "that if I encourage young people to take precautions about pregnancy, it is to help avoid a later decision about abortion."

He deflected my thrust. "Father Carroll, His Eminence is distressed that you are giving public scandal. This letter makes plain that you are notorious, even among those outside the Church." The BU president was not a Catholic. This complaint surprised me, and I did not know what to say. Was the cardinal's problem with the ethical instruction I offered young people, or was it with the fact of my deviance from Vatican norms having drawn notice—especially the notice of the BU president? Was I being told to change what I told young people about sex, or was I being told to be more discreet in my disobedience? Was the cardinal, through his surrogate, simply discharging the duty that was required of him by the fact of his having received that letter? Confused though I was, the event was a moment of awakening. "Scandal." The word was pushed in my face as if it defined the gravest of offenses, yet all that was really being talked about were appearances. Medeiros wanted not my obedience but the semblance of it.

After one or more of my other "infractions" against Church authority were brought to the cardinal's attention—I was publicly worshiping with Protestants; I was letting women distribute Communion; in television interviews, affirming the moral primacy of love, I declined to condemn sex outside marriage; I blasted the Catholic hierarchy's support of the Vietnam War—Medeiros angrily contacted the head of the Paulist Fathers in New York, instructing him to remove me from Boston. *Fired.*

I learned of my banishment from my sympathetic Paulist superior Father Thomas Stransky, whom we saw at the Vatican Council as an author of the decree on religious liberty. Stransky told me that, adopting a ploy favored by Vatican bureaucrats, he would carry out the order only when Medeiros repeated it. That did not happen. Cardinal Medeiros, I realized, was not actually trying to impose his authority on me or get me out of his archdiocese. With a simple phone call to Newman House, he could have exiled me from Boston himself. He was simply purging his responsibility to have done something about my "scandalous" behavior, hoping to intimidate me into stopping it, while taking no real action to force me to.

In this refusal to be serious about authority, Medeiros embodied the slow collapse of moral structure which had been set in motion by *Humanae Vitae.* Abortion was an ethical issue on which Catholic assent was more or less maintained, but not contraception.[5] Few really believed that condoms, diaphragms, and the birth control pill were intrinsically evil, but the encyclical imposed a cloud of pretense on the Church. Bishops pretended to promulgate the teaching, priests pretended to impose it, and laypeople pretended to listen to them. It was a tissue of lies.[6] But that did not matter, because the appearance of conformity on the issue was all the hierarchy wanted, since the "issue" was not the issue. Birth control, that is, was not the real subject of *Humanae Vitae.* Papal power was, and by extension, episcopal power and priestly power—the power structure of clericalism. That was what I had violated, not by disobeying *Humanae Vitae* but by being *seen* disobeying it.

3. PAUL SHANLEY AND HIS PROTECTORS

The culture of clerical power was the absolute, and Medeiros saw its protection as his most solemn duty. That explains the far more serious lapse of authentic authority of which he was guilty in that same period—a lapse of which I and everyone I knew were ignorant, even though it involved another of my fellow presumptuous priests.

Reverend Paul R. Shanley was the campus minister at Boston State College, a blue-collar school (formerly Boston State Teachers' College, now the University of Massachusetts at Boston) a mile or two away from BU. Shanley, ordained to the priesthood in 1960, had taken the Vatican Council revolution to heart, and by the late sixties, having angled for an assignment to a relatively unfettered campus ministry, he reinvented himself as one of the new breed of Catholic priests.

Boston State was a gritty urban school with no real campus, and its students were commuters. Mostly they were older, and holding down jobs. Therefore much of what occupied chaplains in more traditional colleges like BU was irrelevant to Shanley's work. Instead he used Boston State as a base from which to freelance in a variety of ad hoc ministries in downtown Boston. Chief among these was reaching out to the then swelling population of runaway teenagers—would-be flower children—who, especially in the spring, summer, and fall, gravitated to the benches and bushes of Boston Common. In the late sixties and early seventies there were hundreds of them. Drug use by these young people was epidemic. They were dangerously exposed and vulnerable.

Shanley organized a broad response to this homelessness, attracting a legion of volunteers, especially from Boston's medical community. He was a founder of Bridge over Troubled Waters, a drug crisis project centered around a mobile clinic—a roving van in which doctors and nurses would drive through the night, on the lookout for bad-tripping kids. Shanley himself spent countless nights wandering the paths of the Common and the back alleys of downtown, searching for children to rescue. In drawing attention to their plight, he also drew attention to himself. He was regarded as a hero, an icon of the new priest in the reformed Catholic Church.

I saw Shanley a number of times during that period, mainly at meetings of campus ministers. He was a tall, good-looking Irishman, one of the staunchest rebels against clericalism. He carried himself with a deliberate swagger, but his stylized embrace of the counterculture—ill-kempt hair, shaggy sideburns, a fringed leather jacket, motorcycle boots—seemed over the top to me. What I saw as fake, others saw as charismatic. The nuns in our circle were drawn to him, and it seemed no accident that the most devoted Bridge over Troubled Waters volunteers were women. I suspected that Shanley might fall in love with one of them.

Wrong. I would not learn it until the sexual-abuse crisis broke in 2002, but Paul Shanley was even then, when I knew him, taking boys home from the Boston Common and raping them. And Cardinal Medeiros was his enabler. As the crisis sparked by stories published in the *Boston Globe* would ultimately reveal, a significant, if relatively small, percentage of Catholic priests, over the decades, had sexually abused children. Shanley was one of the most lecherous. The revelation of such "unpriestly" behavior was staggering enough. But what the crisis laid bare with equal power was that almost every Catholic bishop, beginning in Boston but reaching west to California and east to cities in Europe, responded to the abuse by protecting the priests instead of the children. The first of such bishops was Cardinal Medeiros, and among the first of his wards was Shanley.

At age seventy-four, in 2005, Shanley was tried and convicted of raping a child and sentenced to from twelve to fifteen years in prison. This crime involved actions he committed in the mid-1980s, but it was clearly only one criminal act among dozens. Shanley's first assaults against underage boys had occurred twenty years before the crime of which he was convicted. The vulnerable runaways he had "rescued" were simply his prey. Various lawsuits settled by the Archdiocese of Boston established that Shanley was raping boys from the mid-sixties on.[7] Typically, he brought them to his weekend cabin in the woods of the Blue Hills south of Boston, or, later, once funders were drawn to his work, to a farm they provided him in Vermont. In such "safe" places, he put boys "in touch" with their bodies. He offered them drugs, and even demonstrated ways to inject drugs with needles. Once Shanley's victims were sexually initiated, he passed them along to other men. This was all unknown at the time, at least to me.

After I had left the campus ministry, Shanley became strident in his defiance of Cardinal Medeiros—on the issue of homosexuality. Never an antiwar protester, an advocate of the equality of women, or a critic of the hierarchy's retreat from the reforms of Vatican II, Shanley emerged in the 1970s as a figure preoccupied with gay rights. He publicly criticized Catholic teaching that sex between people of the same gender was intrinsically wrong. It seemed that the resolutely macho Shanley was just defending a group that was unfairly marginalized in the Catholic Church, the hero selflessly risking himself for the sake of victims. But his concern was narrow.

In Shanley's secret homosexuality, he was like a significant percentage of Catholic priests.[8] Their dilemma shows that what we are considering here is not just a question of a "personal problem." The Church condemns homosexuality in no uncertain terms, yet it simultaneously accommodates homosexuals in the ranks of its leadership. The camaraderie of community life that forms the idealized essence of the priestly fraternity has, as we've seen, been marked through the centuries by a sublimated homoeroticism, a not surprising consequence of all-male exclusivity. This has been especially true of religious and monastic orders, but it stamps the overall clerical culture. I saw it myself, if mainly in the distorting mirror of the rules we lived by.

Through the years of seminary training, we Paulists, following Vatican-imposed regulations, were forbidden to cross the threshold into another seminarian's room. We were warned against "particular friendship" and instructed not to take walks in pairs. Eagle-eyed obsessiveness on the part of those in charge made us seminarians aware that they expected us to fall in love with each other. And why not? As long as such male bonding did not express itself in openly sexual acts, same-sex love was not only permitted but considered normal. Although "homos" were detested, the currents of life in our exclusively male world ran strenuously in the direction of homosexuality. This contradiction—condemn what you live—was a version of the corrupting falsehood that surfaced with *Humanae Vitae*, even if in the birth control case the context was heterosexuality.[9]

If homosexual feelings are a routine part of the culture and circumstances in which you live, and if, simultaneously, you are taught—and bound to teach—that such feelings are evil, the resulting moral discord can be crippling. Many priests were secretly broken by this tension—"broken servants" indeed. That woundedness surely accounts for such typically self-punishing responses as alcoholism or the retreat into the harsh impersonality that marked many a man in the Roman collar. A few, however, broke under these stresses in ways that victimized those who were readily and defenselessly at hand—children.

How could priests have been capable of such heinous acts as they were revealed by the thousands as having committed? The dynamic is simple: if an inclination is evil and yet so powerful it cannot be denied, that contradiction can secretly sanction the urge to act on it. There is a difference between pederasty and homosexuality, and, in accounting for the priest abuse crisis, the distinction must be insisted on. The Vatican has tried to blame homosexual priests for the problem,[10] but its roots sink deep in the Catholic sexual imagination itself. We have seen repeatedly how sexual totalitarianism is a main mode of clerical power, an organizing principle of the institution. Heterosexuals are vulnerable to this kind of power, and so are homosexuals. Without scapegoating homosexuals, it can be acknowledged that a key aspect of the priest abuse crisis involves the social pathology of a massively denied homosexuality that, when seeking release, targets available victims, who are youngsters of the same sex.

Cardinal Medeiros had reason to know Shanley for the victimizer he was, but he did nothing either to stop Shanley or to puncture his pose. Indeed, archdiocesan officials had received complaints, beginning before Shanley was famous as a "street priest," that he was bringing teenage boys to his cabin in the woods and having sex with them. But no such complaints were made public or acted upon. Records opened during Shanley's 2005 criminal trial show that Church officials did nothing to investigate these charges, though they dated to the mid-1960s and at least one came from a fellow priest.[11]

What finally pushed Medeiros to act in the Shanley case, as in mine on the question of birth control, was the fear of scandal. In a 1977 lecture in Rochester, New York, Shanley openly advocated man-boy sexual relations, asserting that children could handle all kinds of sexual intimacy. He claimed, in fact, that children were often the ones to coyly initiate sexual intimacy with men, and that men were right to respond. Grown men as the true victims.

Rochester was a long way from Boston, and though Medeiros was informed of what Shanley was saying, he did not take action until contacted a year later by a lawyer from New York, after Shanley had repeated his advocacy of child-adult sex. That the notice came from a lawyer raised an implicit threat of legal consequences. This was a stimulus finally to do something.

And what action did Medeiros take? He closed down Shanley's freelance ministry in the inner city and assigned him to a posh parish in the prosperous Boston suburb of Newton. That church was blessed with a legion of bright-faced altar boys. From his niche as curate in Newton, and then, after being promoted to pastor by Medeiros's successor, Cardinal Bernard Law, Shanley continued abusing young people for another fifteen years, including the boy whose rape case eventually came to trial.

In response to the sex-abuse crisis in 2002, the Catholic bishops established the National Review Board for the Protection of Children and Young People to investigate the real scope of the Catholic failure. When the board issued its findings in 2004, the nightmare was even worse than Catholics thought. From the Church's own numbers (and therefore, if anything, undercounted), it became known that more than ten thousand minors had been violated. More than four thousand priests had committed the crimes, about four percent of all priests who served. The vast majority of bishops protected the priests instead of the children.[12]

Catholics could not hear this news the way other people did. For us, the devastation and anger involved a measure of personal remorse. It was not only that our entire Church stood indicted—from its system of authority to its clerical culture to its tradition of secrecy to its basic teachings about morality—but also that each Catholic had reason to feel implicated. I am not talking about a generalized corporate guilt here, nor do I mean to take away from the particular responsibility of the individual perpetrators. But this massive failure could not have happened if we the Church had not enabled it. I have been a layman for thirty-five years, but for five years—as this crisis was brewing—I was a priest among priests who were victimizing children. To say that I did not know does not say enough.

When Catholics cooperated in the climate of dishonesty that polluted the Church's teachings about sex—not making an issue, for example, of the absurd birth control prohibition—we were shoring up the dishonest atmosphere in which abusive priests thrived. When we declined to hold bishops accountable for their excessively autocratic exercise of authority in small matters (forbidding girls from serving at Mass with altar boys) and large (closing parish schools without consultation), we supported the power system that bishops were protecting in protecting abusers. When we failed to make an issue of the unjust discrimination against women embodied in the male-only priesthood, we were part of what allowed patriarchal clericalism to reach a state of calcified corruption. When we passively accepted the hierarchy's refusal to implement the Vatican II reforms aimed at empowering the laity, we gave the abusive priests a place to hide and their sponsoring bishops a way to keep them hidden.

"The terrible history recorded here today," the head of the U.S. bishops' conference, Bishop Wilton Gregory, said when the review board's report was issued in 2004, "is history." That was his way of saying it was over. Done with. If anyone presumed to ask about the sources of the abuse scandal, bishops talked vaguely about homosexuals, an obsessive media, or the permissive 1960s. They baldly asserted that celibacy has nothing to do with the priesthood's problems, and as for women, the bishops averred that the second-place status of females was set by Jesus. That question was still closed. Meanwhile, on subjects ranging from gay marriage to the closing of parishes, bishops resumed their old autocratic habit of giving orders from on high. In all of this the bishops showed every sign not only of wanting a return to "normal," but of thinking it was possible.

But what if normal was the problem? Were Catholics going to enable this refusal to deal with the Church's real crisis? Were Catholics going to pretend that deep questions of moral teaching, lay empowerment, homophobia, and sexism had not been raised? Were they actually going to allow the avoidance of consequences by the particular bishops who enabled abusers to continue their crime sprees? Catholics assured one another and the world that, across fifty years, we had not seen what was happening in so many rectories and in so many church-sponsored youth activities. But we could no longer claim such moral blindness. The corruptions of our Church had been made plain.

The Shanley case told it all. By the early 1990s he and another priest had cultivated a life apart from Boston, running the Cabana Club, a "clothing optional" motel for gay men, in Palms Springs, California. Cardinal Law knew everything about Shanley that Medeiros knew; Law had even authorized secret payments to some of Shanley's victims. Yet in 1997 Law wrote a letter of recommendation for him, for the position of director of a Catholic homeless shelter in New York, a post Shanley would have had if Cardinal John O'Connor of New York had not intervened to stop the appointment.[13] When Shanley formally retired from the priesthood in 1996, having raped dozens of boys over thirty years, Cardinal Law, who knew that history, wrote to him: "Without doubt over all of these years of generous and zealous care, the lives and hearts of many people have been touched by your sharing of the Lord's Spirit. You are truly appreciated for all that you have done."[14]

4. THE BASILICA OF DENIAL

Cardinal Law's protection of Shanley was central to the legal case that was ultimately built against Law himself, but there were numerous other abusers whom he shielded. The attorney general of Massachusetts issued a finding that said, but for technicalities, Law would have been indicted as an accomplice to these crimes. "State's Top Lawyer Accuses Boston Church of Cover-up," a *New York Times* headline read.[15] To protect abusers and his own power, the cardinal did not stop short even at sacrilege, as this example shows: A victim named Tom Blanchette encountered Law at the funeral of Father Joseph Birmingham in 1989. When Blanchette described to Law the way Birmingham had abused him as a child, Law, as Blanchette recounts it, "laid his hands on my head for two or three minutes. And then he said this, 'I bind you by the power of the confessional never to speak about this to anyone else.'"[16]

The so-called seal of the confessional defines the absolute obligation of *priests* to maintain the secrets of penitents. In Catholicism that seal is sacred. Law's reversal of its meaning, and his readiness to use such mystical mumbo-jumbo to manipulate a desperate and broken man, exposes the depth of this scandal. The sacraments themselves could be twisted to serve the silence. But Law had been behaving this way for years. A decade before the Shanley story broke, the actions of a priest named James Porter, abuser of more than two hundred children, had been laid out by the *Boston Globe*.

That brought Law's wrath down on the paper. At a 1992 press conference, using a bizarre phrase, the cardinal "called down the Holy Spirit" on the paper in what felt like a kind of curse. I was by then a columnist for the *Globe*. There may be something off-key in referring to my own work here, but the timing of my observations, and the content, have larger relevance for the point at issue. I wrote at the time, "The Church's impulse toward cover-up—always under the rubric of 'not giving scandal'—was chillingly displayed by Cardinal Bernard Law when he attacked the media, especially the *Globe*, as if public interest in the allegations was somehow anti-Catholic. The news coverage, in fact, was even then enabling dozens of Porter's alleged victims to drop the chains of secrecy, guilt, and loneliness he had imposed on them, chains that the Church had helped to keep bound tight." In that column, I suggested what was being revealed. "The Porter case savagely demonstrates how in need of broad reform our Church remains. Why have we Catholics so passively allowed the clerical establishment to resist the changes begun at Vatican II? In its effort to maintain outmoded, sexist structures of priesthood and hierarchy, the Church is killing itself and harming its members. Its deeply dishonest posture on most matters of sexual morality involves the same cult of denial that cloaked Porter."[17]

As if the cardinal's "curse" worked, the *Globe* did, in fact, back off the priest abuse story, although there was plenty to cover. Finally, in 2001 the *Globe* began to publish the scathing series of articles, including the Shanley story, that set the public crisis in motion. Because this time the *Globe* refused to let the abuse story rest, a disgraced Cardinal Law was forced to resign his position as archbishop of Boston in 2002. But, as he had protected abusive priests, the Vatican protected him. Law was named archpriest of the Basilica of St. Mary Major in Rome by Pope John Paul II. It is no wonder. In pursuing his illegal policy of obfuscation, denial, and protection, Law was carrying out instructions from the Vatican itself.

In May 2001, within months of the scandal's breaking open in Boston, Cardinal Joseph Ratzinger, in his role as prefect of the Congregation for the Doctrine of the Faith, sent a secret letter to every Catholic bishop in the world. The letter made the astounding claim that crimes "perpetrated with a minor by a cleric" fall under Church jurisdiction, not civil law enforcement. The letter decreed that "cases of this kind are subject to the pontifical secret," the violation of which was punishable by excommunication. In other words, bishops were to report cases of priestly sex abuse not to civil authorities but only to the Vatican. This clear attempt to obstruct justice failed, but not before dozens of Catholic bishops, not only in the United States but in Mexico, Ireland, Austria, and elsewhere in Europe, had disgraced themselves by trying to keep the Church's grievous failures hidden, at the cost of allowing abusive priests to go on with their crimes. Ratzinger's secret letter became public when he was elected pope in 2005. Asked about it, a Vatican spokesperson replied, "This is not a public document, so we would not talk about it."[18] Pontifical secret indeed.

Some embarrassed defenders of Law's appointment to St. Mary Major described his sinecure in Rome as not really important, yet the basilica is one of the greatest churches in the world (Bernini contributed to its decoration and is buried there) and its palace was once home to the popes. With Law ensconced there, it seems especially significant that St. Mary Major is not only an emblem of Church triumphalism but, from its earliest days, was an instrument of it.

Although renovated repeatedly over the centuries, the basilica dates to the year 438. Its stunning fifth-century mosaics enshrine the aesthetic marvel that occurred when faith was joined to beauty, but those same artworks served a darker purpose. In dozens of panels, scenes from the Hebrew Bible (Abraham, Isaac, Moses) are counterpoised to scenes from the life of Jesus (Annunciation, nativity, flight into Egypt), a deliberate contrast to show that Christian revelation has fulfilled, and therefore replaced, Jewish religion. The mosaics are the first visual representation of the supersessionist theology that took hold once Christians could use the power of the state against their religious rivals. "The Jew carries the book from which the Christian takes his faith," St. Augustine preached. "They have become our librarians, like slaves who carry books behind their masters."[19]

As St. Mary Major was being completed, the Christian emperor Theodosius II issued an edict forbidding Jews to hold office and making proselytizing by Jews a capital crime. Bishops then justified the burning of synagogues, and history's first pogroms occurred. The Basilica of St. Mary Major both signified and advanced this violent triumphalism.

It took the Holocaust to lay bare the terrible corruption of Christianity's contempt for Jews and Judaism. In the past sixty years, Christians, in dialogue with Jewish partners, have begun to dismantle the structures of antisemitism, including the replacement theology that reduced Judaism to a Christian library. One need not equate the Holocaust to the sex-abuse scandal to see that an analogous exposure of deep corruption had occurred again. As St. Mary Major was being built, the Church was choosing power over love, and that choice, as Law's survival near the top of the Church pyramid shows, remains a pillar of the clerical establishment. The Basilica of St. Mary Major is a symbol of one Church disaster, which is being reckoned with. Its archpriest is the symbol of another, which is still being denied.

5. THE CHURCH ON FIRE

To my surprise, I experienced the sex-abuse crisis as a second shoe dropping, and only then did I appreciate what the first shoe had been. Much as I loved being a priest, and humbled as I was by the privilege, I was also crushingly ill at ease with the world I had to live in as a priest. There was a gap between the image and the reality.[20] Long after I acted on that unease, I finally understood.

As the *Boston Globe* laid out the history of priests' crimes and bishops' collusion, I saw with stark clarity how the Catholic clergy had compromised itself for the sake of its own continuance. The crisis at last illuminated, in hindsight, the moral crisis I *had* been aware of: the blatant Catholic dishonesty surrounding *Humanae Vitae*, promulgated in 1968 for no better reason than to protect papal primacy. That primacy capped a pyramidal structure that included all of us clergy, guaranteeing each one a share in the power. Protecting that power was priestly Job One. Hence *Humanae Vitae*. Hence the cover-up of clerical crimes.

I, alas, had not known how to protect the system, which at bottom was what made Cardinal Medeiros so "peesed off" at me. No wonder membership in the clerical fraternity had given me no pleasure, and no wonder the black suit and clerical collar had been a uniform from which I instinctively shied away. Something in the priestly way of life was rotten, and even as a young man I could smell it.

But first I smelled smoke. The fire came on the very night when Humberto Medeiros was installed as archbishop of Boston, in October 1970. A BU colleague whose apartment had a view of the Charles River called me at midnight (by then I had my own phone) to say that flames were lighting up the night sky downriver, coming from a fire raging near Newman House. I threw on clothes and made my way there as quickly as I could. When I arrived, the street was blocked by fire trucks, hoses were snaking everywhere, water was gushing along the curbs, the stench of smoke and ash was in the sky, red lights flashed on trucks as if they, too, were burning. It was not Newman House that was on fire, but the building next door. As I made my way up the block, approaching the scene, I became aware that the fire had engulfed my chapel. The little red church that students and I had reinvented, and that we had together rededicated to a new vision of our religion, was being destroyed.[21]

I stood watching from across the street. Word passed quickly that no one was in the building except firefighters. No loss of life, thank God, and the firefighters would be safe. I had no need of a metaphor-making mind to grasp the meaning of what was happening, even if, at that moment, I could not quite admit that meaning fully to consciousness. The stained-glass windows that one of my students had made were smashed, simply gone, and flames licked the air from inside the chapel. As the fire tore through the roof of the building, I saw the moving shadows inside, the firefighters selflessly at work. I fixed on their raw courage as a way of seeing something wonderful in the midst of what otherwise was pure horror. It was evident that the building was lost, and along with it our red carpet, our hand-wrought table, our mural and confessional corner, our midnight Masses, and our prayers for peace. I watched my church burn, bare ruined choirs.

Arson investigators established that the fire had been set. That same night, intruders broke into Newman House and ransacked my office. Some people associated the fire with that day's installation of Humberto Medeiros as Boston's archbishop, as if Irish racists were protesting the "Portogee."[22] Catholic radicals assumed that FBI agents were responsible, having targeted an institution known to support draft resisters and antiwar organizing. The arson investigators never identified a suspect in the case, nor did police have a clue about the break-in. I myself never came to firm conclusions about the cause. All I knew was that the sight of flames against the black sky marked yet another before-and-after moment of my identity.

In another room, in Newman House next door, I would say Mass again. I would clasp the bowed heads of students again. I would stand among a cluster of cross-legged kids, speaking of Jesus again. And of peace. But I would never be fully at home again, either as a Catholic priest or as an American citizen, and I knew it that night. Later, I would read what Pope Paul VI said about the dissent-wracked Church he had created, and I would think of my own red chapel. "Through some crack in the temple of God," he said, "the smoke of Satan has entered."[23]

6. THREE REASONS

In 1974, I resigned from the ministry at BU, then formally applied to the pope for a dispensation from my vows. After I left the priesthood, people would ask me, Why? Putting the question off, I would answer with a joke: "Three reasons." Beat. "Poverty. Chastity. And obedience." My riposte always drew a laugh, but the truth was not funny.

Obedience was far more the presenting issue in my situation than chastity was, yet I see now how they were related. Celibacy was a mode of hierarchical control over priests and nuns, as I've said, just as the prohibition of birth control aimed to be a mode of control over couples. Without consciously addressing the question of my relationships with women—I was not "in love" when I left BU in 1974—I nevertheless came to grips with the utter inadequacy of celibacy as what it was defined to be—a spiritual path to God. My peers were vigorous men, and life in community with them was like membership in an intellectually challenging seminar. But the life's limitations had shown themselves. I noted in myself and in my brothers more contradiction than mystery, more narcissism than generosity. I would not grasp the real meaning of what was missing until I had found it.

Yet the great thing about sex is the way it refuses to be spiritualized, a permanent reminder that the glory of creation is its very physicality. When celibates attempt to wax eloquent about its esoteric meaning, they can make it sound, as Garry Wills said of Pope John Paul II's mode of speaking of sex, as if only monks are holy enough to actually do it.[24] Abstract knowledge of the meaning of sexual relations is insignificant compared to the lived experience. And finally, nothing inhibits the understanding of sex like an emphasis on sexual longing as an occasion of sin.

Jansenists in the Catholic tradition, Calvinists in the Protestant—Christianity has been all too ambivalent about sex. Catholicism has affirmed it, at most, from the margins of Church thought and life. Why else are the overwhelming majority of canonized saints virgins? Whatever the positive aspects of celibacy are or ever were—and many priests continue to fulfill them—its deeper meaning now is as a dramatic instance of the repudiation of human sexuality. Against that is the fundamental proposition that loving sexual union, and all that follows from it, is sacred. The body is godly. Sensual mutuality is a sacrament. Physical expression is holy. Pleasure is divine.

Still, in my case chastity was not the issue. Obedience was. Cardinal Medeiros's patent assumption that a simple display of his disapproval would be enough to bring me around was unrelated to the context in which I was actually living. And that was, overwhelmingly, the war in Vietnam. Conditioned as I was by a rigorous upbringing in a military family, and by early training in the disciplines of the Church, I might well have clamped down on the uneasy stirrings of my own will—as if willfulness were my problem. But I was partner to those many young men whose war-induced struggles with conscience became the measure of my own conscience. If I was counseling men to navigate the shoals of politics and morality by the polestar of their own visceral reactions, how could I not apply that standard to myself?

Conscience. Within that faculty, Catholics instinctively sought to reconcile the contradiction with which they were faced. Standing against *Humanae Vitae* was *Dignitatis Humanae*, the Vatican II declaration on religious liberty: "Man perceives and acknowledges the imperatives of the divine law through the mediation of conscience. In all his activity, a man is bound to follow his conscience in order that he may come to God, the end and purpose of life. It follows that he is not to be forced to act in a manner contrary to his conscience. Nor, on the other hand, is he to be restrained from acting in accordance with his conscience, especially in matters religious. The reason is that the exercise of religion, of its very nature, consists before all else in those internal, voluntary and free acts whereby man sets the course of his life directly toward God."[25]

After the council, Church authorities saw what would happen if members took such instruction literally, and they tried to insist that *Dignitatis Humanae* intended to affirm a principle of religious freedom applying outside Catholicism, not inside. Once again, the issue was the clerical power structure—a system that would not stand once the primacy of conscience was elevated above the mindless obligation to obey. Such individual freedom was the satanic smoke Pope Paul VI was worried about, but it was ludicrous to think the Church could uphold conscientious integrity for everyone but Catholics. "Every man has the duty, and therefore the right"—the Vatican II declaration could not have been clearer—"to seek the truth in matters religious in order that he may with prudence *form for himself* right and true judgments of conscience"[26] (italics mine). Even without knowing the formal names of the documents involved, Catholics instinctively took this teaching to heart, and as a priest I shaped both my ministry and my own personality around it. When it became clear to me that I was expected to join in the thwarting of the movement that began with Vatican II, I simply refused. That was what leaving the priesthood meant. Thousands of us did it.[27]

7. HANS KÜNG VS. JOHN PAUL II

Vatican II began with the articulate explanations of the young Swiss theologian Hans Küng. We saw how his book *The Council, Reform and Reunion* gave expression to Pope John XXIII's own vision, and how, consequently, Küng had embodied the Church's vital new understanding of itself. The first to see the hope, Küng was also the first to see the danger of its betrayal.

In 1970, as I was confronting the absurd blowback of the Vatican's birth control prohibition, Küng launched a powerful counterattack against it. He published *Infallible? An Inquiry.* In that book, responding to trends in Catholic responses to the birth control encyclical, he already saw the handwriting on the wall. *Humanae Vitae*'s "unforeseen and unintended side-effect was a widespread major examination of conscience about the meaning of the Church's authority—in particular, its teaching authority . . . Nowhere has the Achilles' heel of the Roman doctrine of infallibility been more revealed than in connection with this encyclical."[28] Küng's book was pointedly published on July 18, one hundred years to the day after the Vatican I declaration on papal infallibility.

We saw how one of the leading prelates in the Catholic Church had warned at Vatican II, when Pope Paul VI removed contraception from the "competence" of the council fathers, that the Church could not stand to have another Galileo affair, yet now Küng argued that was just what the Church had given itself. "Just as the Council of Trent assumed the validity of the Ptolemaic universe, so did Vatican I assume a particular conception of the truth."[29] It was that conception that Pope Paul VI was trying to uphold in 1968. Assumptions of a static universe, bound by an inflexible set of natural laws, undergirded the world that His Holiness was trying to protect. The prohibition of birth control may never have been formally proclaimed by a pope speaking *ex cathedra*, Paul VI reasoned, but bishops and popes had held it with such consistency that the teaching achieved the infallibility of *magisterium ordinarium.*[30] Pope Paul could not change it—here was the crux—because to do so would undermine not only his own claim to infallibility but the Church's, a claim that presumably went back to the Apostles of Jesus. But that was the point. It simply didn't.

Küng argued that the people on whom Jesus depended at the start of his movement were described in the New Testament "neither as heroes nor as geniuses, but as weak and frail human beings who carried their treasure in earthen vessels (2 Corinthians 4:7) and could do nothing of themselves (John 15:5)."[31] He highlights the story of Peter, the head of the Apostles, who is seen in the Gospels as making one large mistake after another, culminating in his thrice-repeated denial of Jesus during the Passion. Yet this same Peter is regarded, in the Tradition, as the first pope. Küng made this foundational argument against the triumphal excesses of Church authority in a spirit far more positive than negative, arguing that the fallibility of the Church and its leaders is not scandalous but a consolation. Because the Church, too, is human, each human can claim a place in it. And attention to the origins of the Church in the New Testament, in the light of contemporary methods of Scripture study, immediately drew deeper attention to the fact that the real successors to the Apostles are not bishops and popes, but Christians themselves. Humans.

Such a reading of Church authority was not, to put it mildly, what Church authority was looking for, especially from a figure of Küng's standing. After Pope John XXIII embraced his program of reform, Küng had emerged as perhaps the most widely admired theologian in the Catholic world. Very simply, he was inviting readers to shift the focus of debate away from the teaching on birth control to the underlying reason for that teaching: upholding the absolute authority of the hierarchy. Indeed, Küng was presuming to ask whether such a claim to absolute authority could, in fact, be maintained. Artificial birth control, ironically, was destroying infallibility. Küng was saying aloud what "the inner emigration"[32] of so many married Catholics had already registered—that the popes and bishops were men without clothes, or vestments.

In 1978, the fifteenth year of his pontificate, Paul VI, the Hamlet Pope, died. He was succeeded, after the brief reign of John Paul I, by a figure who was inclined to do more than wring his hands in anguish. Karol Wojtyla, as a young man in his native Kraków, had defied the Nazis. He had become a respected philosopher as a young priest. His election as pope, when he was only fifty-seven, was itself historic, since, as a Pole, he was the first non-Italian pope since the sixteenth century. After having spent his life standing up to dictators—first German, then Soviet—he was not about to be timid in asserting himself. He regarded *Humanae Vitae* as a line drawn in sand, and he set about at once to engrave it in stone.

Within weeks of becoming Pope John Paul II, he solemnly celebrated the tenth anniversary of the birth control encyclical, leaving no doubt that he intended to enforce it. It was instantly clear that no priest who manifested ambivalence on the question would be promoted to bishop or brought into his Curia (this word for the Vatican bureaucracy is thought to come from the Latin *co-* plus *vir*, meaning "men together"). That demand of doctrinal conformity on this issue would trump every other consideration in the pope's evaluation of his clergy, a standard that eventually destroyed the integrity of the episcopacy, the bishops collectively, while condemning the priesthood to a slavish dishonesty. The result would become tragically evident when the entire cohort of bishops appointed by John Paul II, especially in the United States, showed itself to be incapable of dealing with the sex-abuse crisis. Their uniform dread of scandal, by which they meant embarrassing the boss, and in the name of which they protected abusers instead of children, showed them to be weak and frightened men, concerned only with the approval of their superior in Rome.

But the most powerful early signal the new pope sent was what he did to Hans Küng. In December 1979, John Paul II ordered Küng's *missio canonica*, his license to teach as a Roman Catholic theologian, withdrawn. Clearly, it was Küng's challenge on infallibility that sparked this. And it was just the beginning of John Paul II's campaign to rescue the absolute authority not so much of the Church, but of his own office. The climax of that determination came with John Paul's tenth encyclical, published in 1993 and titled *Veritatis Splendor* (The Splendor of the Truth). The document was addressed to the bishops and not much noted by laypeople. If the laity had bothered to take it in, they would have been astounded by the pope's claims.

In *Veritatis Splendor*, John Paul II utterly rejected the idea that moral consciousness can evolve through history. Forgetting the pilgrim metaphor of Vatican II, he swept aside any notion of truth as somehow unfinished or incomplete. The custodian of that "splendid truth" was the pope himself. John Paul asserted that his own sexual teachings were moral absolutes of the highest order, that there were no circumstances that could influence moral choices. Certain acts were "intrinsically evil." Traditional notions that intention and context must always be taken into account in evaluating the moral meaning of behavior were jettisoned. And chief among such intrinsically evil acts was artificial contraception.

The pope's salvo was double-barreled. He later issued *Evangelium Vitae* (The Gospel of Life). In this encyclical, the Polish pope drew a stark distinction between the "culture of death" and the "culture of life." The vision was a stinging repudiation of much of what was taken for granted by Europeans and Americans living in a secular and pluralistic world. John Paul condemned the "cultural, economic and political currents" that amounted to "a war of the powerful against the weak . . . a kind of conspiracy against life." It was not only that this sweeping anathema lumped together obvious but generalized evils like the desperation of poverty or the cruel violence of militarized societies with morally complicated individual decisions involving the ambiguities of the beginning and end of life. Under its sweeping rubric "culture of death," the encyclical effectively equated genocidal murderers and couples using birth control, state executioners administering lethal doses of poison and genetic scientists inventing reproductive technologies. The divorced, the gay and lesbian, the bisexual and transgendered, the women forced to choose abortion, the ex-priests, the boys who masturbate, the thinkers who defend notions of relativism, the pluralists—such were the citizens of the culture of death. The Manichaean divide embodied in the cultures of death and life boiled down to the distinction between the fallen world and pope-obeying Catholicism.

As with morality, so with politics. Replacing the collegiality of bishops was the strict rule from the center, with the long tradition of semiautonomous local churches redefined as mere branch offices. Replacing Vatican II's affirmation of the modern world was a spirit of negation and rejection. Replacing the new theological sophistication that the council had generated among laypeople was the old devotionalism. Replacing hopes for reunion of the Christian denominations was a triumphalist assertion of Roman Catholic supremacy. Not since the nineteenth-century war on modernism—not, perhaps, since the Middle Ages—had such extreme moral and political claims been made for the Roman Catholic Church.

But if Wojtyla was stern in his reaction to Küng, the Swiss critic proved the Polish pope's match. "The great ship of the Catholic Church which set sail into the future with strength and hope during the Council of Pope John XXIII has gone off course." These words appeared in the widely read Italian newspaper *Corriere della Sera* in 1996 during a week of celebrations on the fiftieth anniversary of John Paul II's ordination. Küng chose that moment to post what he called "Ten Theses on the Future of the Papacy" in a forum designed to confront the pope directly. And the word "theses" was meant to invoke the memory of Martin Luther.

But Küng was a Luther who refused to leave the Church. In his

"Theses," staying with the ship analogy, he reiterated his complaint against the "despotic" pope. "Longing for his homeland, the captain wishes to forcibly take the ship back to the harbor of medieval Catholic pseudo-security. The Church is neither a warship, where a military drill holds sway, nor a galley, where a single individual beats time for all with a hammer . . . Someone must dare to look the captain in the face and, when they know better, to contradict him. The highest authority . . . is not the captain, but the Lord, the owner of the ship."[33]

Within days of that challenge appearing in the Roman newspaper, I visited Küng at his home in Tübingen, a university town a half hour southwest of Stuttgart, in the foothills of the Swabian Jura. The professor had given me an appointment so that I could interview him for a magazine article I was writing. Tübingen has been Küng's home since 1960; his house sits on a hill above a river valley, with a view of turreted rooftops and towers and, in the distance, the mountains. In contrast to this open view, the entrance to the house is hidden by a screen of juniper trees and arborvitae, as if for anonymity.

I was greeted by Küng's assistant, a well-tailored fiftyish woman, who showed me to his study. The most striking feature of the room was a large window framing the mountain vista. Books lined the other walls. One set of shelves held many dozens of volumes, including one copy each of the translations of Küng's more than fifty books. I had first seen him at a lecture he gave in Washington, D.C., in 1963. Now, as the theologian entered the room, he was wearing stylish glasses, a blue Lacoste shirt, and a trim tan cardigan. He came forward with an easy smile and an outstretched hand. His face was no longer youthful—he was sixty-eight—but he was more handsome in person than I'd remembered. He still had a great shock of hair, but it was now gray.

After greeting me, Küng indicated a table near the window. As I sat down, he disappeared into a far corner, then returned with a half bottle of champagne and two glasses. "To welcome you," he said. His English was precise, but his voice was warm. Any impulse I'd had to see him as a firebrand Luther evaporated. We toasted each other, then he said, "Let's get right to work."

"Infallibility," I said.

"And the ordination of women," he replied at once.

"I declare," John Paul II had written in his 1994 "Letter on the Ordination of Priests," "that the Church has no authority whatsoever to confer priestly ordination on women and that this judgment is to be definitively held by all the Church's faithful." Within months, in 1995, as if to drive a stake through the heart of any remaining reluctance to accept this teaching, the Vatican's Congregation for the Doctrine of the Faith defined this rejection as "irrevocable." No, more. "This teaching requires definitive assent, since, founded on the written Word of God, and from the beginning constantly preserved and applied in the Tradition of the Church, it has been set forth infallibly by the ordinary and universal magisterium."[34]

In 1996, days before my visit, Küng had pounced. The Vatican's explicit claim that the Church's rejection of women for ordination was infallible teaching doubled the bet that the popes had placed on the square of artificial contraception. Küng delighted in the "wriggling" of Catholic theologians who felt obligated to defend this proposition, yet who already knew at some level that the ruling would not stand the test of time. After all, the Second Vatican Council had declared with equal fervor, "Any type of social or cultural discrimination in basic personal rights on the grounds of sex, race, color, social condition, language or religion must be curbed and eradicated as incompatible with God's reign."[35] By tying the doctrine of infallibility to the women's ordination issue, Küng was sure, the Vatican had already undermined it.

Küng explained: "'It is because,' they say, 'the bishops and popes through all the centuries agreed as a matter of faith that women cannot be ordained. Therefore—' That is Ratzinger's logic."

8. RATZINGER AND GALILEO

Cardinal Joseph Ratzinger was, at the time, the head of the Congregation for the Doctrine of the Faith. Where John Paul II had, in his youth, defied the Nazis, the Bavarian-born Ratzinger, in his, had been conscripted into the German army. In 2005, he would be elected as Pope Benedict XVI, but he had already been exercising authority in the Catholic Church for a generation.

As John Paul II's chief theological adviser, Ratzinger was a kind of theological Henry Kissinger. Küng was Ratzinger's nemesis, which was ironic, since they began as friends and colleagues. They were together at Vatican II. As dean of the theology faculty at the University of Tübingen, Küng hired Ratzinger in 1966. Tübingen was a hotbed of student radicalism, which appalled Ratzinger. In 1969, he left for the new, more conservative, and far less distinguished university at Regensburg, in Bavaria. As the Church began to renege on the promises of Vatican II, Ratzinger emerged as the chief sponsor of the conservative restoration. It was he who had instigated John Paul II's insulting attack on Küng in 1979, when the theologian was stripped of his license to teach as a Catholic. But by 1996, Küng saw Ratzinger as a man who had overreached. "They all told me, 'If you keep quiet, you can be what you want! But keep quiet!'" Küng said. "Of course, when I saw that, I had to say, 'Well I cannot just keep quiet about infallibility,' and now we see more and more that it is the crux of the whole system. It is the main reason why they are unable to correct themselves." Correct themselves, I saw, on any question.

Küng was leaning across the table toward me. Our champagne glasses stood between us, practically untouched. "In order to solve this problem, they would have to say, 'This is the wrong kind of teaching.' They would have to say, 'It proved to be an error.'"

But where is the mechanism for admitting error? I asked Küng whether the absolutism with which the Church defends this tradition reduces infallibility to the absurd. "Yes," he replied. "Exactly." He went on, "I mean, it is the same way for Galileo. He [John Paul II] said, 'Yes, there were errors on both sides.'[36]

"What?" Küng banged the table. "Galileo was right! The others were wrong! Now they have acknowledged Darwin finally, but they never say, 'We made a terrible mistake. We censored books,' and so on. It is always a half-truth: 'Some of us sinned,' yes. But John Paul II will never say, 'My predecessor made a serious mistake.'"[37]

Galileo was right! The others were wrong! It struck me how this story kept coming back to Galileo and Darwin, and how, in my sojourn through the history this book recounts, I had recapitulated the journey of which those two are patrons. For so many in the Church, that journey is incomplete, a saga of interruption. Any authentic religious message, like any scientific method, presupposes fallible minds and tolerance. Despite the affirmations of basic science that have become part of the Church's official conventional wisdom, including heliocentrism and evolution,[38] there is an inability to reckon with the deeper meaning of such insights. Finally, religion and science are both grounded in mystery, and when religion and science insist on seeing each other as antagonists, the truth in the mystery is lost. What we call revelation is obscured. For Catholicism, that has boiled down to the misbegotten notion of infallibility, which, ironically, is a profound denial of that most Catholic of doctrines, Original Sin. The Church, too, is of the human condition. Here is the real smoke of Satan that has been befouling the sanctuary for centuries, the fire consuming each pillar on which pope-centered Catholicism so unsteadily stands.

No, the earth is not the center of the cosmos, nor, for that matter, is the sun a particularly significant star in its insignificant galaxy, the Milky Way. No, the universe is not eternal; it had a datable beginning, about fifteen billion years ago. It is continually expanding, but it could also come to an end as abrupt and mysterious as its beginning was. No, nature is not unchanging, nor therefore is natural law.

Nuclear physics shows that matter itself, at the subatomic level, far from being stable, is in constant motion—or, rather, matter itself is motion. Change, therefore, is essential to all that exists. The play of energies defines the cosmos, and those energies are by definition unpredicted and unpredictable. Thus, however accounted for, an undesigned randomness is part of the experimentally unfolding diversity of life. Notions of freedom and responsibility, which are so central to moral thinking, must be measured against the constraints of genetic prehistory and cultural determination that are part of the evolutionary process. Just as life-form species have evolved over the last nearly four billion years, so have forms of human consciousness, including the religious impulse and morality.

Both Galileo and Darwin point to the same revolution-generating fact—that motion, not unchanging stability, is the ground of being. The shift to dynamics is comprehensive, with Renaissance humanists like Machiavelli having applied the insight even to the social order. Politics, too, is evolving. Being is becoming. That dynamism is ongoing and open-ended. It follows that ethical awareness and sensitivity to the numinous will continue to develop, leading to fuller understanding of what is right and wrong, leading also, for those who continue to live by faith, to ever more intimate acquaintance with the intuited and revealed reality humans call God.

But that moves the question: Can ideas of God and language about God adjust to the new understandings? A positive answer presumes a humility of the present in the face of the future, a humility, alas, that remains foreign to Church authorities, whose search for a triumphal restoration of the broken myth is as constant as it is desperate.

But Galileo was right. And so, I presume to add, is Küng.

CHAPTER NINE

RELIGION AND TERROR

1. CRUSADE AND JIHAD

THE BIOGRAPHERS OF John Paul II uniformly credit him with a central role in his era's great drama, the nonviolent demise of Soviet communism.[1] The blocks of that story are firmly in place: Karol Wojtyla's Polish origins; his fierce opposition to totalitarianism, beginning in the Nazi era; his rejection of *ostpolitik* accommodation; the 1981 assassination attempt, rumored to have been ordered by the KGB; his personal (and perhaps financial) sponsorship of Lech Walesa's Solidarity; his at least implicit collaboration with Ronald Reagan in giving the calcified Kremlin empire a last, shattering shove. It was Mikhail Gorbachev who decisively and heroically repudiated violence at the crucial moment of Cold War endgame, and he was able to do that only because the democratic resistance that challenged him from within, embodied in Poland's Solidarity movement, had resolutely embraced nonviolence from the first. And that was enabled by nothing more than the moral witness, and stern insistence, of the Polish pope.

Having established, against the prevailing *realpolitik* of the era, that nonviolence could have such political force, John Paul II remained a fervent opponent of every form of war, which in the end made him Washington's critic, too. The pope opposed the Gulf War in 1991, the post-9/11 attack on Afghanistan, and the 2003 invasion of Iraq. The significance of this consistent papal rejection of coercive violence as an instrument of political power was not sufficiently understood in the pope's time, certainly not in Washington. John Paul II was a prophet of the late-twentieth-century epiphany that the nonviolent alternative to war is no longer a moralist's dream but a practical option, humanity's only realistic hope.

The conventional assessment contrasts John Paul's liberalizing work outside Catholicism with his antiliberal governance of the Church itself. Thus his support of democratic movements against totalitarian regimes stood in stark relief to the rigid authoritarianism with which he squelched theological dissent (the pinnacle of which was his treatment of Küng) and the regional autonomy of bishops (which in part accounts for the bishops' grievous failure to act against priestly abuse of children). His global promotion of human rights was seen against his rejection, say, of the demands of Catholic women for equality (which contributed to the collapse of the Church's moral authority on all matters having to do with sex). The profound shift implied in his respect for Judaism's covenant with God as complete and permanent (embodied in his historic reverencing, in 2000, of the Western Wall in Jerusalem) seemed impossible to square with his reassertions of pope-centered Catholicism as the only fully authentic religion (which set back all efforts at interreligious reconciliation). John Paul II, one of whose numerous books was titled *Sign of Contradiction,* embraced contradiction as a self-identifying note, and many commentators, myself included, often picked up the theme.

It is not enough to say that John Paul was a force for good outside the Church even though he stifled an overdue renewal within the Church. The shattering events of September 11, 2001, exposed the dangers of mixing zealotry and politics—a combination that was evident in the campaign of Al Qaeda, while it was implicit in George W. Bush's reactive "global war on terrorism," which bled into his catastrophic wars against Afghanistan and Iraq. No Christian with a bare acquaintance of Church history needs any warning about the lethal effects of such mixing, yet its first consequence can be amnesia. In an age of religiously inspired violence, the ultimate impact of John Paul II's long reign, by sowing seeds of a related zealotry in the world's largest and most cohesive religious institution, may yet prove to have been profoundly negative.

The rise of religious fundamentalism as a sponsor of political violence defines a major new threat. Fundamentalism, like other movements, might expect to be understood and even respected on its own terms, but in fact, fundamentalism has a way of drawing out of some people extreme and intolerant responses. This is so because fundamentalism obliterates the epistemological underpinnings of tolerance. To tolerate such intolerance anyway is not to leave it uncriticized.[2]

In the late twentieth and early twenty-first centuries, regimes that have overtly fundamentalist rationales have come to power in nations such as Iran, Sudan, and India. In diverse manifestations around the globe, fundamentalist religion can mix with nationalism and hyperethnicity, with xenophobia or tribalism. Political leaders can be clerics or cult figures or warlords exploiting the piety of their subjects. Resistance movements defined by fundamentalist religious doctrines include antiabortion radicals in the United States who kill doctors, Sikh extremists in India who assault government buildings, the so-called Jewish underground known for murdering Arab political leaders, the Armed Islamic Group in Algeria that has slaughtered countless innocents, religiously motivated Muslim revolutionaries in Chechnya—not to mention Al Qaeda. The problem is obvious in Islam, within which a cult of suicide-murder has taken hold. But Christianity, too, has a long history of mingling fervor and violence, not least in its early celebration of martyrdom as the supreme manifestation of virtue. In the martyrology, it is pagan Rome that is accused of savaging the saints, but more Christians died at the hands of Roman emperors *after* the conversion of Constantine in 312 than had died before. They, of course, were heretics.[3]

Ideological violence begins in intolerance, which begins in dogma. Even apart from overt programs of sacralized physical attack, a retrogressive "re-Islamicization" defines itself as medievalist and antimodern. But there is an echo of that in Europe, where a campaign of "re-evangelization" seeks to restore an overtly Christian identity after two generations of ascendant secularism, and in the United States, where right-wing politicians (including some so-called neocon Catholics[4]) have enlisted evangelical zeal as a tool. And fundamentalist Christians are savagely at war with fanatical Muslims in the Philippines, Indonesia, Sudan, and elsewhere along the southern fringe of the Sahara Desert. These political, ethnic, and economic battles are increasingly defined in almost exclusively religious terms. The most apocalyptically minded are the most violent, which, in military terms, often means the most successful.

Within Roman Catholicism, the conservative reaction against the reforms of Vatican II can be understood as a "re-Catholicization,"[5] an attempt to restore the Church of the antimodernist nineteenth century, if not of the Middle Ages. Contemporary Roman Catholic rejection of pluralism, feminism, clerical reform, religious self-criticism, historical theology, and the scientific method as applied to sacred texts all exacerbate dangerous trends in world Christianity. This is perhaps especially so in the nations of the Southern Hemisphere, where Catholicism sees its future (between 1985 and 2001, for example, Catholic membership increased in Africa by eighty-seven percent; in Europe it increased by one percent) and where proselytizing evangelical belief —Protestant and Catholic both—is spreading rapidly.[6]

John Paul II, in his determination to restore the medieval European Catholicism into which he was born (especially in post-Communist Poland) ironically made any such recovery impossible. That is because, while offering himself to the world, through travel and the celebrity media, as the beau ideal of the Catholic priest, he presided over the destruction of the Catholic priesthood. Rather than changing its structures, he allowed the priesthood to wither. This is nowhere more the case than in the developing nations toward which the Church looks. In Honduras, for instance, there is one priest for every sixteen thousand Catholics, and in the Philippines, overextended itinerant priests sometimes have to celebrate up to nine Masses on a Sunday.[7] John Paul II was the global priest because, increasingly, there is no parish priest.

But below that organizational crisis is an ideological one. The Polish pope, for all his savoir-faire, became an inadvertent leader of a new Catholic fundamentalism. The great question now is whether his defensive, pre-Enlightenment view of the faith will maintain a permanent grip on the Catholic imagination. An apostle of peace—yet the last contradiction may be in how, if this narrow aspect of John Paul II's legacy takes hold, he will have helped to undermine peace, not through political purpose but through deeply felt religious conviction.

2. CATHOLIC FUNDAMENTALISM

"Catholic fundamentalism" once might have seemed a contradiction in terms, since the origins of fundamentalism lie in the anti-Catholic wing of conservative Protestantism. Usually the movement is traced to the 1910 General Assembly of the Presbyterian Church, which affirmed adherence to five "fundamentals" of faith: inerrancy of the Bible, the virgin birth and divinity of Jesus, the doctrine of substitutionary atonement, the bodily resurrection of Jesus, and the authenticity of the miracles of Jesus (sometimes the fifth fundamental is given as the imminent return of Jesus). Commonly associated with American Protestantism, fundamentalism also had its British adherents. In fact, between 1910 and 1915, British and American Christian conservatives jointly produced a multivolume manifesto, *The Fundamentals: A Testimony to the Truth.* The movement can be understood as a Protestant reaction against the historical-critical method of reading the Scriptures, which was central to the explosive controversies sparked by the theories of Charles Darwin. These characteristics still animate Protestant fundamentalism everywhere.

Roman Catholicism, in that same early-twentieth-century period, was gripped by an analogous impulse, and the condemnations of modernism, as we have already noted, were signs of that. Yet the Catholic Church had never embraced the *sola scriptura* idea, and its insistence on Tradition as a coequal source of doctrinal authority kept the otherwise antimodern Church from falling into the trap of extreme biblical literalism. As we saw, the Church seemed able to accommodate the insights of Darwin, taking the creation account in Genesis metaphorically. It was as if the Church had learned something from Galileo after all.

Roman Catholicism, even in the throes of its own antimodern reaction under John Paul II, has remained mostly antifundamentalist when it comes to biblical texts, with the glaring exception of the contemporary Vatican's claim of a Gospel mandate for its rejection of women as priests because, according to the texts, all of the Apostles were male. We saw earlier how this violates a historical appreciation of Jesus' own egalitarian position, but in its rank literalism, this appeal to Scripture as justification for an all-male priesthood also violates the Church's normal way of reading the texts. (No Celts were among Jesus' Apostles, but the Irish can be ordained.)

That normal Catholic approach to biblical interpretation is reflected in this 1993 declaration of the Pontifical Biblical Commission: "In its attachment to the principle of 'Scripture Alone,' fundamentalism separates the interpretation of the Bible from the tradition which, guided by the Spirit, has authentically developed in union with Scripture in the heart of the community of faith." The commission's statement did not mince words in describing what it saw as the hazards of this way of thinking: "The fundamentalist approach is dangerous, for it is attractive to people who look to the Bible for ready answers to the problems of life. It can deceive these people, offering them interpretations that are pious but illusory, instead of telling them that the Bible does not necessarily contain an immediate answer to each and every problem. Without saying as much in so many words, fundamentalism actually invites people to a kind of intellectual suicide. It injects into life a false certitude, for it unwittingly confuses the divine substance of the biblical message with what are in fact its human limitations."[8]

The phenomenon of fundamentalism has made an extraordinary impact on the world. But what precisely is it? The scholar Gabriel A. Almond defines fundamentalism as "religious militance by which self-styled 'true-believers' attempt to arrest the erosion of religious identity, fortify the borders of the religious community, and create viable alternatives to secular institutions and behaviors."[9] Some fundamentalists pursue openly political agendas (Northern Ireland, Israel, Iran). Some are apolitical (Latin-American Pentecostalism). In war zones (Sudan, Afghanistan, Palestine, Sri Lanka) fundamentalism is energizing conflict. Most notably, the warring groups in Iraq jelled around fundamentalist religion.

Obviously these manifestations are so varied as to resist being defined with one word, which is why it is better, as Almond suggests, to speak of "fundamentalisms." But they all have something in common, and as the Vatican critique of biblical fundamentalism suggests, all are dangerous. The impulse may begin with good intentions, the wish to affirm basic values and sources of meaning that seemed threatened. All fundamentalisms, rejecting a secular claim to have replaced the sacred as the chief source of meaning, are skeptical of Enlightenment values, even as the Enlightenment project has begun to criticize itself.[10] Ironically, fundamentalism is antimodernism that is grounded in modernist simplifications, holding to, for example, the goal of restoring a premodern idyllic state that never actually existed.

But now "old-time religion," of whatever stripe, faces a plethora of threats: new technologies, globalization, the free-market economy, rampant individualism, diversity, pluralism, mobility—all that makes for twenty-first-century life.[11] And fundamentalisms thrive wherever there is violent conflict or stark poverty, because these ultrareligious movements promise meaning where there is no meaning. For all these reasons, fundamentalisms are everywhere.

Even in contemporary Roman Catholicism, whose condemnation of fundamentalism we just noted—and not only in the exceptional biblical literalism about women. Catholic fundamentalists are more likely to be called traditionalists, and this book has given a history of their influence. Like other fundamentalists, they are attuned to the dark consequences of Enlightenment assumptions, from the Pandora's box opened by science unconnected to morality, to the grotesque inequities that follow from industrialization and, more recently, globalization. Where others celebrate new information technologies, traditionalists, while they use those technologies, warn of the coarsening of culture, the destruction of privacy, and especially threats to the family. In nothing more than its emphasis on a rigorous and comprehensive sexual ethic—antifeminist, pro-life, contemptuous of homosexuality—does this brand of Catholicism echo a broader fundamentalism. The "splendor of the truth," to use John Paul II's phrase, lies in its objective and completely knowable character. Though, as we noted above, he was asserting papal supremacy in the 1993 encyclical of that name—pope-centered Catholicism as sole custodian of fully authentic truth—John Paul II was, in fact, articulating an idea of truth to which every fundamentalist could assent. Yet this was the same year that the Vatican commission denounced biblical fundamentalism.

In the immediate aftermath of the Second Vatican Council, Catholic traditionalists, with their attachment to the Latin Mass, fiddleback vestments, clerical supremacy, the entire culture of Trent, were rebels. Today the Vatican is their sponsor.[12] Instead of reading the Bible uncritically, in search of "ready answers to the problems of life," Catholic traditionalists read papal statements that way, finding in encyclicals the very "false certitude" that the Vatican warns biblical literalists against. To affirm the eternal validity of prior papal statements, as we have seen in the case of artificial birth control, traditionalists willingly sacrifice common sense and honesty. They do this not in defense of the values being upheld ("natural" procreation) but in defense of papal authority. They caricature the more democratic alternative to such authoritarianism ("the Catholic Church is not a democracy"), as if other institutions—like, say, the university—do not offer examples of authority that is earned, collegial, and accountable. (The university, recall, originated in the Church.) As Protestant fundamentalists effectively make an idol of biblical texts, Catholic fundamentalists, in obedience to the Vatican, make an idol of the papacy.

3. MEMBER OF THE LAITY

As the conservative reaction to Vatican II took hold in the Church, I was making my life as a layperson, a family man, and a writer. While my Catholic identity remained central, I imagined that religious questions would move to the margin of my concerns. As a writer, I took up political and literary themes: my first two novels treated the Irish question, and my third involved a mentally unbalanced actor who takes on the crazy-making role of Richard III.

I married an Episcopalian at an ecumenical service, imagining that before we had children—or before they were old enough for it to matter—the Catholic and Anglican communions would have completed the then promising process of interdenominational reconciliation. But the U.S. Episcopal Church had begun ordaining women to the priesthood, and Canterbury joined in. For Rome, that soon posed an insurmountable obstacle to reunion. I occasionally attended the Episcopal Eucharist with my wife, or alone, while continuing to worship at Catholic Mass. When we had children, we raised them to regard the two traditions as equally valid: our son made his First Communion at the Episcopal Cathedral of St. John the Divine in New York; our daughter made hers at the Paulist Center in Boston, where I still worship. Theologically there was no longer any substantial difference between Rome and Canterbury, with the one exception of Rome's claim to supreme ecclesiastical authority. Given Vatican II's emphasis on collegiality, not even that might have hindered a denominational rapprochement, but as it happened, the question of women's ordination certainly did. Open differences over recognizing homosexual rights would follow.

On such issues I was more in line with the Episcopal Church than with the Vatican, and indeed, my conclusions about the overreaching authority of the modern papacy made me more like an Anglican than a traditional Catholic. So why did I not follow the path that so many Catholics took in those years and become an Episcopalian?

In fact, I considered it, to the point of taking counsel on the question from friends like James Parks Morton, then dean of the Episcopal Cathedral of St. John the Divine in New York. My decision to remain a

Catholic was more than a visceral reckoning with native Irish identity. (In famine Ireland, British hunger relief was administered through Anglican churches, with conversion as a price tag. "Taking the soup," or joining the Church of England, known as the Church of Ireland, was mortal treason.) Rather than leftover Irish chauvinism, my choice to be what I was involved an awareness that such "conversion" was no longer to the point in the post–Vatican II Church. By remaining a Catholic and advocating reunion of these two traditions (and ultimately of other Christian denominations), I am keeping faith with the widely held and profoundly Catholic conviction that the scandalous divisions of the Reformation must end. Over the years, as I have entered into serious interreligious dialogue and returned to formal study of theology and Church history, my Catholic identity has only deepened. It has matured.

Obviously there is a place for a diversity of religious practice and belief within the Church, and some of the cultural traditions embedded in post-Reformation denominationalism can be maintained without insult—much as within the Roman Catholic Church there are various rites that preserve national and cultural differences. In any case, the Christian Church is one, and the time for its organization and theology to reflect that unity is now, even if it does not yet seem so in Rome. As this book shows, the dominant experience I have had of Roman Catholicism has been of its vitality. I revere Jesus and believe in him. But I am a Catholic, and not another kind of Christian, because Catholicism is a necessary realm of community responsibility and historical consciousness. If we are not committed to a particular decision-making commonwealth, how can we hope to hold the world together?

My commonwealth is the Catholic Church. The culture of this particular tradition is too precious to be abandoned, and its coherence is too powerful to be underestimated. That only democratic procedures of the sort initiated by Vatican II (and aiming to dismantle everything from antisemitism and misogyny to pederasty) will allow this institution to continue its evolution, and that those procedures have so far been stifled by the narcissism of Church leadership, are not the whole story. My criticisms of the Church's hierarchy were generated in the first place, as we saw, by figures of that hierarchy. And my criticisms have been steadily tempered by gratitude for the hierarchy's prophetic teachings on social justice, with, for example, the American bishops' decisive turn away from war (1983) and their rejection of an unjust economy (1986). In the era of Vatican II, the Catholic laity came into their own as people of conscience, unafraid to think for themselves. I was one of those.

As my writerly concerns returned to religion—an accidental development tied to religion's emergence as a public question in the past dozen or so years—I found myself making public the private conclusions I had reached as a believer. This was especially so with the book I published in 2001: *Constantine's Sword: The Church and the Jews—A History.* After September 11 of that year, the connection between religion and violence surfaced as a world-historic problem, and my work as a writer of books and newspaper columns became more centered on religious questions than ever.

This is an ironic turn in my own life story. As a former priest, my religion is as much to the point as it was when I was a priest. Yet my understanding of Catholic faith, violating as it does the neoconservative dogma that holds sway in the Church, became controversial. In a *Constantine's Sword* symposium held by the theology faculty at Boston College, one priest dismissed my work as "Protestant." Aware as I always am of the life-shaping influence I have been fortunate enough to feel from Protestant writers like Dietrich Bonhoeffer and Reinhold Niebuhr, and from Protestant friends like William Sloane Coffin, Jr., and Krister Stendahl—not to mention from my Protestant wife—I was taken aback to hear the word used as an epithet. I replied that, in my view, the time had come for the Catholic Church to take up the Protestant challenge, learn from it, and do its part to end the conflict. It was no longer necessary to drive from the Catholic Church those who raised questions about belief and practice, any more than it was necessary for such questioners to banish themselves. The depth of relief I felt when, even as a Catholic out of step with the newly conservative hierarchy, I laid public claim to my place in the Church brought home to me how very much I love it.

4. A GERMAN POPE

So, to the disappointment—although not despair—of Vatican II Catholics, the medieval paradigm of doctrine and discipline was restored during the long pontificate of John Paul II. His fiercely autocratic character meshed with an irresistible charisma, a penchant for absolute pronouncements, and a savvy knack for exploiting the celebrity culture's every technological innovation. The astounding personality of this one man rescued the antimodern papacy.

But John Paul II could not have achieved this startling rollback by himself. For theological justification and temperamental reinforcement, he depended for the full quarter century of his pontificate on the German scholar and prelate Joseph Ratzinger, whose interventions we have noted. In fact, on several key questions, like liberation theology and the pluralistic implications of interreligious dialogue, Ratzinger was far more reactionary than the pope, and, especially during the latter's long physical decline, the German defender of the faith was wholly able to impose his views on the Church.[13]

We have considered Ratzinger's role already, as Küng's former colleague at Tübingen, as a critic of the liberalizing consequences of Vatican II, and as a chief sponsor of denial during the sex-abuse crisis. But emphasis belongs on Ratzinger's authority, beginning in 1981, as the prefect of the Congregation for the Doctrine of the Faith, the Vatican office (formerly known as the Holy Office, and before that as the Inquisition) charged with maintaining orthodoxy in theology and discipline in religious practice. We have seen how this agency was central to the repudiation of the spirit of Vatican II, and central, as it turns out, to my own reconscription into the Church's public argument with itself. The point is that the Congregation was Ratzinger's congregation, a simple fact of contemporary Catholic life that took on enormous significance when the theological sentry was elected pope in 2005.

In the spring of 2008, arriving on an airplane christened *Shepherd One*, Pope Benedict XVI made a triumphant visit to the United States. The heretofore obscure Vatican figure emerged not only from the shadow of his former function as a theological enforcer, but from the shadow of his immensely popular predecessor. Benedict was as personally withholding as John Paul had been expressive, but, from the White House rose garden to Yankee Stadium, his shyness was taken as a signal of benign authenticity. Soft-spoken, smiling, physically tentative, the pontiff's image as a man of exceptional goodwill was solidified. It was impossible to square this picture of Pope Benedict with the snarling inquisitor Ratzinger, and so, during the visit, no one tried.

"Dear friends, *shalom*," the pope said to New York's Jewish community. Yet when he visited the Park East Synagogue and described his emotion "to recall that Jesus, as a young boy, heard the words of Scripture and prayed in a place such as this," it would have seemed rude to point out that Jesus, the fully grown man, never stopped reading Scripture and praying in such a place (leaving aside the question of Temple observance, not synagogue, in the lifetime of Jesus). That Pope Benedict's religious imagination prevents his understanding the full and permanent Jewishness of Jesus, who never became a "Christian," does not mark him as a person of ill will, but such a perception is thoroughly outmoded now. In this detail inheres a cosmos of implication. The idea that young Jesus outgrew Jewish faith can be labeled for what it is: an integral part of the Church's supersessionist anti-Judaism. "He was very sincere," one of his Jewish hosts said of the pope later, "in expressing his wish for improved relations between our faiths."[14] One wonders how such improvement will come if basic theological obstacles are reestablished.

During his visit to the United States, Pope Benedict spoke repeatedly of the sex-abuse scandal. He was "deeply ashamed," he said, and expressed contempt for the abusive priests. He met with five victims, who expressed gratitude for his sympathy. But again, basic problems remain. "It is not power but love that redeems us," Benedict said in his first homily as pope,[15] but in fact Ratzinger was elevated to the papacy on a platform of power, not love. His 2008 visit to America, like his generally benign approach to the pontificate—his first two encyclicals concerned love and hope—poses a troubling question: Can this good man also be the man who has put in place over thirty years the structures of cruelty that have come to define so much of Catholic life?

Ratzinger is a German who came of age during the years of the Nazi nightmare. He was a member of the Hitler Youth and, after being conscripted, served in the Wehrmacht, in an antiaircraft unit. His biographers uniformly define these youthful associations with Nazism as having occurred against Ratzinger's will, under the pressures of life in a savage totalitarian nation. Much is made of Ratzinger's desertion from his Wehrmacht unit, although that took place after the German fighting machine had collapsed, just before or after Hitler's suicide in late April 1945.[16] One need not pass judgment on the Ratzinger boy to hear the dissonant chord struck when someone with such a personal history is elected to the papacy, especially since the Catholic Church's reckoning with its own failures during World War II is incomplete. Powerful figures in the Vatican still look forward to the canonization of Pius XII, the pope of the "silence."[17] That would be an act of moral denial, but it would be consistent with the way Ratzinger himself remembers the events of his youth.

In 1998, the Vatican published a document that was purported to be an account of the Church's record during the Holocaust. Titled "We Remember: A Reflection on the Shoah," it could easily have been called "We Forget." The document said, for example, that while "some" Catholics participated in the genocide, or passively stood by, "many" actively resisted. The truth is exactly opposite: some resisted, many participated. One of the statement's most egregious assertions was to praise as an example of anti-Nazi resistance "the well-known Advent sermons" of the archbishop of Munich, Cardinal Michael von Faulhaber, in 1933. In the sermons, the cardinal defended the Old Testament against Nazi assaults on Jewish Scripture, and the Vatican, in "We Remember," put that defense forward as an example of heroism in behalf of the Jewish people. However, Faulhaber explicitly declared that he was concerned only with "Israel of biblical antiquity," not Jews alive in his own day. Faulhaber's secretary went so far as to say that the cardinal "had not taken a position with regard to the Jewish question of today."[18]

That careful distinction between Jewish texts, which the Church would defend, and Jewish people, about whose fate the Church declared it had nothing to say, signaled to the Nazis that, as far as Roman Catholicism was concerned, the road ahead to assaults on Jews was clear. In fact, Faulhaber was the avatar of Catholic Germany's ambivalence about Hitler, with its positive aspect rising to the point of the Munich prelate's celebrating a Mass of thanksgiving when the Führer escaped an assassination attempt in 1939.

Faulhaber a forthright defender of the Jewish people? How did such a dubious claim come to be in the Vatican's 1998 document? I was present at a meeting in Chicago of Jewish and Catholic Holocaust scholars when one of the main authors of "We Remember," Cardinal Edward Cassidy, was asked that question by an aged rabbi, a Holocaust survivor originally from Munich. The old man's eyes filled with tears and his voice shook with anger at the exoneration of Faulhaber.

The rabbi declared that he had been present in Munich when the sermons were delivered, and he remembered them as an abandonment. Visibly embarrassed, Cardinal Cassidy, who headed the Vatican office concerned with Jewish-Catholic dialogue, made plain that the claim for the Munich archbishop was Ratzinger's doing.[19] The German cardinal intervened when the document was being written and imposed his own reading of Faulhaber's behavior. That intervention led to the whitewashing of history, which caused that rabbi such hurt and anger.

But again it seems clear that, instead of purposeful dishonesty, Ratzinger was motivated by the wish to honor a man who was dear to him. Faulhaber, who ordained Ratzinger to the priesthood in 1951, was his beloved mentor. "What moved me deeply about him," Ratzinger wrote, recalling Faulhaber's experience as a seminarian after the war, "was the awe-inspiring grandeur of his mission, with which he had become fully identified."[20] Ratzinger eventually succeeded Faulhaber as archbishop of Munich, and remains devoted to his memory.

As this intervention and numerous other statements on the subject show, Ratzinger remains equally devoted to the proposition that the German Catholic Church was a consistent center of resistance to the Nazis. Whatever accounts for Ratzinger's memory, it is not true. What Catholic resistance showed itself in Germany was exceptional. What does it say about Roman Catholicism that a man so tied to the Church's most grievous failure, and so typical of the element in the Church that wants to whitewash that failure, should have been elected as pope in 2005?

It is not enough to contrast Cardinal Ratzinger's harsh zealotry with Pope Benedict's mild-mannered good intentions. The main fact of Catholic life in these years has been cruelty, for that is the effect of the decrees that have come from Rome. I am not thinking here of the direct and pathological cruelty of an Iago, but more of the cruelty of bureaucratic remoteness. There can be cruelty in the dry satisfaction of fidelity to an abstraction—no blood on the hands, but indifference to suffering in the soul. Ratzinger once derided those who want "a nice Church," and flaunted instead what he called "the hard sayings" of Jesus.[21] But was there perhaps an unseemly edge in such "truth-telling"?

In his quarter of a century as prefect of the Congregation for the

Doctrine of the Faith, Ratzinger redefined Roman Catholicism in ways both major and minor. Here is a summary of what he did:

He stopped the use of inclusive language ("people" instead of "men") in Scripture translations and liturgy; killed the movement toward Catholic reconciliation with the Church of England (and, by extension, with other Christian denominations) by declaring that the Roman rejection of Anglican orders is an infallible teaching; condemned joint prayers with other believers (even when, in Assisi in 1986, Pope John Paul II did it); announced that the Virgin Mary, in her appearance to children at Fátima in 1917, had predicted the assassination attempt against John Paul II in 1981; was first to declare that Hans Küng should forfeit his license to teach as a Catholic theologian; led the prosecution of other theologians with whom he disagreed, silencing and even excommunicating them; single-handedly dismantled what he called the "heresy" of liberation theology; condemned the use of the word "martyr" for Archbishop Óscar Romero, who was assassinated at the altar while saying Mass by a Salvadoran government death squad; saw to the Vatican's recognition of the military coup that overthrew President (and former priest) Jean-Bertrand Aristide of Haiti (the Vatican was the only government in the world to do so); declared that the Catholic prohibition of women as priests is infallible teaching; condemned the use of condoms to prevent the spread of AIDS, even by married couples one of whom is infected with HIV; defined masturbation as "intrinsically and gravely disordered"; equated religious pluralism with communism; denounced the "subtle seductions" of J. K. Rowling's Harry Potter novels; affirmed neoconservative American bishops in their right-to-life alliance with the Republican Party (helping to reelect George W. Bush in 2004); was, in general, the author of Pope John Paul II's most reactionary statements and actions. More than John Paul II, Ratzinger was the architect of reaction.[22]

It seems harsh to say so, but cruelty underlies the shy pope's evident goodwill. That is because the ideology he advances for Roman Catholicism cares less for actual people (men and women in the hopeless dead end of a failed marriage, say) than for esoteric abstractions (the absolute indissolubility of matrimony). It is this aspect of Pope Benedict's mindset that qualifies him as the chief sponsor of the new Catholic fundamentalism, enforced with no regard for the real cost to human beings. "In essentials, unity"—here is how St. Augustine defined Catholic life—"in nonessentials, diversity; in all things, charity."[23] But not in the Church of Pope Benedict XVI, where essentials and nonessentials are all blurred together, and where charity is mocked with the word "nice."

I say "new" fundamentalism, but, alas, there is something very old at work here—a return to the preference for dogma over ethics that was reversed, as we saw earlier, by Cardinal Cushing. If the most sincere defense of abstract theological or philosophical principle results in cruelly imposed suffering, then something is wrong with it. Cushing rejected "No salvation outside the Church" because he saw the pain in his Jewish brother-in-law's eyes. Ratzinger, for all his good intentions, has inflicted Feeney-like pain in countless lives across a generation, and in order to defend what I learned from Cushing, I have returned to the Catholic fray.

This is a matter not of liberal versus conservative, but of the very meaning of the Gospel. What set Jesus apart, more than any "hard sayings," was his rejection of the well-meant assertion of religious principle—rejecting, say, the condemnation of the woman taken in adultery—if its effect was cruel. "Let the one without sin cast the first stone." The Gospel is riddled with examples of this, from the parable of the Good Samaritan to the acts of healing on the Sabbath. Dogma must be tested against ethics, and not the other way around. This is what St. Augustine meant by charity in everything.

One sees Ratzinger's mistake even when he sets out less to enforce discipline than to encourage devotion. The "Apostolic Exhortation" on the Eucharist issued in early 2007, for example, began as a contemplative appreciation of the Eucharist but ended as an exercise in "border fortification," a manifesto designed to keep many Catholics from receiving Holy Communion at Mass. The *Domine, non sum dignus* was back. With this teaching, homosexuals, divorced Catholics, and dissenters on sexual teachings of various kinds were put on notice. The ticket to draw near the altar for the sacred bread and wine was an uncritical acceptance of what the pope's statement called, in a striking echo of those early-twentieth-century Protestants, "fundamental values." These included, especially, the defense of human life "from conception to natural death." The document's key declaration was that "these values are not negotiable."[24]

5. THE NEGOTIATION OF VALUES

But culture consists precisely in the negotiation of values, and change in how values are understood is part of life. Moral reasoning is not mere obedience but lively interaction among principles, situations, and the "human limitations" referred to in the 1993 Vatican statement rejecting biblical fundamentalism. (Benedict himself showed this. His rejection of sharing Holy Communion with non-Catholics did not prevent him, at the Mass of his consecration as pope, from personally giving the sacred bread to his friend Brother Roger Schultz, the saintly, elderly—and Protestant—founder of the ecumenical community of Taizé in France.[25])

There is negotiation even on a question as basic to Catholic teaching as conception, the key issue when it comes to any moral conclusion about abortion. The great Thomas Aquinas, from whom so many theological absolutes derive, depended on thirteenth-century notions of biology and did not believe that human life began at conception. Indeed, he had little or no idea of fertilization occurring when the male sperm penetrates the female ovum. For him, "ensoulment" occurred at birth, and the logic of this position led him to oppose the baptizing of fetuses.[26] Aquinas, that is, did not believe what the Vatican asserts today.

Science trumped Thomas's biological ideas, the meaning of "conception" changed, and, in effect, negotiation followed. The Roman Catholic conviction that the human person comes into existence at the instant of conception *evolved*, and so, therefore, did the absolute Catholic prohibition of abortion. Negotiation assumes a negotiator, and Catholics understand their Church to occupy that position. Abortion is not a matter *only* of individual conscience. But conscience, from the Latin for "to know with," is the seat of an individual's knowing-with, or negotiating with, the community. For Catholics, that prohibition represents a humane affirmation of life, and Catholic opposition to abortion is a morally proper position. Even so-called Catholic dissidents like myself affirm it, although not with the same level of absolutism as the hierarchy, and not necessarily on the same grounds, since the moral equation of a fertilized ovum with a fully realized person is biologically debatable.

Indeed, it matters that the hierarchy's position is based—not on Scripture, which never mentions abortion—on a particular philosophical tradition and a certain understanding of the biological sciences, both arrived at over time.[27] Both arrived at, that is, by negotiation. Such negotiation continues today as new methods of human reproduction are invented and as philosophical assumptions shift. But the real flaw in the Vatican's teaching on abortion is in the way that instruction is paired with its equally absolute rejection of birth control. Here is where the "sense of the faithful," the moral judgment of the Catholic people, comes into play, for any serious opposition to abortion, a teaching that most Catholics accept, requires the promotion of contraception, not the condemnation of it. The Catholic people see that, and have made their ethical judgment accordingly.

So too with "natural death," the other pole of the papal exhortation's linear structure. We needn't appeal to Thomas Aquinas or to Scripture to detect powerful disagreements over the meaning of natural death even within the Catholic community. Such differences were made vivid in 2005 in the case of Terri Schiavo, a Florida woman who had lain in a vegetative state for fifteen years. Her husband wanted her feeding tube removed, and her parents argued that depriving Terri of nourishment would violate her Catholic faith. A tense negotiation followed involving courts and legislatures; even the U.S. president intervened.[28] Catholic bishops weighed in on both sides of the dispute, with Vatican spokesmen expressing appreciation for the right-to-life aspects of the case, while the Church's catechism continued to allow the cessation of end-of-life medical procedures that are "extraordinary or disproportionate to the expected outcome."[29]

I had myself experienced the compassion of Catholic teaching on this question when my father lay dying. My mother, brothers, and I were confronted with the painful question of whether and when to remove the feeding tube that was sustaining him. The priest who ministered to us was the soul of sensitivity, and so was the teaching he laid out for us. But official Catholic pronouncements during Terri Schiavo's last days, tying her fate to the right to life, were cruel in the way they reflected an unwillingness to imagine the consequences of such abstract dogmatism. More to our point, such decrees were clearly out of sync with the mainstream of Catholic moral theology. The cruelty of the newly conservative Church was on full display.

Meanwhile, as the battle raged over the meaning of Terri Schiavo's "natural death," Pope John Paul II lay dying, too. Unlike what happened in Florida, though, no "burdensome, dangerous, extraordinary," or "overzealous" procedures were imposed in the name of prolonging the pope's life.

Even the idea of nature must be constantly negotiated. In his 2007 exhortation on the Eucharist, Pope Benedict XVI affirmed universal and unchanging "values grounded in human nature," as if human nature is fixed instead of evolving. The political philosopher Michael Sandel reminds us of a basic truth of nature by saying, with eloquent simplicity, "Not everything given is good."[30] Diseases are natural, yet human ingenuity is arrayed against them. The human project itself can be said to have begun when our Neolithic ancestors began to intervene in nature. Began, that is, to change nature, even if, across the millennia, humans did not recognize that as what they were doing.

In returning to a premodern notion of reality, the Vatican is disqualifying itself from any meaningful role in the urgent task of ethical reflection as humans confront risk-laden choices on the two great frontiers of morality—the start of life and the end of life. Stem cell research, cloning, biological "enhancement," genetic engineering, organ transplants, growth hormones, life extension—it is not enough to issue blanket condemnations of such revolutionary techniques. They and many others present ethical challenges that require intellectual engagement and moral humility. The lessons of the past—of tradition—are essential to a humane, if as yet undefined, future. But Pope Benedict, offering not argument but assertion, removes himself from the building of that future. At bottom, one detects in this brilliant and erudite Church leader, too, a suspicion of Darwin, an invitation to intellectual suicide.

6. THE WEST AGAINST THE REST

The restrictive effects of such reactionary governance in the Church are obvious—from the quiet exodus of educated Catholics to the further alienation of women to the decline in quality of the clergy—but in the age of religiously animated terror, the consequences of the German pope's policies for the wider world are more drastic. "Oh, East is East, and West is West, and never the twain shall meet." This old dictum comes to mind in connection with the Eurocentric Pope Benedict's attitudes toward everything from religion to politics. His suspicion of Asian thought and religion were evident in his Holy Office vendetta against pluralism, which was mainly a campaign to snuff out Catholic attempts to bridge the gulf with Hinduism and Buddhism.[31] One of his early acts as pope was to shut down the Vatican office charged with fostering better relations with Islam. The Ratzinger-Benedict campaign gave dramatic *theological* expression to the broader impulse embodied in Samuel P. Huntington's essay "The Clash of Civilizations?" The Roman Catholic Church would reclaim its lost power and glory by being a bulwark in the epic contest of "the West against the rest."[32]

The conviction that the East-West divide is unbridgeable is a mark of European defensiveness, the flip side of which is European aggressiveness. "The Ballad of East and West," from which the "twain" line comes, was written, after all, by Rudyard Kipling, the troubadour of European imperialism.

What is Europe, anyway? When Cardinal Ratzinger took "Benedict" as his papal name, much was made of the fact that that saint was the patron of Europe. By this name, the pope was making clear that the central purpose of his pontificate would be to reclaim the ever more apostate continent for Christianity. Shortly before being elected pope, Ratzinger wrote, "While Europe once was the Christian Continent, it was also the birthplace of that new scientific rationality which has given us both enormous possibilities and enormous menaces . . . In the wake of this form of rationality, Europe has developed a culture that, in a manner hitherto unknown to mankind, excludes God from public awareness . . . A culture has developed in Europe that is the most radical contradiction not only of Christianity, but of all the religious and moral traditions of humanity."[33]

But Ratzinger's concern was never the religious and moral traditions of humanity, nor was it even with Christianity. His program of "reevangelizing" Europe, the very watchword of his pontificate, was aimed at nothing less than reclaiming the continent for Roman Catholicism, which meant, in his view of Catholic ecclesiology, for himself as pope. The story of Europe's Christian past is more complex than it appears, however, and more complex than the new pope seemed to think.

St. Benedict, the father of Western monasticism, died in about 543, but he was not named Europe's patron until 1964, in the middle of the Cold War. At that point, East-West conflict was all about the contest between communism and capitalism, with "Europe" defined primarily by what fell on the western side of the Iron Curtain. That the patron of Europe could be a man from Rome, associated with the Benedictine monasteries that flourished from Italy to Ireland and back (with the medieval flowering of monasticism occurring in Ratzinger's Germany), was an implicit affirmation less of the whole culture than of the NATO alliance. It is NATO, after all, that began referring to central Europe as "Eastern" Europe. That is why St. Benedict as the continental patron was taken as an insult by European Catholics beyond the Danube. And that is why, when a Pole became pope, one of his early acts, in 1980 (before he fell fully under Ratzinger's influence), was to correct the slight by naming as Europe's "copatrons" St. Cyril and St. Methodius, the ninth-century Greeks who brought Christianity to the Balkans and the Slavic north.[34]

The end of the Cold War presented a rare opportunity to reintegrate Europe, and the European Union has been a magnificent signal of reconciliation—former antagonists flourishing together. Leaving behind the East-West conflict on the continent (the Berlin Wall) meant that now larger East-West barriers could be dismantled. The move away from narrow nationalisms in Europe offered the world an image of a new and expansive politics, globalization without imperialism.

The first test of this vision was Turkey, and that posed a special problem for Pope Benedict. Turkey belonged to NATO, yet its admission to the European Union was a flashpoint, with many of Europe's leaders, including the pope when he was Cardinal Ratzinger, warning that the large Muslim nation (with about seventy million people, Turkey would be second in population only to Germany, which has about eighty million) would irrevocably compromise Europe's cultural identity. "Europe is a cultural continent," Ratzinger said in 2004, "not a geographical one."[35] In fact, the growth of Muslim populations already in Europe has been dramatic (there are about twenty million Muslims in the nations of the European Union, a figure expected to double in the next fifteen years).[36] Most Europeans who expressed unease over such a large Muslim population were concerned about preserving a democratic and secular identity; Ratzinger explicitly worried about Europe's loss of its ancient Christian character—the one he, as pope, had set out to restore.

Late in 2006, Benedict traveled to Istanbul to meet with Ecumenical Patriarch Bartholomew I, the titular head of Eastern Orthodoxy. With this visit, Pope Benedict was aiming to overcome the schism that divided Christendom into East and West almost a thousand years before, but many observers had the impression that his real purpose was to enlist the nearly three hundred million Orthodox Christians as a "first line of defense against radical Islam."[37] The pope deplored the secularity of Europe, but that was a secondary concern. His primary one was with Islam. That had become clear only two months before when he chose to celebrate the fifth anniversary of the September 11, 2001, attacks against the World Trade Center and the Pentagon by citing, the next day, a fourteenth-century slur that Muhammad brought "things only evil and inhuman, such as his command to spread by the sword the faith he preached."

The pope's speech, delivered at his former university at Regensburg, in Bavaria, was instantly notorious. In a putative defense of rationality in faith, he declared that Islam had no such capacity. "For Muslim teaching," he said, "God is absolutely transcendent. His will is not bound up with any of our categories, even that of rationality."[38] The patently false characterizations of Muhammad's teaching, displaying an ignorance of the Koran, of the magnificence of Islamic devotion, and of history, were offered almost as an aside in the pope's otherwise esoteric lecture about reason and faith. But it was not an aside, and it was not accidental. Advisers who saw his text ahead of time sent warnings to the pope that the slur was "incendiary"[39] and recommended its deletion. The warnings were ignored, and the rhetorical conflagration followed. After the predictable Muslim uproar, the pope, while not really apologizing, insisted his intentions had been misunderstood. Here is the pattern: a nice man whose abstractions are in effect cruel. In fact, Benedict's intention was to draw a stern line in the sand against Islam, and in that he was understood very well.

Leaving the offending citation aside, Benedict's lecture revealed a deeper and still insulting problem. He properly affirmed the rationality of faith, and the corollary that faith should therefore be spread by reasoned argument and not by violent coercion. But he did so as a way of positing Christian superiority to other faiths. That was the point of the passing comparison with Islam—which supposedly is irrational and so is intrinsically violent, unlike Christianity, which is rational and intrinsically eschews coercion.

But this ignored history. It was not only that Christianity, beginning with Constantine, continuing through the Crusades, and up until the Enlightenment, routinely "spread by the sword the faith" it preached (with many popes as military commanders, right into the modern era), or that, on the other hand, Islam sponsored rare religious amity among Jews, Christians, and Muslims in the very period from which Benedict drew the insulting "evil and inhuman" quote. More significant for any discussion of reason and faith was the fact that Christian theology's breakthrough embrace of the rational method, typified by St. Thomas Aquinas's appropriation of Aristotle and summarized by Benedict as "this inner rapprochement between biblical faith and Greek philosophical inquiry," was made possible by Islamic scholars, like Averroës, whose translations of Aristotle rescued that precious tradition for the Latin West. At Regensburg, Benedict made no mention of this Islamic provenance of European and Christian culture. Indeed he could not, because the main purpose of the lecture—as of his papacy—was to emphasize the exclusively Christian character of that culture. The "convergence" of Greek philosophy and biblical faith, "with the subsequent addition of the Roman heritage, created Europe and remains the foundation of what can be rightly called Europe." Europe remains Christian.

Benedict seemed to have forgotten that the European rejection of violent coercion in religion came about through the secular impulses of the Enlightenment, not through religion. Take, for example, Benedict (Baruch) Spinoza (b. 1632). In reaction to oppressive religious institutions—his own Jewish as well as Christian—he gave primal expression to human rights and the ideal of tolerance in his *Theological-Political Treatise.* Spinoza's heirs included John Locke and, later, Thomas Jefferson. The separation of church and state, in defense of the primacy of individual conscience, was the *sine qua non* of that rejection of religious coercion—an idea the Catholic Church fought right up to the twentieth century. As the defender of what we have already noted as a Catholic fundamentalism for a quarter of a century, and then as pope, Ratzinger consistently campaigned against basic tenets of Enlightenment politics—nowhere more stridently than in the streak of anathemas he aimed at pluralism and relativism.

The latter word had become a kind of battle cry for Ratzinger, but he used "relativism" imprecisely. His attack targeted the idea that one morality or belief system is no better or worse than any other—an idea that is put forward by no mainstream thinkers, secular or religious—as well as the much more widespread notion that even general truths are perceived according to individual perspectives. This kind of relativism might better be called perspectivalism.[40] Therefore, absolute truth is available to humans only relatively. In the homily he preached at the funeral Mass of John Paul II—remarks that probably sealed Ratzinger's election as pope—he said, "We are moving toward a dictatorship of relativism which does not recognize anything as for certain and which has as its highest goal one's own ego and one's own desires."[41]

Benedict draws on his own past as a German to bolster his warnings about the "dictatorship of relativism," as if the world that ignores his definitions of the absolute is repeating the error that led to Hitler. Here we begin to see the fuller significance of Benedict's refusal to reckon with facts of history that contradict Catholic moral primacy, especially in connection with the Church's past with the Jews. During a visit to Cologne in 2005, he said Nazi antisemitism was "born of neo-paganism," as if Christian anti-Judaism were not central. If Hitler presided over a dictatorship of relativism, he was in part enabled to do so by the supersessionist and triumphalist dogmas of the absolute religion into which he was christened. At Auschwitz in 2006, Benedict went further, blaming the Holocaust on a "ring of criminals," exonerating the German nation in a way that is almost never done in Germany. By exterminating Jews, Pope Benedict decreed, the Nazis were "ultimately" attacking the Church. He decried God's silence, not that of his wartime predecessors.

In Ratzinger's declarations, and then in Pope Benedict's, a pattern had begun to show itself. Forget Church offenses against Jews. Denigrate Muslims. Caricature modernity and dismiss it. If in doing all of this—especially expressing a blatant contempt for Islam—the Catholic pope provided an incidental theological underpinning for an American president's "crusade" ("This crusade," George W. Bush said, "this war on terror"), so be it.

When Benedict went to the White House in 2008, George W. Bush displayed the oversimplifications of "relativism" when he embraced the pope's polemic. "In a world where some no longer believe that we can distinguish between right and wrong," the president told Benedict, "we need your message to reject this dictatorship of relativism." Yet Bush, a president whose adherence to moral law was selective, was a defender of torture and aggressive war. Bush, emblematic of moral relativism, drew no criticism from the pope. Indeed, the pope had honored him. After Benedict's remarks Bush said, "Thank you, Your Holiness. Awesome speech."[42]

In pursuing his narrow agenda, Benedict was defending a hierarchy of truth. Faith is superior to reason. Christian faith is superior to other faiths (especially Islam). Roman Catholicism is superior to other Christian faiths. And the pope is supreme among Catholics. Ratzinger had made this schema explicit with his document *Dominus Iesus,* issued in 2000. People outside Christianity, it said, lived "in a gravely deficient situation in comparison to those who, in the Church, have the fullness of the means of salvation." The faith of non-Catholic Christians was "defective." Pope John Paul II had approved *Dominus Iesus,* but when many non-Catholics and Catholics took it to be a return to the exclusivism of "No salvation outside the Church," the pope had to issue clarifying statements himself, pulling back on Ratzinger to affirm Vatican II's teaching that Christ's salvation is offered to all, whether they know him or not. Ratzinger, however, had made his much narrower position clear. But such an abstract schema can be defended only at very human costs, costs to which the cerebral Ratzinger has shown himself to be indifferent.

As prefect of the Congregation for the Doctrine of the Faith, for example, he had personally pronounced the excommunication of a Sri Lankan Catholic priest named Tissa Balasuriya, a seventy-two-year-old theologian and dialogue partner with Hindus and Buddhists. In showing respect for these religions, Balasuriya was accused of relativism, of placing the presuppositions of Christian revelation "on the same level as those of other religions." Balasuriya denied that this was so, yet a participant in dialogue presumes the dialogue partner's right to his or her own point of view without prejudging it. Not so for Ratzinger: "There can be no dialogue at the expense of the truth," he said. He is a man who enters dialogue knowing he already has the truth. His task, in charity, is to present it.

But where was charity in the way Balasuriya was treated? The evident injustice—not to say cruelty—of his punishment (Balasuriya is the only theologian to have been excommunicated since Vatican II; not even Küng was excommunicated) led to protests in his behalf from throughout the Catholic world, and the Vatican relented.[43] But the Balasuriya case made Ratzinger's position plain. He rejected the pluralism that regarded various religions as offering, each in its own way, authentic avenues of access to God, and he dismissed the Vatican II assertion that Christ's salvation was available to all, beyond religion, through the mysterious workings of God's grace.

Dominus Iesus was one thing, but in his first major address as pope, Benedict reiterated the denigrating theology, and he did so explicitly in relation to Islam. He did not seem to care, even on that anniversary of the September 11 attacks, that such triumphalism came attached to a fuse. The dynamite, of course, was the escalating clash of civilizations for which, inadvertently or not, Benedict had begun to serve as a kind of field marshal and theoretician both. The post–Cold War dream of a new Europe was undercut by tensions associated with those large populations of Muslims living in European cities, who were suspected of being culturally, if not militarily, allied with self-proclaimed Islamic enemies of the West. It turned out that tensions with Islam, more than with the "schismatics" to whom Benedict deferred during his trip to Istanbul, still defined the European mind.

History tells us why this was so. Europe became "Europe" in the first place only in response to a challenge from Islam. Muslim armies, moving north and west from the Arabian Peninsula, reached as far as Tours, in France. It was there, in 732, that a Frankish warrior won the decisive battle. His name was Charles Martel. The significance of his defeat of Muslim forces, famously summed up in Edward Gibbon's remark that, without Martel, the Koran would form the content of studies at Oxford, is further shown by the fact that Europe's political dynasty comes from Martel. His grandson was Charlemagne, who solidified his power by giving his allies grants of land—the origin of Europe's landholding nobility. When the pope crowned Charlemagne as Holy Roman Emperor in Rome in 800, the emperor in Constantinople took offense, the true origin of the East-West divide in Christendom. But it was the external contest with Islam that gave Europe its internal cohesion.

The psychological mechanism was basic: group identity followed from group threat. Humans know who they are by knowing whom they oppose. From tribalism to nationalism, this polarity shaped human responses, with the dynamic taking extreme form in Europe after Charlemagne. What began in the Crusades reached a tragic pinnacle with the wars of the twentieth century. That Europe was both instigator and victim of those wars was the precondition of its astounding conversion, begun at the end of World War II and continuing through the end of the Cold War—a conversion that amounted to a recognition that the East-West battle was unwinnable. Pope Benedict saw moral rot in the fact that the magnificent churches of Europe were mostly empty, without asking why the world-historic European renunciation of violence (including the abolition of the death penalty, the condemnation of abuse in marriage, the final end of colonialism, not to mention the Soviet empire's refusal to save itself through war) was accomplished by the generation that walked away from religion. Did that generation walk away from religion, and from Christianity in particular, because it was necessary if violence was to be fully left behind?

7. MONOTHEISM, VIOLENCE OF

It can seem an outrageous, insulting question, but a brief investigation into the foundations of European religious attitudes points to the problem that inheres in Benedict's campaign to restore to Europe an uncriticized Christianity. Take something as basic to Judaism, Christianity, and Islam as the tradition of exclusivist supersessionism—the idea, in mythic terms, that, as the Jewish scholar Jon D. Levenson puts it, "a late-born son dislodges his first-born brothers."[44] The rivalries between Cain and Abel, Isaac and Ishmael, Jacob and Esau, Joseph and his brothers, Israel and Canaan all establish the theme as grounded in Judaism. One brother lodges an exclusive claim to the familial legacy, condemning the other brother to nothing, often to death. This is what, after Jesus, the Church does to the Synagogue. The New Israel replaces the Old, consigning it to history's waste bin. The claim to God's favor now excludes the older sibling and, soon enough, everyone else.

This supersessionism was picked up, in turn, by Islam, asserting dominance over Judaism and Christianity, and then by Protestantism, which claimed to be the true Church, the successor to Roman Catholicism. After reviewing this litany of sibling rivalry, with one brother replacing the other, the Scripture scholar Krister Stendahl comments, "In no case is complementarity or coexistence an option chosen: there is always the claim to exclusive legitimacy."[45]

Judaism, especially once it entered the Diaspora and permanent minority status in the Roman Empire, and then Christendom, did not make exclusive claims for its relationship to God,[46] but it was out of this "one and one only" impulse that the Catholic Church developed its dogma of *Extra Ecclesiam nulla salus.* The New Testament texts that described the grace of Christ as intended for all people were read to mean that all people were bound to submit to that grace as popes and bishops defined it, and the definition became ever more exclusive. In the Christian tradition, Jesus is remembered as having given his followers a last command just before ascending to heaven. Because the words are attached to the moment of his final disappearance, they have always rung in the Christian ear with transcendent authority. The declaration assumes an absolute universality and points to the educational mandate—missionizing—that inevitably follows from it. "All authority in heaven and on earth has been given to me," Jesus said. "Go, therefore, make disciples of all nations; baptize them in the name of the Father, and of the Son, and of the Holy Spirit. And teach them to observe all the commands I gave you."[47]

While it is true that the proselytizing impulse of the Jesus movement led to an astoundingly rapid spread of Christian devotion —"Church membership"—in the Mediterranean world, the "commands" that were learned in this early missionizing program were not nearly so univocal as is commonly assumed today. Despite the supersessionist impulse, hard and fast distinctions between the Synagogue and the Church, to take one example, were not consistently observed in the first three centuries after Christ. The command Jesus gave was not necessarily to leave the old religion for the new. Neither was the even more fundamental distinction between the monotheism of Christianity and Judaism and the polytheism of the Roman Empire nearly so sharp as is imagined now—as the Trinitarian formula attributed to Jesus by Matthew indicates, on one side, and as the then emerging primacy of the Roman sun god indicates, on the other. The command to honor the one God was not necessarily what we assume it was.

In reading the words attributed to Jesus in Matthew (a text dating to about 90 C.E.), one should note that those words meant something very different after the emperor Constantine, more than two hundred years later, turned the project of Christian missionizing into a method of expanding his control over the far-flung Roman Empire. His universalizing of the faith (establishing the cross as its symbol, imposing a univocal creed, making heresy a capital crime, absolutizing the difference between Synagogue and Church) served a political purpose.

The word "monotheism" is a clue. The work it does as a noun is like the work "universal" does as an adjective. The biblical tradition from which rabbinic Judaism, Christianity, and Islam derive was unlike the tenets of other religions of the ancient world in asserting that its God was one—that is, its God was the only God, was everybody's God, whether they knew it or not. Genesis is unique among ancient creation myths in that it accounts for the creation not of the tribe's world, or even of humankind's world, but of the very cosmos. This God is the universal God, and claims made in this God's name are believed to be universally authoritative. This is why the three monotheistic religions are themselves absolute religions, and why, not incidentally, so-called holy war has regularly found a place in the accepted practice of these religions. Absolute claims come to be enforced absolutely.

But does the common understanding of this tradition do it justice? Does the "one" implied in "universal," or in "monotheism" for that matter, have a numerical character—as in "We're number one!"—or does it have a moral character—meaning, as the U.S. motto has it, "Out of many, one." If the latter, then the unity being celebrated is not the lonely singleness of a digit but the communal solidarity of a group. "Universal," in this sense, is inclusive rather than exclusive. An essential pluralism is implied in such a notion of universality, a ready acknowledgment that, however absolute the claim being made, there is more than one way to understand its meaning.

At the beginning of his *Ethics,* Aristotle suggests that the good is that "to which all things aim." So the truth. Universal truth may be understood as referring to a truth that applies across time, place, and culture, but time, place, and culture shape every perception and every expression of such truth. This is the fuller meaning of what we already called perspectivalism. Any given—"one"—statement of truth must be offered and taken in awareness of truth's inevitable contingency. Therefore, truth, to use another essentially numerical word deriving from "one," is not univocal. If it were, then education, whether religious or secular, would simply amount to the student's conforming his or her mind to the truth as stated by the teacher (whether speaking for the established religion, the state power, or merely the conventional wisdom). There is an elusive aspect even to something regarded as universal truth, and education begins and ends with respect for that elusiveness, which means a teacher's goal is not the student's mind conforming, but its engaging.

There is, of course, a profound cultural assumption embedded in this idea of the essential elusiveness of truth, and in the pedagogy—and preaching—that follows from it. That assumption is itself a matter of fierce debate in all societies and cultures. One way to articulate that assumption is to contrast static ontology with a philosophical view that gives emphasis to process: is "being" primary, or is "becoming"? As we have seen numerous times before, the difference here shapes thinking in such diverse arguments as that between "creation science" (which sees reality as having been established once, in that originating act of creation) and evolution (which sees reality as unfolding), or that between opponents of abortion (who see human life as beginning at conception) and advocates of "choice" (who see the growth of fetal life into fully human as gradual). Each side in such disputes will stake its claim to universality.

But what divides these contestants, perhaps most fundamentally, is that an understanding of universality that is inclusive, not exclusive, assumes the contingency of truth and affirms that reality is a process. The consequent necessity of pluralism must leave room for the point of view that denies all of this. Universalism, to be truly universal, must have a built-in acknowledgment that the ideal of universality, in addition to being humane and politically germane, is also problematic. Such an approach to education in everything from religion to politics would be consistently self-critical, aware of the implications of power, and permanently alert for a gnostic imposition by those who know on those who do not—all the pitfalls that have turned previous efforts at universalism into exercises, however nobly defined, of imperial triumphalism. And of course the teaching of such intellectual humility amounts, finally, to the most important act of universal education of all.[47]

Return to Matthew, where Jesus calls his followers "the salt of the earth . . . the light of the world,"[48] images that suggest that Christianity does not make universal claims after all. (What if all the earth turned to salt?) But that exhortation with which Matthew concludes—"Go, therefore, make disciples of all nations!"—would be read as a mandate for the *exclusive* universalism that consigned non-Christians to hell. A return to such exclusive universalism is the antidote that Pope Benedict offers for the poison of an undifferentiated relativism, and again, this inevitably involves cruelty. Transcendent cruelty. We saw early in this book how fear of hell dominated the Catholic imagination before Vatican II—hell as the place to which the superseded siblings are consigned. And so it should be no surprise that, in 2007, Benedict resurrected that image, too. "Hell," he declared, "of which so little is said in our time, exists and is eternal."[49] The threat of hell, with its assumption of a monstrous God, backs up the supersessionism-plus-universalism that became the mark of state-sponsored Christianity and then of politically charged Islam. The violence of hell served, in effect, as the afterimage of the violence that this theology ultimately justified, the violence of crusade and jihad.

8. PEACE AMONG THE RELIGIONS

How can religion be detached from violence? How can peace be achieved in a religiously inflamed world? That question surfaced with surprising urgency in the early twenty-first century. Ironically, one man who had been preparing to take it up—arguing against the viewpoint put forward by Cardinal Ratzinger—was Hans Küng. The further irony is that Ratzinger's late-twentieth-century vendetta against him, which had culminated in his loss of the license to teach Roman Catholic theology at Tübingen, was the very thing that prepared Küng for a new role. "Because we had the big fight in 1979, I was liberated," he told me when I visited him in Tübingen. "I had to leave the Catholic faculty . . . which was considered a punishment, but it was a liberation." It was then, he said, that he could turn his attention "to Judaism, Islam, Hinduism, Buddhism, Chinese religion . . . to think through all these problems."[50] Küng, while still at Tübingen, undertook a study of world religions with the purpose of understanding their relationship to violence. "The survival of humanity is at stake," he said.

As a man whose own horizon had been upended by the Holocaust, Küng started with the question of Christianity's connection to violence, and then he went on to consider Judaism and Islam.[51] He grasped before many others that the problem of world peace had a religious component. He defined his project with the mantra "No peace among nations without peace among the religions. No peace among the religions without dialogue between the religions. No dialogue between the religions without investigations of the foundation of the religions."[52]

The third stage of Küng's program is the critical one. Interfaith dialogue is often discussed as if the goal were mere civility, people from different religious traditions getting together over tea, taking up questions of no particular threat or import. The main object of dialogue, in this view, is for each party to achieve a new appreciation and respect for the other's beliefs. But in the experience, dialogue has been more far-reaching than that, and that is what Küng points to. His mantra reflects authentic religious dialogue, how a believing person who encounters the different beliefs of someone else inevitably winds up reexamining the foundation of his own beliefs. Here dialogue enters a new stage. "The most significant basis for the meeting of men of different religious traditions," wrote Rabbi Abraham Joshua Heschel, "is the level of fear and trembling, of humility and contrition, where our individual moments of faith are mere waves in the endless ocean of mankind's reaching out for God, where all formulations and articulations appear as understatements, where our souls are swept away" and the human spirit is "stripped of pretensions and conceit." It is then, Heschel concludes, that "we sense the tragic insufficiency of human faith."[53] God, Heschel says with staggering simplicity, is greater than religion.

Moving from civil exchanges between two separate groups, focused on a sharing of dogmas and traditions that are assumed to be beyond criticism, dialogue becomes the self-critical examination of one's own dogma and tradition in the presence of the other, and in the light of the other's experience and belief. Dialogue, that is, leads to change. That, of course, is why reactionaries reject the entire enterprise, and why conservatives want to restrict dialogue to matters that are not, in Küng's word, foundational.

The principle of dialogue, in Hans Küng's scheme, applies within as well as without. When his old nemesis Ratzinger was elected pope, Küng immediately asked to see him. They met privately at Castel Gandolfo, the papal summer residence. Küng, recall, had given Ratzinger his first major job as a theologian nearly forty years before. The two men did not discuss "the persistent doctrinal questions" that separated them, nor did the rehabilitation of Küng as a Catholic theologian come up. The meeting was personal, a tribute to Pope Benedict's civility, and to Küng's.[54]

But Pope Benedict generally imagines that civility, as opposed to substantive exchange, is sufficient, an understanding reflected in his wanting to restrict the realm of interreligious dialogue, distinguishing between theology, which is off-limits, and culture, which is not. Human rights questions can be discussed, but not their religious underpinnings. Anthropology, yes; theology, no. The problem here is that distinguishing between theology and culture is like distinguishing between halves of a walnut. This is perhaps clearer in the House of Islam, where there is no hard and fast distinction between life and religion, or between culture and theology. But among Christians as well, such distinctions are more theoretical than real. Benedict's dichotomy, in fact, does justice to neither culture nor theology. Neither does the distinction he wants to draw between virtuous values of a culture, from which religion can learn, and the amoral culture in which those values exist. Affirm one, reject the other. "This is breathtaking in its superficiality," the Church historian Eamon Duffy commented. "'Values' are not detachable entities which can be removed from the structures—intellectual, social, political, economic—which give them shape and coherence. They are not pills which (suitably gilded) can be swallowed painlessly, taking care not to exceed the stated dose. Really to 'take on' the 'best values of liberal culture' would involve for the Church deep structural transformations."[55]

Benedict, as Ratzinger, was appalled when Pope John Paul II seemed to recognize the validity of non-Catholic and non-Christian religions while praying at Assisi in 1986 with other spiritual leaders—everyone from a Crow medicine man to the Dalai Lama, from the archbishop of Canterbury to the chief rabbi of Rome. That gathering was defined by its organizers as "an unconditional opening to the religion of the other,"[56] a version in Italy of the stance Tissa Balasuriya had taken in Sri Lanka. That is surely why Ratzinger took the extraordinary step of criticizing it, despite the pope's sponsorship. "This cannot be the model," Ratzinger said.[57]

At the next interreligious gathering at Assisi, in 2002, during the time of John Paul's decline and after the promulgation of the exclusivist *Dominus Iesus*, Ratzinger saw to it that there was no praying "with." Instead, as far as the Roman Catholic participants were concerned, the praying was "beside." What this means is unclear, especially if more than a moment's thought is given to the significance of prayer itself. Speaking as one who has prayed "with," not "beside," intimate friends and family members of other faiths for decades, I wonder what kind of God was imagined in Assisi, and what kinds of channels were seen to separate the hopes and fears that rise to God from the human heart.

"The contemplative dimension of life, present in all the great religions," observed the Trappist abbot Thomas Keating, "is the common heart of the world. There the human family is already one."[58] But not in Assisi. Oddly, this gathering took place only a few months after the September 11 attacks, when the relationship between peace and interreligious understanding had been made so dramatic, yet for the Roman Catholic Church "Assisi II," as it was called, represented a rejection of the interfaith progress that had been made over the previous thirty years. Roman Catholicism would in no way enter into a relationship with other religions that might imply recognition of non-Catholic religious claims. This is resistance to the "dictatorship of relativism."

9. "CATASTROPHE" MEANS "TURNING POINT"

Pope Benedict is right. His theology admits of no need for self-criticism, no possibility of foundational change. And so authentic religious interaction must be avoided, especially in relation to Islam. Much that has happened over the past half century must be renounced, going all the way back to the story of Archbishop Richard Cushing and his brother-in-law Dick Pearlstein. Their encounter—an informal act of interreligious dialogue—led directly to Cushing's rejection of "No salvation outside the Church," and indirectly to the Catholic Church's rejection of that same dogma. Similarly, if more broadly, the momentous interfaith encounter between Jews and Catholics after World War II led eventually to the Catholic renunciation at Vatican II of the "Christ killer" charge and the replacement theology of supersessionism—two pillars of a true theological revolution. The change in Church teaching about Jews and Judaism represents the ultimate instance of the "investigation of foundations" of which Küng speaks. But by the early twenty-first century, the question had to be confronted: Was that theological revolution's most lasting consequence the conservative reaction that was then mounted against it?[59]

Cushing's dogma-changing excommunication of Father Leonard Feeney, in 1953, took place two years after Joseph Ratzinger was ordained to the priesthood. On Pope Benedict's calendar of relativism, it seems reasonable to observe, Cushing's act was when things began to go wrong.[60] Pope Benedict has single-handedly thrown into doubt much of the interfaith progress that had been made between the Catholic Church and various other religious bodies.[61] We have already noted the destructive effect of Benedict's pronouncements on Islam at Regensburg in 2006, but even in areas where historic strides toward reconciliation had been made, Benedict's impact has been negative. After all, his Regensburg lecture was mainly given over to an attack on non-Catholic Christians and secularists for their submission to the dictatorship of relativism.

But it is the Church's relationship with Jews and Judaism that has perhaps suffered the most damage. Jewish dialogue partners are loath to criticize the pope, but the rollback is under way. The key emblem of this was the Catholic embrace, when Ratzinger was at the peak of his power as a cardinal, of the antisemitic film *The Passion of the Christ* by Mel Gibson. It is not necessary here to rehearse the litany of offenses represented by that pornographically violent movie—just to note that, upon its release in 2004, the seriously impaired Pope John Paul II was approvingly quoted by Vatican sources as saying, "It is as it was." Later that year, in a move widely regarded as having been carried out with Ratzinger's blessing, the Vatican beatified Gibson's main antisemitic source, Sister Anna Katharina Emmerich. She was a nineteenth-century mystic whose visions featured wild caricatures of hyperviolent Jews. The "cause" of her beatification had been gathering dust in Vatican drawers for more than a century, but was brought forward now as a signal of approbation for Gibson. In 2005, driving the point home, the U.S. Conference of Catholic Bishops named the film as one of its top ten of the year—this despite the overwhelmingly negative response *The Passion* received from every mainstream theological and scriptural scholar, and despite Gibson's own status as a reactionary Catholic who rejected the authority of the Second Vatican Council. Or was such approval offered *because* of that status?[62]

In all of this the Catholic hierarchy was putting its own interests before the crucial tasks of combating antisemitism and rejecting violence in religion, using the extremely popular film as a bridge to an increasingly alienated population of Christians—especially in the Southern Hemisphere, where proselytizing fundamentalism had mass appeal. Catholic fundamentalism, courtesy of Mel Gibson, whose worldwide DVD sales broke records, would match evangelical Protestantism in the remote villages and teeming cities of the Third World. No matter that the violent theology of *The Passion of the Christ* meshed perfectly with the bloodthirsty apocalyptic aims of post-9/11 terrorism. As for the Jews, by 2007 there could seem to be no real surprise when the papal homilist who preached that year's Good Friday sermon in the papal chapel, in Benedict's presence, openly repudiated the most important elements of the breakthrough Vatican II declaration *Nostra Aetate.* The homilist said, in effect, *The Jews were, too, guilty of the murder of Jesus!*[63] As if following the tradition, the pope's response to this reiteration of the "Christ killer" charge was silence.

But what if Küng is right and interreligious dialogue, leading to religious self-criticism, is essential to peace among nations? In that case, the world is presented with the spectacle of the Catholic Church protecting its view of truth rather than promoting an urgent global need for pluralist mutuality, and the leader of the Church protecting his own position at the expense of Catholics instructed by Vatican II to understand themselves as the people of God.[64] How can this be? In fact, the determination of the Catholic Church's clerical hierarchy to protect itself at all costs had already been made as clear as day during the years when Ratzinger was solidifying his hold on power.

The catastrophe of the priests' sex-abuse scandal should have been a turning point in the clerical culture—"turning point" being the meaning of the Greek word "catastrophe." In Aristotle's analysis of narrative form, catastrophe is also the moment of recognition, the epiphany in which the hidden action of the drama is revealed for what it is.

After September 11, 2001, the world saw with stark clarity how ideology and even theology can lead to violence, showing the link between interreligious understanding and peace. In just such a way, after the horrible revelations of the Catholic hierarchy's failures to protect children, the connection between the Church's power structure and violence against the most powerless was made plain. There is a global connection between religion and terror, and there is an intensely personal one. For all his civility, as Pope Benedict XVI inhibits any resolution of the first, so he keeps in place the structures of the second. More because of Ratzinger than anyone else, the urgently needed confrontation with the catastrophe of clergy sexual abuse, what might have made it a turning point, did not occur.

Basic questions about the all-male and celibate priesthood, about the totalitarian style of Church authority, as well as about the way the clerical power structure consistently protected itself, without regard for the thousands of young victims of predatory priests—such questions were efficiently deflected by the Vatican. More than one prelate actually blamed the scandal on the dominance of Jews in the American media, with Ratzinger himself declaring ominously, in 2002, "I am personally convinced that the constant presence in the press of the sins of Catholic priests, especially in the United States, is a planned campaign."[65]

When Benedict became pope, it was widely assumed that he would move quickly to deal with this crisis, and he did. In the first year of his pontificate he issued a formal order forbidding further admission to the priesthood of any man having a "gay orientation" or "deep-seated homosexual tendencies." For centuries, Catholic dioceses and monastic orders had welcomed homosexual men (as convents welcomed homosexual women), with the proviso that, like their heterosexual comrades, they would observe the rule of celibacy. No more. This new prohibition was itself a stark proclamation: the abuse of young people by priests was caused by homosexuals in the priesthood.[66] No other change in the priesthood or ecclesiastical culture was necessary. Indeed, no other change was allowed. One cruelty was multiplied by another.

Based on what? Pope Benedict, while still a cardinal, had been asked if he had met any homosexuals personally. "Yes, in Berlin," he replied. "They were demonstrating against the pope."[67]

The limits of such a perception—or the self-deception of it—make plain that the empathetic tradition of the Catholic Church runs deeper than the thinking of those who now govern from its margin. The resistance to Catholic reform, no matter how well intentioned, is a signal more of an era's ending than of one being restored.

CHAPTER TEN

A WRITER'S FAITH

1. BAD CATHOLIC

I LEFT THE PRIESTHOOD to be a writer. This is the very definition of my life. People sometimes refer to that choice as my having "left the Church," and I habitually explain that I did not leave the Church. I remain a practicing Catholic. Indeed, my Catholic faith was rescued by my decision to leave the priesthood, because it is only as a layman that I have the intellectual and moral freedom to dissent from the reactionary trends in the post–Vatican II Church. And, although this was unimagined, it is as a writer that I have discovered a way of being that goes to the core of Catholic faith as I live it—that largeness of the Church that is so much more than governance. The redemptive shape of narrative form, the unquenchable thirst for meaning, the implication-laden tension between language and what remains forever unspoken, the contemplative habit of absorbedness, the dark night of the soul as a source of illumination, God as the author of creation, why we call Jesus "Word," the final inadequacy of all expression, which is the first value of it—such momentous experiences had eluded me until I became a writer.

That this life emerged in the form of a renewed Catholic identity may seem all too particular to the writer's vocation, but I aim to show here how a basic understanding of faith as rooted in imagination and expression can brace every Catholic's identity. My assumption throughout this book has been that one Catholic's personal journey can illuminate the pathways taken by—and now open to—all.

In leaving the priesthood—a breaking of my vows, even though I was eventually dispensed;[1] a violation of the Church's ancient insistence that the vocation is for life—I took up a place in the Church's shadowy vestibule. To other Catholics, including certain friends, my status became unclear.

"Spoiled" is a word that was once applied to my kind. I understand why non-Catholics take for granted that I have left the Church behind, or that it has somehow banished me. Such complications mark me as a writer, and they give me my subject. "How many Roman Catholics have been good novelists?" George Orwell asked. "Even the handful one could name have usually been bad Catholics. The novel is a Protestant art form; it is a product of the free mind."[2] Orwell had apparently not noticed the novels of Georges Bernanos, François Mauriac, or, for that matter, Cervantes. He did not know the work of Walker Percy, Flannery O'Connor, or Mary Gordon. I have written ten novels myself, and take for granted my version of that free mind, whether Orwell could imagine my doing so or not. I'll leave assessments of my novels to others, but I recognize that by Orwell's ranking (as by the hierarchy's) I would surely qualify as a bad Catholic.[3] For one thing, as an ex-priest my appointed role was to shrink into those shadows of disapproval, drink heavily, and not be heard from again. Certainly not on any subject having to do with the faith.

What is a bad Catholic anyway? Once it was clear. Orwell probably had Graham Greene in mind, or perhaps Evelyn Waugh—admired novelists but famously unbridled Catholics. Hard drinkers, womanizers, men with a public taste for sin. Late in life, writers like Eugene O'Neill and F. Scott Fitzgerald were haunted by their status as bad Catholics. O'Neill nearly saw a priest on his deathbed, but his domineering wife refused to allow it.[4] Bad Catholics were in bad marriages, or they were openly gay, or they had had abortions, or they practiced artificial birth control. They were condemned by their own heart-rending personal circumstances.

The issue is murkier now. Members of Catholic reform groups, like Voice of the Faithful, Future Church, and Call to Action,[5] are labeled as bad Catholics by some. Lay movements generally are looked on askance, even though they are thriving in the Church around the globe.[6] In Latin America, priests who organize campesinos without permission of the bishop are bad. So are Latin-American laypeople, for that matter, who organize themselves into "base communities" without a priest; Dutch theologians who invoke Erasmus; and women who preside at unofficial Eucharists without waiting to be ordained. On the other hand, Governor Frank Keating of Oklahoma would seem to be a good Catholic, since the American bishops appointed him head of their National Review Board on Clergy Sexual Abuse in 2002. Yet Keating had authorized dozens of death row executions, and Pope John Paul II, in his encyclical *Evangelium Vitae,* had said justification for the death penalty is "rare, if not virtually nonexistent." Supreme Court Justice Antonin Scalia is regarded as a good Catholic, yet he is openly contemptuous of the pope's teaching here. And what about Catholics who supported George W. Bush's war in Iraq, and his program of torture, despite the grave misgivings expressed by Church leaders? Was Pope Benedict's honoring of Bush with an unprecedented papal visit to the White House consistent with those misgivings? Not long ago bad Catholics were also known as cafeteria Catholics, choosing beliefs as much by conscience as by the menu of authority, but it seems now that Catholics from left to right approach the cafeteria line, eyeing options.

This confusion is a good thing. It undermines the moralistic polarity that infected the Church's thinking about itself. Because there was an identifiable group of bad Catholics, those not in it could smugly bask in the self-approval of being good. In the old days, they were the few who presented themselves at the altar rail for Communion. Early in this book, I recalled how most Catholics were at the mercy of that *Domine, non sum dignus* ("Lord, I am not worthy")—a built-in feeling of shame. But at bottom, the good-bad division's real purpose was to protect the pyramidal authority of the hierarchy. That is why, in former times, the label "bad" was reserved for those attitudes and behaviors that challenged Rome's own emphasis, especially regarding sex. You could be excommunicated for having an abortion, but not for being a Nazi. You could be homosexual in the Church, but not in a public way that would call into question Church prohibitions. You could remarry after divorce, but only if your divorce could be labeled "annulment." You could practice birth control, but only the method deemed "natural." Administering such distinctions from the confessional, the clericalized Church controlled the inner lives of Catholics by making sexual ethos the one area of moral absolutism. That is why abortion still trumps the death penalty as a matter of Catholic concern, why contraceptive gel draws Church fire and jellied gasoline (also known as napalm) does not.

As the girder of a power structure, the system was ingenious because sexual restlessness defines the human condition. Once that restlessness was made a matter of eternal damnation or salvation, every layperson, even a Fitzgerald or an O'Neill, became psychologically subservient to every priest. Every priest moved within an aura, and around an ex-priest that aura could still be glimpsed. Here we return to the economy of unworthiness to which, as a child, I watched the people around me submit. I myself abandoned that economy only when I left the priesthood, which was possible only when I realized that worthiness and unworthiness are alike in meaning very little. That the priestly aura, in the view of others, clings to me is a measure of its strength. This aura depended on the myth that priests are creatures set apart from the human condition, and that myth broke when priests, like me, left their orders. It broke for the larger community when priests became known as abusers of children, when bishops protected those priests instead of the children.

Who are the bad Catholics now? That there was ever such a category obscured the basic truth that every Catholic is a sinner, because every human being is. This is what the Catholic writers of whom Orwell disapproved have known so well—Greene with his whiskey priests, Waugh with his fey pansies, O'Connor with her mad mothers. From life to literature and back, the Catholic story celebrates our noblest impulses by lifting up the opposite inclinations that betray them. And churchgoing American Catholics are now well acquainted with this aspect of the human condition. While a majority of them are "bad," in the sense of rejecting core hierarchical teachings, up to eighty percent of them regularly receive Holy Communion at Mass.[7] Whether they feel that their unauthorized moral choices are wrong or not, they have come to understand that the main note of this community must be repentance, the main hope forgiveness.

2. ALLEN TATE

As it happens, my ultimate decisions—first to be ordained as a priest, and then to leave the priesthood to be a writer—were intimately tied to a relationship with a writer who, at a critical moment, was labeled bad. That was where I came in, and where we were both changed. I have already recounted how, in the early 1960s, as a novice and seminarian, I was drawn to priest-writers like Thomas Merton and Daniel Berrigan, sources of a new ideal. Their conviction that the Kingdom of God is within was reflected in their preference of writerly introspection over obedience to an external magisterium, but in that they were only a later manifestation of an ancient Catholic impulse defined by none other than Augustine, for whom "spirals down into memory" were the most reliable way to God.[8] Augustine, acknowledged at the beginning of this book as one of its sentries, still stands by, as witness and authority. Indeed, he is the author of the writer's faith, and all the rest of us are his imitators.

I have described the impact of Allen Ginsberg's "Howl," but its shattering force depended, in my case, on hearing the word "howl" as "holy." The writers whose wanderings kept circling back to God became my spiritual reading—T. S. Eliot and W. H. Auden, among others. Around the time Eliot had become an Anglican, scandalizing the unchurched literary establishment, his friend and peer in the United States, Allen Tate, had converted to Roman Catholicism. Tate teased Eliot for settling, in his trek to Canterbury, for near beer, while he himself, swimming the Tiber, took a full draft of the real thing.[9] Tate's high-flown celebrations of what he called the "Catholic aesthetic" drew me to him.

"Nature the casual sacrament," I read in his masterpiece "Ode to the Confederate Dead," "to the seasonal eternity of death." I recognized that the religious significance of poetry, as I experienced it, was not defined by its subject matter—Francis Thompson's *The Hound of Heaven*—but by the state of awareness it created, a transformation, in Tate's phrase, of "the heaving air."[10] In the writing of poetry, I discovered a way to navigate the oceanic vastness of my feelings, and at last I began not so much to understand myself but to come into myself, as if I could be the harbor against my own storms. The works of Allen Tate became a particular companion.

Tate was born in Kentucky in the last year of the nineteenth century. As a student at Vanderbilt, his circle included Robert Penn Warren and John Crowe Ransom. His influence as a poet and critic was centered on three journals he edited over the years: the *Fugitive*, the *Kenyon Review*, and the *Sewanee Review*. As his reputation grew, he was known as a generous mentor of younger poets, like John Berryman, Richard Blackmur, and Robert Lowell (whose *For the Union*

Dead was written in tension with Tate's poem on the Confederate dead. Tate also influenced Lowell's decision to become a Catholic, though Lowell, too, became a bad one).

In the 1950s Tate became a teacher of poetry at the University of Minnesota. Learning that, I conjured a dream of going there so that he could mentor me. In 1966, in an astounding act of independence for a seminarian of that time, I put in a request with my religious superiors to be allowed to spend a summer term enrolled in Tate's class in Minneapolis. And astoundingly, permission was granted. I was twenty-three years old.

After the first class, I showed up at his office with a sheaf of the poems I had written over the previous two years. Tate was nattily dressed and carried himself like a southern gentleman. His forehead was high, and his blue eyes twinkled. His formal manner intimidated me, but then I noticed that his fingernails had been chewed. I took that signal of his anxiousness as evidence of what we had in common. We talked for an hour, at the end of which he invited me to come back each week, each time with a single poem. I did that, and he regularly took my work apart, leaving me steadily determined to put it back together. Over the course of the term, in addition to the challenging class on modern American poetry, I was the beneficiary of a private tutorial with one of the great literary figures of the age.

Even then, I did not kid myself about why Tate found me interesting. His was a high-medieval Catholicism, and what he saw in me was more priest-in-training than poet-to-be. But it was an unlikely match. Tate was innately conservative, a contributor to William F. Buckley's *National Review.* He was a Buckley-style Catholic, and so he should have despised the new-breed Vatican II liberalism that enthralled me. By the standards set at the Council of Trent, standards he defended, I belonged in my cloister. Yet he welcomed me.

I had no way of knowing it ahead of time, but a personal crisis was blowing those fixed categories open in Tate's life just as I showed up in it. Among my fellow students in the university's English department, Tate was the subject of gossip that summer. He was rumored to have had an affair with one of his students from a course a year or two before, and tongues had really clucked when, that year, his wife, the poet Isabella Gardner, divorced him. He promptly married his former student. What really spiced the gossip, and what had unexpected relevance for Tate's readiness to receive me, was the fact that the object of his passion was a young Catholic nun, who, reciprocating his feelings, had just left the convent for him.[11] How could Tate not have found a Catholic seminarian intriguing? The Vatican II revolution, having allowed nuns to leave convents for secular classrooms, had already upended his life.

Whatever motivated Tate, however, I was greatly affected by his steady affirmation. In our meetings I learned that I could not possibly know what I thought or felt until I had expressed it with images and the music of language. Then I learned how the expression itself transforms thought and feeling both, the discovery and invention of meaning. For Tate, meaning was sacramental, an opening to more than was meant. The very act of writing was a creating *ex nihilo,* an exercise of pure imagination, which was, in the words of Samuel Taylor Coleridge, whom Tate loved to cite, "the repetition in human beings of the creative 'I AM' of God." In Tate's view, poetry was the sacred vocation of the human race. We are the medium through which all that exists becomes conscious of itself, and the unending reach for clarity of that consciousness, for knowledge and for truth, defines each person's purpose. Poetry, I learned from Tate, is the intensification of this broader human project.

Once I began to appreciate the from-nothing creativity of the imagination, I could extend the insight from poetry to the narrative form itself. Humans live by the stories they tell, and for a very good reason. In storytelling, the imagination composes the disordered notes of experience—through the form of beginning, middle, and end; through conflict, crisis, and resolution—in narrative structures that affirm order and meaning. Extending Coleridge's dictum about the "I AM" of God, one can understand creation itself as the story God is telling. God, in a phrase of the Anglican John Macquarrie, is "Expressive Being."[12] Expression as such, that is, points beyond itself to the wholly—and holy—inexpressible.

A feeling for the self-transcendence of art, and its home in imaginative expression, had been Tate's way into religion. The words he used in describing this were familiar to me, but, focused as we were on my own poems, I heard the familiar words as a new language. A new language, but also as natural to me as my native language—and Catholicism was its syntax. Incarnation means not that God is in the details of life, but *only* in the details. It was the old lesson of the universal in particularity, but I learned it as a lesson in belief and writing both. I offer the lesson here, suggesting that its relevance goes far beyond a writer's work to the impulse, innate in every person, to put experience into words.

At the end of that summer, I asked Tate to autograph my copy of his *Collected Poems.* He wrote, "For James, with best wishes for your two vocations." He handed me the book; I read the inscription and looked up at him. "Poet and priest," he said, three words that dazzled me—a dream come true. With that simple statement, Allen Tate gave me permission to think of myself as a poet, which was the true beginning of my life as a writer. Before I could react, he added, "But you can't have both, you know."

You can't have both the vocation to poetry and the vocation to priesthood. They are mutually exclusive. This surprising statement was something akin to what Orwell had written. I thought Tate was wrong. Merton had both vocations, so did Berrigan, and so, for that matter, had Gerard Manley Hopkins. The cardinal archbishop of New York, with the laying on of hands, would make me a priest. Allen Tate had just ordained me a poet. But that was 1966, just after the Vatican Council had concluded in such hope, and just before what the Vietnamese were already calling "the American war" showed itself for what it was. Before long, Merton was absurdly dead and Berrigan was a true (not literary) fugitive, and New York's cardinal was the war's blesser in chief.

Earlier in this book, I wrote about the impact of the two assassinations in the spring of 1968, with Robert Kennedy being felled just as I was to deliver my first sermon. The feeling then, and afterward, was that any sermon at such a time could only be false. A couple of days after Kennedy's murder, I stood in the throng that lined the railroad tracks outside Washington to watch the train carrying Bobby's coffin from New York to Arlington. I was one of tens of thousands who had spontaneously, across a couple of hundred miles, taken up that position by the tracks, and as the funeral train passed slowly by, we too picked up the low refrain that accompanied it all the way, a chain of voices singing "The Battle Hymn of the Republic." But what mine eyes saw that day seemed the farthest thing from the glory of the Lord.

In *Nausea,* Jean Paul Sartre offered the terrifying thought that presenting human experience in the ordered form of a story is inevitably to turn it into a lie, but what was most striking about Sartre's assertion is that he wrote it not in a philosophical treatise but in a novel.[13] Only in narrative do we understand ourselves, which I learned from what I was reading, from what I was going through. My year of hitting bottom—the year my dread conflict with my father broke open, the year "the sixties" became a nightmare—was the year I came into myself as a writer.

"Art begins in a wound," the novelist John Gardner wrote, adding that the art is itself the medicine. In that year of the wound, I really began to write—really began, that is, to order the chaos of my experience by creating form and structure, through meter, rhyme, and the epiphanies of mental freedom. I could not write a sermon, but I wrote poems, which Tate himself later characterized as concerned with "the conflict between belief and existential disorder." A poem I wrote about Merton, Tate publicly declared, announced my arrival as a poet.[14]

For Catholics, the climactic distress of 1968 came with the promulgation of *Humanae Vitae*, the encyclical condemning birth control about which we have already seen so much. It can be no coincidence that that was the summer of my great vocational crisis. Self-expression, yes. But talk of God and the Church? It no longer seemed possible to me. If suffering and death were routes of redemption, why were the deaths of King and Kennedy so without meaning? The war between the races in America and the war in Vietnam were both set loose, and now so was the Catholic Church's war against itself. *Humanae Vitae* made a mockery of the religious reform on which I had, until then, pinned my life. I have described how I embraced, in that following autumn, the new image of priestly ministry defined by political (and also religious) resistance and embodied in the figure of the Reverend William Sloane Coffin, Jr. But before that happened I nearly quit the seminary, months short of my ordination. Only an encounter with Tate stopped me from bailing out.

That summer, I was assigned to a pastoral education program at a clinic in Atlanta, part of my training to be a counselor. I was away from the incubator of Catholic life, surrounded by social workers, medical professionals, and secular psychologists—not to mention by the clinic's alcoholic and drug-addled patients. Some of my peers on the staff were young women, and I was far from immune to their charms, although I behaved myself. My identity as a counseling intern was not religious, and to my surprise I liked it that way. With a detached eye, I saw in a new way the absolutes on which my priestly vocation rested, and I realized that I cared more for my writing desk than for the chapel. *Humanae Vitae* fell like a deciding blow. I remembered what Allen Tate had said to me about my two vocations—"You can't have both"—and decided that he was the one to whom I had to declare myself.

By then, Tate had retired from the Minnesota faculty and returned to Sewanee, Tennessee, only a couple of hours from Atlanta. I wrote to him and asked if he would see me. He replied promptly with an invitation, setting a date.

I had read the news earlier that year that he and his young wife had had twin sons, and so I brought a pair of crib toys with me when I hitched a ride to Sewanee. I showed up at his house at the appointed hour, rang the doorbell, and waited. It was a sweltering afternoon. No one appeared at the door, and I felt a twinge of panic that I had the date wrong. I dared to ring the bell again. Finally the door opened to reveal Allen Tate standing in his bedroom slippers. I had never seen him without a jacket and tie, and now he was wearing a rumpled short-sleeved shirt, revealing scrawny pale forearms. His oversized forehead was glistening and his eyes were rheumy. He looked at me without a clue who I was or what I wanted, and I was sure he was drunk. I introduced myself, apologizing profusely and offering to come back some other time, but with a snap of recognition, his habitual courtesy took over, and he insisted that I come in.

The house was recently built, in a modern style. The window shades were drawn, and the flagstone floor was cool. Tate showed me to a sitting room, and we took places on a couch side by side. As I always had in Minnesota, I carried a folder with a batch of recent poems, but I sensed at once that we would not be turning to them. My business was far more urgent than that. The reason I was so nervous wasn't the great man; it was what I'd come to declare to him: "You were right. And if I can't have both vocations, the one I choose is the one you chose. I want to be a writer, not a priest."

But before any of that could come forward in my consciousness, much less my throat, I opened my bag to take out the pair of crib toys I had brought. When I proffered them, Tate gasped.

"You don't know what's happened," he said. With a cracking voice and a fresh flood of water to his eyes, he told me that his infant son Michael had, that very week, choked in his crib and died, and was buried only a day or two before. Tate grasped my arm, apparently remembering at last who I was. "I could have used you yesterday," he said. Then he blurted out the story of how the local Catholic priest —"the monsignor"—had refused to let Michael be buried in a Catholic ceremony. I felt the full horror of this and asked why. "Because I am a bad Catholic," Tate said. "My marriage is 'notorious.'" Michael's funeral was held in a Protestant church, Tate told me, weeping.

Instantly, and instinctively, I began to explain to Tate all that made the Catholic priest's cruel decision wrong and improper, even according to the Church's own rules. The rules, as I explained them, of course, reflected the adjustments made by Vatican II, but the most momentous change was not in rules. At the extremity of loss, Tate was desperate for a word that would establish the meaningfulness of life, and I knew that that word was God, the one who establishes meaning as the ground of experience, including the experience of death. Either God's existence had relevance for the death of Michael or God did not exist.

But what God? The all-powerful monarch who knows nothing of human suffering? Who condemns on the basis of regulation? Who wants only to be obeyed? But in that God's name, Tate's child had been abandoned. At once I saw all that was wrong with the tradition into which I had been born, and from which, over the years of my training for the priesthood, I had been struggling to be free.

I do not have a detailed memory of what I said to Tate on that day, but the burden of my words—their weight and significance—is very clear to me today, and was then. All that poured from me showed that my faith had been transformed. The God of judgment and condemnation, so vividly incarnate in the excommunicating priest, had nothing to do with the God whom Jesus preached. Human love, Jesus said, which seeks not to command but to lure, is the great signal of who God is. And wasn't it in Jesus' own life, as those who loved him told the story, that we saw that? Nor had I ever seen more clearly the significance of the fact that this revelation comes to us as *story*. The Gospels are stories! Narrative form is the mode of God's presence to us, and so, with utter naturalness, I reminded Allen Tate of how the story goes.

How Jesus talked. How he lived. How he died. Jesus whose first public act was to be baptized in repentance (yes, Jesus, too, was contrite!); who then made his unselfrighteous way among the "bad" ones, the hookers, the divorcées, the collaborators with the hated Roman occupiers, identifying with those outsiders instead of condemning them; and who spoke the truth to power, rejecting sovereignty and every form of coercion. And then the story of Jesus reached a climax with the one experience that calls all other experience into question: the experience of death. The agony of Jesus—first in contemplating death in the garden, then undergoing it on the cross—was nothing but the agony that Allen Tate was feeling in front of me. Jesus was God's decisive word to human beings that the nothingness of death is neither the whole story nor its end.

Not that I reassured Tate that his infant son was now waiting for him in heaven. According to the theology of the Council of Trent, the unbaptized Michael would have been consigned to limbo, a middle place, neither heaven nor hell, in which blameless but "unsaved" souls do not suffer. Compared to the torments of hell—infinite pain, experienced with infinite sensitivity—limbo was not so bad, but it meant nothing to me, and would have meant nothing to Tate. Even less so hell, and not even heaven was to the point. Nor was praying for Michael's soul, as if God needed interventions from us. It would take me some years to understand this, but I had already moved away from the simple notion of intercessory prayer, as if, in consequence of earnest petition, a friendly God will favor one person over all others (sparing hell, or zapping a tumor, or working miracles with college admissions, or influencing the lottery draw). Such a God, treated as merciful, is, in fact, arbitrary and unjust (my lottery win means your loss). Such a God is unworthy of belief.

What consolation I could offer Tate had nothing to do with answered prayers, immortality, or the afterlife; not liberated souls or angelic beings; not the idea that death is just a bump in the road on the way to the bliss of paradise. Paradise, heaven, the pearly gates, the many mansions, the streets paved with gold, winged creatures, the beatific vision—all metaphors aiming to express something else. All poetry. Not that I disbelieved it, but that I saw how far short it fell of expressing our faith. Our faith, I knew by then, was not in *what* followed death, but *who.* To pray for Michael was to hand him over, without condition, into the care of the One who created him in the first place.

This is not to crudely debunk intercessory prayer, but to suggest that its purpose is less to alter God's attitude than ours. And a way of praying that emphasizes the omnipotent otherness of God instead of the inwardness of God—closer to us, as St. Augustine put it, than we are to ourselves—can actually be more alienating than affirming. Prayer, if it is anything, is the opposite of alienation. And praying for Michael was simply to recall that he was already beloved of God, as his very existence had demonstrated. As for the afterlife, it was not that Michael had a future, but that God did. And Michael's link with God remained unbroken.

God had been progressively speaking both to and through creation—the creation God beheld in the beginning as "very good." That creation included the radical fact of mortality, not only mortality of individuals but, across the eons, of species on earth, of earth itself, and ultimately of planets and galaxies beyond. There was a time when humanity did not exist, a time that is surely coming again. And so, perhaps, with the very cosmos. Death is built into the structure of being, and the instinct of belief is to see that death-including structure, as God does in Genesis, as good, very good. All that God had been saying since "the beginning," however defined, was *trust.*

Trust even now. Even this. Trust me. I am the one, God says, *who creates out of nothing.* Not only at the alpha of the cosmos, whatever and whenever that was—but now, in the dance of time, as being overwhelms nonbeing at every instant. Nothingness, therefore, is not to be feared—not even the nothingness of death. What God did at the beginning, measured as human time, God does at the end. *I am the one,* God had been saying all along, *who draws life out of death.*

God's "word," saying those things, became a human being—"incarnate"—not by coming down from heaven, from a preexisting state of supernatural being, but by being fully human, living his life, and confronting his death in such a way that God's self-expression was complete. I had already learned this from writing: that *expression* is the part of our being made in God's image. What the word is to me, the world is to God. And it is an ingenious intuition that enables us to call the world God's "word." As with the world, so with Jesus. The "word became flesh," that is, not when Jesus was born, but when he lived his whole life, even to death. Jesus lived by loving and Jesus died by trusting. Jesus trusted the one whom he called Father, even when his father had forsaken him. *Deus absconditus.* "My God, my God, why have you abandoned me?" gave way—here is the heart of the story—to "But into your hands I commend my spirit." *Jesus handed himself over to the God who was not there.* And found God there. In trusting the One who was not there, Jesus was resurrected, lifted into the status of being God's very own, or, as the Church calls him, God's Son.

What Jesus offers is not salvation, conceived only as a negative rescue from damnation. Instead Jesus offers a positive completion of life—"life," as he said, "to the full." This was the meaning of the promised "eternal life"—not some endless Sunday afternoon, stretching on toward an omega point that never comes, but the fullness of life here and now. Past, present, and future, experienced in the light of God's promise, change the meaning of time, and that same promise changes the meaning of space. But the point is, *it happens here.* Not in some afterlife. By being *fully* human, Jesus became God's real presence.

Presence, I presumed to say to Allen Tate in the center of the heartbreak that was choking him. Michael was dead. Utterly without future. Final. Gone. But God was not dead, and Michael still had God. Michael was in the eternal bosom of that love now. I firmly believed that, and found ways to say as much to the broken old man.

3. DEATH IS THE OPENING

In the mists of long ago, humanoid creatures began to distinguish themselves from other animals in the ways they responded to what was left of dead companions. It may well be that the emotional and intellectual confrontation with the physical fact of death was a context within which human consciousness evolved. We can imagine our Neolithic ancestors bent over the fallen, forcing open eyelids, feeling for a heartbeat, the rise of breath. Even once the finality of lifelessness was clear, the bereaved refused to treat such inert remains as insignificant. The reverencing by survivors of the corpses of their fellows was a defining act. Gravestones are a vestige of the prehistoric practice of covering lifeless corpses with rocks to protect them from the indignity of being assaulted by scavenging animals. Burial itself involved a kind of protection, a deliberate refusal to forget the one who had died. And in what does that refusal consist but the act of telling stories of the dead?

All such rituals enshrined the imaginative leap that survivors had made, grasping that the mysterious experience that had befallen some was coming to all. The eternal present of animal consciousness thus gave way to a feeling for the future. Awareness of death is the precondition of the sense of time.[15] When a living creature drew conclusions from the fate of its intimates to understand its own mortality, it had become a human being.

And so also the believing human being. Religion was born in the refusal to accept death as final. It was as if human consciousness, once achieved through the astounding adaptations of natural selection, could not accept itself as pointless. Confronted with the apparent pointlessness of death, human consciousness invented ways to think about it that mitigated the absurdity. Myths of the afterlife and immortality populated the human mind like clusters of figments and wishes, but again and again the harsh fact of death undercut such hope. But never permanently. Beginning in the Iron Age (around 1500 B.C.E.) and continuing for a thousand years, humans around the globe were alike in their intuitive efforts to mitigate the finality of mortality. Confucianism, Buddhism, Hinduism, Greek rationalism, and the monotheism of Israel all gave expression to the questions put by corpses: Why is there something and not nothing?[16] What is the purpose of a life that passes so quickly?

By the time an obscure nomadic people settled in the land between the Jordan River and the sea, they had learned to put their hope not in any idea of an undying soul or gods at play on Olympus or the calculations of rewarded virtue, but in a personal promise from One who was heard claiming the name "I AM." One whose wont was to draw being out of nothingness. If the long-gone fathers of this people—Abraham, Isaac, and Jacob—lived, it was because the promise lived. And that promise would continue to be offered and received across time, even as the simple assumptions of a primitive worldview—gods in the sky, miraculous interventions, man as the center of the cosmos—gave way to the subtleties of Philo, Augustine, Maimonides, Aquinas; ultimately to the complexities of Galileo, Darwin, Einstein, Watson and Crick. Death remains as much a problem in the Internet Age as it was in the Iron Age, and despite humanity's much-vaunted progress, it offers the same opening to transcendence as it ever did.

Out of the faith of Israel came the faith of the Church. The primordial pattern—humans rejecting the meaninglessness of death—reasserted itself when the grief-struck friends of Jesus contemplated what had happened to him. Their contemplation expressed itself in stories, which became sacred texts. The Jewish-Roman historian Josephus, who lived a generation after Jesus, and whose *Antiquities of the Jews* provides independent, if not entirely undisputed, confirmation of key elements of the Gospel story, offered a simple but crucial observation about Jesus and his friends: "Those who in the first place had come to love him did not give up their affection for him."[17] It was in that not giving up affection for the dead that human consciousness had been born in the first place, and it was in such loyalty that the Jesus movement was born. The death of Jesus was what required explanation, which is why the story that emerged from that first grief was organized around the Passion narrative, which in turn achieves its climax in the story of the Resurrection.

I do not recall discussing the Resurrection with Allen Tate, but I might have. Just as I would never have spoken of Michael at play in the streets of heaven, I would not have spoken of some miraculous resuscitation of the dead body of Jesus—as if the reorganization of molecules and atoms forms the content of Christian hope. I had learned from Tate himself the power of metaphor and symbolism, and was at home in understanding my religious impulse in those terms. Resurrection is the symbol pointing beyond itself to the intuition that, as his friends could not give up their affection for Jesus, neither could God. God's permanent affection is for life, life over death, resurrection. It is not that God intervenes to counter the normal course of nature, but that the normal course is itself the intervention.

4. LANGUAGE IS GOD

What the writer knows, in using such language, is that language is not merely the medium in which such hope is expressed; language is itself the hope. All knowledge and self-knowledge come through signals, signs, symbols, gestures, words, and text. Through language, that is. And what I had learned from Tate, a master of language, was that language itself is an opening to the world we cannot see.

What is language anyway? For humans to ask that question is like a fish asking "What is water?" We swim in language. We think in language. We live in language. We love in language. In language we are together. And with language we know the true meaning of being alone. Language is what makes us human. But language, or so the writer thinks, makes us more than that.

As the fish is ignorant of the water in which it has its being, so we miss the significance of the language within which we are aware. The use of words in expressing even the most absolute of convictions or hopes suggests that there is no absolute apart from the interpretive function of what the philosopher Paul Ricoeur calls "the mediating terms." Language, that is, is distinct from what language aims to express. "The chart," as an old Maine fisherman once told me after my boat had run aground because a rock was not marked on my navigational map, "is not the sea." Humans have a tendency to forget this, like fish forgetting water, but once they pay attention again to the medium in which all expression—all thought, for that matter—occurs, they cannot use it innocently. This is not only the limit of language, but the glory of it. The Christian story, the account of what the bereaved friends of Jesus experienced once they refused to give up their affection for him, quickly became a story of language—language as the mediating term of nothing less than God. Yet that story, because of its mediating character, is not nearly so absolute as Christians, forgetting that character, have commonly thought.

Pentecost, which Christians experienced as the birth of their movement, is the feast of language, when an assembly of foreigners—"Parthians, Medes, and Elamites," it says in the Acts of the Apostles[18]—understood one another despite not sharing a common tongue. The story of the miraculously comprehended preaching of Pentecost is deliberately constructed to celebrate the reversal of the Fall, as related in Genesis—the true Fall. Not Adam and Eve and their reach for the knowledge of good and evil. Certainly not, as Augustine had it, Adam and Eve and their carnal knowledge. No. Genesis 11, the story of the Tower of Babel, gives us the primordial definition of human fallenness—human beings divided by words, broken by words, "scattered" by separate tongues. "What we've got here," as Paul Newman says in *Cool Hand Luke,* "is a failure to communicate."[19] Language as the condition of alienation. The fish swimming in a sea of polluted water. Poison.

What is God? Who is God? If we conceive reality only in physical terms, then God may indeed be, as the Enlightenment scientist Pierre-Simon Laplace put it, the hypothesis we do not need. But what the Church has always understood is that God is the hypothesis we very much *do* need—not to explain physical events (other than creation itself) but to explain love, truth, beauty, gratitude. Here is where the perceptions of the neo-atheists show their limits, and where the

Church's skepticism about Galileo's extreme defenders, for that matter, shows its deeper significance. How can humans put into language our intimations of the beyond? Intimations, that is, of the *meta*physical. Any language we use of God falls short. And any language implies the act of interpretation. Therefore every person uses it, hears it, believes it differently. The common images: Father, Lord, king, sky, sun, horizon, ground—as in ground of being—Being itself, *ipsum esse.* Images of the poetic, not the scientific.

At Mass, we Catholics recite the Nicene Creed, a summary of belief that dates to the fourth century.[20] It is a litany of language that can now seem outmoded but that still enters the believing mind with power: "God of God, Light of Light, True God of True God." In the unencumbered way these words fall on the contemporary ear, we can sense what the Catholic Church has become in my lifetime—a people that has reclaimed its lyrical expression, even if at the expense of rigid orthodoxy. I have never heard anyone ask what "Light of Light" means, but neither have I heard anyone object to saying the phrase. Indeed, it fairly rolls off the tongues of the Sunday throng.

This is what it means that, every week, many American Catholic churches are filled with brightly intelligent worshipers who understand the meaning of the words they use, and their larger significance accumulates more through implication and connotation than dogmatic precision. "God of God" is another phrase that has precious gravity, even if we cannot explain it. We are in the realm of poetry here, not doctrine. Thus the liturgical reform enacted in the era of Vatican II, despite efforts to thwart it, has had its effect—not only on the Catholic faith but on the Catholic mind. The faith *is* rational. But in a profoundly sacramental tradition like Catholicism, it is no denigration to say that faith operates most powerfully at the pre-rational level of symbol and art—the realm of imagining as much as thinking.

The post–Vatican II renewal shows this. In the old days, the baptismal font in churches occupied a shadowy corner, but now it shares prominence in the sanctuary with the crucifix, a move whereby life (Easter) pushes death (Good Friday) aside. When, similarly, the priest comes down from the high altar to stand amid the worshipers, strict hierarchy becomes relative. When the altar, for that matter, becomes a table, the Mass becomes less a grim sacrifice than a festive meal. When the tabernacle, the golden receptacle that holds the consecrated bread, is moved to a side vestibule, Christ's "real presence" is shown to be as much in the people as in the sacrament.[21]

With the Church's commitment to the intellectual life enshrined in American Catholic universities, which have only improved over the years, post–Vatican II Catholics tend to be somewhat better educated in religious ideas than other Americans,[22] but like those Americans, their commitment to democratic values, individual responsibility, freedom of conscience, and respect for the convictions of others provides a firmer foundation for vital religious life than doctrinaire submissiveness ever did.

Because religion is centrally concerned with the God who is wholly Other, and is therefore necessarily cloaked in mystery, the imprecision of the poetic language of the Nicene Creed is its great advantage. That is why the Mass is language and symbol that serve well as the organizing center of a Catholic life that is more chosen than inherited, more a mode of relating to God and less a matter of ethnic identification. Where I worship the pews are crowded. People stand more than kneel, with eyes lifted rather than lowered. No longer bent chest-thumpers proclaiming our unworthiness, we raise our voices in new ways.

"Begotten, not made," the creed continues. "Being of one substance with the Father by whom all things were made." The words draw attention to themselves in their very archaism, as if to acknowledge that the Transcendent One is beyond contemporary expression. Everything we say of God—including "God"—is in some way untrue. Why? Because we *say* it. To put God into language is to take the fish out of water. Language by definition points beyond itself. Idolatry is the act of confusing language with what it aims to express. This idea is a liberation not only from what we believe but from where and when we believe it, and with whom. For idolatry is also the confusing of the here-and-now Church with the timeless One for whom the Church (and the ashram and the mosque and the temple) exists to point. Just as every word of God falls short, so does this—and every—people of God.

This awareness is the mark of a Catholic community that has been shaken loose of its antimodern triumphalism. The privilege of living happily in the age of science is that religious language has been forced to undergo a kind of purification, a calling-into-question, in a phrase of Einstein's, of "the dross of anthropomorphism."[23] The anthropomorphic image of the Creator as a kind of potter, creating the cosmos at a moment in time, quickening the creation, and setting it on its way, occasionally intervening in nature, has been debunked. But how much more wonderful is the creativity of a God who works through atoms, stars, supernovas, gravity, RNA, DNA, randomness, and all else that we mean by evolution.[24] Evolution—and here is the point—even unto language. In this age we have also become conscious, in ways that have eluded humans in the past, of the complexities—the advantages and limits—of language itself.

This experience of a new consciousness of language is the mark of a cultural mutation far larger than the world of Roman Catholic theology. That is why the kinds of basic changes that Catholics have lived through have occurred in all religion. Take one example: When language becomes relative, so does denominationalism. As the word indicates, we put certain names on our religious particularity. Once those names were regarded as divine; once, that is, denominations dominated Christian identity. But no longer, at least for many. When Catholics say they do not believe that God restricts grace and salvation to the Catholic Church—and after Vatican II they say so overwhelmingly—they are demonstrating a kind of post-denominationalism. If no one need be Catholic to be saved, neither do Catholics. Therefore, we are in and of the Church not because we must be, but because we want to be. I learned this for myself, as I said before, when I realized that embracing a different Christian denomination would not only be pointless, given what I believe; it would absolutize denominationalism. That I am Catholic is both all-important and not all that important. Such expansiveness is the precondition of the freedom required to welcome the whole Church's own evolution into unpredicted forms, with, for example, the vastly reshaped authority structure that must be coming.

To repeat Rabbi Heschel's words: God is greater than religion. Greater than *every* religion. Every denomination. Every time-bound ecclesiastical manifestation. And today many religious people see that. Certainly including many Catholics. God is greater than any language used of God.

Not that this way of thinking is new, exactly. The genius of the biblical faith, which, in its renewal, the Catholic Church is reclaiming, lies in its unexpected answer to the question What is God? The Bible's answer is: God is language. The Acts of the Apostles makes the claim explicitly, if symbolically: God is "tongues." God is words afire. God is the meaning in which strangers—speaking strangely—discover each other as friends. But the Pentecost story in Acts, reversing the Tower of Babel (babble) story in Genesis, is the least of it. For the entire Bible (Babel? Bible?) answers the question—Who is God? What is God?—with itself.

"In the beginning was the Word, and the Word was with God, and the Word was God." So begins the Gospel of John.

"The Word was God." John here echoes the Bible's own first words: "In the beginning God created . . ." And how? God created by *saying*. "God said, Let there be light, and there was light." God does not create by throwing lightning bolts. God does not create by thunder. God creates by language. More: God *is* language. Or so say the "people of the Book." I speak as a Christian, observing of our Jewish brothers and sisters that in Torah, the living word and the act of its study and interpretation— the Talmud—one does not so much learn of God but encounter God. God is the language of Torah.

Again observing as a Christian, what our Muslim brothers and sisters do in reciting the sacred words revealed to the Prophet, the Koran, is not so much pray to God, or praise God, but rather enter into God. God is the language of the Koran. The language itself. If this is true of Judaism and Islam, it is more so of Christianity, which finds in its sacred texts the very presence of Christ. "These writings," the sixteenth-century humanist and theologian Erasmus observed of the New Testament, "bring you the living image of his [Christ's] holy mind and the speaking, healing, dying, rising Christ himself, and thus they render him so fully present that you would see less if you gazed upon him with your very eyes."[25]

What does this reveal? Language differs from the set codes of animal communication. Birds and dogs have wondrous ways of signaling, but human language—more than the sending of a simple message: the whistle of danger, the yelp of pain, the purr of pleasure—is a cosmos of implications.[26] When we catch the connotation and the flash of images—*Light of Light*—we go ever deeper into understanding. And understanding points beyond itself to something else. What?

5. THE MEANING OF MEANING

All language is adaptive and contingent and dynamic. No word ever means the same exact thing to every person using it or hearing it. That is why all truth is elusive, and why we must respect the subtle differences between each person's grasp of truth. No word ever means the same thing every time it is used, its shade of meaning depending on who the speaker is, who the listener, what the context. Every word, that is, is forever new.

Understanding is therefore forever unfinished, forever in the process of coming to be. Creation, too, is forever unfinished. Forever happening, even as we write. Which is *why* we write. Every writer is a member of an imagined congregation, with notional readers and a language that aims for shared truths. What would be the point of writing if we didn't believe that there is a community in which we live in a language that has a common meaning? That is what is happening here, through these words on the page. Attending to it, we can sense that we, writer and reader, are meeting at a rare depth of meaning. Or, I should say, meanings. Elusive, yes. Complex, yes. But what simplicity. What intimacy. For we have moved—in our language, in my writing, in your thoughtful reading—from understanding to communion, which, finally, is the business of language.

Who is God? What is God?

I cited before the Gospel of John. John is the poet laureate of the Word.

But "Word," which translates the Greek *logos,* does not quite catch the significance of all of this. Here, in their full length, as given in the Revised Standard Version, the great opening lines of the Gospel of John:

> In the beginning was the Word, and the Word was with God, and the Word *was* God. He was in the beginning with God. All things were made through him, and without him was not anything that was made. In him was life, and life was the light of men. The light that shines in the darkness, and the darkness has not overcome it. The true light that enlightens every man was coming into the world. He was in the world, and the world was made through him, yet the world knew him not. He came to his own home, but his own received him not. But to those who received him, to those who

> believed in his name, he gave power to become children of God; who were born not of blood, nor of the will of the flesh, nor of the will of man, but of God. And the Word became flesh and dwelt among us, full of grace and truth; we have beheld his glory, glory as of the only Son from the Father. And from his fullness we have all received, grace upon grace. For the Law was given through Moses; grace and truth came through Jesus Christ. No one has ever seen God; the only Son, who is in the bosom of the Father, he has made him known.[27]

Words are the tools of the writer, but words are not the purpose of writing. So perhaps "word" is an inadequate expression here. The purpose of writing is meaning, and that idea comes closer to expressing John's bold declaration. This brings us to the human-defining question: What is the meaning of meaning? What if God is present to the world the way meaning is present in the word? Here is another translation of the same opening lines of John's Gospel—perhaps, in an age after Galileo, Darwin, and Einstein, a more accurate one:

> Fundamental to everything is Meaning. It is closely connected with what we call God, and indeed Meaning and God are virtually identical. To say that God was in the beginning is to say that Meaning was in the beginning. All things were made meaningful, and there was nothing made that was meaningless. Life is the drive toward Meaning, and life has emerged into self-conscious humanity as the (finite) bearer and recipient of Meaning. And Meaning shines out through the threat of absurdity, for absurdity has not overwhelmed it.
>
> Every human being has a share in Meaning, whose true light is coming into the world. Meaning was there in the world and embodying itself in the world, yet the world has not recognized the Meaning, and even humanity, the bearer of Meaning, has rejected it. But those who have received it and believed in it have been enabled to become the children of God. And this has happened not in the natural course of evolution or through human striving, but through a gracious act of God. For the Meaning has been incarnated in a human existent, in whom was grace and truth; and we have seen in him the glory toward which everything moves—the glory of God. From him, whom we can acknowledge in personal terms as the Son of the Father, we have received abundance of grace. Through Moses came the command of the Law, through Jesus

Christ grace and truth. God is a mystery, but the Son who has shared the Father's life has revealed him.[28]

Somehow, in the anguished exchange that occurred between me and Allen Tate in Sewanee, Tennessee, within a day or two of the funeral of his infant son, "meaning" took on this kind of significance. The uppercase significance: Meaning. In my encounter with Tate, a return to a basic—classic—proclamation of the Good News had its effect. Life is meaningful, even in the face of meaningless death. The love of God cannot be undone by the cruelty of God's self-appointed hierarchs. Trust in the One who is not there, precisely as Jesus did. Hand Michael over into the care of One who, in creating him, promised him, too. The promise holds. Such words, however banal they seem on this page, mattered enormously to Tate, and the authority with which I spoke them as a Catholic mattered, too. He listened to me, he asked questions, and he allowed the silence to grow pregnant at times—pregnant with Meaning. Meaning rescued Tate. Meaning rescued Michael. Finally, I realized that we were finished. When I said I should go, he nodded. He accepted the crib toys, both of them. At the door, his thanks—mostly unspoken—were more heartfelt than any I'd ever been offered.

I walked away from Allen Tate's door only partly conscious of what had just occurred. I had come here to declare myself a writer, but the poet had needed me to be a priest. He needed a word of meaning, which, for Tate, required a word, not out of silence, but out of a certain tradition.

The tradition had become an obstacle to its own treasure, yet that treasure remained alive, more so for me than ever before. Promulgating the reforms of Vatican II—preaching a God of love instead of a God of doom; ethics ahead of dogma—had never seemed more urgent, but what I preached was the oldest news of all. Around that double awareness—an old faith made new—I have composed myself ever since, an awareness that goes deeper into who I am than either of my impossible vocations had when they seemed to be in contradiction. None of this was clear when I left Tate's house, yet, given what he'd asked of me, and what I'd offered, it was the most natural thing in the world for me then to be ordained to the priesthood that year.

Clarity has come slowly across the years. I understand the meaning of the encounter with Tate more clearly than I did a decade and a half ago when I first wrote of it. I realize today exactly how that event was decisive for my faith. That monsignor who rejected Tate's infant son, inflicting an additional wound on the heartbroken parents, embodied a sort of spiritual malice that I had never confronted before. Yet now I understand that that monsignor's moralizing cruelty had its equivalent in attitudes of mine. I knew his kind, but his kind had been the first to draw me into the life of the Church. My first hope, in entering the seminary, was to be like him. But no more. My visceral certainty that the monsignor had nothing to do with God, and was in no way to be obeyed or even respected, blew open the hatch of my conscience. With that, I moved from being a submitter to authority to being a possessor of it. But now I see that I cannot condemn that monsignor without condemning something of myself.

The free play of the mind, which Orwell defined as essential for the writer, became mine. I would never yield unthinkingly to Church oppressiveness again, but—and this sets me apart from a legion of apostates and rebels—I came to such freedom of conscience in the heart of Catholicism, not against it. Within weeks of my visit to Tate, Cardinal Patrick O'Boyle of Washington would demand assent to *Humanae Vitae* of all priests and seminarians in his archdiocese, and I would openly refuse it, but that decision, too, was made inside the Church, in concert with the bulk of the Catholic people. Birth control was the wedge issue that would make us "anti-institutional believers." And we would go on to form, as Catholics, whole networks of "anti-institutional congregations."[29]

Within months, I would kneel at my ordination before Cardinal Terence Cooke of New York—as military vicar he was the bishop in charge of blessing the war in Vietnam—and I would knowingly dissemble when the ritual required me to promise to "obey and respect" him, since I disrespected him at that moment. But peace, I see now, is the very meter of the language Jesus came to speak, and if it is my mother tongue, I have it from the Church. In my lifetime, the Church has become a defender of peace, which is why I prize it most.

As a priest, and then as a writer, I would have no trouble discerning which commands of the hierarchy were worthy of obedience and respect. But that was possible because the deeper authority of this tradition—conceived historically and critically—had impressed itself on me. I could understand, for example, both that abortion is not the black-and-white moral slam dunk the hierarchy said it was and that abortion is nevertheless almost always wrong. Indeed, it is because I take the Church's rejection of abortion seriously that I so firmly reject its teaching on birth control, which leads to countless abortions.

Take another example: That Tennessee monsignor was in the back of my mind when I denounced Cardinal Bernard Law for his protection of a child-abusing priest a full decade before Law was forced to resign for having done so numerous times. Such failure, roundly to be condemned, is still the occasion, for me and many others, not of a Church-rejecting moralism but of a Church-purifying reckoning with the truth. "In their response to the sins of the hierarchy," the sociologist Alan Wolfe wrote, "American Catholics are unlikely to leave their faith behind . . . What they are seeking is a Church that is more responsive and open, a Church, in short, like the rest of America."[30] Americanists after all.

And so I left Allen Tate's house having glimpsed through the lens of his brokenness the brokenness of our shared community. That lens became a mirror in which I saw my own brokenness, what the seminary priest who disapproved of me called my "soft middle." The Gospel of John declares, "The truth will set you free." First it will break your heart, yes, but the truth is what counts. And so is the freedom. I was alive as never before to the meaning of my faith, which itself released me to be a writer. Released me, ironically, to be a lifelong man of the Catholic Church.

6. A SECOND NAÏVETÉ

Once a believer has learned to think historically, as we have been doing throughout this book, it is impossible any longer to think mythically. And now we can see how deeply into belief historical consciousness takes us. Defenders of the "Deposit of Faith" insist that no ideas or beliefs have been added to the bank account of orthodox doctrine since the time of the Apostles, but that goes out the window when one learns, for example, that none of the actual Apostles thought Jesus was divine. The New Testament is "inspired," but what does that mean for appeals to apostolic authority when one learns, as we did earlier, that it was not even identified as such until three hundred years after Jesus? Once we remember that our symbols are invented, we stop bowing before them. Once we understand ourselves as belonging to a religious tradition, we can no longer belong to it as we did when we simply took the tradition for granted. Once our internal geography recognizes that, however much we are a center, we are not the only one, we have no choice but to affirm the positions of others not as "marginal to our centers, but as centers of their own."[31]

Faced with such recognitions, we can retreat into fundamentalism, into the indifference of stark relativism, or into aggressive rejectionism. Or we can deliberately embrace what Paul Ricoeur calls a "post-critical naïveté." Innocence is no virtue unless, after failure and disillusionment, it is chosen. Ricoeur also calls this state of mind a "second naïveté,"[32] which implies a movement through criticism to a renewed appetite for the sacred tradition out of which we come, while implying that we are alive to its meaning in a radically different way—alive to its limits, and its corruptions as well. Ironically, there can be an imprisoning literalism to critical thought, as much as to fundamentalism, and that is what Ricoeur rejects. To be fully aware of the flaws of one's tradition is to know the flaws of one's own thinking. What the genius knows is that no one is a genius. Important as the objective explanation of critical thinking is, it is not the only authentic way of knowing. This essential intellectual (and moral) humility involves moving beyond a disenchantment with sacred texts or symbols—the disenchantment that comes with knowing they *are* symbols—to a renewed embrace of the sacred meaning that the texts and symbols intend to express.[33]

In speaking of classical religious symbols like the Trinity or the Incarnation, the Real Presence in the Eucharist or even the divinity of Jesus, we can acknowledge that these symbols were invented over time (none of them are affirmed in the Gospels of Matthew, Mark, and Luke, and John's Gospel knows nothing of the Trinity or of, say, the doctrine of transubstantiation) and accept them anew precisely for their meaning. The Trinity affirms, within monotheism, that community is fundamental to being. The Incarnation, locating the divine in the human, posits the goodness of fleshly existence. And so on. As Ricoeur helps us understand, meaning itself is created; its creation is the noble task of human intelligence.

That does not mean that religious faith is mere projection, as if God were nothing but a figment of the human imagination. Indeed, the essence of faith is to see in the human capacity for such invention a sign of the luring that God does. Yes, God is a figment, but a figment that points to something real. The human intuition that evolved from a first primitive imprinting of consciousness to speak of God in these ways is itself—this is the affirmation of faith—a response to God. There is no proving such conviction, but there is no disproving it either. Blaise Pascal, one of the fathers of modern science, wrote in his *Pensées*, "When I think about the shortness of my life melted into the eternity that came before me and into the eternity that will come after . . . I'm frightened and astonished to awaken in this place rather than that, and I see no reason why I should be here and not there, now and not then." And this sensibility prompted in Pascal the question "Who put me here?" He answered it by saying "God," but others, judging from available evidence, and from a like sense of the profound insignificance—on a cosmic scale—of each human life, may well answer by saying "Who knows?"[34]

The distinguished biologist Edward O. Wilson sums up the scientific-secular worldview: "Life was self-assembled by random mutation and natural selection of the codifying molecules."[35] In rejecting the deist God who is assumed to have done the assembling, Wilson skims over that half word "self." The wonder to which the religious sense responds springs from the experience implied in selfhood, which is nothing but awareness. And what awareness points to is far more subtle than the easily rejected "God in heaven"—watchmaker, potter, ruler—that has dominated both secular and religious discourse about God since the Enlightenment. "Man is but a reed," Pascal observed, "the most feeble thing in nature. But he is a thinking reed."

In an obscure corner of the vast cosmos, for the briefest period in the vast stretch of time, all that exists became aware of itself when humans became self-conscious, and that awareness, I would argue, is what we mean by worship.[36] The religious person sees the religious affirmation as a fulfillment of a profoundly human impulse, without which the human impulse is incomplete. Faith, as St. Anselm put it, seeks understanding, yes. Hence the real necessity of critical thought. But understanding also seeks faith. Critical thought is not everything.

"God does not merely create something other than himself. He also gives himself to this other." Here is a summary of the argument I am making, offered by the greatest Catholic theologian of the twentieth century, Karl Rahner: "The world receives God, the Infinite and the ineffable mystery, to such an extent that he himself becomes its innermost life."[37] Human beings are the creatures who—inventing symbols, imagining, and, yes, projecting—instinctively respond to that innermost life. "This mystery," Rahner writes, "is the inexplicit and unexpressed horizon which always encircles and upholds the small area of our everyday experience . . . We call this God . . . However hard and unsatisfactory it may be to interpret the deepest and most fundamental experience at the very bottom of our being, man does experience in his innermost history that this silent, infinitely distant holy mystery continually recalls him to the limits of his finitude and lays bare his guilt yet *bids him approach;* the mystery enfolds him in an ultimate and radical love which commends itself to him as salvation and as the real meaning of his existence."[38]

Meaning is the point, and the capacity to create meaning is a gift. The gift implies the giver. Meaning, to the believer, is the sacrament of God's presence to creation. It makes a difference to know who you are, and who you are is the beloved of God. The sign of that status is your capacity for meaning. But meaning is always and by definition elusive. While it is not necessary to understand meaning in religious terms, as the work of science shows, meaning is inevitably a sign of transcendence, however defined.[39] What the philosopher Gabriel Marcel calls "transcendental desire" is built into the human condition, though transcendence is elusiveness itself. Therefore we believers no longer see the sacred tradition in which (through a second naïveté) we find our meaning as the only sacred tradition. Instead we see it as one of many, each of which is to be respected on its own terms. The other traditions include the various religions—and "the religion of no-religion,"[40] certainly including science. And these other modes of understanding are not necessarily more limited than our own.

This shift from exclusiveness to pluralism, from triumphalism to modesty, is also a shift from a faith of certitude to a faith that includes ignorance and doubt. We cannot know God not because we are ignorant or finite, but because the word "God" applies to one who is beyond categories of knowledge (therefore beyond the deist God of the Enlightenment) and beyond categories of imagining (therefore beyond Michelangelo's God on the ceiling). Beyond the capacity of these very words to do more than imply. Therefore the God we worship is always the God beyond "God."

"The God who is with us," as Dietrich Bonhoeffer wrote from a Nazi prison, "is the God who forsakes us. The God who lets us live in the world without the working hypothesis of God is the God before whom we stand continually. Before God and with God, we live without God."[41] Because this incomprehensibility is built into the faith as its core, believers respond to the skepticism of modernity with a skepticism of their own—especially about claims to ultimate truth that often come cloaked in the language of classical science. Contemporary physicists aim, for example, at a grand unified theory, a final theory that will explain everything, banishing mystery at last.[42] But a religious person, attuned to the essentially mysterious nature of existence (embodied in the mysterious nature of language), believes *a priori* that no such theory is possible. Science, too, can be at the mercy of mythical thinking, even when (or perhaps especially when) debunking myth. Mystery is the essence of religion, but science has all too often attempted to dismiss mystery as, at best, nothing but the frontier of further discovery, and at worst, as primitive superstition. But in this science manifests its own superstition.

To observe the limits of the scientific view, however, is in no way to accept the widely touted dichotomy between science and religion. The believer can firmly accept all that science lays bare, and can celebrate as fully as any physicist the importance of "testable learning." The assertions of faith can and must be tested, too (for example, testing them against their consequences for violence or bigotry; testing, as we have throughout this book, theology against ethics). That the religious and scientific views differ does not mean they are necessarily contradictory. My religiously informed humanism is based on science, on knowledge of the creation that points—points me—to a Creator.[43] I mean no disrespect to my nonbelieving colleagues when I say that science, too, points beyond itself. Science, too, is worship.

7. THE CATHOLIC IMAGINATION

Catholics are those who have developed a particular approach to this radically unknowable God, finding the Creator's "traces," to use an image that originates with St. Augustine, in creation itself. Catholics are well known for organizing their religious practice around sacraments, which are defined as "outward and visible signs of an inward and invisible grace." As we have seen, this was a point of contention during the Reformation, when some Protestants rejected most sacraments and diluted the transcendental character of the two (Baptism and Eucharist) that they retained. The Protestant revolution was addressed, in large part, to this defining characteristic of Catholicism—the sacramental imagination, which had been reflected in the Church's celebration of the visual arts for centuries. Indeed, the Roman Catholic culture was like the pagan culture of the Roman Empire in its preference for the visual (statuary, buildings, paintings, elaborate rituals) over texts as the main medium of encountering divinity. The Protestant reformers would reverse this.

Perhaps because they were tied to the abuses of Renaissance popes, whose lavish artworks spawned the raising of money through the hated—blasphemous—sale of indulgences, such visual expression was jettisoned by most reformers,[44] and with it the expressly religious idea of sacramentalism. Interestingly, the Protestant traditions realized a whole new *audible* genius in celebration of the faith. The scholar John W. O'Malley observes that "Johann Sebastian Bach is almost a second founder of the Lutheran tradition."[45] It is not only that there are seven sacraments, or that Jesus himself is taken to be the sacrament of God's presence, which is what we mean, after all, by the Incarnation. It is that, in the Catholic imagination, the very stuff of life, in its visible, touchable, smellable ordinariness, is the mode of God's presence: water (Baptism), bread and wine (the Mass), oil (Anointing of the Sick), sexual intercourse (Matrimony), words (Absolution in Confession), touch (Imposition of Hands in Confirmation and Ordination). "Smells and bells," in the argot.

One sees in every Catholic church how the Catholic idea remains centrally tied to the imagination (and one also sees that this Catholic sensibility was retained or reclaimed in some Protestant traditions, especially in the Church of England and related Episcopal churches). In the unfolding of reality through time, also known as the evolution of the universe, the Creator has been communicating in creation and, with the advent of human consciousness, *to* creation. Creation, in other words, is God's self-expression. The created world points beyond itself to the Creator, even if only part of that world (humanity) is capable of knowing it. The rational and affective faculties of human beings are joined, or "reconciled," in Coleridge's word, in the imagination. Humans grasp the significance of what surrounds them, and what is in them, through images and stories, which appeal to intelligence and emotion both. This is what Genesis hints at when its author has God defining human beings, alone of all creatures, as made in God's image.[46] Creation itself is God's great self-communication.

The Catholic Church is organized around this idea. Its most magnificent manifestation occurred, not incidentally, during the time of great criticism of Church failures, the Reformation. It is commonly said that the Roman Catholicism of that period did not have theologians of the stature of Martin Luther and John Calvin, but perhaps the greatest theological expression of the age was rendered not doctrinally but visually. I am referring to Michelangelo's work in the Sistine Chapel. His painting of *The Creation* on that sanctuary's ceiling may send the religious imagination down the dead end of a literal anthropomorphism—God as superman, with that radiating fingertip. Still, the frescoes are a joyous celebration of what Genesis affirmed in having the Creator deem creation as "good, very good."[47]

But *The Creation* frescoes by themselves are not what make the Sistine Chapel immortal as art and as theology. It is *The Last Judgment* that does that, the mural that covers the mammoth wall behind the high altar, a completion of the uncritically joyous rendition on the ceiling. At its center is the figure of a stern Jesus who, in his Second Coming, is rebuking not humanity in the abstract, and not, as one would expect, the enemies of Rome, but Rome itself. There are angels and saints in the picture. Mary, to her son's right, wears an expression of horror at what she is beholding. Below her, the damned are being dragged into hell by demons, one of whom is recognizably Cardinal Biagio, the papal master of ceremonies. The judging Christ makes eye contact with no one, suggesting that Borgia popes, Medici cardinals, warrior bishops, and hedonist priests are alike in being consigned to hell, and their corruptions—the money, the lust, the abusive power, the worship of self instead of God—are all vividly implied.

Michelangelo created this fresco between 1534 and 1541, long after painting the far more optimistic *Creation*. The point is, given the state of the Church during those years, there was no reason for optimism, and a beaten Michelangelo saw that. As he worked on the painting, Pope Paul III excommunicated Henry VIII of England, moving the Reformation dispute away from theology (grace versus works) to papal power, pure and simple. The defense of the prerogatives of the papacy would from now on be the single defining note of Roman Catholic faith, a kind of papalolatry, which it remains. When Pope Paul III, who commissioned *The Last Judgment*, first saw the painting, he fell to his knees and exclaimed, "Lord, charge me not with my sins when Thou shalt come on the Day of Judgment."

Copernicus, who died in 1543, was just then publishing *On the Revolutions of Heavenly Bodies,* which defined a new cosmology, a definitive rejection of the cosmology of the Sistine Chapel's ceiling. Copernicus's ingenious act of scientific imagination, as we saw, represented the birth of modernity, and though it came from the heart of the Church (recall that Copernicus was dean of the Kraków Cathedral), the Church was preparing to reject this new vision of the universe —even as Michelangelo painted. The consequences of this rejection are still being felt, as the Church today continues to defend a theology (heaven above, hell below; the earth, and therefore humanity, as the center of all that exists; a God who, in response to prayers, abrogates the laws of nature; and so on) that assumes a cosmos that does not exist. The cosmos of Copernicus, by contrast, is an infinite stretch of galaxies in which the earth is the merest speck, and humanity is but a passing phenomenon of no significance to the vast and indifferent universe.

The paint on *The Last Judgment* was barely dry when the Council of Trent convened in 1545. This gathering of bishops, in a long-overdue response to the crisis engendered by Luther, countered his impassioned plea for renewal with the cold logic of Aristotelian syllogism.[48] The ambiguity of paradoxical knowledge, which is essential to a faith rooted in the poetic expression of the Bible, not to mention in the unknowability of God, was jettisoned in favor of a polemical precision of doctrine—not Thomism but scholasticism—that would stunt Catholic theology and life. And most momentously, it was during the Council of Trent that the Jew-hating grand inquisitor Gian Pietro Caraffa became Pope Paul IV, and immediately established the Roman ghetto. Popes would enforce that prison for Jews until nearly the twentieth century, and from it Jews would be rounded up by the Nazis in 1943, beneath the windows of a silent pope. Caraffa, when he first saw *The Last Judgment,* demanded that the entire fresco be removed, but the conscience-stricken Paul III overruled him. By the time Caraffa became pope, the painting's genius was accepted and he could not remove it, but he commanded that the genitals of naked figures be covered, which led to the creation of a new Vatican profession, "the underpants painters."

It is as if Michelangelo foresaw all this in producing the judging Christ—judging the Church, which is the point. Against any notion that the Church was exempt from the human condition, the reformers had denounced its sinfulness—and not only the reformers. The religious upheavals of the day, together with this achievement of the religious imagination, exposed the ways that the Church was, in a formulation Luther applied to the individual believer, *simul justus et peccator*—both justified and sinful. The juxtaposition of *The Creation* and *The Last Judgment* in the Sistine Chapel makes an equivalent statement. But the Council of Trent, in its traumatized defensiveness, launched the Church on its sorry detour, with its *Extra Ecclesiam nulla salus*, its blind rejection of any criticism of Catholicism—both of which would culminate in nineteenth-century declarations of papal infallibility, under Pope Pius IX, and the Church as a "perfect society," under Pope Leo XIII.

8. FAR SURPASSING HUMAN HOPES

This was the church into which I was born, and with which this book began. It can seem that we are back to it. Pope Benedict XVI is seeking to resuscitate the culture of the Council of Trent, restoring its liturgy—the pre–Vatican II Latin Mass, including a pointed hint of its anti-Judaism—and its imperialist exclusivism: pope-centered Roman Catholicism as the only authentic path to God. Perhaps more disturbing, as we saw, is the way that Pope Benedict exacerbates political and religious conflict by emphasizing the Christian character of Europe—this at a time when antisemitism and hatred of Islam are on the rise and when Bible-sponsored violence is blessed by fundamentalists.

Never has the world needed a rational, energized, and fully reformed Catholic Church more, yet never has the Catholic Church's need for reform been more manifest. From the sexual neurosis that abets a multitude of preventable deaths from AIDS, to the ongoing scandal of a hierarchy that refuses to attend to the deeper sources of abuse of children by Catholic priests, to the antifemale bigotry enshrined in the all-male priesthood, the Catholic Church is doing serious damage. The pope sits atop a clerical structure that is set against change in any of this. But unlike the time of Michelangelo, the whims and initiatives of the men in charge no longer determine whether change will come.

The Catholic people have already changed, and this book is that story. Catholics came to understand that they themselves—not their priests, bishops, and pope—are the Church. We understand full well that our Church is *simul justus et peccator*, both saved and sinner, and that it is therefore *semper reformanda*, always in need of reform. Reform is coming not from the collapsing clerical establishment but from the people. We maintain our loyalty to the Church because we cannot live without it. The Church gives us a language with which to speak of God, a Meaning that is God. The Church feeds us in the Eucharist, keeps the story of Jesus alive in the preaching of the Word, marks our journey through life with the sacraments, and underwrites our participation in the community that transcends space and time.

We love the Church for its global reach. Those of us who live in the affluent Northern Hemisphere especially value this singular mode of solidarity with those of the impoverished South, so many of whom believe what we believe, though they may do so differently. In the Church we hear the authentic voice of the poor, and we have a way to respond. But the emphasis on "Catholic" is no longer the whole story. To be Catholic today is to be in the act of leaving behind the narrow denominationalism of the now finished Reformation. We affirm our communion with all the baptized, and look forward to increasing the ecumenical fellowship of the larger Church. The hope for Christian unity is itself the unity.

The most striking thing about *The Last Judgment* is not the furious Christ or the condemned papal master of ceremonies. Rather, it is the way Michelangelo included himself in that drastic scene. The fresco contains a rare self-portrait of the artist, and what a portrait it is. In a corner of the painting, drawing no attention to itself, the close observer sees that the artist has put his own face on the otherwise shapeless, flayed flesh of a martyr, St. Bartholomew, who had been skinned alive. Michelangelo's message is clear: I, too, have betrayed the Lord; unlike all these others, I am unworthy of the human form. *Of everything I presume to accuse the Church in this painting, I first accuse myself.* But this signal of the artist's own humility is a minor note in the otherwise devastating vision. Michelangelo, the master of man's beauty, rendered himself as the totality of degradation, an impulse that displays his complete lack of self-righteousness.

We are back to the members of my first congregation thumping their chests, *Domine, non sum dignus.* But in coming full circle, we arrive at a different place, for Michelangelo's humility was not the source of timid obeisance, of unworthiness, but of a prophetic denunciation of all that he saw as wrong. It was not Christ whose judgment so unsparing, but the artist. With this masterpiece, Michelangelo was echoing the great declaration of Martin Luther, made at the Diet of Worms: "Here I stand, I cannot do otherwise, God help me." As Michelangelo knew, the diet condemned Luther, but that did not stop the artist.

Yes, to be a member of this community is to stand openly in need of forgiveness, which is why every Mass begins with the penitential prayer. But now it is clear that instead of isolating us under the unbearable burden of individual guilt, this community, responding to the Father's prodigal love, the antidote to judgment, invites us to put that burden down. That the Church is sinful is why, finally, each of us can feel at home in it. But more to the point in a Church that is still tempted to betray its founder, we, like Michelangelo, seize every opportunity to demand its purification, and its reform. In the end, the Church is the community of the forgiven, but that forgiveness is itself the condition of change. At last we can complete the *Domine, non sum dignus* prayer, all of us, together: *Sed tantum dic verbo et sanabitur anima mea.* Say but the word, and my soul will be healed.

Healed not merely for the sake of consolation, but to take responsibility for the vision that braced our youth, the humane and hopeful agenda laid out by Pope John XXIII, which still demands our loyalty. In the momentous speech with which he opened the Second Vatican Council, he denounced not only the naysayers and "underpants painters" of his own time, but, as it were, those who would come after him. Pope John showed us the move from judgment to hope: "In the daily exercise of our pastoral ministry, and much to our sorrow, we sometimes listen to those who, consumed with zeal, have scant judgment or balance. To such ones the modern world is nothing but betrayal and ruin. They claim that this age is far worse than previous ages . . . We feel bound to disagree with these prophets of doom who are forever forecasting calamity . . . *Today, rather, Providence is guiding us toward a new order of human relationships, which, thanks to human effort and yet far surpassing human hopes, will bring us to the realization of still higher and undreamed-of experiences.*"

Amen.

A TWENTIETH-CENTURY AMERICAN CATHOLIC CHRONOLOGY

1896 Pope Leo XIII publishes the encyclical *Satis Cognitum*, declaring the Roman Catholic Church to be a "perfect society."

1899 Leo XIII issues the apostolic letter *Testem Benevolentiae Nostrae*, condemning the heresy of "Americanism." The First Amendment of the U.S. Constitution is particularly indicted.

1907 Pope Pius X publishes the encyclical *Pascendi Dominici Gregis*, condemning Catholic biblical scholars and theologians labeled as "modernists."

1908 The Paulist Fathers open Newman Hall, at the University of California at Berkeley, spawning a movement of Newman Clubs for Catholic students at non-Catholic universities.

1928 Al Smith, the first Catholic candidate for the presidency, is defeated by Herbert Hoover, sealing a sense among American Catholics of being discriminated against.

1930 Pope Pius XI publishes the encyclical *Casti Connubii*, condemning "artificial contraception."

1936 The Spanish Civil War breaks out, leading to the murders by republicans of hundreds of Catholic bishops, priests, and nuns.

Thomas More, the opponent of Henry VIII of England, is canonized.

1940 The St. Benedict Center is established at Harvard by Catholic students, including Avery Dulles. Under Father Leonard Feeney, S.J., the center will be a bastion of conservative Catholicism.

1943 Pope Pius XII publishes the encyclical *Mystici Corporis*, defining the Catholic Church as the "Mystical Body of Christ," reinforcing the claim to perfection. But the encyclical also says non-Catholics can be attached to the Church "by some kind of unconscious desire and longing."

1944 Richard Cushing is named archbishop of Boston.

The pope publishes *Divino Afflante Spiritu*, encouraging Catholic scholars to take up modern methods of biblical criticism.

1948 The Trappist monk Thomas Merton publishes *The Seven Storey Mountain*. It becomes a bestseller, and over the next decade thousands of Catholic men enter seminaries and monasteries, carrying this and other books by Merton.

1949 "The Boston Letter" from the Vatican to Archbishop Cushing says that Church membership is necessary for salvation, but that membership can be a matter of "desire and longing . . . God also accepts implicit desire."

1953 Cushing orders Feeney to stop preaching "No salvation outside the Church." When Feeney disobeys, Cushing excommunicates him. The Vatican upholds the excommunication, although for disobedience, not heresy.

Cushing presides at the wedding of Jacqueline Lee Bouvier and John F. Kennedy in Newport, Rhode Island.

1954 The American theologian John Courtney Murray, S.J., is silenced by Rome for advancing ideas thought to be too "American," like religious liberty and separation of church and state. Murray obeys.

1955 The Catholic historian Monsignor John Tracy Ellis, in the article "American Catholics and the Intellectual Life," criticizes the mediocrity of American Catholic thinking. Catholic universities take note and begin to improve.

1958 Pope John XXIII is elected. He quickly names Richard Cushing to the College of Cardinals. He announces plans for the Second Vatican Council.

The Jesuit poet Daniel Berrigan, S.J., wins the Lamont Prize for Poetry, announcing his arrival as a major literary figure.

1960 The Swiss theologian Hans Küng publishes *The Council, Reform and Reunion*, which will help shape the agenda of the Vatican Council.

John F. Kennedy affirms his free Catholic conscience before the Houston Ministerial Association in a speech cleared in advance with John Courtney Murray.

1961 Kennedy is sworn in as president. He declares "that here on earth God's work must truly be our own."

1962 The Second Vatican Council opens. Pope John XXIII decries his Catholic critics as "prophets of doom."

Within days of the council's opening, the Cuban Missile Crisis begins. The pope's appeal helps Soviet and American leaders to back down. Catholic bishops see the need for a relevant and updated Church.

1963 *The Deputy*, a play by Rolf Hochhuth, accuses Pope Pius XII of remaining silent in the face of the Holocaust. It becomes an international sensation.

Dr. John Rock, inventor of the birth control pill, publishes *The Time Has Come: A Catholic Doctor's Proposals to End the Battle over Birth Control.*

John XXIII appoints a commission of three priests and three laypeople to reconsider Church teaching on birth control.

John XXIII publishes the encyclical *Pacem in Terris,* a resounding criticism of war. Weeks later, he dies of stomach cancer.

John Kennedy gives his own resounding critique of war at American University. Months later, he is assassinated.

Betty Friedan publishes *The Feminine Mystique.* In *Pacem in Terris,* John XXIII had approved the women's movement as one of the "signs of the times."

1964 Pope Paul VI orders the bishops of the Vatican Council not to take up the birth control question. Bishops protest, with one warning of a new "Galileo affair."

Paul VI expands the Papal Commission on Birth Control to seventy-two members, almost all of whom are clergy and prelates.

The Vatican Council publishes *Lumen Gentium,* which effectively repudiates "No salvation outside the Church."

1965 A small group of Catholic activists, including Daniel and Philip Berrigan, meet with Thomas Merton at Gethsemani, in Kentucky—the beginning of the Catholic peace movement.

Merton publishes *Conjectures of a Guilty Bystander* and *Raids on the Unspeakable.*

Vatican II publishes *Dignitatis Humanae,* the declaration on religious liberty that affirms the primacy of conscience. Its principal author is the formerly silenced John Courtney Murray. The declaration effectively reverses the condemnation of "Americanism."

The Vatican Council publishes *Nostra Aetate,* a formal renunciation of the "Christ killer" charge against the Jewish people, and an affirmation of the ongoing validity of the Jewish religion.

Cardinal Cushing, declining to instruct Catholic legislators in how to vote on a bill repealing the Massachusetts ban on birth control, says, "I should not impose my position upon those of other faiths."

Pope Paul VI, addressing the United Nations, cries, "War no more! War never again!"

1967 Cardinal Francis Spellman of New York supports the war in Vietnam, saying, "My country right or wrong."

The *National Catholic Reporter,* a lay-run U.S. Catholic weekly, reveals that all but six of the members of the Papal Commission on Birth Control, including dozens of priests and prelates, voted to change the Church's teaching on birth control.

Paul VI publishes the encyclical *Populorum Progressio,* a blast at capitalism, which puts the Church firmly on the side of "the hungry peoples of the world."

1968 Martin Luther King, Jr., is murdered.

Daniel and Philip Berrigan and seven others burn draft files at Catonsville, Maryland.

Robert F. Kennedy is murdered.

Paul VI publishes the encyclical *Humanae Vitae,* reiterating the Church's condemnation of birth control. Hundreds of Catholic theologians and priests openly reject the teaching.

Boston College theologian Mary Daly publishes *The Church and the Second Sex.*

The Reverend William Sloane Coffin, Jr., and four others stand trial in Boston for supporting draft resistance to the Vietnam War.

Thomas Merton dies in Bangkok, Thailand, electrocuted by a faulty wire.

1970 Hans Küng publishes *Infallible? An Inquiry,* on the centenary of the First Vatican Council's declaration that the pope is infallible in matters of faith and morals.

1978 The Pole Karol Wojtyla is elected as Pope John Paul II, the first non-Italian pope since the sixteenth century.

1979 John Paul II says Mass for a million Poles in a field outside Kraków. An unknown electrician, Lech Walesa, attends. John Paul preaches "Be not afraid!" Months later, Walesa starts Solidarity, the beginning of the democracy movement that will bring down Soviet communism.

Encouraged to do so by Cardinal Joseph Ratzinger, prefect of the Congregation for the Doctrine of the Faith, John Paul II withdraws Hans Küng's license to teach as a Roman Catholic theologian. Küng had hired Ratzinger as a young theologian.

1983 The American Catholic bishops publish "The Challenge of Peace: God's Promise and Our Response," raising questions about American attitudes toward war. The bishops support a nuclear freeze and criticize Ronald Reagan's war in Central America.

1989 The Berlin Wall is dismantled nonviolently. John Paul II is widely credited as key to the resolution of the nuclear standoff between Washington and Moscow.

1991 John Paul II condemns the first Gulf War. The Vatican consistently opposes American warmaking.

1992 Father James Porter, a Catholic priest of Fall River, Massachusetts, is convicted of sexually abusing a child. Boston's Cardinal Bernard Law condemns the *Boston Globe* for its reporting about the Porter case.

1993 The Archdiocese of Boston pays $40,000 to a man who claims to have been raped as a child in 1972 by Father Paul Shanley, who remains in good standing as a priest.

1996 Cardinal Law writes a letter to Shanley, who is retiring. Law praises him: "the lives and hearts of many people have been touched by your sharing of the Lord's Spirit."

2000 John Paul II observes the new millennium by repenting of Catholic sins, especially antisemitism and violence "in defense of the truth."

2001 The *Boston Globe* begins reporting on the sexual abuse of minors by priests.

A new Catholic lay movement is born in response to the clergy abuse scandal, led by a Boston group calling itself Voice of the Faithful.

Cardinal Ratzinger sends a secret letter to the world's bishops, ordering them to report crimes "perpetrated with a minor by a cleric" to the Vatican, not to civil authorities.

Islamic militants crash hijacked airliners into the World Trade Center and the Pentagon, sparking widespread concern about connections between religious intolerance and violence.

2002 Cardinal Law is forced to resign as archbishop of Boston for having protected abusers instead of the abused.

2004 John Paul II names Cardinal Law the archpriest of St. Mary Major Basilica in Rome.

2005 Paul Shanley is sentenced to prison for raping a child, one of dozens of his victims.

Cardinal Ratzinger is elected as Pope Benedict XVI. Traveling to his native Germany, he blames Nazi antisemitism on "neo-paganism," with no mention of Christian anti-Judaism.

2006 Marking the fifth anniversary of 9/11, Benedict XVI cites a medieval source to say Islam brings things "only evil and inhuman."

2007 Benedict XVI restores the Latin rite that Vatican II had abandoned. The Good Friday liturgy includes a prayer for the conversion of the Jews.

2008 Benedict XVI travels to the United States, displaying his sincere goodwill. He affirms the Bush administration with an unprecedented visit to the White House.

ACKNOWLEDGMENTS

I wrote this book at Suffolk University, Boston, where I am a scholar-in-residence. I drew essential support from Dean Kenneth Greenberg and my faculty colleague Fred Marchant. I gratefully acknowledge them, the librarians of the Mildred F. Sawyer Library and its director, Bob Dugan, and the whole Suffolk community.

My life as a Catholic has been shaped by my early membership in, and nearly half century association with, the Paulist Fathers. I hope that readers of this book will take it as a tribute to that extraordinary Catholic order. I acknowledge especially Fathers Thomas Stransky, Michael McGarry, Paul Lannan, and the priests of the Paulist Center in Boston.

Parts of this book were the basis of columns I wrote for the *Boston Globe.* I gratefully acknowledge my editors there: Renée Loth, Marjorie Pritchard, Don Macgillis, and Dante Ramos. I wrote about Hans Küng in an article for *The New Yorker,* where my editor was Jeffrey Frank. An early version of the section on Mary Magdalen appeared in *Smithsonian,* where my fine editor was Thomas Frail. And some material on Cardinal Cushing appeared in a privately published *Festschrift* in honor of Father Stanislaus Musial, S.J., edited by John Pawlikowski and Doris Donnelly. Some of these reflections informed the writing I did for the American Academy of Arts and Sciences; I acknowledge its director, Leslie Berlowitz, and my editor, Martin Malin. I drew from this work in progress for lectures at Boston College; Loyola University of Chicago; Brandeis University; the Catholic community at Harvard University; Merrimack College; the Thomas Merton

Foundation in Louisville, Kentucky; Voice of the Faithful; Call to Action; All Saints Episcopal Church in Pasadena, California; and Trinity Church on Wall Street in New York. Thanks to each of these communities for receiving my work generously.

The manuscript of this book was read in its entirety by Askold Melnyczuk, William Gibson, Mark U. Edwards, Kenneth Greenberg, Fred Marchant, Bernard Avishai, Padraic O'Hare, Larry Kessler, and Alexandra Marshall. Each one offered astute responses and some corrections. I cannot properly express my thanks except to say this book is better because of them. At Suffolk, I had the invaluable help of Charles Ryan and Bora Hajnaj, and I convey my gratitude to them as well. The Boston Public Library, as so often in the past, was my invaluable resource, and I thank its magnificent staff. At Houghton Mifflin Harcourt, I had the expert editorial support of Deanne Urmy and Larry Cooper. Special thanks to them, and to all at HMH who have brought this book to the public.

I have been an associate of the Humanities Center at Harvard University, where my large debt is to Homi Bhabha and Mary Halpenny-Killip. My privilege has been to serve on the Dean's Council of the Harvard Divinity School during the writing of this book. I gratefully acknowledge Dean William Graham, Professors Mark U. Edwards, Karen King, Kevin Madigan, Diana Eck, Peter Gomes, and other members of the divinity school faculty for steady encouragement. My thanks go in particular to Harvey Cox, whose work has transformed my thinking for forty years, and still does. My most valued conversation partner, and dear friend, was the former Harvard Divinity School dean Krister Stendahl, who died before I was able to show him what he had helped me do. I remember him with love, and humbly commend this work to Brita Stendahl.

My friends Jim and Pam Morton have been a steady support. Ed Bacon is an inspiration. Padraic O'Hare is my personal prophet. Jack Smith and Mac Gatch are the best preachers I hear. Larry Kessler teaches me what being Catholic means for social justice. This is the sixteenth book that I have written with the unstinting support of my agent and friend, Donald Cutler. The work itself is my thanks to him. And this book, like all of my work, comes of the life I share with my daughter Elizabeth, my son Patrick, and my wife, the novelist Alexandra Marshall. To them this final word of thanks and love.

NOTES

Introduction: Practicing Catholic

1. Cullen Murphy, *Are We Rome? The Fall of an Empire and the Fate of America* (Boston: Houghton Mifflin, 2007), 190.
2. The broader national culture is not only implicitly pietistic but also implicitly (and sometimes explicitly) Reformed, in H. Richard Niebuhr's sense of "Christ transforming culture." This gives rise to the particularly American impulse to realize the Kingdom of God here on earth, an imperial impulse we will see more of later. I owe this insight to Mark U. Edwards.
3. *Time,* August 21, 1964.
4. David Gibson, *The Rule of Benedict: Pope Benedict XVI and His Battle with the Modern World* (San Francisco: HarperSanFrancisco, 2006), 310.
5. A Notre Dame study reported in 1990 that about sixty percent of American Catholics were white and about thirty percent were Hispanic; Asian and African-American Catholics amounted to about five percent each. Notre Dame Study of Catholic Parish Life, University of Notre Dame, Report #15, http://www.nd.edu/~icl/study_reports/report15.pdf. In 2008, the Pew Forum on Religious and Public Life reported that the percentage of Hispanic Catholics has steadily increased since then. "U.S. Religious Landscape Survey," http://religions.pewforum.org. *New York Times,* February 26, 2008.
6. The percentage of self-identified Christians in the United States surpasses the percentage of Jews in Israel. In 2007, the U.S. Congress passed a bill that "expresses support for Christians in the United States" and affirms that "Christmas is celebrated in recognition of God's redemption, mercy, and grace." Sally Quinn, "Congress's Bullying Pulpit," *Washington Post,* December 23, 2007.
7. See, for example, Mary Jo Weaver and R. Scott Appleby, eds., *Being Right: Conservative Catholics in America* (Bloomington: Indiana University Press, 1995).
8. Republican presidents appointed eleven of the most recent thirteen justices. Richard W. Garnett, "Law, Lawyers, the Court, and Catholicism," *American*

Catholic Studies Newsletter 33, no. 2, Fall 2006. The Roman Catholic justices, in addition to Alito, are Clarence Thomas, Antonin Scalia, Anthony Kennedy, and Chief Justice John Roberts. Including these five, there have been only eleven Catholic justices in the court's history.

9. For a discussion of the alliance of Protestant fundamentalists and Catholic neoconservatives, see Garry Wills, *Bush's Fringe Government* (New York: New York Review of Books, 2006).

10. I find the word in Robin Marantz Henig, "Darwin's God," *New York Times Magazine*, March 4, 2007, 39.

11. Richard Dawkins is an evolutionary biologist at Oxford University and the author of *The God Delusion* (Boston: Houghton Mifflin, 2006). Sam Harris is a student of neuroscience and the author of *The End of Faith* (New York: W. W. Norton, 2004). Christopher Hitchens is a journalist and literary critic and the author of *God Is Not Great: How Religion Poisons Everything* (New York: Twelve/Warner Books, 2007). Hitchens asserts that religion is "violent, irrational, intolerant, allied to racism, tribalism, and bigotry, invested in ignorance and hostile to free inquiry, contemptuous of women and coercive toward children." All true. For a rebuttal of these works, see Christopher Hedges, *I Don't Believe in Atheists* (New York: Free Press, 2008). A deeply instructive and comprehensive reflection of the themes raised in this debate, on the new condition of religious belief, is found in Charles Taylor's *A Secular Age* (Cambridge: Belknap Press of Harvard University Press, 2007).

12. A Catholic instance of such a reaction came two years into his papacy from Benedict XVI. It was then that he issued two unexpected decrees, restoring the atavistic Mass of the Council of Trent, the sixteenth-century gathering of bishops to oppose Luther and other Protestants, and resuscitating an outmoded Catholic exclusivism, the notion of a pope-centered Catholicism as the only authentic way to God. On July 7, 2007, Pope Benedict issued a decree known as a *Motu Proprio*, which in Latin means "of his own accord." Titled *Summorum Pontificum*, the decree restored the Latin Mass, according to rubrics published in 1962, but preserving in essence the rite established by the Council of Trent. Significantly, the restored ritual includes references to Jews as "blind" and "walking in darkness," and offers prayers for Jews to finally recognize Jesus as their Messiah. The ritual makes no requirement, as the Vatican II reformed liturgy does, that passages from Hebrew Scriptures be read at every Mass, a key element in building respect for Judaism. "I can't fight back the tears," an Italian bishop said upon hearing of the ruling. "It's a day of mourning, not just for me, but for the many people who worked for the Second Vatican Council. A reform for which many people worked, with great sacrifice and only inspired by the desire to renew the Church, has now been canceled." *National Catholic Reporter*, July 20, 2007, 24. The *Motu Proprio* followed by three days an official Vatican declaration titled "Responses to Some Questions Regarding Certain Aspects of the Doctrine of the Church." That statement said that Protestant churches are merely communities, not to be regarded as churches "in the proper sense." Orthodox churches, while closer to the truth, are nevertheless "wounded" by being separated from the pope. Only the

Roman Catholic Church is a true church. Indeed, the word "Church" fully applies only to Catholicism.

13. Peter Steinfels, "Modernity and Belief: Charles Taylor's *A Secular Age*," *Commonweal* 135, no. 9, May 9, 2008.
14. That Catholics have adopted this more liberal attitude shows up in polls. For example, a 2007 Catholic University poll found that eighty percent of students at Catholic universities in the United States reject the idea that the Catholic Church "contains a greater share of truth than other religions." Even among their parents and grandparents, the change is clear. Sixty-one percent of Catholics who came of age before the 1960s believe a person can be a good Catholic without accepting the teachings of the hierarchy. William V. D'Antonio et al., *American Catholics Today*, cited in *National Catholic Reporter*, March 9, 2007, 5.
15. In 2001, Cardinal Ratzinger, as head of the Congregation for the Doctrine of the Faith, sent a secret letter to all Catholic bishops, ordering them to refer all charges of sexual abuse by priests to the Vatican, not to secular authorities. This secrecy was enforced with a threat of excommunication. The letter became public only when Ratzinger was elected pope in 2005. We will return to this later in this book. Jamie Doward, "Pope 'Obstructed' Sex Abuse Inquiry," *Guardian*, April 24, 2005.
16. For documentation of the clergy sex-abuse scandal and the bishops' response to it, see Investigative Staff of the Boston Globe, *Betrayal: The Crisis in the Catholic Church* (New York: Little, Brown, 2002).
17. I owe this observation to Professor Padraic O'Hare of Merrimack College, North Andover, Massachusetts.

Chapter One: Born Catholic

1. Jurgen Moltmann, *The Way of Jesus Christ: Christology in Messianic Dimensions*, translated by Margaret Kohl (Minneapolis: Fortress Press, 1993), 12.
2. See James Kugel, *How to Read the Bible: A Guide to Scripture Then and Now* (New York: Free Press, 2007).
3. Augustine's famous works include *Confessions*, *City of God*, *The Trinity*, and numerous treatises on the Scriptures, the sacraments, and other Christian beliefs. But much of his writing has not been translated into English. He left behind more than five million words. See Garry Wills, *Saint Augustine* (New York: Viking, 1999).
4. Richard E. Leakey and Roger Lewin, *Origins* (New York: Dutton, 1977), 10. The physicist Stephen Hawking said, "We are just an advanced breed of monkey on a minor planet of a very average star. But we can understand the universe." Quoted by George Johnson in "The Theory That Ate the World," *New York Times Book Review*, August 24, 2008, 16.
5. In 1963, the Lutheran scholar Krister Stendahl suggested that the "introspective conscience of the West" began with Augustine's reading of St. Paul. The emphasis on sin, guilt, and dread of judgment that marked Luther's work be-

came typical of Western Christianity generally—the obsessive idea of the "self" that ultimately spawned modern individualism. "The Apostle Paul and the Introspective Conscience of the West," *Harvard Theological Review* 56, no. 3, July 1963, 199–215.

6. Original Sin for Augustine was not sex as such but selfishness (*curvatus in se*, turning in on oneself). The tendency to give in to sexual temptation was the main manifestation of that selfishness, but not the essence of it. I owe this point of clarity to Mark U. Edwards.
7. Genesis 3:10.
8. John 6:68.
9. I recounted a version of this sense-memory of the stockyards in my novel *Memorial Bridge* (Boston: Houghton Mifflin, 1991), 3–6.
10. Jon D. Levenson, *The Death and Resurrection of the Beloved Son: Transformation of Child Sacrifice in Judaism and Christianity* (New Haven: Yale University Press, 1993), 207.
11. Matthew 8:8. A centurion approaches Jesus, concerned that his servant is gravely ill. The text reads, "Sir, I am not worthy to have you under my roof; just say the word and my servant will be cured."
12. See Tom Hayden, *Irish Hunger* (Boulder, CO: Roberts Rinehart Publishers, 1997).
13. Mary Gordon makes this kind of insecurity vivid in her memoir *Circling My Mother* (New York: Pantheon, 2007).
14. I first gathered the biting significance of this question from the writer Andrew Greeley.
15. Kenneth C. Jones, *Index of Leading Catholic Indicators: The Church Since Vatican II* (St. Louis: Oriens Publishing Co., 2002).
16. Genesis 22:1–19.
17. Genesis 1:25, 31. In Genesis, God "sees" the goodness, but I take the text itself as God "saying."
18. Psalm 130:7.
19. Matthew 27:46. Mark 15:34.
20. Luke 24:21.
21. The week I was born saw the opening of Los Alamos, the start of U.S. strategic bombing against cities, and the total-war declaration by Franklin Roosevelt of unconditional surrender. See my book *House of War: the Pentagon and the Disastrous Rise of American Power* (Boston: Houghton Mifflin, 2006), 1–5.
22. Luke 23:46.
23. My point here is not to make an exclusive claim for Catholicism. Lutheranism, for example, makes much of the *deus absconditus*, the absent God. This shows up powerfully in the writing, say, of Dietrich Bonhoeffer: "Before God and with God, we live without God." *Letters and Papers from Prison*, edited by Eberhard Bethge (New York: Macmillan, 1971), 360.
24. Roman missal, "Preface of Christian Death."
25. The liturgical Protestant churches, defined as Lutheran and Anglican, tended to keep the corpus on the cross.

26. Otto Zoeckler, *The Cross of Christ: Studies in the History of Religion and the Inner Life of the Church,* translated by Rev. Maurice J. Evans (London: Hodder and Stoughton, 1877), x. See also, Jaroslav Pelican, *The Christian Tradition,* vol. 3 (Chicago: University of Chicago Press, 1971–89), 132.
27. Pelikan, *Christian Tradition,* vol. 3, 118.
28. I Corinthians 15:55.
29. Philippians 2:5–11. This passage is called the Kenosis Hymn, from the Greek word Paul uses to say, in verse 7, that God "emptied Himself" to become human.

Chapter Two: The God of My Youth

1. Leo XIII called the Catholic Church a "perfect society" in his 1885 encyclical *Immortale Dei,* in his 1890 encyclical *Sapientiae Christianae,* and again in his 1896 encyclical *Satis Cognitum* (On the Unity of the Church). The phrase originates with St. Robert Bellarmine, S.J. (1542–1621).
2. The culture of midcentury Catholicism is evoked in such books as Mary McCarthy, *Memories of a Catholic Girlhood;* Eamon Duffy, *Faith of Our Fathers;* Eugene Kennedy, *Tomorrow's Catholics, Yesterday's Church;* Sebastian Moore, *God Is a New Language;* and Brian Moore, *Catholics.*
3. Al Smith "received the votes of millions of Protestants and carried six states in the southern Bible Belt." Rodney Stark, *One True God: Historical Consequences of Monotheism* (Princeton, NJ: Princeton University Press, 2001), 239.
4. The original hangs in the Frick Collection in New York, where, to this day, I am jolted by seeing it titled as *Sir Thomas More* instead of as *St. Thomas More.* Holbein painted More in 1527, when Henry VIII and he were still solidly aligned with the pope.
5. Robert Bolt's play and film *A Man for All Seasons* brought Thomas More back into fashion in the 1960s, when a mass audience, not just Catholics, could appreciate a story of a man of principle risking everything to resist a tyrant.
6. For an account of More's life written by a non-Catholic, see Richard Marius, *Thomas More: A Biography* (New York: Knopf, 1984).
7. Evelyn Waugh, *Edmund Campion* (London: Cassell, 1947), 47.
8. The "Bull Against Elizabeth" reads, in part, "Therefore, resting upon the authority of Him whose pleasure it was to place us (though unequal to such a burden) upon this supreme justice-seat, we do out of the fullness of our apostolic power declare the foresaid Elizabeth to be a heretic and favourer of heretics, and her adherents in the matters aforesaid to have incurred the sentence of excommunication and to be cut off from the unity of the body of Christ. And moreover (we declare) her to be deprived of her pretended title to the aforesaid crown and of all lordship, dignity and privilege whatsoever. And also (declare) the nobles, subjects and people of the said realm and all others who have in any way sworn oaths to her, to be forever absolved from such an oath and from any duty arising from lordship, fealty and obedience; and we do, by authority of these presents, so absolve them and so deprive the same Elizabeth

of her pretended title to the crown and all other the abovesaid matters. We charge and command all and singular the nobles, subjects, peoples and others afore said that they do not dare obey her orders, mandates and laws. Those who shall act to the contrary we include in the like sentence of excommunication."

9. In 2007, Queen Elizabeth's oldest grandson, Peter Phillips, announced his intention to marry a Roman Catholic, Autumn Kelly. According to the still valid 1701 Act of Settlement, either Phillips had to renounce his place in the line of succession to the throne (he was tenth) or Kelly had to renounce her Catholicism. As of 2008, they have not married, and neither renunciation has been made.
10. Blair announced, in December 2007, about six months after leaving office, that he had been received into the Catholic Church.
11. "Catholic-baiting is the anti-Semitism of the liberals." Peter Viereck, *Shame and Glory of the Intellectuals* (Boston: Beacon Press, 1953), 45.
12. John Tracy Ellis, "American Catholics and the Intellectual Life," *Thought*, Fall 1955.
13. Leo XIII condemned "Americanism" in his 1899 apostolic letter *Testem Benevolentiae Nostrae.*
14. For more on the significance of the Council of Trent, see John W. O'Malley, *Trent and All That: Renaming Catholicism in the Early Modern Era* (Cambridge: Harvard University Press, 2000).
15. Thomas Aquinas defined Jesus Christ as "the absolutely necessary way to salvation." But access to Jesus is available only through the Catholic faith, and "it is for the Pope to define what [that] faith is. [Therefore] it is necessary for salvation to submit to the Roman Pope." *Contra Errores Graecorum*, 2.36.
16. The Cathari, a Manichaean sect in southern France, condemned as heretical, might have qualified as being outside the Church, but an early-thirteenth-century Crusade, authorized by the Fourth Lateran Council, wiped them out.
17. *Mirari Vos*, in Leonard Swidler, *Freedom in the Church* (Dayton, OH: Pflaum Press, 1969), 45.
18. *Syllabus of Errors*, http://www.papalencyclicals.net/piuso9/p9syll.htm.
19. The extremity of Civil War violence is underappreciated. More than 700,000 men, women, and children died in those four years, when the U.S. population was around 30 million. An equivalent mortality rate today would be about 7 million dead.
20. I owe this insight to Mark U. Edwards.
21. "When the Roman Pontiff speaks *ex cathedra*, that is, when . . . as the pastor and teacher of all Christians in virtue of his highest apostolic authority, he defines a doctrine of faith and morals that must be held by the Universal Church, he is empowered through the divine assistance promised him in blessed Peter, with that infallibility with which the Divine Redeemer willed to endow his Church." *Pastor Aeternus*, http://www.ewtn.com/faith/teachings/papae1.htm.
22. *Pastor Aeternus.*
23. Matthew 16:18.

24. For more on this, see R. Scott Appleby, "Modernism as the Final Phase of Americanism: William L. Sullivan, American Catholic Apologist, 1899–1910," *Harvard Theological Review* 81, no. 2, April 1988, 171–92.
25. U.S. Census Bureau, "Poverty Working Papers," http://aspe.os.dhhs.gov/poverty/papers/htrssmiv.htm.
26. "The erroneous opinions and 'principles' of the so-called Americanism Pope Leo XIII reduced to one proposition: 'In order the more easily to bring over to Catholic doctrine those who dissent from it, the Church ought to adapt herself somewhat to our advanced civilization, and, relaxing her ancient rigor, show some indulgence to modern popular theories and methods.'" R. Scott Appleby, "The Triumph of Americanism," in *Being Right: Conservative Catholics in America*, edited by Mary Jo Weaver and R. Scott Appleby (Bloomington: Indiana University Press, 1995), 43.
27. The phrase is from the 1907 decree *Pascendi Dominici Gregis*. The pope condemned the idea "that certain liberties ought to be introduced into the Church so that, limiting the exercise and vigilance of its powers, each one of the faithful may act more freely in pursuance of his own natural bent and capacity." *Documents of American Catholic History*, edited by John Tracy Ellis (Milwaukee: Bruce Publishing Co., 1964), 534–43.
28. The first great American statement against coercion in religion came from Roger Williams, who wrote *The Bloody Tenent of Persecution for Cause of Conscience, Discussed* in 1644. For questioning the use of force in promoting belief, he was banished from Massachusetts. There is a line from Williams to Thomas Jefferson, who advanced the argument in 1786 with "The Virginia Statute for Religious Freedom."
29. Indeed, one of the condemned Americanists was a priest-scientist, John Zahm, whose 1896 work *Evolution and Dogma* "embodied the link between Americanism and evolutionism." Appleby, "Triumph of Americanism," 46.
30. Newman published his *Essay on the Development of Christian Doctrine* in 1878, the year before he was named a cardinal by Pope Leo XIII. Johann Joseph Ignaz von Döllinger, writing "Letters from Rome" in 1870, at the time of the Vatican Council, was excommunicated in 1871 for refusing to accept the newly defined doctrine of papal infallibility. Döllinger accepted the excommunication.
31. Walter Elliott, *The Life of Father Hecker* (New York: Columbus Press, 1891). For more on Americanism, see Thomas T. McAvoy, *The Great Crisis in American Catholic History, 1895–1900* (Chicago: H. Regnery Co., 1957), and David O'Brien, *The Renewal of American Catholicism* (New York: Paulist Press, 1972).
32. Luke 17:20.
33. For more on Hecker's democratic theology, see David O'Brien, *Isaac Hecker: American Catholic* (New York: Paulist Press, 1992).
34. For an account of that argument, see John T. Noonan, *A Church That Can and Cannot Change: The Development of Catholic Moral Teaching* (Notre Dame, IN: University of Notre Dame Press, 2005).
35. The Father Feeney Internet Archive, http://www.fatherfeeney.org.

36. In September 1907, Pope Pius X issued *Pascendi Dominici Gregis*, condemning Catholic biblical scholars and theologians labeled "modernists." It said they were "the most pernicious of all the adversaries of the Church [who used] a thousand noxious arts . . . poisonous doctrines . . . the synthesis of all heresies." The most famous of the Paulist modernists was William L. Sullivan, who became a Unitarian in 1910, reversing the journey that Isaac Hecker had made. "Our purpose was in no sense destructive," Sullivan wrote of himself and fellow modernists. "We hoped to bring to the knowledge of intelligent priests and lay-folk some of the critical and philosophical questions which, sooner or later, they would have to face anyhow, and to give these questions such solutions as a liberal and loyal Catholic scholarship could discover." Appleby, "Modernism as the Final Phase of Americanism," 183.

Chapter Three: Coming of Age

1. Thomas H. O'Connor, *Boston Catholics: A History of the Church and Its People* (Boston: Northeastern University Press, 1998), 239–83. Thomas O'Connor is the dean of Boston Irish historians, and I acknowledge my debt to him. See also "The Unlikely Cardinal," *Time*, August 21, 1964.
2. For more on Cardinal O'Connell, see James O'Toole, *Militant and Triumphant: William Henry O'Connell and the Catholic Church in Boston, 1895–1944* (Notre Dame, IN: University of Notre Dame Press, 1992).
3. "The Unlikely Cardinal," 36.
4. John Cooney, *The American Pope: The Life and Times of Francis Cardinal Spellman* (New York: Times Books, 1984), 249, 262.
5. Clare Boothe Luce was the wife of the founder of *Time*, Henry Luce. She became famous as the editor of *Vanity Fair* and as a Broadway playwright. During World War II she served in Congress as a Republican from Connecticut. In 1944, her nineteen-year-old daughter, a student at Stanford, was killed in an automobile accident. This shattered Luce. She resigned her congressional seat. It was in this crisis that she discovered her Catholic faith.
6. See Avery Dulles, *A Testimonial to Grace: Reflections on a Theological Journey* (Kansas City, MO: Sheed & Ward, 1996).
7. Stephen J. Whitfield, *The Culture of the Cold War* (Baltimore: Johns Hopkins University Press, 1991), 77. See also William M. Newman and Peter L. Halvorson, *Atlas of American Religion: The Denominational Era, 1776–1990* (Walnut Creek, CA: AltaMira Press, 2000). Other sources put churchgoing rates in 1955 somewhat lower. See "Secularization and Religious Revival," http://www.jstor.org/stable/1386577?seq=2.
8. Fr. Leonard Feeney, *The Point*, October 1953, http://www.fatherfeeney.org/point/53-oct.html.
9. Rodney Stark, *One True God: Historical Consequences of Monotheism* (Princeton, NJ: Princeton University Press, 2001), 236.
10. The nephew is Steve Pearlstein, a Pulitzer Prize–winning reporter for the *Washington Post*. I recounted what he told me about Cardinal Cushing in "Boston's Jews and Boston's Irish," *Boston Globe*, January 12, 1992.

11. J. Anthony Lukas, *Common Ground: A Turbulent Decade in the Lives of Three American Families* (New York: Random House, 1985), 379.
12. John 14:6.
13. John 8:44.
14. An early articulation of "Baptism of desire" came, in fact, in response to Cushing's initial appeal to Rome. The so-called Boston Letter, issued by the Holy Office in 1949, stated that Church membership is necessary "at least in desire and longing (*voto et desiderio*) . . . God also accepts implicit desire." Richard McBrien, *Catholicism* (Minneapolis: Winston Press, 1980), 753.
15. He said this in an interview with Diane Sawyer on *Primetime Live*, February 17, 2004.
16. The Congregation for the Doctrine of the Faith issued *Dominus Iesus* in 2000. Pope John Paul II got his distance from what was taken to be that document's implication that *Extra Ecclesiam nulla salus* was making a comeback. But then Pope Benedict, in 2007, issued what was taken to be a "clarifying" reiteration of *Dominus Iesus*, with a decree titled "Responses to Some Questions Regarding Certain Aspects of the Doctrine of the Church."
17. The phrase "anonymous Christian" was introduced in the mid-1960s by the theologian Karl Rahner. He defined the anonymous Christian as "the pagan after the beginning of the Christian mission, who lives in the state of Christ's grace through faith, hope and love, yet who has no explicit knowledge of the fact that his life is oriented in grace-given salvation to Jesus Christ." *Theological Investigations*, vol. 14, translated by David Bourke (London: Darton, Longman & Todd, 1976), 283.
18. The Book of Joshua explicitly defines the sun's movement. "So the sun stood still, and the moon stopped, till the nation avenged itself on its enemies, as it is written in the Book of Jashar. The sun stopped in the middle of the sky, and delayed going down about a full day. There has never been a day like it before or since." Joshua 10:13–14.
19. The Immaculate Conception was proclaimed as doctrine in 1854. In 1858, Mary was reported to have appeared to a peasant girl named Bernadette Soubirous in Lourdes, France, the first of eighteen apparitions over six months. Mary reportedly said to Bernadette, "I am the Immaculate Conception." *On the Origin of Species* was published in 1859.
20. Indicative of the Vatican's capacity to take in the new knowledge, the Reverend George Coyne, S.J., the astrophysicist and director of the Vatican Observatory, told an interviewer in 2002 that "to imagine a Creator twiddling with the constants of nature is a bit like thinking of God as making a big pot of soup . . . [a regression to] a watchmaker God." Mary Beth Saffo, "Accidental Elegance," *American Scholar* 74, no. 3, 27. "For Father Coyne," Dr. Saffo comments, "no conflict exists between God and a world of evolutionary surprise."
21. See Karen Armstrong, *The Great Transformation: The Beginning of Our Religious Traditions* (New York: Knopf, 2006).
22. This evolutionary understanding of consciousness does not imply inevitable progress, as if the present is necessarily better than the past. Nor does it mean

that later religions "supersede" earlier ones—a mistaken idea that shows up in Christian contempt for Judaism.

23. John 1. As we will see later, the Greek word *logos* can be profitably translated as "meaning."
24. Elaine Pagels, *Beyond Belief: The Secret Gospel of Thomas* (New York: Random House, 2003), 144.
25. I heard the late theologian Paul Van Buren offer this tongue-in-cheek definition of mysticism at a conference in Jerusalem in 1998.
26. The first great organizer of "orthodox" Christianity was Irenaeus, a second-century bishop of a Roman settlement in Gaul, now Lyons, France. He saw the factionalism of the Christian movement throughout the empire as its mortal flaw, and worked to exert doctrinal and organizational control. This would ultimately lead to the canonization of certain Christian texts (the New Testament) and the suppression of many others. The texts that survived were to be interpreted only by bishops, their meaning eventually codified in the creed. See Pagels, *Beyond Belief*, 74–141.
27. See Krister Stendahl, "The Apostle Paul and the Introspective Conscience of the West." Luther realized through his reading of Paul that the righteousness of the judging God was manifest in Christ, through whom God reckons humans as righteous. Lutherans strive to get beyond the damning judge to the merciful God revealed in Christ. But for Lutherans, as for Catholics, that striving is fitful.
28. I learned about the distinction between Calvin's covenant maker God and Catholicism's judge God in conversation with Krister Stendahl.
29. John Courtney Murray, *We Hold These Truths: Catholic Reflections on the American Proposition* (Lanham, MD: Rowman & Littlefield, 2005).
30. Lukas, *Common Ground*, 380.
31. John T. McGreevy, *Catholicism and American Freedom: A History* (New York: W. W. Norton, 2004), 229–32.
32. http://www.americanrhetoric.com/speeches/johnfkennedyhoustonministers speech.html.
33. Theodore C. Sorensen, *Kennedy* (New York: Harper & Row, 1965), 190.
34. That a profound reversal was accomplished here is indicated by the fact that the Paulist Fathers, whose founder, Isaac Hecker, had nearly been condemned as an Americanist heretic early in the twentieth century, put Hecker's name before the Vatican as a candidate for sainthood early in the twenty-first.

Chapter Four: The Council

1. Christopher Ruddy, "Good Pope, Bad Pope," *Commonweal*, March 8, 2002.
2. Peter Hebblethwaite, "John XXIII," in *The HarperCollins Encyclopedia of Catholicism*, edited by Richard P. McBrien (San Francisco: HarperSanFrancisco, 1995), 709.
3. James Carroll, *An American Requiem: God, My Father, and the War That Came Between Us* (Boston: Houghton Mifflin, 1996), 76–79.

4. "Pius XII Ordered: Do Not Give Back the Jewish Children. The Future Pope Roncalli Disobeyed," *Corriere della Sera*, December 28, 2004.
5. Quoted in Hannah Arendt, *Men in Dark Times* (New York: Harcourt, Brace and World, 1968), 63.
6. Jules Isaac, the author of *Jesus and Israel*, for example, was warmly received by Pope John in June 1960. After that meeting, the pope put the Church's relationship with the Jewish people on the agenda of the Vatican Council.
7. John Cooney, *The American Pope: The Life and Times of Francis Cardinal Spellman* (New York: Times Books, 1984), 283.
8. See my account of their experience in *House of War: The Pentagon and the Disastrous Rise of American Power* (Boston: Houghton Mifflin, 2006), 255.
9. Thomas Merton, *The Waters of Siloe* (Garden City, NY: Image Books, 1962), 72.
10. Thomas Merton, "The Sign of Jonas," in *A Thomas Merton Reader*, edited by Thomas P. McDonnell (Garden City, NY: Image Books, 1974), 202.
11. Hans Küng, *The Council, Reform and Reunion*, translated by Cecily Hastings (New York: Sheed & Ward, 1962).
12. Peter Hebblethwaite, *John XXIII: Pope of the Council* (London: Geoffrey Chapman, 1984), 375.
13. There is no doubt that John XXIII was influenced by Küng, but it is not clear which of Küng's works the pope read. Given the hostility to Küng's ideas among Vatican insiders, his book was not published in Italian until 1965. Hebblethwaite, *John XXIII*, 373.
14. Hebblethwaite, *John XXIII*, 200.
15. John XXIII complained that the officials around him "have refused the Pope." Hebblethwaite, *John XXIII*, 341.
16. Hebblethwaite, *John XXIII*, 431.
17. J. Anthony Lukas, *Common Ground: A Turbulent Decade in the Lives of Three American Families* (New York: Random House, 1985), 381.
18. Hebblethwaite, *John XXIII*, 386.
19. "Man of the Year," *Time*, January 4, 1963, 51.
20. Hebblethwaite, *John XXIII*, 444.
21. http://www.jfklibrary.org/jfkl/cmc/j102262.htm.
22. Kenneth R. Himes and Lisa Sowle Cahill, eds., *Modern Catholic Social Teaching: Commentaries and Interpretations* (Washington, DC: Georgetown University Press, 2005), 218.
23. Hebblethwaite, *John XXIII*, 445.
24. Hebblethwaite, *John XXIII*, 445–47.
25. "Man of the Year," *Time*, 52.
26. Lest Cushing's two interventions seem paltry, note that of the 2,135 bishops present at the council, only 200 ever rose to speak. John L. Allen, Jr., *Cardinal Ratzinger: The Vatican's Enforcer of the Faith* (New York: Continuum, 2000), 63.
27. John M. Oesterreicher, *The Rediscovery of Judaism: A Re-examination of the Conciliar Statement on the Jews* (South Orange, NJ: Institute of Judeo-Christian Studies, Seton Hall University, 1971), 197–98.

28. *Lumen Gentium*, http://www.vatican.va/archive/hist_councils/ii_vatican_council/documents/vaticanii_const_19641121_lumen-gentium-en.html.
29. Thomas O'Connor, *Boston Catholics: A History of the Church and Its People* (Boston: Northeastern University Press, 1998), 264.
30. The letter was addressed to Ernesto Cardenal. Thomas Merton, *Courage for Truth: The Letters of Thomas Merton to Writers*, edited by Christine M. Bochen (New York: Farrar, Straus and Giroux, 1993), 128.
31. Merton, *Courage for Truth*, 30–31.
32. Merton, *Courage for Truth*, 130.
33. Daniel Berrigan, *Portraits of Those I Love* (New York: Crossroad, 1982), 19.
34. http://www.jfklibrary.org/Historical+Resources/Archives/Reference+Desk/Speeches/jfk/003pof03americanuniversity06101963.htm.
35. "The Unlikely Cardinal," *Time*, August 21, 1964, 37.

Chapter Five: A New Language

1. By far the most influential reporting on the council appeared in *The New Yorker*. The writer was a Redemptorist priest named F. X. Murphy. His "Letters from Vatican City" were well informed, full of insider insights, and irreverent. No one knew he was a priest. He published under the pseudonym Xavier Rynne. See his *Vatican Council II* (New York: Farrar, Straus and Giroux, 1968).
2. Marshall McLuhan, *The Medium and the Light: Reflections on Religion* (Toronto: Stoddart, 1999), 144–48.
3. This effect unfolded gradually, since a large majority of Reformation-era Europe was illiterate. But the combination of movable-type printing and Protestantism spawned a great rise in literacy, so that by the seventeenth century, reading and *reading the Bible* had spread from the elites to the masses.
4. "Since between 95 and 97 percent of the Jewish state was illiterate at the time of Jesus, it must be presumed that Jesus was also illiterate." John Dominic Crossan, *Jesus: A Revolutionary Biography* (San Francisco: HarperSanFrancisco, 1994), 25. I acknowledge my large debt to Crossan for my understanding of contemporary Scripture scholarship.
5. Athanasius, the bishop of Alexandria, who died about 373, had compiled a list of twenty-seven books that he called the New Testament, a first formal "canonization" of Christian writings. There were probably dozens more texts from which he chose. In the interest of establishing an orthodox reading of Christian origins, Athanasius, in the year 367, ordered those other texts to be destroyed. It was almost certainly this order that prompted an anonymous monk at Nag Hammadi, in Egypt, to take more than fifty other "books" and hide them in a cliffside cave, where they were discovered in 1945. Among these books are the so-called Gnostic Gospels. Elaine Pagels, *Beyond Belief: The Secret Gospel of Thomas* (New York: Random House, 2005), 96–97.
6. David Daniell, *The Bible in English: Its History and Influence* (New Haven: Yale University Press, 2003), 11.
7. Daniell, *The Bible in English*, 152, 129.

8. "Decree on Sacred Books and on Traditions to Be Received," session IV, 1546, quoted in Richard P. McBrien, *Catholicism*, vol. 1 (Oak Grove, MN: Winston Press, 1980), 214.
9. Limbo was a vaguely defined netherworld conjured for the sake of those who, while not guilty of mortal sin and therefore not deserving of hell, were also not baptized members of the Catholic Church, and therefore not eligible to be saved. Souls in limbo did not suffer, exactly, but they were deprived for all eternity of the "beatific vision," the true bliss of heaven. In 2007, a Vatican commission declared that there was no such thing as limbo, with unbaptized infants consigned to God's mercy. (It was theorized that the Vatican renounced limbo in response to pressures from African bishops whose parishes were burying so many babies who had died of AIDS-related diseases.) See John Thavis, "Vatican Commission: Limbo Reflects a 'Restrictive View of Salvation,'" *Origins* 36, no. 45, April 20, 2007.
10. Augustine says, for example, that the four rivers in the Garden of Eden, as recounted in Genesis, are an allegorical reference to the four Gospels. *The City of God*, bk. 13, ch. 21.
11. J. L. Heilbron, *The Sun in the Church: Cathedrals as Solar Observatories* (Cambridge: Harvard University Press, 1999), 24–45.
12. The Copernicus-Galileo dispute is the main example given by Thomas Kuhn of a "paradigm shift" in his influential book of 1962, *The Structure of Scientific Revolutions.*
13. Joshua 10:13.
14. Giorgio de Santillana, *The Crime of Galileo* (Chicago: University of Chicago Press, 1976), 45.
15. De Santillana, *Crime of Galileo,* 99.
16. In 1992, a Vatican commission declared that "Galileo was right in adopting the Copernican astronomical theory." Alan Cowell, "After 350 Years, Vatican Says Galileo Was Right: It Moves," *New York Times,* October 31, 1992.
17. *Divino Afflante Spiritu,* quoted in McBrien, *Catholicism,* vol. 1, xxix.
18. Karl Marx's celebration of this event, written from his table at the British Museum in London, was his first writing that drew notice. The anticlerical violence of the Communards would, in the Church's mind, be associated from then on with the Communists who took their inspiration from Marx.
19. Among the condemned, as we saw, was John Zahm, for his work *Evolution and Dogma,* a reconciliation of Darwin and Catholicism that was formally approved by Archbishop John Ireland of St. Paul, Minnesota—which heightened Vatican alarm. R. Scott Appleby, "The Triumph of Americanism," in *Being Right: Conservative Catholics in America,* edited by Mary Jo Weaver and R. Scott Appleby (Bloomington: Indiana University Press, 1995), 45.
20. "Fundamentalism" was a new word, coined in the early twentieth century by conservative American Protestants committed to defend the five "fundamentals" of their faith. We will see more of this later in the book.
21. *Nostra Aetate,* quoted in *The Documents of Vatican II,* edited by Walter M. Abbott (New York: Guild Press, 1966), 666.
22. John 19:6–7, 15.

23. John 1:11.
24. Pontifical Biblical Commission, "Instruction on the Historical Truth of the Gospels," April 21, 1964, quoted in *Catholic Biblical Quarterly* 26, July 1964, 305–12.
25. Crossan, *Jesus: A Revolutionary Biography,* 25. Sections of the Gospel of Thomas were discovered in 1897, but the complete text was not found until 1945.
26. John Dominic Crossan and Jonathan Reed, *Excavating Jesus: Beneath the Stones, Behind the Texts* (San Francisco: HarperSanFrancisco, 2001), 13.
27. Crossan and Reed, *Excavating Jesus,* 13.
28. Elaine Pagels used this phrase in conversation with me.
29. John 2:19.
30. Barbara H. Geller Nathanson, "Toward a Multicultural Ecumenical History of Women in the First Century/ies C.E.," in *Searching the Scriptures,* vol. 1, *A Feminist Introduction,* edited by Elisabeth Schüssler Fiorenza (New York: Crossroad, 1993), 274.
31. Susan Haskins, *Mary Magdalen: Myth and Metaphor* (New York: Harcourt, Brace, 1994), 13.
32. Matthew 27:56.
33. Mark 16:9.
34. John 20:18.
35. Haskins, *Mary Magdalen,* 37.
36. Karen L. King, *The Gospel of Mary of Magdala: Jesus and the First Woman Apostle* (Santa Rosa, CA: Polebridge Press, 2003), 153.
37. King, *Gospel of Mary of Magdala,* 3. Raymond E. Brown, *An Introduction to the New Testament* (New York: Doubleday, 1997), 350.
38. John 11:1–44.
39. Matthew 27:56.
40. John 19:25–26.
41. Luke 7:36–50.
42. John 4:5–43.
43. John 8:3–11.
44. See John Dominic Crossan, *The Birth of Christianity: Discovering What Happened in the Years Immediately After the Execution of Jesus* (San Francisco: HarperSanFrancisco, 1998), 49–121.
45. Luke 8:1–3.
46. Haskins, *Mary Magdalen,* 18.
47. Luke 7:36–50.
48. Matthew 26:6–13.
49. Brown, *Introduction to the New Testament,* 241.
50. Mark 14:3–9.
51. Crossan, *Birth of Christianity,* 558.
52. For example, Matthew 27:61.
53. Matthew 26:14–16.
54. John 12:1–9.
55. John 11:32–37, 48.

56. Crossan, *Birth of Christianity,* 268.
57. Crossan and Reed, *Excavating Jesus,* 268.
58. John 20:1–18.
59. Crossan, *Birth of Christianity,* 573.
60. Richard A. Horsley and Neil Asher Silberman, *The Message and the Kingdom: How Jesus and Paul Ignited a Revolution and Transformed the Ancient World* (New York: Grossett/Putnam, 1997), 99.
61. King, *Gospel of Mary of Magdala,* 152.
62. John 20:11–18.
63. Crossan, *Birth of Christianity,* 573.
64. Haskins, *Mary Magdalen,* 155–56.
65. In the Letter to the Philippians, for example, he honors "these women, for they have labored side by side with me in the gospel." Philippians 4:3.
66. The Church "holds that it is not admissible to ordain women to the priesthood for very fundamental reasons: the example recorded in Sacred Scripture of Christ choosing his Apostles only from among men, the constant practice of the Church which has imitated Christ in choosing only men, and her living teaching authority which has consistently held that the exclusion of women from the priesthood is in accordance with God's plan for his Church." Apostolic letter of Pope John Paul II (citing Pope Paul VI in 1975), *Ordinatio Sacerdotalis,* 1994. http://www.vatican.va/john_paul-ii/apost_letters/documents/hf_jp-ii_apl_22051994_ordinatio-sacerdotalis_en.html.
67. Pagels, *Beyond Belief,* 175.
68. King, *Gospel of Mary of Magdala,* 184.
69. Mark 16:17.
70. Mary 6:1–4, in King, *Gospel of Mary of Magdala,* 15.
71. Mary 10:7–9, in King, *Gospel of Mary of Magdala,* 17
72. Haskins, *Mary Magdalen,* 69–74.
73. King, *Gospel of Mary of Magdala,* 170f.
74. With Gregory, her image "was finally settled . . . for nearly fourteen hundred years." Haskins, *Mary Magdalen,* 93.
75. Homily XXXIII, quoted in Haskins, *Mary Magdalen,* 93.
76. Haskins, *Mary Magdalen,* 94.

Chapter Six: Sex and Power

1. Peter Hebblethwaite, *Paul VI: The First Modern Pope* (New York: Paulist Press, 1993), 394.
2. My discussion of this controversy is informed by John Noonan, *Contraception: A History of Its Treatment by the Theologians and Canonists* (Cambridge: Belknap Press of Harvard University Press, 1986).
3. Sanger founded the American Birth Control League in 1921; in 1942, it became the Planned Parenthood Federation of America.
4. Ironically, St. Augustine condemned the timing of intercourse and the use of coitus interruptus to avoid conception.

5. Hebblethwaite, *Paul VI*, 445.
6. For a discussion of this case, see John W. Johnson, *Griswold v. Connecticut: Birth Control and the Constitutional Right of Privacy* (Lawrence: University Press of Kansas, 2005).
7. In his "Memo to the Cardinal," Murray wrote, "It is not the function of a civil law to prescribe everything that is morally right and to forbid everything that is morally wrong." http://woodstock.georgetown.edu/library/Murray/1965F.htm.
8. The Cushing quotes are cited, disapprovingly, by Thomas A. Droleskey, "A Champion of the Americanist Spirit," *Seattle Catholic: A Journal of Catholic News and Views*, March 22, 2004.
9. What the writer Amy Sullivan calls "John Kerry's religion disaster," when bishops discouraged Catholics from voting for Kerry in 2004, was rooted in his claim to privately uphold Catholic teaching on abortion while publicly affirming the right of women to choose. The "wafer watch," attention drawn to whether Kerry was receiving Communion, was key to his loss of the presidency to George W. Bush. Amy Sullivan, *The Party Faithful: How and Why Democrats Are Closing the God Gap* (New York: Scribner, 2008), 121.
10. The pope's statement goes on, "Our intention is not only to preserve this ancient law as far as possible, but to strengthen its observance." Hebblethwaite, *Paul VI*, 441.
11. Jansenism takes its name from Cornelius Jansen, a French bishop of the early seventeenth century who taught that humans are incapable of virtue without the intervening grace of God. When Catholic seminaries were outlawed in British-occupied Ireland, Irish clergy were trained in France, where the flesh-hating virus of Jansenism was picked up, and thence carried to America by the Irish clergy.
12. The other two "signs of the times" were the movement for full economic rights by workers and the end of colonialism.
13. J. Anthony Lukas, *Common Ground*, 389.
14. "Reveal Papal Birth Control Texts," *National Catholic Reporter*, April 19, 1967.
15. "Something inside of me kept saying, 'There was the Sunday school, you could 'a gone to it; and if you'd 'a done it they'd 'a learnt you there people that acts as I'd been acting about that nigger goes to everlasting fire.' It made me shiver. And I about made up my mind to pray, and see if I couldn't try to quit being the kind of boy I was and be better. So I kneeled down. And the words wouldn't come . . . You can't pray a lie—I found that out." The lie was that slavery was right. Mark Twain, *The Adventures of Huckleberry Finn* (New York: Airmont Books, 1962), 188–89.
16. This is one translation of the name God claims in response to Moses's question "Whom shall I say sent me?" Exodus 3:13–15.
17. Daniel Berrigan's first volume of poetry, *Time Without Number*, had won the Lamont Poetry Prize in 1958. Marianne Moore said his poems "seem as much revealed as written."
18. Merton and Ginsberg, as well as Kerouac, had in common formative experi-

ences at Columbia University. All three were protégés of Mark van Doren, and all three benefited from the publishing connections of another Columbia figure, Robert Giroux. Kerouac published "A Poem Dedicated to Thomas Merton" in an upstart literary journal called *Monk's Pond.*

19. Russell Fraser drew my attention to the significance of this stage direction.
20. Stephen Prothero, "On the Holy Road: The Beat Movement as Spiritual Protest," *Harvard Theological Review* 84, no. 2, April 1991, 205–22.
21. Allen Ginsberg, *Howl: 50th Anniversary Edition* (New York: HarperPerennial, 2006), 8.
22. James W. Woelfel, *Bonhoeffer's Theology: Classical and Revolutionary* (New York: Abingdon Press, 1970), 20. Harvey Cox, a Baptist theologian teaching at the Harvard Divinity School, published *The Secular City* in 1965.
23. For the connection between the Beat movement and the transcendentalists, I am grateful to Stephen Prothero.
24. *Populorum Progressio,* March 26, 1967. http://www.vatican.va/holy_father/paul_vi/encyclicals/documents/hf_p-vi_enc_26031967_populorum_en.html.
25. For a contemporary exploration of the distinction between "curing" disease and "healing" illness, see John Dominic Crossan, *God and Empire* (San Francisco: HarperSanFrancisco, 2007), 119.
26. Matthew 26:52.
27. John 8:11.
28. Quoted in Thomas C. Fox, *Sexuality and Catholicism* (New York: George Braziller, 1995), 68. For a more positive view of *Humanae Vitae* than I offer here, see John L. Allen, Jr., "The Pope vs. the Pill," *New York Times,* July 27, 2008.
29. Fox, *Sexuality and Catholicism,* 77–79.
30. John T. Noonan, Jr., *The Morality of Abortion: Legal and Historical Perspectives* (Cambridge: Harvard University Press, 1970), 23. See also Robert McClory, *Turning Point: The Inside Story of the Papal Birth Control Commission and How* Humanae Vitae *Changed the Life of Patty Crowley and the Future of the Church* (New York: Crossroad, 1995).
31. Within five years of *Humanae Vitae,* eighty-seven percent of priests refused to enforce it in Confession. Fully sixty percent of them rejected it as doctrine. Fox, *Sexuality and Catholicism,* 81.
32. A 2007 Catholic University poll found that eighty-nine percent of Catholic college students, and sixty-one percent of their grandparents, believed that being a "good Catholic" did not require accepting the hierarchy's teaching on birth control. Rich Heffern, "The Bookend Generations," *National Catholic Reporter,* March 9, 2007. One of the theologians who joined in Curran's dissent against *Humanae Vitae* was Daniel Maguire. By 2007, he was a professor at Marquette University in Milwaukee. That year, the Catholic bishops of the United States formally denounced him for teaching that Catholics are justified in dissenting from the hierarchy's prohibition of birth control. That showed less about what Catholics believe than about the kind of bishops John Paul II had appointed—all men whose conformity on this question was a

given. "Catholic Bishops Condemn Maguire on Birth Control, Gay Marriage," *National Catholic Reporter,* April 6, 2007, 5.

33. Noonan, *Morality of Abortion,* 36. Thirty-seven years later, Church figures were still pretending to enforce the ban. In "Married Love and the Gift of Life," issued in 2006, the American Catholic bishops formally declared, "Suppressing fertility by using contraception denies part of the inherent meaning of married sexuality and does harm to the couple's unity." Not only did the bishops reiterate the ban on contraception, which by their own assessment ninety-six percent of married Catholics reject, but they went on to say that any Catholic rejecting this teaching should not receive Communion at Mass. If they thought for a moment that ninety-six percent of married Catholics would stop receiving Communion, they would never have made this decree. It was simple posturing, done with an eye on Rome, not on the Catholic people. Michael Paulson, "Bishops Stress Sexual Issues and Warn on Communion," *Boston Globe,* November 15, 2006. In 2008, Catholics ignored the pressures from conservative bishops and voted for the pro-choice Barack Obama by a margin of 52 to 45 percent, an increase of 7 percent over Catholics voting for John Kerry in 2004. Hispanic Catholics, whom bishops regard as relatively docile, voted for Obama by 67 percent. Peter Steinfels, "Catholics and Choice (in the Voting Booth)," *New York Times,* November 8, 2008.

Chapter Seven: Thou Art a Priest

1. Thomas Merton, *Conjectures of a Guilty Bystander* (New York: Doubleday, 1966), 156.
2. The father general, Merton had written at the time, "objected to this kind of dialogue between a member of the Order and Buddhists, Protestants, Jews, and so forth. He does not think, apparently, that I have sufficiently the mind of the Church to be able to engage safely in dialogue of this kind." Letter to Jacques Maritain, 1960.
3. Patrick Hart and Jonathan Montaldo, eds., *The Intimate Merton: His Life from His Journals* (New York: HarperCollins, 2001), 247.
4. Thomas Merton, *A Thomas Merton Reader,* edited by Thomas P. McDonnell (New York: Image Books, 1989), 345.
5. Thomas Merton, *The Seven Storey Mountain: Fiftieth Anniversary Edition* (New York: Harcourt Brace & Co., 1998), 406.
6. Hart and Montaldo, eds., *Intimate Merton,* 287.
7. Hart and Montaldo, eds., *Intimate Merton,* 287.
8. M. Scott Peck, introduction to *A Thomas Merton Reader,* edited by Thomas P. McDonnell (New York: Doubleday, 1996), 3.
9. Thomas Merton, "Two Asian Letters," *A Thomas Merton Reader,* 446.
10. The others were Benjamin Spock, Michael Ferber, Mitchell Goodman, and Marcus Raskin.
11. Coffin cited Luther often in those days. He did so in a sermon at Yale, in the presence of Yale President Kingman Brewster, an implicit justification of his

crimes. Warren Goldstein, *William Sloane Coffin: A Holy Impatience* (New Haven: Yale University Press, 2004), 205.

12. I describe this scene and what it meant to me in my memoir, *An American Requiem* (Boston: Houghton Mifflin, 1996), 236–40.
13. *Time,* November 1, 1968.
14. J. Anthony Lucas, *Common Ground,* 390. "Furor over Defense of Jacqueline Leads Cardinal Cushing to Resign," read the headline in the *Harvard Crimson,* October 23, 1968.
15. *Boston Pilot,* April 29, 1969.
16. Not everyone was so edified by the astronauts' reading from Genesis. The professional atheist Madalyn Murray O'Hair sued NASA for the violation of the separation of church and state, an action, like much of O'Hair's program, that prompted much comment but came to nothing.
17. John 21:15–17.
18. John H. Yoder, "Conscientious Objection," in *The HarperCollins Encyclopedia of Catholicism,* edited by Richard P. McBrien (San Francisco: HarperSanFrancisco, 1989), 357.
19. Quoted in Andrew O. Shapiro and John M. Striker, *Mastering the Draft: The Comprehensive Guide for Solving Draft Problems* (New York: Avon Books, 1970), 249.
20. The application form for CO classification included this instruction: "Describe the nature of your belief which is the basis of your claim, and state why you consider it to be based on religious training and belief." Applicants were instructed to explain "from what source you received religious training and acquired the religious belief which is the basis of your claim." Shapiro and Striker, *Mastering the Draft,* 256.
21. *Pacem in Terris,* http://www.vatican.va/holy_father/john_xxiii/encyclicals/documents/hf_j-xxiii_enc_11041963_pacem_en.html.
22. "Pastoral Constitution on the Church in the Modern World," *Gaudium et Spes,* http://www.vatican.va/archive/hist_councils/ii_vatican_cons_9651207/gaudium-et-spes_en.html. The council declaration called for making "humane provision for the care of those who for reasons of conscience refuse to bear arms," but this was read as a repudiation of selective conscientious objection.
23. http://www.priestsforlife.org/magisterium/bishops/68-11-15humanlifeinourdaynccb.htm.
24. "In assessing our country's involvement in Vietnam, we must ask: Have we already reached, or passed, the point where the principle of proportionality becomes decisive? . . . Would not an untimely withdrawal be equally disastrous?" On the question of conscientious objection, they were equally tortured: "Nor can it be said that such conscientious objection to war, as war is waged in our times, is entirely the result of subjective considerations . . ." http://www.priestsforlife.org/magisterium/bishops/68-11-15humanlifeinourdaynccb.htm.
25. One of these, Pat Farren, went on to a life career as a peace activist. While

working at Newman House, Pat founded *Peacework*, a publication of the American Friends Service Committee. He edited it until he died in 1998.

26. Shapiro and Striker, *Mastering the Draft*, 257.
27. Lucas, *Common Ground*, 390.
28. *Boston Pilot*, April 11, 1970, 2.

Chapter Eight: The Scandal

1. J. Anthony Lukas, *Common Ground*, 374.
2. According to the U.S. Conference of Catholic Bishops, in 2002 there were 35.3 million Catholic Hispanics. Hispanics comprise 12.3 percent of the U.S. population and make up 39 percent of American Catholics. Hispanics account for 71 percent of U.S. Catholic growth since 1960. http://www.nccbuscc.org/hispanicaffairs/demo.html.
3. In 1990, Pope John Paul II beatified Juan Diego, the Mexican peasant to whom Our Lady of Guadalupe is supposed to have appeared. Mainstream historians agree that no such person existed.
4. Lukas, *Common Ground*, 399.
5. In 1974, polls showed that barely more than fifteen percent of American Catholics accepted the teaching of *Humanae Vitae.* That percentage continued to decline. Thomas C. Fox, *Sexuality and Catholicism* (New York: George Braziller, 1995), 300.
6. Garry Wills calls this a "structure of deceit." *Papal Sin: Structures of Deceit* (New York: Doubleday & Co., 2000).
7. "The Boston archdiocese has paid at least five settlements to Shanley's victims, including a $40,000 payment in about 1993 to a man who notified Church officials that he had repeatedly been anally raped by Shanley around 1972, when he was twelve or thirteen. Another man received a $100,000 settlement in 1998 after reporting a four-year sexual relationship with Shanley that began in 1965, when he was in the fifth grade." Investigative Staff of the Boston Globe, *Betrayal: The Crisis in the Catholic Church* (New York: Little, Brown, 2002), 66.
8. Donald B. Cozzens, a former seminary rector, puts the figure of homosexual priests at as high as forty percent. *The Changing Face of the Priesthood: A Reflection on the Priest's Crisis of Soul* (Collegeville, MN: Liturgical Press, 2000), 95–99. Others put the figure at something like twenty-five percent.
9. The context would become decidedly homosexual during the AIDS epidemic, when pressure built against *Humanae Vitae* for the sake of approving condoms for safer sex. Even then, the Vatican held the line, with drastic consequences, especially in Africa.
10. In 2005, Vatican investigators interrogated seminarians at all U.S. seminaries, focused especially on rooting out homosexuals. In the same year, after Ratzinger's election as pope, a document he had supervised was published forbidding men "with deep-seated homosexual tendencies" from being ordained to the priesthood. For gays, it would no longer be enough to be celibate. They could not be priests.

11. Investigative Staff of the Boston Globe, *Betrayal*, 68.
12. National Review Board for the Protection of Children and Young People, "A Report on the Crisis in the Catholic Church in the U.S.," http://www.usccb.org/nrb.
13. Investigative Staff of the Boston Globe, *Betrayal*, 71.
14. Investigative Staff of the Boston Globe, *Betrayal*, 69.
15. *New York Times*, December 13, 2002.
16. Investigative Staff of the Boston Globe, *Betrayal*, 96.
17. James Carroll, "Catholicism After Porter," *Boston Globe*, September 29, 1992. When the *New York Times* acquired the *Globe* later in the 1990s, Cardinal Law asked the paper's new publisher to fire me. The publisher declined to do so, and subsequently told me the story. I continue to write the column today.
18. Jamie Doward, "Pope 'Obstructed' Sex Abuse Inquiry," *Guardian*, April 24, 2005.
19. Margaret R. Miles, "Santa Maria Maggiore's Fifth-Century Mosaics: Triumphal Christianity and the Jews," *Harvard Theological Review* 86, no. 2, April 1993, 155–75.
20. After many priests like me had left the priesthood, priests who remained often described themselves as fulfilled. It is not up to an ex-priest to speak for those who chose to remain. In 2002, for example, a *Los Angeles Times* survey reported that ninety percent of responding priests said they would choose the priesthood again. This was before the full force of the abuse crisis was felt. Stephen J. Rossetti, "Post-Crisis Morale Among Priests," *America*, September 13, 2004, 8–10.
21. I described this fire in my 1996 memoir, *An American Requiem*. It remains a defining moment in my life, which is why I return to it here.
22. Lukas, *Common Ground*, 373.
23. Peter Hebblethwaite, *Paul VI: The First Modern Pope* (New York: Paulist Press, 1993), 595.
24. Wills, *Papal Sin*, 101.
25. *Dignitatis Humanae*, http://www.vatican.va/archive/hist_councils/ii_vatican_council/documents/vat-ii_decl_19651207_dignitatis-humanae_en.html.
26. *Dignitatis Humanae*.
27. In 1965, there were 58,632 priests in the United States. By 2001, that number had fallen by 23 percent, to 45,191. By 2007, the majority of priests were over sixty years old. Center for Applied Research in the Apostolate, Georgetown University, quoted in Investigative Staff of the Boston Globe, *Betrayal*, 195.
28. Hans Küng, *Infallible? An Inquiry*, translated by Edward Quinn (Garden City, NY: Doubleday, 1983), 29, 145.
29. Küng, *Infallible?*, 124.
30. Küng, *Infallible?*, 51.
31. Küng, *Infallible?*, 66.
32. Küng, *Infallible?*, 213.
33. Hans Küng, "Ten Theses on the Future of the Papacy," *Corriere della Sera*, November 10, 1996.
34. The document goes on, "Thus, in the present circumstances, the Roman Pon-

tiff, exercising his proper office of confirming the brethren (cf. Luke 22:32), has handed on this same teaching by a formal declaration, explicitly stating what is to be held always, everywhere, and by all, as belonging to the deposit of faith." Maureen Fiedler and Linda Rabben, eds., *Rome Has Spoken: A Guide to Forgotten Papal Statements and How They Have Changed Through the Centuries* (New York: Crossroad, 1998), 119–20.

35. "Pastoral Constitution on the Church in the Modern World," *Gaudium et Spes.*
36. In a 1992 address to the Pontifical Academy of Sciences, which had issued its report on Galileo, which we noted earlier, John Paul II spoke of "a tragic mutual incomprehension."
37. James Carroll, "The Silence," *The New Yorker,* April 7, 1997, 57–60.
38. In 1893, Pope Leo XIII, in his encyclical *Providentissimus Deus,* distinguished between biblical accounts of creation and Darwin's theory of evolution, helping Catholics avoid the dead end of reading Genesis as a scientific account. Nevertheless, Catholic thinkers have been slow to confront the implications for theology of evolutionary science. One of the few who did was the Jesuit paleontologist Pierre Teilhard de Chardin (1881–1955), author of *The Phenomenon of Man,* which was censored during his lifetime.

Chapter Nine: Religion and Terror

1. John Cornwell, *The Pontiff in Winter: Triumph and Conflict in the Reign of John Paul II* (New York: Doubleday, 2004). Tad Szulc, *Pope John Paul II: The Biography* (New York: Scribner, 1995). Jonathan Kwitny, *Man of the Century: The Life and Times of Pope John Paul II* (New York: Henry Holt, 1997). Carl Bernstein and Marco Politi, *His Holiness: John Paul II and the Hidden History of Our Time* (New York: Doubleday, 1994). George Weigel, *Witness to Hope: The Biography of Pope John Paul II* (New York: HarperCollins, 1999).
2. Fundamentalists make the point that antifundamentalism *is* a form of bigotry. See Louis Bolce and Gerald DeMaio, "A Prejudice for the Thinking Classes: Media Exposure, Political Sophistication, and the Anti-Christian Fundamentalist," *American Politics Research* 36, no. 2, 155–85.
3. My discussion of fundamentalism is informed by Gabriel A. Almond, R. Scott Appleby, and Emmanuel Sivan, *Strong Religion: The Rise of Fundamentalisms Around the World* (Chicago: University of Chicago Press, 2003), 1–20.
4. Neoconservative Catholics in alliance with the evangelical right wing include Michael Novak, George Weigel, Joseph Fessio, and Richard John Neuhaus. See Garry Wills, "Fringe Government," *New York Review of Books,* October 6, 2005.
5. I find the word in Hans Küng, *Judaism: Between Yesterday and Tomorrow* (New York: Crossroad, 1992), 624.
6. Dean R. Hoge, "The Current State of the Priesthood: Sociological Research," lecture presented at Boston College, June 15, 2005. In the early twenty-first century, Christians numbered 480 million in Latin America, 360 million in Africa, 313 million in Asia, and only 260 million in North America. Of the 18

million Catholic Baptisms recorded worldwide in 1998, 8 million were in Latin America, 3 million in Africa, and nearly 3 million in Asia. Philip Jenkins, "The Next Christianity," *Atlantic Monthly*, October 2002, 54, 59.

7. David Gibson, *The Rule of Benedict: Pope Benedict XVI and His Battle with the Modern World* (San Francisco: HarperSanFrancisco, 2006), 334.
8. Maureen Fiedler and Linda Rabben, eds., *Rome Has Spoken: A Guide to Forgotten Papal Statements and How They Have Changed Through the Centuries* (New York: Crossroad, 1998), 39–40.
9. Almond, Appleby, and Sivan, *Strong Religion*, 17.
10. Using a term taken from architecture, thinkers now embrace a "postmodernism" that repudiates fundamental tenets of Enlightenment modernity. Postmodernism "is a decisive rejection of modernity's myth of progress, breakthrough, and renewal . . . Both Christianity and Enlightenment, belief and modernity, are grand universal accounts—'metanarratives,' to use Lyotard's term . . . The displacement of Christianity by Enlightenment was the substitution of one universal narrative for another; postmodernism, however, not only offers no new universal narrative in place of modernity, it also denies the possibility of any such narrative—that is, it denies the possibility of any universally accepted and acceptable account of the world and humanity's place in it." Frederick Mark Gedicks, "Spirituality, Fundamentalism, Liberty: Religion at the End of Modernity," *DePaul Law Review*, Summer 2005.
11. There is an equivalent revolution in the way humans obtain their news, with newspapers and broadcast networks being challenged by a plethora of new media, which are often grassroots-driven, radically democratic, change-minded—and sorely in need of editing. In religion, mainstream denominations are being surpassed by megachurches, televangelists, and anti-institutional charismatic movements—all in need of critical theology.
12. Archbishop Marcel LeFebvre, for example, had been excommunicated after Vatican II for refusing to abandon the so-called Tridentine Mass, the Latin ritual as set by the sixteenth-century Council of Trent. But in 2007, when Pope Benedict XVI formally authorized a return to the Tridentine Mass, he was seeking to be reconciled with LeFebvre's followers.
13. Having been central to the campaign against liberation theology, Ratzinger attempted to finish it off in 2007 when, as Pope Benedict XVI, he censured the much-admired, and by then elderly and ailing, Spanish Jesuit Jon Sobrino. The priest had almost been murdered in 1989 when his six confreres were gunned down by a Salvadoran death squad. He was condemned by Benedict for "not sufficiently emphasizing the divinity of Jesus." David Gibson, "His Own Pope Yet?," *New York Times*, April 23, 2007, A21.
14. *New York Times*, April 19, 2008.
15. Gibson, *Rule of Benedict*, 267.
16. In his memoir, Ratzinger writes that "at the end of April or the beginning of May—I do not remember precisely—I decided to go home." *Milestones: Memoirs, 1927—1977* (San Francisco: Ignatius Press, 1998), 36.
17. In the spring of 2007, the Vatican announced that the "cause" of Pius XII's beatification was on track, with the completion of the formal canonical inves-

tigation into his life and work. On October 9, 2008, the fiftieth anniversary of Pius XII's death, Benedict prayed that the process of beatification "may continue smoothly." Frances D'Emilio, Associated Press, October 9, 2008.

18. Guenther Lewy, "Pius XII, the Jews, and the German Catholic Church," in *Betrayal: German Churches and the Holocaust,* edited by Robert P. Erickson and Susannah Heschel (Minneapolis: Augsburg Fortress, 1999), 131.
19. I describe this encounter in *Constantine's Sword: The Church and the Jews—A History* (Boston: Houghton Mifflin, 2001), 683.
20. Anthony Grafton, "Reading Ratzinger," *The New Yorker,* July 25, 2005, 44.
21. Gibson, *Rule of Benedict,* 319.
22. The word "architect," applied in this way to Ratzinger, is John L. Allen's: *Cardinal Ratzinger: The Vatican's Enforcer of the Faith* (New York: Continuum, 2000), 296.
23. David Gibson cites this saying as a model for Benedict. *Rule of Benedict,* 345.
24. "Post-Synodal Apostolic Exhortation *Sacramentum Caritatis* of the Holy Father Benedict XVI to the Bishops, Clergy, Consecrated Persons, and the Lay Faithful on the Eucharist as the Source and Summit of the Church's Life and Mission, March 10, 2007." Less than a month after this exhortation was issued, on April 5, the bishop of Cheyenne, Wyoming, sent a letter to a lesbian couple, parishioners at St. Matthew's Parish in Gillette, Wyoming. "I must inform you," the letter read, "that because of your union and your public advocacy of same-sex unions that you are unable to receive Communion." The U.S. Conference of Catholic Bishops had previously published guidelines telling dissenting Catholics to refrain from taking Communion, but this was the first time a bishop had proactively raised the barrier. In 2004, the archbishop of St. Louis had declared that he would withhold Communion from presidential candidate John Kerry because of his pro-choice position, but Kerry never presented himself for Communion in St. Louis. With Pope Benedict's "exhortation," the policy had moved from theory to practice. Kathleen Miller, "Wyoming Church Denies Communion to Lesbian Couple," *Boston Globe,* April 6, 2007.
25. Gibson, *Rule of Benedict,* 245. At Schultz's funeral some months later, presided over by a Catholic cardinal, Holy Communion was distributed without regard to denomination.
26. John T. Noonan, ed., *The Morality of Abortion: Legal and Historical Perspectives* (Cambridge: Harvard University Press, 1970), 54. The Church does not advocate the baptizing of fetuses to this day, which seems at odds with the doctrine that each one is a fully constituted human person.
27. "Catholic ethics uses an absolutist version of deontological natural law ethics when it speaks of abortion, while when it speaks of war it shifts to a consequentialist ethic that carefully balances conflicting values." Rosemary Radford Reuther, "'Consistent Life Ethic' Is Inconsistent," *National Catholic Reporter,* November 17, 2006.
28. George W. Bush made a dramatic return to Washington, D.C., to sign a special law ordering federal courts to take up the case.
29. *The Catechism of the Catholic Church,* paragraph 2278.

30. Michael Sandel, *The Case Against Perfection* (Cambridge: Belknap Press of Harvard University Press, 2007), 101.
31. In 1997, Ratzinger characterized Buddhism as an "auto-erotic" religion, a kind of spiritual masturbation. Leo D. Lefebure, "Cardinal Ratzinger's Comments on Buddhism," *Buddhist-Christian Studies* 18, 1998, 221–23.
32. Samuel P. Huntington, "The Clash of Civilizations?," *Foreign Affairs,* Summer 1993.
33. Quoted in Russell Shorto, "Keeping the Faith," *New York Times Magazine,* April 8, 2007, 43.
34. Peter Hebblethwaite, *In the Vatican* (Bethesda, MD: Adler & Adler, 1986), 3. The exhortation is called *Egregiae Virtutis.*
35. *New York Times,* April 24, 2005, 4.
36. Shorto, "Keeping the Faith," 45.
37. Jane Kramer, "The Pope and Islam," *The New Yorker,* April 2, 2007, 65.
38. Quoted in Shorto, "Keeping the Faith," 45. Shorto adds, "Benedict was taken to task by 38 Muslim scholars, who wrote a joint letter indicating that his words distorted Muslim thought on reason and faith and stating that Muslims acknowledge 'a hierarchy of knowledge of which reason is a crucial part.'"
39. Kramer, "The Pope and Islam," 60.
40. I find the word in Richard Holloway, *Looking in the Distance: The Human Search for Meaning* (New York: Canongate, 2004), 123.
41. Quoted in Shorto, "Keeping the Faith," 58.
42. *Washington Post,* April 17, 2008. Benedict went out of his way to affirm Bush, both in the papal visit to Washington and in Bush's visit to the Vatican later the same year. Bush was the first head of state to be received in the pope's private garden. "This is fantastic," Bush said. "Your Eminence, you're looking good." *Boston Globe,* June 15, 2008.
43. I was one of those who protested. James Carroll, "By Excommunicating a Sri Lankan Priest, Vatican Spurned a Prophet," *Boston Globe,* January 28, 1997. The Boston archdiocesan newspaper, the *Pilot,* responded to my column by calling for the *Globe* to fire me. "The Angry Mr. Carroll," *Boston Pilot,* February 3, 1997.
44. Jon D. Levenson, *The Death and Resurrection of the Beloved Son: The Transformation of Child Sacrifice in Judaism and Christianity* (New Haven: Yale University Press, 1993), x.
45. Krister Stendahl, "Qumran and Supersessionism—and the Road Not Taken," *Princeton Seminary Bulletin* 19, no. 2, new series, 1998, 139.
46. Against religious exclusivism, the rabbis began to emphasize such passages as this one from Micah (4:5): "For all people will walk every one in the name of his god, and we will walk in the name of the Lord our God forever and ever."
47. I offered a version of these reflections for the Project on Universal Basic and Secondary Education, at the American Academy of Arts and Sciences, 2007.
48. Matthew 28:17–19. Scholars suggest that this command may have been added well after the composition of the Gospel, since it reflects a Trinitarian understanding that evolved over time.

49. Matthew 5:13–16.
50. Quoted in Shorto, "Keeping the Faith," 41.
51. James Carroll, "The Silence," *The New Yorker,* April 7, 1997, 67.
52. Küng's project was built around the writing of three magisterial books. *Judaism* was published in 1991; *Christianity* in 1995; the third volume, *Islam,* appeared in 2007.
53. Hans Küng, *Christianity: Essence, History and Future* (New York: Continuum, 1995), epigraph.
54. Quoted in Edward K. Kaplan, *Spiritual Radical: Abraham Joshua Heschel in America, 1940–1972* (New Haven: Yale University Press, 2007), 283.
55. Gibson, *Rule of Benedict,* 186. "It's clear that we have different positions," Küng said after the meeting. "But the things we have in common are more fundamental." The ban on Küng's right to teach theology was not lifted. *National Catholic Reporter,* September 26, 2005.
56. Grafton, "Reading Ratzinger," 48.
57. Kramer, "The Pope and Islam," 63.
58. Allen, *Cardinal Ratzinger,* 296.
59. Thomas Keating, *The Heart of the World: A Spiritual Catechism* (New York: Crossroad, 1981), 1.
60. The *New Yorker* writer Jane Kramer asked this question. Kramer, "The Pope and Islam," 61.
61. Father Feeney, as we noted, was the chaplain of the St. Benedict Center, an organization of conservative Catholics at Harvard. We saw that one of its founders in 1940 was a student named Avery Dulles, the convert son of John Foster Dulles. Avery Dulles became a prominent theologian, and was named a cardinal by John Paul II in 2001. He was Ratzinger's ally in seeking to roll back the ecumenical spirit of Vatican II. For example, in 2002 he rebutted a statement by the U.S. Conference of Catholic Bishops' Committee on Ecumenical and Interreligious Affairs, "Reflections on Covenant and Mission." The document stated that "targeting Jews for conversion to Christianity [is] no longer theologically acceptable in the Catholic Church." Dulles cited Hebrews 8:13 to declare that Jesus Christ abolished the first covenant "in order to establish the second." Scholars quickly showed that Dulles's use of Scripture in this way was incorrect. It was a Feeney-Cushing replay. Padraic O'Hare, *Spiritual Companions: Jews, Christians, and Interreligious Relations* (New London, CT: Twenty-third Publications/Bayard, 2006), 19.
62. A year into his pontificate, Benedict told a German journalist, "Let's say that my basic personality and even my basic vision have grown, but in everything that is essential I have remained identical." *New York Times,* April 23, 2007.
63. My reaction to Gibson's movie took the form of making one of my own. With the documentary film director Oren Jacoby I made *Constantine's Sword,* based on my book of the same name. It was shown in theaters across the United States in 2008. See http://www.constantinessword.com.
64. Edward Kessler, "A Deafening Silence," *Tablet,* April 14, 2007.
65. "The holy people of God shares also in Christ's prophetic office . . . The entire body of the faithful, anointed as they are by the Holy One, cannot err in mat-

ters of belief." *Lumen Gentium,* Dogmatic Constitution of the Church, *The Documents of Vatican II.* This declaration is the core of the Church's new teaching that other religions are authentic, and that the Christian people (not just Catholics) are themselves the Church. For a discussion of "Ratzinger's rather acrobatic interpretation" of this Vatican II document—how he is imposing a meaning on it that is the clear opposite of what the council intended—see Grafton, "Reading Ratzinger," 42–43. The meaning of *Nostra Aetate* was also undercut when, as we saw, Benedict restored the Tridentine liturgy, in 2007, with its provision for a "prayer for the conversion of the Jews" on Good Friday.

66. Shorto, "Keeping the Faith," 63. Gibson, *Rule of Benedict,* 294.
67. Commenting on this conclusion, Benedict's biographer David Gibson wrote, "That was an empty rationale, most obviously because the number of abuse cases was dropping sharply in recent decades even as the percentage of gay priests was rising. Above all, the decision unjustly denigrated a group of people simply for who they are. And it was akin to hoisting the ladder after one is safely aboard ship given that there are already plenty of gay priests and bishops serving the church faithfully, many in the Vatican itself." "His Own Pope Yet?," A21.
68. Gibson, *Rule of Benedict,* 313.

Chapter Ten: A Writer's Faith

1. In 1975, after a year's "leave of absence," I applied in writing to the Vatican for dispensation from my priestly and religious vows. In 1977, I received a letter, the "rescript" from Rome, written in Latin, granting my request.
2. George Orwell, "Inside the Whale," Part II, http://www.ourcivilization.com/smartboard/shop/orwellg/whale2.htm.
3. In 2001, Cardinal Sean O'Malley, then the bishop of Fall River, Massachusetts, published a decree in the diocesan newspaper telling Catholics not to attend a lecture I was to deliver at Stonehill College, a Catholic college south of Boston. The college refused to cancel the lecture, and the hall was filled to overflowing. Sean O'Malley, "Stonehill Forum for Catholic-Bashing Speaker Shocks Bishop," *Anchor,* April 2001.
4. As it happened, O'Neill's last days were spent in a Boston hotel, which by my time had been converted to a BU dormitory. "I knew it! I knew it! Born in a goddam hotel room," he declared, "and dying in a hotel room!" The priest who responded to the dying O'Neill was Father Vincent Mackay, pastor of a nearby parish. Years later, Mackay was my putative boss when I was BU chaplain. Louis Shaeffer, *O'Neill, Son and Artist* (Boston: Little, Brown, 1973), 669–70.
5. Voice of the Faithful was founded in the wake of the priestly abuse scandal in Wellesley, Massachusetts, in 2001. It has tens of thousands of members, with chapters in all fifty states. Call to Action was founded in Chicago in 1978, and it too is a national organization with tens of thousands of members. Future

Church, focusing on calls for women's ordination and a married priesthood, was founded in Cleveland in 1990.

6. The Community of Sant'Egidio, founded in Rome in 1968, is typical. An antiwar, antipoverty, anti–capital punishment movement, Sant'Egidio has tens of thousands of members, with chapters throughout Europe, North America, and Africa. *National Catholic Reporter*, May 11, 2007, 12.
7. One study found that Catholics use birth control at the same rate as non-Catholics, and white Catholic women have fewer children than white Protestant women. Seventy-five to eighty percent of Catholics received Communion in the observed parishes. Notre Dame Study of Catholic Parish Life, University of Notre Dame, Report #15, http://www.nd.edu/~icl/study_reports/report 15.pdf.
8. "Allow me this, I beseech you," Augustine prayed in the fourth book of his *Confessions*, "to trace again in memory my past deviations." Bk. 4, ch. 1, 71.
9. George Orwell described Eliot's conversion to the Anglican Church, instead of the Roman, as equivalent to his joining the Trotskyites, instead of the full-bore Bolsheviks.
10. Allen Tate, "Ode to the Confederate Dead," *Poems* (New York: Scribner, 1960), 19–20. I first recounted Allen Tate's influence on my life in my memoir, *An American Requiem* (Boston: Houghton Mifflin, 1996), 106–7, 205–10.
11. One of the more astonishing changes of the Vatican II revolution was the sudden liberation of nuns. Their arrival in the classrooms of secular universities like the University of Minnesota would have been unthinkable before the mid-1960s.
12. John Macquarrie, *Principles of Christian Theology* (New York: Scribner, 1966), 182.
13. See Alasdair MacIntyre, *After Virtue: A Study in Moral Theory* (South Bend, IN: University of Notre Dame Press, 1981), 199. We make sense of what we experience only "to the extent that it is articulated through a narrative mode, and narrative attains its full significance when it becomes a condition of temporal existence." Paul Ricoeur, *Time and Narrative*, vol. 1, translated by Kathleen McLaughlin and David Pellauer (Chicago: University of Chicago Press, 1984), 2. "The narrative constructs the identity of the character, what can be called his or her narrative identity, in constructing that of the story told. It is the identity of the story that makes the identity of the character." Ricoeur, *Oneself as Another*, translated by Kathleen Blamey (Chicago: University of Chicago Press, 1992), 147–48.
14. "'Resurrection Poem' and half a dozen others announce a new, original talent"—Allen Tate blurb for my book of poems, *Forbidden Disappointments*.
15. "So we stand before the Mystery of this moment, terrified and awestruck as this moment dies and is reborn as the next. The mysteries of time and death are at the center of the human condition, and it has been so since we first achieved consciousness. This is the beginning place." James A. Connor, *Pascal's Wager: The Man Who Played Dice with God* (New York: HarperCollins, 2006), 209.
16. For the importance of the "axial age" (a term originating with Karl Jaspers),

during which the great religions were conceived, see Karen Armstrong, *The Great Transformation: The Beginning of Our Religious Traditions* (New York: Knopf, 2006).

17. Flavius Josephus, *Antiquities of the Jews*, bk. 18, ch. 3, para. 3. Note that some of Josephus's assertions about Jesus (that he was the "Christ," for example) are understood to be emendations by later Christian editors, but there is no reason to doubt the authenticity of the line "Those that loved him did not give up their affection for him." http://www.earlyjewishwritings.com/josephus.html.
18. "Parthians, Medes, and Elamites; people from Mesopotamia, Judaea, and Cappadocia, Pontus and Asia, Phrygia and Pamphylia, Egypt, and the parts of Libya round Cyrene, as well as visitors from Rome—Jews and proselytes alike, Cretans and Arabs: We hear them preaching in our own language about the marvels of God." Acts 2:9–11.
19. Newman, as Luke, is repeating the line first uttered in the film by the captain, played by Strother Martin. The film was written by Donn Pearce and Frank Pierson.
20. The Nicene Creed was composed by bishops meeting at the Council of Nicea in 325–326. They were responding to pressure from the newly converted Emperor Constantine, who needed a clear statement of faith so that he could enforce Christian orthodoxy on his now Christian empire.
21. According to a 1993 Gallup poll, only about thirty percent of U.S. Catholics adhere to a "literal" belief that the Communion bread is the body of Christ. Conservatives decry this, but the key question is what "literal" means. Catholics may simply have adopted a more sophisticated appreciation of the connection between the symbolic and the real. See R. Scott Appleby, "The Triumph of Americanism," in *Being Right: Conservative Catholics in America*, edited by Mary Jo Weaver and R. Scott Appleby (Bloomington: Indiana University Press, 1995), 59.
22. "Fifty-eight percent of Americans cannot name five of the ten commandments, just under half know that Genesis is the first book of the Bible, fewer than that can tell interviewers about the meaning of the Holy Trinity, and ten percent of them believe that Joan of Arc was Noah's wife." Alan Wolfe, *The Transformation of American Religion* (New York: Free Press, 2003), 247. My positive description of post–Vatican II Catholics may not apply to younger Catholics. The scholar Christian Smith finds Catholic teenagers to be less knowledgeable about religion than non-Catholic teens. Christian Smith with Melinda Lundquist Denton, *Soul Searching: The Religious and Spiritual Lives of American Teenagers* (New York: Oxford University Press, 2005), 193–218.
23. "Science not only purifies the religious impulse of the dross of its anthropomorphism, but also contributes to a religious spiritualization of our understanding of life." Albert Einstein, quoted in Chet Raymo, *Skeptics and True Believers: The Exhilarating Connection Between Science and Religion* (New York: Walker, 1998), 164. I acknowledge my debt to Chet Raymo for this discussion of the relationship between rationality and faith.
24. "God is that-without-which-there-would-be-no-evolution-at-all; God is the

atemporal undergirder and sustainer of the whole process of apparent contingency and 'randomness,' yet—we can say in the spirit of Augustine—simultaneously closer to its inner workings than it is to itself. As such, God is both 'within' the process and 'without.'" Sarah Coakley, "God and Evolution: A New Solution," *Harvard Divinity School Bulletin*, Spring/Summer 2007, 10. The usual assumption that there is necessary conflict between religion and evolutionary theory does justice to neither. For example, here is Darwin's key statement from chapter four of *On the Origin of Species:* "It may be said that natural selection is daily and hourly scrutinizing, throughout the world, every variation, even the slightest; rejecting that which is bad, preserving and adding up all that is good; silently and insensibly working, whenever and wherever opportunity offers, at the improvement of each organic being in relation to its organic and inorganic conditions of life." Quoted in E. O. Wilson, *The Creation: A Meeting of Science and Religion* (New York: W. W. Norton, 2006), 114. Note that Darwin, in the thematic phrase "It may be said," is positing an analogy, attributing to natural selection the kind of agency and, yes, "design" that traditional believers attribute to God.

25. Quoted in John W. O'Malley, *Four Cultures of the West* (Cambridge: Harvard University Press, 2004), 161.
26. We should be modest in making assertions about animal communication. Chimpanzees, for example, seem to achieve rudimentary skill in using American Sign Language.
27. John 1:1–18, omitting 6–8 and 15.
28. John Macquarrie, *Jesus Christ in Modern Thought* (Philadelphia: Trinity Press International, 1990), 105.
29. Wolfe, *Transformation of American Religion*, 37, 49.
30. Wolfe, *Transformation of American Religion*, 263.
31. David Tracy, *On Naming the Present: Reflections on God, Hermeneutics, and Church* (Louisville, KY: SCM Press, 1994), 4.
32. Paul Ricoeur wrote of surrendering "the immediacy of belief. But if we can no longer live the great symbolisms of the sacred in accordance with the original belief, we can, we modern men, aim at a second naïveté in and through criticism." *The Rule of Metaphor: Multi-disciplinary Studies of the Creation of Meaning in Language*, translated by Robert Czerny, with Kathleen McLaughlin and John Costello (Toronto: University of Toronto Press, 1977), 318. See also Tracy, *On Naming the Present*, 138, and Gerald Bednar, *Faith as Imagination: The Contribution of William F. Lynch, S.J.* (Lanham, MD: Rowman & Littlefield, 1996), 31.
33. Flannery O'Connor is often cited as saying, in defense of the Mass, "If it's a symbol, to hell with it." But it is inconceivable that she would have said, "If it's a sacrament, to hell with it." Sacrament and symbol are words that get at the same mystery—and each ever so imprecisely.
34. Connor, *Pascal's Wager*, 179.
35. Wilson, *The Creation*, 166.
36. "There was a message written in pencil on the tiles by the roller towel [in the men's room of a movie house]. This was it: WHAT IS THE PURPOSE OF

LIFE? Kilgore Trout plundered his pockets for a pen or pencil. He had an answer to the question. But he had nothing to write with, not even a burnt match. So he left the question unanswered, but here is what he would have written, if he had found anything to write with: TO BE THE EYES AND EARS AND CONSCIENCE OF THE CREATOR OF THE UNIVERSE, YOU FOOL." Kurt Vonnegut, *Breakfast of Champions* (New York: Dial Press, 1991), 66.

37. Karl Rahner, *Theological Investigations*, vol. 5, *Later Writings*, translated by Karl-H. Kruger (London: Darton, Longman & Todd, 1975), 171–72.
38. Karl Rahner, *The Rahner Reader*, edited by Gerald McCool (New York: Seabury, 1975), 20.
39. "The term transcendence simply refers to what surpasses the limits of experience. As such, it inevitably raises the question of what lies beyond the limit. The person may respond to that question by embracing a theist view of transcendence, or he may refuse to respond where no sufficient evidence for any system is available." Louis Dupré, "A Fateful Separation of Philosophy and Theology," *Harvard Divinity School Bulletin*, Spring/Summer 2007, 56–57.
40. See Jeffrey J. Kripal, *Esalen: America and the Religion of No Religion* (Chicago: University of Chicago Press, 1997).
41. Dietrich Bonhoeffer, *Letters and Papers from Prison* (New York: Macmillan, 1971), 360–61.
42. See, for example, Steven Weinberg, *Dreams of a Final Theory*. Here is Chet Raymo on Weinberg: "No theory conceived by the human mind will ever be final. The universe is vast, marvelous, and deep beyond our knowing; its horizons will always recede before our advance. All dreams of finality are (probably) futile." *Skeptics and True Believers*, 207.
43. Edward O. Wilson posits a different view: "You (believer) and I (scientist) are both humanists in the broadest sense: human welfare is at the center of our thought. But the difference between humanism based on religion and humanism based on science radiates through . . . the very meaning we assign ourselves as a species. They affect the way we separately authenticate our ethics, our patriotism, our social structure, and our personal dignity." *The Creation*, 167. On the contrary, I insist that the two humanisms are one: critical religion takes sciences for granted as the source of its knowledge of the world, knowledge that is the basis for all values, from patriotism to personal dignity.
44. Luther and Lutheranism and much of what became Anglicanism retained pictures and images, as Mark U. Edwards reminded me, while the more Calvinist or "reformed" traditions rejected such representation.
45. O'Malley, *Four Cultures of the West*, 217.
46. "And God said, Let us make man in our image, after our likeness . . . So God created man in his *own* image, in the image of God he created him." Genesis 1:26, 27.
47. I first offered reflections on Michelangelo's work in the Sistine Chapel in *Constantine's Sword*. I return to the image here because its power is clearer to me now, after recognitions gained in writing this book.
48. "Luther's discourse is psychological and relational, the theologians at Trent logical and metaphysical." O'Malley, *Four Cultures of the West*, 112.

INDEX